Advance praise for
Key Account Management and Planning

"A valuable tool for transforming the art of account management into a science. Companies wishing to move up their customer's value chain would be well advised to follow the principles and processes contained in this comprehensive work."
—**David Macaulay,** Senior Vice President, Information and Communications Group,
   Siemens AG

"A detailed framework for servicing customers through a key account management process . . . a valuable and useful book for organizations contemplating a change to their sales organization."
—**Richard J. Potter,** Director, Vital Strategic Program, Deloitte Consulting

"Comprehensive and authoritative . . . offers a powerful framework for developing superior key account strategies."
—**Professor Christoph Senn,** University of St. Gallen, Switzerland

"Provides a strategic planning process that can build business success. . . . Capon understands that all business is global and that being globally competitive will determine who will ultimately survive. A must read for any business leader who hopes to generate the sales revenues needed to compete both locally and globally."
—**William M. Klepper, Ph.D.,** Academic Director, Executive Education,
   Columbia University Graduate School of Business

"The prescription for success is carefully, objectively, and comprehensively defined in this book. What Capon describes today will be a required competence for every business executive tomorrow."
—**Howard Stevens,** Chairman and CEO, The H.R. Chally Group

"A wise and insightful book. . . . Describes approaches used by organizations to reach key customers. . . . Capon's unique vision of the planning process, strategic issues, partnering, and global account management will make this book a classic."
—**Tony Carter,** Chair, Business Administration and Professional Programs,
   Wagner College

"Strategic account management has become the leadership force that brings companies close to their business customers. Capon has assembled the tools that companies will need to achieve this critical objective."
—**Jordan D. Lewis,** author of *Trusted Partners*

"This book is must reading for anyone who really cares about building a first-rate key account sales capability."
—**Gary Tubridy,** Vice President and Founder, The Alexander Group

"Provides a soup-to-nuts guide to key account management, applicable to any business. If key accounts are in your future (and they should be), read and act immediately upon the precepts in this book."
—**Laurie Charlton,** Business and Operations Director, Corning Museum of Glass

"A practical guide that presents a comprehensive overview and concrete action steps on an important strategic issue facing corporations today."
—**Peter Mathias,** CEO, Mathias and Co., Strategic Customer Consultants

"Embraces this new world of global account management and provides breakthrough perspectives for any global account manager or global team."
—**Tim Love,** Managing Partner, Saatchi & Saatchi

"It's better than a Clancy novel if you enjoy business as much as I do. . . . Practical insights and a wealth of examples that will work for any business in any industry. The bottom line is delivering more value through demonstrably differentiating our company from our competitors in our key accounts. Capon's business acumen has provided the insight and the motivation to improve on both."
—**David Lambers,** Channel Business Development Manager, Eastman Kodak Company

*f***P**

KEY ACCOUNT
MANAGEMENT
AND PLANNING

The Comprehensive Handbook
for Managing Your Company's Most
Important Strategic Asset

NOEL CAPON

The Free Press

New York   London   Toronto   Sydney   Singapore

THE FREE PRESS
A Division of Simon & Schuster, Inc.
1230 Avenue of the Americas
New York, NY 10020

For information regarding special discounts for bulk purchases,
please contact Simon & Schuster Special Sales at 1-800-456-6798
or business @simonandschuster.com

Manufactured in the United States of America

1   3   5   7   9   10   8   6   4   2

LIBRARY OF CONGRESS CATALOGING-IN-PUBLICATION DATA
Capon, Noel.
Key account management and planning : the comprehensive handbook for managing
your company's most important strategic asset / Noel Capon.
p.   cm.
Includes index.
1. Marketing—Key accounts.   I. Title.
HF5415.122 .C36 2001
658.8'1—dc21   2001033430
ISBN 0-7432-1188-X

TO DKNY

CONTENTS

Preface, xi   Acknowledgments, xiii

I. INTRODUCTION

CHAPTER ONE: The Rationale for Key Account Management   3

II. STRATEGY, ORGANIZATION, AND HUMAN RESOURCES FOR KEY ACCOUNT MANAGEMENT

CHAPTER TWO: Developing Strategy for the Firm's Customers   39

CHAPTER THREE: Organizing for Key Account Management   70

CHAPTER FOUR: The Key Account Manager   106

III. SYSTEMS AND PROCESSES

CHAPTER FIVE: Key Account Planning: Analysis of the Key Account   141

CHAPTER SIX: Key Account Planning: Analysis of Competition and the Supplier Firm, Planning Assumptions, and Opportunities and Threats   190

CHAPTER SEVEN: The Key Account Strategy   221

CHAPTER EIGHT: Managing the Key Account Relationship   251

IV. CRITICAL ISSUES FOR KEY ACCOUNT MANAGEMENT

CHAPTER NINE: Partnering with Key Accounts   281

CHAPTER TEN: Global Account Management   308

Exercises, 345   Appendixes, 381   Notes, 415   Index, 451

PREFACE

As we enter the twenty-first century, senior management in corporations around the world is realizing that customers are critical firm assets. Notwithstanding the continuing importance of controlling costs and making effective investments, the task of securing and retaining customers is increasingly taking center stage at the highest corporate levels. Nowhere does this task emerge in such clear focus as in key account management. Although the firm's entire customer base may be important as a source of revenues, key accounts typically comprise those customers that currently do, and in the future will, purchase the majority of the firm's products and services. Key accounts are the firm's single most important asset inasmuch as they supply the majority of sales revenues to support its investment and cost structures. As such, they require special emphasis.

During the past fifteen years I have both worked with many companies on key account management issues and developed teaching materials for key account management programs. In the early days of this work the focus and terminology in key account management was typically one of national accounts, and many companies developed national account programs. Of late, however, as global competition has become a reality for so many firms in so many industries, a national account focus has become too restrictive. Many suppliers must now deal with their customers on a global rather than just on a national or even multicountry basis and hence are developing global account programs.

This book lays out a congruence framework for key account management that focuses on the relevant dimensions and issues with which key account managers and directors must struggle as they develop and enhance their key account management programs. In addition, we present a planning process that points the way to gaining deeper insight into these accounts, and so enables the firm to develop solid key account strategies. When properly implemented, these strategies should lead to improved returns. I hope that the material in this book will enable firms to manage their key accounts more appropriately and, by protecting and enhancing their current and future revenue streams, will ensure continued profitability, organizational survival and growth and, consequently, improved shareholder value.

The book contains numerous examples. In many cases the organizations are named. Where anonymity was appropriate, an artificial name is used, indicated by an asterisk, for example, Maple Company*.

Noel Capon
Professor of Business and *Chair of the Marketing Division*
Graduate School of Business,
Columbia University, New York, NY
keyaccountmanagement.com
strategicaccountmgt.com
globalaccountmgt.com

ACKNOWLEDGMENTS

Many people have contributed to the development of this book. Most important are William K. Brandt, Robert Christian, and Mac Hulbert who first introduced me to the importance of key account management and who later formed the highly successful Impact Planning Group. In addition, I have long had a valuable association with the Alexander Group, a sales management consulting company, especially with principals Dave Cichelli, Robert Conti, and Gary Tubrity, each of whom has taught under my direction in the Columbia Business School Sales Management Program. In addition, Gary was particularly helpful in forming and chairing workshops of industry experts on the Columbia Business School Key Account Management Program. Jerry Colletti, now a principal with Colletti Fiss, was also very helpful.

Over the years, many colleagues in Columbia's Sales Management and Key Account Management programs have provided insight into the challenges, opportunities, and difficulties in these areas. In particular, I should like to acknowledge Eric Abrahamson, Bill Klepper, Schon Beechler, Bob Bontempto, Sunil Gupta, Betta Mannix, Nachum Melamud, and Peter Palij from Columbia, and Grant Ackerman, Arthur Anderson, Eric Baron, Henry Bergmans III, Tony Carter, Dee Gaedert, Mel Ingold, Howard Katzen, LaVon Koerner, Douglas Lambert, Jordan Lewis, Steven Lewis, Peter Mathias, Paul Newbourne, John Neuman, Cliff Schorer, and Bill Zimmerman from other organizations.

In addition, many executive participants at these programs and various in-company seminars provided insight into key account management issues and were more than willing to share their experiences. In particular, I should like to thank Laurie Charlton from Corning. Laurie and key account managers Jean-Pierre Lormeau, John Wahl, and Bob Walker both confirmed the value of the planning process presented here, and provided insights into key account management in a technologically turbulent environment.

Several people gave freely of their time to educate me in global account management. They include J. Michael Brown at MVE, Inc., Lance Davis at Schlumberger, Bill Etherington and Fred Schnidler at IBM, Timm Hammond at 3M, Guian Heintzen at Citibank, Tim Keane at Betz Dearborne, Paul Newbourne at CSX, and Dave Potter at Xerox. In addition, members of the Columbia Initiative in Global Account Management who have educated each other and me include Timm Hammond and Michael W. Graff at 3M, David Bowerin, Mary Corkran, Gary Greenwald, and Arnold Ziegel at Citibank, Dane Owen and Peter Kirk at Milliken & Co., Dick Potter at Deloitte & Touche, Mike Cohn and Alan Nonnenberg at Hewlett-Packard, Patricia Brecciaroli, Corinne Clark, David Heckman, Joy Kieschke, Michael Rec and Bill Radwill at Lucent Technologies, Geoff Williams at Square D–Schneider Electronics, and Tim Love at Saatchi and Saatchi.

The Strategic Account Marketing Association (SAMA) (formerly the National Account Management Association [NAMA]) and its executive director, Lisa Napolitano, were extremely helpful in the formative stages of writing this book. They cheerfully supplied many documents for my review, mainly reproduced-presentation graphics from various meetings. Among the authors of these documents were Richard P. Aschman, Tony R. Coalson, David J. Cornelius, Douglas A. Decker, G. Wayne Henderson, Raymond C. Howick, Mark A. Moon, John H. Nordloh, Susan K. Pieper, Charles C. Poirier, Kathleen Quasey, and Thomas R. Wotruba. Other documents of this type were unidentified by author but identified by company—Appleton Papers, Freddie Mac, Goulds Pumps, and Xerox.

Finally, I should like to thank Tom VanHootegem, director of national accounts for Boise Cascade Office Products and past president of SAMA, Lisa Napolitano, independent consultant Peter Mathias, international author and lecturer Jordan Lewis, and Christoph Senn from the University of St. Gallen, Switzerland for reading the entire manuscript and providing feedback. In addition, Bill Klepper and Dave Potter provided valuable feedback on Chapters 4 and 10 respectively. Finally, Sullie Sherman, Joe Sperry and Jim Guilkey of S4 Consulting, and Bob Shullman of Willard & Shullman were very helpful on separate aspects of Chapter 8.

I am very grateful for the interest and support of all those mentioned above.

I. INTRODUCTION

The Rationale for Key Account Management[1]

On August 21, 1998, it was announced that telecommunications supplier Ciena would not be receiving an expected $100 million worth of business from key account AT&T. As a direct result of this news, Ciena's stock price plunged 45%, from $56.78 to $31.25. On August 28, a planned merger between Ciena and Tellabs based on a one-for-one stock swap that valued Ciena at $7.3 billion was being renegotiated at $4.7 billion. Shortly afterwards, Ciena announced the loss of a $25 million sale to key account Digital Teleport. On September 14, the merger was abandoned with Ciena's share price at $13.19.[2]

On January 4, 2000, General Motors announced that it was ceasing participation in B2B auctions managed by Freemarkets Inc. Freemarkets' share price dropped from a high of $370 that week to $164, two weeks later.[3]

In August 2000, AT&T's stock price hit a fifty-two-week low. An article in *The Wall Street Journal* attributed the decline to problems in the Business Services Group, responsible for over half of AT&T's 1999 revenues and profits. Among the causes: lack of service to major customers in part due to severe downsizing and layoffs to meet short-term profit targets.[4]

Securing and retaining customers is increasingly recognized as the fundamental requirement for improving shareholder value, the primary objective for many corporations around the world. All firms develop their own methods of communicating with customers, but typically in business-to-business marketing, an on-the-road sales force is a critical element in this process. However, in recent years significant pressure has been placed upon the traditional sales force system. As powerful forces have raised the perceived importance of sales and customer management, many firms are reevaluating their sales force processes. As a result, the traditional sales force system is fragmenting and many corporations are developing key account management programs as a new way of organizational life.

In this chapter, we discuss traditional communication systems, the pressures facing them, and the nature of the resulting fragmentation. We see that the development of key account management is a natural response to these pressures, with benefits for both supplier firms and key accounts. We also raise a series of cautions. Finally we present a structure for guiding those firms wishing to invest in key account management; this also doubles as the structure of the book.

ORGANIZATIONAL OBJECTIVES

The critical objective for most publicly held corporations is increased shareholder value. To increase shareholder value, the organization must survive and grow. However, survival and growth are possible only if the firm both makes profits today and is perceived as likely to make profits tomorrow. Profits are earned only when the firm outperforms its competitors in securing and retaining customers (Figure 1.1).

Over the years, corporations have developed numerous forms of *nonpersonal* and *interpersonal* communications in attempts to influence both the purchase and recommendation behavior of current and potential customers. Nonpersonal communication embraces such methods as advertising, direct mail, publicity and public relations, and, more recently, the Internet, in which an individual or group within the firm typically controls the firm's message. Interpersonal communication, by contrast, has traditionally been largely under the control of individual sales representatives. In many industries, the sales force is the principal vehicle for contact between the supplier firm and its customers, and has historically enjoyed the sole responsibility for managing long-term customer relationships.

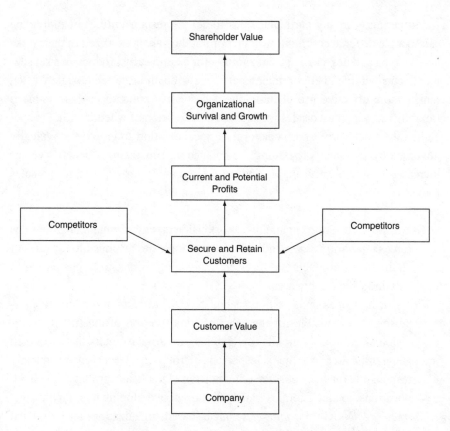

FIGURE 1.1: A Hierarchy of Organizational Objectives

THE TRADITIONAL SALES FORCE SYSTEM

The traditional sales force system typically comprises a hierarchical organization in which a number of "on-the-road" salespeople report to a first-line sales manager. First-line managers in turn report to more senior managers, for example, regional or zone, ultimately to a national sales manager. The number of managerial levels varies from firm to firm and depends on such factors as sales force size and management's philosophy regarding decentralization and salesperson empowerment. In recent years, downsizing efforts have led to increases in managerial spans of control and a flattening of the hierarchy in many sales organizations.[5]

Furthermore, in any particular sales force, the responsibilities of individual salespeople differ according to whether or not they are specialized in their tasks and the type and degree of specialization—for example, by product, market segment, channel member, or maintenance–new business. Specialization often makes more effective use of individual salespeople but also leads to reduced flexibility and increased sales force costs. The decision of whether or not to specialize the sales force and what form of specialization to employ is typically governed by judgments regarding the balance of effectiveness benefits versus increased costs.[6] Several major options are available for organizing the sales force:

Geography. The simplest and most cost efficient way of organizing the sales force is *geographically.* Individual salespeople are responsible for sales of all the firm's products and services,[7] in all applications, to all customers, in a defined geographic area.[8]

Product. In a sales organization specialized by *product,* an individual salesperson is responsible for the sales of some portion of the firm's (or division's) products, in all applications, to all customers in a defined geographic area. Another salesperson or group of salespersons is typically responsible for sales of some other portion of the firm's products, in all applications, to all customers in the same or an overlapping geographic area.

Market segment. In the *market segment*–based organization, an individual salesperson is responsible for sales of all the firm's (or division's) products to all customers in a particular market segment, for example, industry or product application. Another salesperson is typically responsible for sales of all the firm's products to all customers in another market segment, in the same or an overlapping geographic area.

Channel member. In the *channel member*–based organization, one salesperson is responsible for developing and maintaining relationships at a specific level in the channel system, for example, distributors; another salesperson is responsible for developing and maintaining relationships at another level, for example, wholesalers or retailers.

Maintenance/new business. In the *maintenance–new business* sales organization, a distinction is made between existing versus new accounts. Salespeople responsible for generating sales to new accounts and initiating firm/customer relationships later hand these customers over to a maintenance sales force.[9]

Although these various methods of managing sales force effort have served supplier firms well,[10] increased competition is giving rise to a series of pressures that is transforming this traditional system into a new system for managing firm/customer relationships.

PRESSURES ON THE TRADITIONAL SALES FORCE SYSTEM

We conceptualize pressures on the traditional sales force system as comprising three types: increased competition, internal pressures from the firm's sales organization, and pressures from customers (Figure 1.2).

Increased Competition

Today, virtually all business organizations around the world face vastly increased levels of competition, making the task of securing and retaining customers ever more difficult. Competition has grown in both depth and scope as separate national economies have become more closely integrated. These linkages have been enhanced by increased global capital flows, and the actions of such supranational global organizations as the World Trade Organization (WTO) (and its predecessor GATT) that promote economic growth by focusing on free trade, by lowering tariff barriers and by reducing other obstacles to competition. In addition, several multinational regional organizations such as the European Union (EU), the North American Free Trade Area (NAFTA), the Association of South East Asian Nations (ASEAN), and Mercosur in South America are leveraging firms out of their national markets, perhaps for the first time, and setting the stage for broader participation in the world economy.[11]

Other factors driving increased competition include denationalization (privatization) of government-owned corporations, relaxed levels of regulation, and increasingly available low-cost, high-quality communications and transportation. Competition is increasing in the supply chain via forward and backward integration, and the greater willingness of firms to engage in various forms of partnership—joint ventures, research consortia, cross-licensing and supply chain alliances. Notwithstanding the recent difficulties of many "dotcoms," the growth of electronic commerce via the Internet is having a major impact on competition in many industries, not least by the development of exchanges. Relatedly, the increasingly widespread diffusion of new information technologies enables executives to better manage far-flung enterprises, and faster technological change is leading to competition not just among firms but among entire industries.

Another significant factor is the increasing spread of the shareholder value philosophy. Although primarily a U.S. creation, this philosophy is increasingly making major inroads in such countries as Germany, France, and Japan where alternative corporate governance models have long held sway. As shareholder interests gain preeminence, profit pressures grow for all firms and competition increases.

Heightened competition in their domestic markets is leading increasing numbers of corporations either to venture abroad for the first time, or to enhance their multicountry scopes to become truly global enterprises. Regardless, at home and abroad, they face new competitors that may operate in unexpected ways. Indeed, in many parts of the world, as corporations strive to identify new opportunities by seeking to satisfy ever more complex customer needs, the increasingly global economy is bringing domestic competitors face-to-face with highly skilled and well-financed foreign firms.

On a day-by-day basis, these competitive pressures take many forms. Prices trend downwards, and product line competition increases via more complex products and shorter product life cycles. Service levels improve in response to the rapidly rising expectations of customers no longer tolerant of bare minimum offerings. Distribution channels shift, and a host of new communication vehicles such as satellite and cable TV, and the Internet, are available to all competitors.

Increases in Selling Costs

An additional factor putting pressure on the traditional sales force system is the increasing cost of sales force effort that, for many years, has outpaced inflation. *Sales and Marketing Management* magazine publishes an annual review of these costs; its data demonstrate that the cost per sales call has been rising in recent years (Figure 1.3).

Driven in part by labor market factors and in part by internal company decisions such as the provision of computers, cell phones, and other technological aids, these cost increases affect all types of sales effort. They are particularly no-

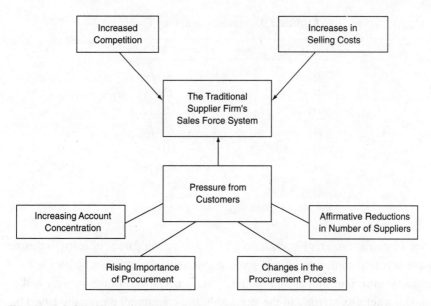

FIGURE 1.2: Pressures on the Firm's Current System for Interfacing with Customers

ticeable for small and mid-size customers where sales revenues are lower. As we discuss below, the increasingly high cost of serving large numbers of small and mid-size customers implies that the firm should explore alternative ways of interfacing with them.

Pressure from Customers

In this section, we highlight four areas: increasing account concentration, the rising corporate importance of procurement, changes in the procurement process, and affirmative reduction in numbers of suppliers.

INCREASING ACCOUNT CONCENTRATION

Sellers face fewer and more powerful customers as the result of many separate environmental forces that are combining to concentrate firm sales with reduced numbers of customers. For example, sales to customers in mature industries are affected by a generalized trend toward oligopolistic market structures as weaker competitors either exit or are acquired by (or merged into) stronger competi-

FIGURE 1.3: Increases in Selling Costs[12]

Year	Average Cost of Sales Call
1986	$57.40
1988	$56.68
1992	$82.18
1994	$96.88
1997	$113.25
1998	$156.71
1999	$164.70

Note: Year 2000 results not available at publication.

tors.[13] International regionalization and globalization forces in many industries have accelerated this trend and some previously domestic oligopolies are now consolidating into global oligopolies.[14] Relatedly, the boom in merger and acquisition activity starting in the late 1980s and continuing during the 1990s has, in many cases, reduced the number of available customers. In part, the rationale for these mergers is to increase bargaining power over suppliers:

> **EXAMPLE:** The North American supermarket industry is undergoing significant consolidation. In late 1998, Kroger purchased Fred Meyer for $13 billion to form the largest U.S. chain. Of the $225 million cost savings, over half was expected to result from *better* buying [emphasis added].[15]

Finally, in many industries, such as health care, buying groups have developed as countervailing forces to the power of suppliers.

RISING IMPORTANCE OF PROCUREMENT

Historically, for many firms in many industries, vertical integration was viewed as a way of increasing profits by capturing large amounts of value added in the conversion process from raw materials to finished goods. In such companies, where the ratio of value-added to revenue was high and, conversely, the procurement spend-to-revenue ratio low, the procurement function was perceived to be relatively unimportant. Indeed, "purchasing" was often viewed as a managerial backwater.

Several factors have led to increases in the procurement spend-to-revenue ratio:

- Corporate downsizing and the increasing replacement of labor by capital has led to relatively greater expenditures on capital equipment, raw materials, and supplies, versus labor.
- Many companies have sought to increase flexibility through reduction in fixed-cost levels via vertical disintegration. For example, at the end of the twentieth century, both General Motors and Ford spun off their parts suppliers, Delco and Visteon respectively.
- Company focus on core competence and the concomitant growth in outsourcing has increased the value of purchased goods and services for organizational use.
- The growth in importance of branding has led many firms to act as resellers for parts of their product line, also raising the purchasing ratio.

In total these changes can be quite dramatic; for example, at IBM, from 1987 to 1997, the ratio of purchasing spend to revenue rose 57% from 28% to 44%.[16]

The profitability implications of this shift have not been lost on corporate management. Consider, for example, two companies with different value-added structures (Figure 1.4): Company A has a 20% ratio of procurement spend to revenue; Company B has a 70% ratio. Assuming that each firm has a 10% profit margin, a 10% increase in procurement efficiency raises Company A's profit by 20%; a 10% increase in procurement efficiency raises Company B's profit by 70%!

In addition, senior management awareness of the importance of procurement has been heightened by margin pressure from increased competition, a sharpened organizational focus, the aftermath of reengineering, increased emphasis

FIGURE 1.4: Illustration of the Impact of Procurement Efficiencies in Companies with Different Cost Structures ($)

	Company A		Company B	
	Original	Procurement Efficiency Increase, 10%	Original	Procurement Efficiency Increase, 10%
Sales revenue	100	100	100	100
Procurement costs	20	18	70	63
All other costs	70	70	20	20
Total costs	90	88	90	83
Profit	10	12	10	17
Profit increase		20%		70%

on supply chain management, cost efficiencies secured following mergers and acquisitions, successful organizational transformations following crisis situations (e.g., IBM, in the early 1990s), and proselytizing consulting firms that offer methodologies for reducing procurement expenditures.[17]

Furthermore, it is important to remember that raw material costs in the supply chain are only one of many types of procurement costs. For example, approximately 52% of Johnson & Johnson's sales revenues represent payments to third party providers of goods and services. However, of those costs, only 33% are for raw materials! Much of the remainder is for support services such as travel, communications, computers, and so forth. Procurement managers believe that these areas, frequently purchased in a decentralized manner with little oversight from procurement professionals, have enormous potential for cost reduction.[18]

The results of increased focus on procurement are starting to come in. For example, in the late 1990s, one $10 billion pharmaceutical company announced a reduction in its inbound supply costs of $1.5 billion.[19]

CHANGES IN THE PROCUREMENT PROCESS

As a result of the growing complexity and importance of procurement decisions, several changes are occurring in the procurement process:

Centralization. A trend to centralization in procurement decision making has been aided by rapid advances in telecommunications, computer technology and the Internet. Whereas, historically, various business units may have operated independently for procurement purposes, the increasing ability of the center to gather data from its disparate units has led to a shift in the locus of procurement practice. For example, in many retail chains, the corporate office is now heavily involved in procurement decisions for individual stores; in previous years these stores may have operated more autonomously.

Increasingly, in these situations, the act of purchase is conduced by an individual through the Internet. The employee simply enters a specially constructed vendor web site (extranet) to place the order. Such systems allow more complete, accurate, and timely data on purchases from individual suppliers to be collected by procurement personnel. Buyers secure greater leverage and are able to track purchasing performance against benchmark databases. These information systems not only track individual suppliers' performance but also monitor employee compliance with centrally negotiated supply contracts.

EXAMPLE: Dell Computer's *Premier Pages* are password-protected customized web sites created for each key account. These sites include approved configurations and negotiated prices for Dell products that key account employees can access to secure the products they require. *Premier Pages* also provide a variety of management reports that enable the key account to track computer purchases.[20]

Globalization. The globalization trend discussed earlier has led firms to search more broadly for suppliers and to add global coverage as a critical choice criterion. Several firms have shifted to global centralization, and national and regional procurement personnel now report to a head of global procurement. Global procurement maintains a master worldwide vendor file that can be used to access previously developed purchasing solutions.

Greater Effectiveness. Historically, purchasing was tactical and transactional, a clerical function with modest educational requirements. Today, the new breed of procurement professional is often a fast-tracker with an MBA, multiple organizational experiences, and headed for increased responsibility in another function. These increasingly proficient procurement staffs, at multiple management levels, often led by newly appointed procurement executives with high corporate visibility,[21] have introduced new strategies to reduce costs, improve quality, and increase efficiencies.

EXAMPLE: The day he arrived at General Motors (GM), incoming procurement czar Jose Ignacio Lopez summoned GM suppliers to a next-day meeting at GM's technology center. Holding up a sample GM contract, he ripped it in two saying, "This is one of your contracts; your new contract *will* incorporate a 20% price reduction!"

Strategic Sourcing. Specific procurement initiatives place great pressure on suppliers via such methods as "strategic sourcing," in which potential suppliers are invited to complete an extensive "Request for Information" (RFI) document before responding to a very detailed "Request for Proposal" (RFP).[22, 23] Highly trained procurement personnel, often using models of suppliers' cost structures, negotiate aggressively to select those suppliers best able to meet specifications at the lowest price.[24]

EXAMPLE: IBM's procurement training embraces an intensive set of courses at three different levels—a basic set of "core" courses, then intermediate and advanced series. Suppliers are invited to some of the more advanced courses to focus on joint cost reduction.[25]

Frequently, the new breed of procurement personnel has little or no regard for long-standing relationships (even if the supplier is an internal division), and may send the firm's own consultants into suppliers' plants to help increase efficiency. Other firms benchmark various supply prices (e.g., raw materials, travel, supplies, printing services) against industry standards to secure leverage in supplier negotiations.[26]

Interface Simplification. In dealing with multibusiness firms, procurement personnel have begun to question whether it is really necessary to meet with salespersons from each of several individual firm divisions, preferring to deal with a single supplier firm representative.

EXAMPLE: Until the early 1990s, salespeople from various divisions of Procter and Gamble (P&G) had relationships with Wal-Mart's procurement personnel. In the new P&G/Wal-Mart partnership, a single key account manager leads a P&G key account team that interfaces with a corresponding Wal-Mart organization.[27]

Concurrently, some suppliers have found they can secure better access to senior management in their major customers by concentrating responsibility for all products and services with a single company contact.

B2B Exchanges. The introduction of these Internet-enabled exchanges has the potential to vastly change companies' procurement practices. The exchanges take several forms, but perhaps the most relevant for key account management is buyer-driven (reverse) auctions. In these auctions, the buyer specifies its requirements, and pre-vetted suppliers place bids to fill the order. A particularly interesting aspect of such auctions is that prices tend to drop dramatically at the conclusion of the auction.[28]

Although much interest has been shown in Internet-enabled exchanges, they are no panacea. For example, in the steel industry, *Business Week* has reported that few buyers use e-steel.com, "preferring to receive bids from the few mills they're interested in, even if that means cutting themselves off from some low bids,"[29] and IBM refuses to hold auctions, believing it "unfair" to solicit quotes from marginal suppliers just to force prices down.[30] In other cases, suppliers refuse to bid. Nonetheless, as auction sites proliferate and key accounts initiate auctions for products they require, suppliers will have to address critical strategic and organizational decisions.

AFFIRMATIVE REDUCTIONS IN NUMBERS OF SUPPLIERS

Concurrent with changes in the procurement process, in recent years, many corporations have made affirmative decisions to forge closer relationships with fewer suppliers and only allow the "best" to compete for their business. These actions run directly counter to the traditional *modus operandi* of sending specifications to a large number of potential suppliers, then selecting a limited number based on such criteria as price and delivery.

Several factors have led to these reductions: the quality movement and a desire by companies to secure tighter control over their raw material inputs; a desire to reduce input costs, including procurement costs; the increased complexity of many purchases involving multiple technologies and customized service, and requirements for increased procurement effectiveness.[31]

> **EXAMPLE:** In the mid-1990s, Patrick Grace, president of Grace Logistics, claimed that high-volume purchasing for MRO (maintenance, repair, and operating supplies) could reduce outlays by 10% to 25%.[32] By 2000, many companies were reducing these types of input costs by purchasing directly over the Internet.

In addition, the adoption of Kanban and just-in-time inventory systems, a concern to reduce working capital, business process reengineering, and an overall focus of improving efficiency and effectiveness in the resource conversion process via supply chain management have all contributed to this trend. Finally, an organizational streamlining movement involving narrowing mission scopes and outsourcing has led many firms to seek closer relationships with suppliers in such matters as product development.

For example, Xerox cut its supplier base 90%, from 5,000 in 1980 to 300 in 1985[33]; at Volkswagen in the mid-1990s, Jose Ignacio Lopez reduced the number of suppliers from 2,000 to 200 (some original suppliers became subcontractors), cutting the purchasing bill by DM1.7 billion (4%)[34]; other examples show similar dramatic reductions (Figure 1.5)

FIGURE 1.5: Reductions in Numbers of Suppliers, Late 1980s to Mid-1990s[35]

Firm	Previous	New	Reduction (%)
DEC	9,000	3,000	70
Ford	1,800	1,000	44
General Motors	10,000	5,500	45
Milliken	19,700	9,200	54
Motorola	5,000	500	90
Texas Instruments	22,000	14,000	36

Furthermore, this trend is expected to continue: in a 1996 study of procurement practices, A. T. Kearney found significant reductions (actual and planned) in numbers of suppliers for both North American and European samples of major firms. Indices formed by setting the number of suppliers in 1992 at 100 were North America, 1995 = 77, 1998 (projected) = 43, and Europe, 1995 = 88, 1998 (projected) = 64.

EXAMPLE: In an extreme example, in late 1996 and early 1997, American, Continental, and Delta Airlines each committed themselves to twenty-year exclusive purchasing agreements with Boeing. In return for the promise of steady business, Boeing agreed to attractive prices and delivery flexibility; the airlines were expected to benefit from significant savings related to training and spare parts inventories. However, these agreements had serious political implications; in July 1997, Boeing agreed to rescind and drop its use of exclusive contracts with major American airlines in a successful effort to win the European Commission's approval of its merger with McDonnell Douglas.[36]

This type of supplier reduction is not only occurring in manufacturing industries. In the advertising agency business, for example, in the mid-1990s, both IBM, and Reckitt and Coleman (a British consumer-goods firm) reduced their numbers of agencies from over thirty to one; Kellogg employs only five agencies worldwide and Nestlé two.[37]

This confluence of pressures discussed above can be especially severe on domestic firms competing with global corporations.

EXAMPLE: Promon Ltd. is a Brazilian firm supplying telecommunications switching equipment and services for all related systems integration. In the

FIGURE 1.6: Percent Sales to Top Five Customers for Firms in Selected Industries[38]

Industry	1972	1996
Biscuits	24%	76%
Board/packaging	16%	64%
Specialty adhesives	14%	39%
Metal bearings	18%	44%

late 1990s, Telesp (Brazil), Promon's largest customer, was privatized and acquired by Spain-based Telefonica España (TE); TE was replacing all Telesp upper management. Promon competed with global suppliers Ericsson, Siemens, NEC, and Alcatel; Ericsson and Alcatel held preferred supplier status at Telefonica España. Telesp was anxious to reduce its supplier base!

Relatedly, many firms are reporting concentration of sales with fewer customers. Figure 1.6 reports the results of a British study.

Significant pressures are impacting the traditional sales force system. Competitive intensity is rising, macroeconomic trends are reducing the number of available customers, and the cost of sales force effort is leading firms to question their traditional ways of dealing with smaller customers. In addition, considerable pressure is being felt from customers for whom procurement is becoming an ever more important issue; they are affirmatively reducing their supplier bases and changing markedly the way they conduct their procurement activities.

During the past quarter century, several major themes can be identified among the myriad of actions firms have taken to deal with these pressures and improve their competitive positions. First, in the early 1980s, the quality movement led to an across-the-board upgrading of quality in firms' products and processes. Second, by downsizing, reengineering, and other approaches, firms attempted to take costs out of their organizations. Third, focusing not only on costs but also on capital employed, management reconceptualized the scope of the firm and its relationship to the supply chain, and began to outsource activities that had traditionally been conducted in-house.

For the most part, these "actions-of-choice" have improved firm functioning in their increasingly fast-changing, complex, and turbulent environments, but increasingly the process of making sales is taking center stage. Supplier firms have developed a heightened awareness of the importance of a small subset of their customer bases, those firms that currently do, and in the future will, account for a large proportion of corporate revenues and profits. As a result, the traditional sales force system is fragmenting and paving the way for a new, emerging system of sales and customer management.[39]

THE EMERGING SYSTEM

The impact of the various pressures discussed in the previous section has led many supplier firms to reevaluate their nonpersonal and interpersonal communication efforts, in particular their sales force systems. Senior management in many corporations now realizes that, across the customer base, not all customers are equal: some customers are more valuable than others.[40]

As a result, the traditional sales force system has become fragmented in the manner described in Figure 1.7. We group customers roughly into three groups: small, medium, and large. Typically, medium-size companies continue to be addressed by the traditional sales force system or some variant; the significant changes concern large customers—key account management—and small customers.

Dealing with Large Customers[41]

For virtually all corporations, some form of 80/20 rule operates. Although this rule can be viewed in several different ways, a typical interpretation is that 80% of the firm's revenues is supplied by 20% of its customers. If this rule, or a close variant (90/10; 75/25), operates in the firm's customer environment, the critical business implication is that these 20% (or 10% or 25%) of customers have an importance to the firm's long-run future that exceeds that of the "average" customer.[42]

These high current (and potential) volume (and profit) customers are the firm's critical assets. Of course, they are not visible on the firm's balance sheet,[43] yet they are more important to long-run survival and growth than many of the firm's fixed assets. Indeed, whereas a firm may have a viable business with many customers but zero fixed assets, a business with many fixed assets but zero customers is not viable. Furthermore, fixed assets may in fact be strate-

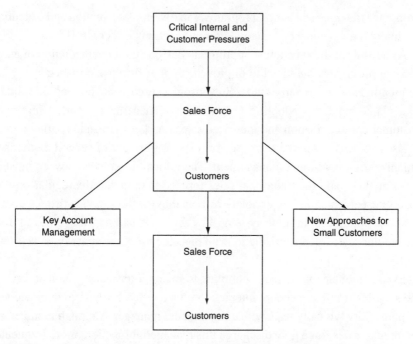

FIGURE 1.7: The Changing Nature of Sales Force Activity

gic liabilities as, for example, when market requirements and technology change; committed to its fixed asset base, the firm may be unable to adapt to changing circumstances. IBM's unwillingness, in the 1980s, to embrace fully a shift from mainframes to work stations and PCs is an exemplar of the liability of fixed assets.

Both the high value of, and increased competition for, this special set of customers suggests that they should be treated differently from the firm's "average" customers. Indeed, they should both receive a disproportionate share of firm resources and are worthy of greater managerial attention. This compelling rationale has led many firms to the development of key account management programs.[44]

Key account management both focuses the firm's attention on those accounts that are especially important for its current and long-run future, and optimizes the use of scarce resources. It provides for the development of more complete information and analysis of customers' strategic realities, critical needs and buying processes, competitive threats, and important supplier firm resources. As a result, the supplier firm better identifies planning assumptions and opportunities and threats, sets more appropriate objectives, and formulates more appropriate strategies and action programs. Finally, implementation and execution are improved via enhanced internal communications and control.

As a result of these benefits, appropriate design and implementation of a key account program should lead to improved supplier firm performance at key accounts. Indeed, in an early study, Stevenson secured data showing that industrial marketing firms adopting key account management reported improved customer communication and increased sales, market share, and profits.[45]

As we discuss later, the supplier firm may employ one of several methods to organize for key account management. The critical difference between most of these methods and the traditional sales force system is that the regular on-the-road salesperson is no longer solely responsible for the supplier-firm/customer relationship. Indeed, in some systems, key account customers are removed from the regular sales force's jurisdiction and placed within a separate organizational unit.

Even if regular salespersons continue to maintain primary responsibility for the supplier-firm/key-account interaction on a day-by-day basis, major account responsibility typically rests with a key account manager. Although members of the regular sales force may discharge this managerial function, more frequently it is placed with a separate key account management group. Managers work with colleagues in other functional departments (including the sales force) as leaders of key account teams and have primary responsibility for the long-run health of the relationship. Fulfilling this function requires a set of skills involving teaching, coaching, mentoring, planning, and facilitating that are typically not required of the average salesperson.

Finally, firms adopting key account programs are developing systems and processes to improve key account management. In addition to a variety of managerial processes designed to coordinate firm efforts at its key accounts, important advances in computer and telecommunications technologies are having a major impact. For example, many firms are using the Internet to enhance key account relationships. Although it is perhaps too early to predict the future effect of the Internet on relationships between supplier firms and their key accounts, there seems little doubt that it will be significant.

Dealing with Small Customers

A logical corollary of the 80/20 rule discussed above is the 20/80 rule. This second rule implies that 20% of the firm's revenues are derived from 80% of its

FIGURE 1.8: Firm Profits (%) by Customer Decile Groups

	Largest 10% of Customers							Smallest 10% of Customers		
	1	2	3	4	5	6	7	8	9	10
1980	15%	17%	16%	13%	12%	10%	7%	6%	4%	1%
1996	–3%	26%	29%	22%	20%	8%	4%	0%	–3%	–3%

customers. It gives rise to the following question: "What does it cost to serve this 80% of the firm's customers?" The answer for most firms is: "A lot!"

A supplier to the European printing industry measured the profit secured from its customers in decile groups in both 1980 and 1996 (Figure 1.8). The later results for this company demonstrate a marked change compared to sixteen years previously[46]:

- Profit is now concentrated largely in the second through fifth deciles (97%).
- The smallest three deciles in total produce a loss.
- The firm now makes a loss with its first decile of customers (the firm's largest). (This item should be treated with care inasmuch as the firm's largest customers may bear a significant amount of the overhead burden.)

(Firms can identify the profit distribution for their own customer bases by completing the table shown in Appendix 1.1.)

Although not the topic of this book, we touch briefly on three ways firms are addressing the increasingly high cost of serving small customers.

Stop serving small customers. A simple way of categorizing small accounts is to identify those likely to grow into larger customers, those likely to continue in business but unlikely to grow, and those whose long-run future looks insecure. A firm using this categorization may decide that the latter group and some portion of the second group should be dropped from its customer list. If the firm makes its selections expeditiously, minimal current and potential sales revenue is lost, but the firm enjoys significant cost savings. On the other hand, dropping customers, who then need a supplier, may remove an entry barrier for competition.

Identify less expensive methods for the firm to deal with these accounts. In this approach, high-cost/low-potential accounts are removed from sales force responsibility and placed with an internal group. Field sales calls are no longer made and supplier firm–customer communication is conducted entirely by such methods as telemarketing, direct mail, and electronic mail. Sales revenue is retained but overall costs are reduced. A recent approach is to serve such customers through Internet web sites.

Assigning accounts to agents and/or distributors. Frequently, because their fixed costs are typically lower, distributors are better structured than suppliers to handle large numbers of accounts purchasing small product volumes. Under this option, the firm advises small customers it can no longer serve them directly but that its products and services can be secured through distribution. Direct sales force costs are eliminated but the firm's revenue stream, less the distributor's margin, continues.

> **EXAMPLE:** A 3M business had over five thousand customers, most of which were small volume users. When a profitability analysis revealed that many of these customers caused losses for 3M, all but the largest customers were handed over to carefully selected dealers. As a result, the customer base was cut to one hundred accounts, some of which were the distributors that acquired the small accounts from 3M.

> **EXAMPLE:** Motorola's Land Mobile Products Sector (LMPS) had 200,000 accounts spread among 2,000 sales representatives. LMPS shifted to a key account management approach by focusing the sales force on the roughly 20% of customers providing 80% of its business. To address the remaining 80% of its customer base, LMPS set up a dealer organization and transitioned these accounts to the dealer channel. By and large, the accounts were pleased with the transition, as it simplified their relationships with Motorola.[47]

Notwithstanding the advantages of this option, the decisions to pass a customer over to a distributor should be made very carefully. Down the road, such an account may be sufficiently successful to warrant reestablishing a direct account-to-supplier relationship. The distributor may object!

THE VALUE OF KEY ACCOUNT PROGRAMS

Key account management can only be a viable approach for dealing with important customers if it benefits both the supplier firm and its key accounts. In this section we discuss the potential benefits available from individual key account programs. We recognize, of course, that their presence, absence, and degree of achievement are functions both of the individual program *per se* and its appropriateness for the two parties. Certainly, key account programs are no panacea; they are not without their problems and issues for both supplier firms and key accounts. After a discussion of the benefits of key account programs for supplier firms and for key accounts, we suggest several cautions.[48] Finally, we identify a series of levers to gain top management's attention on the potential benefits of a key account program

Benefits for Supplier Firms

Key account programs may provide a variety of interrelated benefits for supplier firms that together lead to increased sales and profits.

As the key account reduces its supplier base, possibly moving to sole suppliers for certain products and services, the supplier firm may anticipate receiving increased business, often with multiyear contracts. Recently collected data demonstrate the importance for company growth of identifying the firm's most valuable customers (Figure 1.9).[49]

Though price reductions may occur, price predictability should improve and the supplier firm should enjoy increased efficiencies: in production via scale economies, matching production to demand, streamlining the purchasing/delivery process, and by developing standardized procedures for servicing the key account's multiple locations. In general these benefits follow from:

Improved understanding of the key account's goals, and requirements. As the key account/supplier firm relationship improves, the degree of information sharing across the interorganizational interface increases. The supplier firm enhances its knowledge of the key account's business environment, plays a role in helping to develop the key account's goals and strategy, and better understands

FIGURE 1.9: The Importance of Key Accounts

	High-Growth Firms	Low-Growth Firms
Percent with an "extremely clear view" of the most valuable customers	38%	22%
Percent of revenue from top 10% of customers	46%	32%

its needs so that extra focus may be given to product and service development. Conversely, the key account secures better information on the supplier firm's competencies and developing technologies so that its own strategy development is improved. Greater understanding should lead to improved performance for both organizations.

> **EXAMPLE:** Said a market operations director at AT&T discussing a particular key account, "There is an excellent give and take. We benefit from strong relationships because we share a strategic direction with our customer. I am told how I can help him."

Increased key account switching costs. As the supplier-firm/key-account relationship develops, the key account comes to rely on the supplier firm for critical inputs to its operations via joint projects, customized products and services, and the like. In addition, the number and variety of interpersonal relationships (professional and social/personal) increases both horizontally (multiple functions) and vertically (multiple levels). All of these factors bind supplier and key account closer, increase the difficulty of severing the relationship, and may lock out competitors.[50]

Better Understanding and Management of the Key Account. When the supplier firm has multiple sales relationships with a customer, there may be no single locus for understanding the total supplier/customer relationship. The simple act of measuring revenues and profits at the key account level may reveal a variety of ideas on how to address the key account. In the absence of such focus, on the one hand, potential opportunities may be forgone; on the other, there may be no clear understanding of the supplier firm's risk exposure.

> **EXAMPLE:** The adoption of a corporate accounts program allowed 3M to identify sales opportunities for its individual business units that previously had been opaque to the company.

> **EXAMPLE:** British Aerospace Regional Aircraft (BARA) manufactures 70- to 120-seat jet aircraft. Difficulties in the airline industry in the early 1990s forced several large customers into bankruptcy before completing payment obligations. Many planes were returned to BARA, and parent British Aerospace suffered a $2 billion loss. BARA's functional organization was unable

to pinpoint potential problems sufficiently early; a well-developed key account system would have surfaced them.[51]

EXAMPLE: Historically, the process used by Snowbell Inc.*, a Latin American financial institution, for collecting on loan defaults comprised three disconnected subprocesses—administrative collection, pre-legal collection, and legal collection. Adoption of a key account collection process enabled the institution to focus attention early on the most serious defaults and so improve its overall collection performance.[52]

Enhanced ability to manage complex relationships. As customers attempt to deal with the increased complexities of their business environments, inevitably the complexity faced by supplier firms also rises. Many networks of relationships must be managed—within both the customer and supplier firm, and across the interorganizational boundary. Key account management is a process for dealing with this complexity and managing relationship networks.[53]

Presentation of a company perspective. In addition to providing a single point of contact, an effective key account manager can bring together many supplier firm personnel, possibly from different businesses, to speak with a single "company voice" to a customer that buys, or could buy, multiple products. In addition, an effective key account manager can influence her firm's organizational subunits to take a "company viewpoint" when responding to customers' multiunit RFPs. Failure to present a single face to the customer can cause significant problems.

EXAMPLE: Spun off from AT&T in 1996, Lucent Technologies' share price fell from almost $80 in late 1999 to less than $20 one year later. One contributing factor to this performance was lack of a functioning company-wide key account organization. Broken up into several divisions for the purpose of securing more entrepreneurial behavior, Lucent units competed with each other for individual customers. As one example, a large local phone company seeking to buy an advanced network to carry both voice and data said, "I fully understand what Nortel is doing, and I fully understand what Cisco is offering, but I'm confused on what Lucent is actually offering, because I've heard different descriptions of the same solution from different Lucent teams."[54]

Second-order market benefits. If the supplier firm has chosen its key accounts wisely, they will push it to higher levels of performance on many product and service dimensions. As the performance envelope is pushed outward to serve hard-driving key accounts, internal transfer of best practice makes the supplier firm more competitive in the market as a whole.

> EXAMPLE: Alpha Graphics, a design, copy, print, and networking business, is one of Xerox's major customers. In the mid-1990s, it was entering five new countries per annum with the latest Xerox equipment. Often Xerox would not have appropriately trained personnel in these countries. In order to serve Alpha, Xerox was forced to upgrade service quality and in so doing improved its ability to serve other customers.

Human resource benefits. Introduction of key account programs offers a variety of human resource benefits:

- A rigorous recruitment, selection, training, and retaining process ensures that experienced competent key account managers deal with important customers.
- The key account manager position is developmentally important inasmuch as he gains experience in "running a business," valuable preparation for more senior management positions.
- Key account management is a motivating career opportunity for the sales force and offers an excellent career track for high-performing salespeople who may neither want, nor be competent in filling, a direct line management position, for example, regional sales manager. Indeed, a critical sales force management problem concerns superior salespeople. Frequently, some form of promotion is necessary to retain outstanding performers, yet these individuals may have neither the ability nor the desire to be promoted to manage a group of salespeople. When flawed promotions do occur, the firm may lose a star salesperson and simultaneously gain an ineffective sales manager! Promotion to key account manager may represent a viable alternative both for recognizing outstanding performance and securing an effective individual for a critical organizational role.

Benefits for Key Accounts

As we discussed earlier, key account programs are typically introduced to rationalize the allocation of resources across the supplier firm's entire customer base. Hopefully, major customers will be better served and the benefits discussed above secured. However, this rationale has an internal focus; the supplier firm must be prepared to answer the following externally focused question with specifics:

> "What is the value of a key account program for the individual key account customer?"

Since introduction of a key account program frequently represents a major organizational shift for the supplier firm, an internal focus can easily dominate its decision making. The key account program will certainly have less than its desired impact if the supplier firm is unable to articulate to its key account customers the real value of such a designation! This issue becomes increasingly critical as savvy key accounts realize that, ultimately, they pay the price for increased attention from the supplier firm in the form of higher input costs.

Without doubt, managers at the key account will develop a set of expectations (probably high) regarding the value of being named a key account. A combination of high expectations but less than high perceived performance will lead to dissatisfaction.[55] The supplier firm should clearly spell out the positive benefits of being named a key account (and identify what will not occur), rather than allowing expectations to be formed in the absence of supplier input. In particular, it should be careful not to alert the key account unnecessarily to its power in the relationship such that the account demands excessive resources and/or price concessions.

Clearly, the benefits of being named a key account vary from account to account. Nonetheless, among the sorts of benefits key accounts might expect are:

A single point of contact. A difficulty for customers in dealing with major suppliers is that they often have separate interfaces with individual suppliers' various business units. The appointment of a single individual with responsibility for the entire institutional relationship, the key account manager, should lead to improved communications, fewer surprises, faster access to resources, quicker decisions, improved conflict resolution, and generally increased ease of doing business.

Lower costs of securing input products. This benefit may be derived from lower prices, improved procurement efficiencies via reduction in numbers of suppliers, and the streamlining of key-account/supplier-firm interfaces, often via one-stop shopping.

Enhanced value. A close supplier/key account relationship may provide customers with a trusted advisor, personal attention and a variety of other benefits. These may include access to high-level supplier firm technologists, partnering on new products, early introduction and testing of new products, product design flexibility providing customized solutions to account problems, consistent and high-level service, and specially designed value-added support services.

Indeed, key account relationships may enhance the probability of receiving value through the use of systems that base supplier payments on measurable results.

> **EXAMPLE:** Historically, advertisers paid their agencies a flat percentage of media advertising costs. Nowadays, advertising agencies and their key accounts (often consumer package goods companies) are developing systems for payment based on measurable marketplace results.

Guaranteed delivery when capacity is short. As supplier firms strive to improve operational efficiencies by running production facilities closer to capacity, shortages will inevitably develop. A key account relationship should protect the customer from all but the worst of supply shortages.

Long-term relationship. Increased closeness to the supplier firm results in ability to influence supplier-firm decision making leading to joint identification of opportunities and solutions to problems in a genuine win-win partnership, and may lead to an enhanced market position.

> **EXAMPLE:** Alder Inc.*, a major North American telecommunications firm told its supplier: "We expect you to provide solutions to the problems we face before we know we have a problem."

Nondirectly related benefits. In addition to those benefits that relate to the transactions between supplier and key account, the key account may receive other types of value from the supplier. Indeed, the supplier may be able to offer a myriad of corporate capabilities to the key account, ranging from the ability to get e-businesses up and running to managing the risk associated with changing weather patterns.

Finally, by the creation of a customer advisory board comprising non-competitive key accounts, the supplier firm may offer key account executives a forum to discuss broad topics of interest in a nonthreatening setting.[56]

Cautions for Key Account Management

All forms of key account management try to direct attention to those accounts that are most important for improving value for the supplier firm's shareholders via improved profits, and organizational survival and growth. However, notwithstanding the considerable potential benefits to both supplier firm and key account discussed above, they should be balanced by several major cautions:

Too many eggs in one basket. A focus on key accounts implies a concentration of resources on few customers.[57] If one or more of these customers is lost, the organizational implications may be severe. In the opening of this chapter, we highlighted the Ciena experience. The advertising industry provides another example:

> **EXAMPLE:** In an effort to secure the best possible services, major advertisers are conducting agency reviews increasingly frequently. In the mid-1990s, Ammitari Puris Lintas, a member of the Interpublic group, was awarded the entire Compaq account. Less than one year later, the account was reassigned to a competitor agency.

In an attempt to deal with this type of problem, Abbott Laboratories' account personnel submit nominations for their efforts in recovering troubled or lost relationships. Selected personnel are recognized and rewarded, but the program's major goal is to discuss and learn from negative customer relationships.

Insufficient benefits to the supplier firm. Regardless of the overall importance of a particular account, a key account relationship may have negative rather than positive effects. For example, if critical decisions at the key account, including procurement, are truly decentralized, alerting the customer to the variety, and value, of products purchased throughout its organization may lead to pressure for price reductions, volume discounts, and so forth; a better approach may be to "let sleeping dogs lie." Notwithstanding these concerns, the firm should consider all potential benefits from key account management. "If the dog will wake eventually," it may be better to play a role in its waking, rather than leave matters to chance, or to the competition!

Insufficient benefits to the potential key account. If the supplier firm does not carefully manage key account expectations, not only may the account see little benefit in the relationship, considerable dissatisfaction may ensue. Consider the following example when the status "improvement" required a change in firm contact personnel.

> **EXAMPLE:** A British Telecom regional sales manager received the following letter from a customer:
>
>> Recently, [our account manager, Helen Douglas] informed us that . . . we were scheduled to be "upgraded." I phoned Helen to tell her that we were very happy with the service she provided and did not wish to change to a new account manager. But she told us that the decision was company policy and not hers to change.
>>
>> Subsequently, I called [several other managers within British Telecom]
>>
>> So now I'm writing to you and appealing to your common sense rather than to company rule-books. I know it's your internal policy to reassign customers when they reach a certain size . . . We feel strongly we're better off remaining with Helen.[58]
>
> Certainly for this customer, designation as a more important account carried a significant penalty.

Limitation of opportunities. Successful key account programs are typically based on increasing the degree of interaction between supplier firm and customer organization. The downside of closer relationships is that the key account may insist on developing a list of competitor firms with which the supplier firm may *not* do business. Conversely, other potential customers may be nervous about such a close relationship between a potential supplier and one of their competitors. In either case, limitations are placed on the supplier firm's market opportunities.

EXAMPLE: Procter and Gamble (P&G) insists that any advertising agency with which it does business cannot work with one of its competitors. As a result, agencies with P&G accounts are deprived of the opportunity of working with such major potential customers as Colgate-Palmolive, Unilever, Nestlé, and Philip Morris.[59]

EXAMPLE: In 1999, Coca-Cola forged a major marketing relationship with Universal Studios. According to *Fortune,* Disney executives were "not pleased" to learn about this relationship from *The Wall Street Journal.* The result: a fraying partnership relationship between *Coke* and Disney and increased business for Pepsi.[60]

Cost and Bureaucracy. The addition of a new managerial system to the traditional sales force structure leads to significant out-of-pocket costs. Indeed, supplier firms frequently initiate key account management by focusing on the development of complex sets of policies and procedures. These "top heavy" systems are far too cumbersome. Commencing with relatively few key accounts, then broadening out as the firm gains experience and develops some best practice is a far preferred process.

Significant organizational change. Whether the current system is the firm's first attempt at key account management or represents an evolutionary stage from an earlier process, significant change is typically required—in the line organization and reporting relationships, in processes such as compensation, and in organizational culture. Unless the implications of these changes are well thought through, and steps taken to minimize the otherwise inevitable disruption, serious consequences, including abandonment of key account management, may follow. The sales force is a particular concern:

Sales force resistance. In many key account management systems salespeople lose some degree of autonomy. In some cases, responsibility for key accounts is entirely removed from the sales force's jurisdiction. These territorial issues and related concerns for sales compensation may lead to severe morale problems.

Unclear responsibility and authority. Frequently, key account management implies an additional reporting relationship for salespeople. Rather than reporting solely to a district or regional sales manager, they also report, in a dotted line sense (sometimes weaker, sometimes stronger), to a key account manager. Not only may these dual reporting relationships invoke considerable tension, salespeople may be required to execute action plans that they had only a minor role in developing. In addition, it may be difficult to identify the causes for success and failure at a particular key account and, consequently, to apportion praise and blame correctly. This is a particularly thorny issue when compensation is involved.

In addition to these cautions, over an operating cycle, there are many occasions when difficulties in supplier-firm/key-account management relationships will occur, some driven by the key account, others by the supplier firm. Profit pressures may be extreme: the key account may continually strive for price reductions from the supplier firm, or key account management in the supplier firm may be unwilling to raise prices for fear of adverse reaction. In addition, the key account may be unwilling (or unable) to provide the forecasts that the supplier firm needs to develop its production schedules, yet be furious when delivery is delayed on short-notice orders.

Other difficulties occur when the key account manager is unwilling to accede to a production request to drop an unprofitable product because it is used by the key account. Conversely, wishing to please personnel at the key account, the manager may be aggressive in offering products the supplier firm is unable to produce, or which are not yet ready for delivery. Finally, the smoothest running key account management system will have a difficult time placating customers faced with incomplete order fulfillment, late deliveries, overcharging, poor service, and the like.[61]

For most organizations the benefits of some form of key account program outweigh the associated costs.[62] Some of the factors leading to top management commitment for a key account program are noted in Figure 1.10. Those senior managers committed to key account management must carefully analyze the chosen key accounts and the various available management systems, then make the tough tradeoffs in choosing that system offering the most effective and efficient method for managing the firm's key accounts.

Top management:
- does not know which of the firm's accounts are most important (even in terms of sales revenues)
- recognizes that growth from its largest accounts is critical to achieving ambitious growth targets
- realizes that major customer or supplier consolidation is placing an increased emphasis on managing a particular customer relationship well
- is concerned about the amount of organizational effort being consumed by a demanding account with little evidence of reward
- recognizes that retaining existing customers is far more profitable than securing new customers
- believes that gaining increased share of a customer's business is the most profitable way of gaining market share
- becomes convinced that the firm's efforts at the account's operating units are wasted, duplicated, and inconsistent

FIGURE 1.10: Important Factors in Securing Top Management Commitment to a Key Account Management Program[63]

THE CONGRUENCE MODEL FOR KEY ACCOUNT MANAGEMENT[64]

Key account management embraces the process of identifying the firm's current and future critical customer assets and putting in place management systems designed to increase revenues and profits through enhanced customer loyalty. Because key accounts are so important for the firm's future, the overall manner in which they are addressed is a serious matter worthy of top management concern. Indeed, as management develops strategy for a particular market arena, it may discover that its success or failure depends very largely on the results it achieves with a limited number of key accounts.

Good key account management requires consideration of several complex elements in an overall management process. It is not simply a matter of appointing a few key account managers or introducing a key account planning system. Rather, consideration must be given to several interconnected building blocks that we term the key account congruence model (Figure 1.11).

The basic thrust of the congruence model is that the firm develops strategy in response to its environmental realities.[65] As a result, other elements must fall into line. Here we define the four elements of the congruence model:

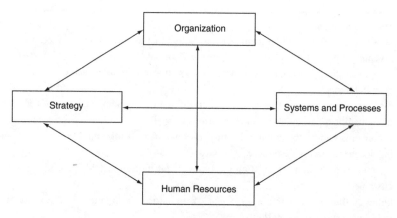

FIGURE 1.11: The Congruence Model for Key Account Management

Strategy: the extent to which the supplier firm is prepared to commit resources to key account management, the development of criteria for selecting key accounts, and building and managing the key account portfolio.

Organization: the line organization designed to support the key account strategy, and the roles and responsibilities of the principal players, in particular, top management, the key account director, and key account managers.

Human Resources: the critical human resource assets involved in managing key account relationships; we focus particularly on the key account manager.

Systems and Processes: the human- and information-technology-based systems and processes required for developing and managing key account relationships. An especially important process is developing the key account plan; related processes for making resource allocation decisions both among key accounts and between key accounts and other customers, are also very important.

The key account congruence model addresses the supplier firm's approach to dealing with key accounts as a whole. Nested within the congruence model are specific processes for managing individual key accounts.

Leading and managing successfully in the context of the key account congruence model is not a simple matter. Success will be achieved only if senior corporate executives fully understand the issues involved in key account management and are prepared to put in place the organizational, technological, financial, and human resources necessary to manage the firm's key accounts on a long-run basis.

The purpose of this book is to provide senior management both with a framework for understanding the critical issues involved in key account management, and a methodology for constructing a key account plan. This plan should function as a living document that drives firm actions by providing serious competitive advantage at the firm's key accounts.

STRUCTURE OF THE BOOK

In Chapter 1 we noted that in its attempts to improve shareholder value, a firm faces many pressures on its existing sales force system. The resulting fragmentation is leading to a focus on key account management. Key account management can offer significant, but different, benefits to both supplier firms and customer organizations but these must be tempered with a series of cautions. As firms move to address their most important customers, they must give serious consideration to the several elements of the key account congruence model.

In Section II, we elaborate on three of four elements of the congruence model. In Chapter 2 we discuss the firm's commitment to a key account strategy, and discuss the nature of key accounts. We examine key accounts at different organizational levels, and discuss various types of relationships between supplier firm and key account. We then move to identifying and using criteria to select key accounts, and conclude by considering different approaches to conceptualizing the firm's key account portfolio with a view to deciding how to allocate resources across the firm's entire key account base. In Chapter 3, we shift to organizational issues and explore the types of organization structure available, and the roles and responsibilities of critical players in the key account management process. Chapter 4 focuses on human resources, in particular on the critical organizational position of key account manager. We identify required skill sets, then discuss a series of issues in recruitment and selection, training, retaining, and rewarding key account managers.

In Section III, we turn to the fourth item in the congruence framework, systems and processes, focusing mainly on the key account planning process. Here we address situation analysis, strategy formulation and execution, and mechanisms for coordination and control. In Chapter 5, we focus on the various elements of the key account analysis. In Chapter 6, we complete the analytic portion of the situation analysis with discussions of competitor analysis and analysis of the supplier firm. We then address planning assumptions, and opportunities and threats for the supplier firm at the key account. These two chapters form the foundation for the key account strategy presented in Chapter 7. Here, we introduce vision, mission and the various elements of the key account strategy. In Chapter 8, we move to other systems and processes and address four major topics—keeping the key account team focused, interfacing with the key account, the role of technology, and performance monitoring.

In the final two chapters of the book, we examine two fast-developing areas in key account management. In Chapter 9, we discuss partnering with key accounts, including the evolution of supplier–key-account partnerships, and present a methodology for identifying partnership opportunities. We highlight the requirements for successful partnerships. In Chapter 10, we turn our attention to global account management, and discuss how managing global accounts differs from, and is more complex than, managing key accounts on a domestic basis.

In addition to the main discussion in the text, a series of seven Exercises contains a guide for developing a key account plan. These exercises comprise several tested sets of questions that enable the key account manager to conduct an in-depth situation analysis and lay out the key account strategy and action programs. Finally, several of the chapters have appendices that elaborate on specific issues.

II. STRATEGY, ORGANIZATION, AND HUMAN RESOURCES FOR KEY ACCOUNT MANAGEMENT

CHAPTER TWO

Developing Strategy for the Firm's Customers

The basic issue in this chapter is the firm's commitment to key accounts as the source of future revenues. In the first part of the chapter we present a framework for analyzing the firm's overall commitment to key accounts and introduce the concept of a vision statement for such a program. We then address the nature of key accounts and discuss the sorts of criteria that may be used to select them. We suggest several issues that should be considered in selecting key accounts and conclude by developing alternative portfolio approaches for managing key accounts.

FIRM COMMITMENT TO KEY ACCOUNTS

As we discussed in the previous chapter, the firm's traditional methods of interfacing with customers are facing many pressures that argue for the introduction of some form of key account management. We may explore the level of firm commitment to key account management by considering two dimensions—breadth and depth.

Breadth of commitment concerns the overall extent to which the firm's customers are assigned key account status.

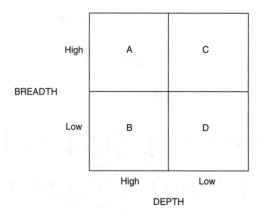

FIGURE 2.1: Firm Commitment to Key Accounts

Depth of commitment concerns the overall level and variety of resource allocation to these key accounts in terms of new and specialized organizational structures, systems, processes, human resources, and so forth.

A simple 2 × 2 matrix developed by arraying two levels each of breadth and depth of commitment to key account strategy produces four strategic archetypes (Figure 2.1):

Low Breadth/Low Depth (Cell D). In this cell, the firm has made no more than a minimal commitment to key accounts. It makes little or no effort to treat its more important accounts any differently from its other accounts. Indeed, it may not even recognize that some form of 80/20 rule governs its sales and profit performance. Even if the firm does recognize the importance of specific customers, it is not prepared to allocate significant organizational resources to treat them preferentially.

High Breadth/Low Depth (Cell C). In this cell, the firm has made the judgment that key accounts are important to its future health and has assigned key account status to a significant number of customers. However, it has not made the concomitant decision to allocate significant firm resources to these key accounts. Rather than make the major changes that are necessary to really make key account management work, it essentially attempts to graft key account management onto existing organizational structures and processes and makes little extra effort in the way of providing additional resources.

Low Breadth/High Depth (Cell B). Here, the firm has assigned key account status to a small number of customers, possibly as an experiment. Furthermore, it is placing significant effort into key account management via organizational redesign, development of specialized systems, processes, and human resources for these few customers.

High Breadth/High Depth (Cell A). In this cell, the firm is totally committed to key account management and focuses relatively greater attention on its major accounts. It identifies a significant number of key accounts and allocates organizational resources disproportionately to these customers.[1] The firm's key account strategy is closely linked to its business and corporate strategies and management makes major efforts in organizational redesign, the development of specialized systems, processes, and human resources to support this strategic direction. Furthermore, the firm may make efforts to rid itself of nonkey accounts.

EXAMPLE: In the late 1980s, Custom Research Inc. (CRI), a national market research firm, completed a thorough revenue and profitability study of all its 157 customers. As a result of this analysis it stopped doing business with over 100 customers to concentrate on its strategic accounts. By the late 1990s, with 80 customers, its revenues had tripled and its margins doubled.[2]

EXAMPLE: In March 2000, Lucent Technologies sold its sales division for small and medium-size business customers to Expanets. These 700,000 businesses thus became Expanets' customers.

EXAMPLE: Button-wood, Inc.*, a Philadelphia-based insurance company, developed profiles of profitable and unprofitable customers. Potential customers provide data that allows the company to classify them into either of the two groups. Those that fall into the unprofitable group are told that, unfortunately, the company cannot meet their needs, but helpfully directs them to close competitors!

DEVELOPING FULL-SCALE KEY ACCOUNT PROGRAMS

Firms in Cell A have made a major commitment to securing future revenues from key accounts. However, suppliers typically do not move from Cell D (minimal effort on key accounts) to Cell A (extensive effort with key accounts) in a single bound. Indeed, those firms attempting to introduce comprehensive key account programs from scratch often fail because they do not understand the necessity for congruence among the four elements of strategy, organization, human resources, and systems and processes introduced in Chapter 1. Neither do they understand the major changes in organizational functioning required to manage large numbers of key accounts. Indeed, firms that put in place organizational superstructures marrying grandiose expectations with high costs frequently find that they produce too little in the way of results and prematurely abandon them.

A more appropriate model for reaching Cell D is to pass through several intermediate stages via "creeping adoption." Initially, the firm focuses on a small number of individual key accounts, then develops its organization structure, systems, and processes as it gains experience in managing those accounts. This "test marketing" allows the firm to support (or reject) hypotheses regarding its efforts with key accounts and iron out organizational issues before broadening its efforts to include other accounts.[3]

EXAMPLE: 3M's corporate accounts program was piloted (1993) with two customers and later expanded to twenty. Xerox's global accounts program commenced with five customers in 1988; by 2000, it had grown to over one hundred accounts.

One experienced practitioner has isolated five phases of internal relationships in developing a key account program.[4]

Phase 1: Start-Up. An exciting (or fun) stage when the value of a key account program is generally recognized and processes are being put in place.

Phase 2: Uncertainty. Other sales channels develop a perception that key accounts may be competitive, significant overhead has been added, but few genuine benefits of the key account program have been identified.

Phase 3: Momentum. Positive sales results are anticipated but key accounts seem to have nonstandard requirements that place pressure on other firm functions.

Phase 4: Success. Substantial new business is earned through efforts of the cross-functional sales team.

Phase 5: Cost of Doing Business. Senior management questions low margins; other employees are concerned about nonstandard requirements that put pressure on their limited budgets. A reevaluation may identify lax criteria for key account assignment and/or a requirement to reengineer the key account process to one that better satisfies customer needs.

See Appendix 2.1 for case studies of evolving commitment to key account management.

VISION STATEMENTS FOR KEY ACCOUNT PROGRAMS

Firms with full-scale key account programs often develop vision statements for those programs as a whole. The best vision statements describe an ideal future state, a picture (in impressionistic form) of what the future should be.[5] Good vision statements should not be excessively restrictive, for employees must find in the vision something to inspire them. An overall statement of vision for the key account program provides focus and direction for the firm's efforts with key accounts. We offer four examples of firms that have grappled with developing visions for their key account programs.

> *Cisco Systems:* To provide best-in-class business practices and support to our worldwide strategic account customers.
>
> *Laidlaw National Accounts:* "To be recognized, and active, as the preferred supplier of innovative environmental resource services for the large, multilocation companies in Canada."
>
> *Olin National Accounts:* "Olin and our National Accounts will enhance its short- and long-term goals through sales, joint ventures, technology cooperation etc. that provide synergistic opportunities for both parties."
>
> *DHL:* "DHL will become the supplier of choice for express and express logistics services to targeted Global Account customers by becoming an essential part of their business plans to achieve their strategic goals."
>
> *Milliken Global Accounts* (carpets): "To develop strategic alliances with our global corporate customers by organizing teams focused on providing total customer satisfaction at the lowest possible process cost."

This last statement specifically identifies the type of customer (global corporate), the type of relationship (strategic alliance), and the organizational mechanism by which these customers will be served (teams). It also states clearly that cost to the customer, rather than the ex-Milliken price *per se,* is the critical issue, and implicitly suggests that process improvement (at Milliken and the customer) is the vehicle for achieving this goal.

THE NATURE OF KEY ACCOUNTS

Our basic definition of a key account is: *any organization that is of strategic importance to the firm.* Using this definition, the loss of a key account's current revenue or the inability to secure potential future revenue has a significant effect upon the firm or the relevant organizational unit. As a result, the key account warrants exceptional efforts from the supplier firm in an attempt to create critical dependencies, far greater efforts than for other important (but not key) accounts.

In this section, we address three issues concerning key accounts—the management of key accounts at different levels in the organization, types of key account relationships, and the degree of closeness of key-account/supplier-firm relationships.

Key Accounts at Different Levels in the Organization

Key account strategy may be developed at different levels within the firm. For example, some key accounts may be strategic at the business (divisional) level, others may be strategic at the corporate level. For global companies, some accounts are strategic at a global level (global accounts); others may be strategic at an international region level (e.g., the European Union). Finally, some accounts may be strategic from the perspective of individual countries (national accounts) or individual within-country regions (regional accounts).[6] As a result, just as strategy in general may be developed at different levels in the firm—for example, corporate strategy and business strategy—so, too, key account strategy may also be developed at several different levels.

> EXAMPLE: Several of 3M's many individual business units may have a key account relationship with a major corporation such as General Electric. In addition, 3M has a corporate accounts program focused on seeking opportunity for all 3M business units at the account.

> EXAMPLE: In the early 1990s, Citibank identified three sorts of account based on size and scope, two of which were key account groupings. The top 300 to 500 multinational corporations worldwide, *global key accounts,* were the responsibility of the World Corporate Group (WCG). In the United States, corporations that were large enough to have access to the capital mar-

kets, but were insufficiently multinational to be the responsibility of WCG, *national key accounts,* were handled by the National Corporate Division. All other companies were the responsibility of the Commercial Bank Division.[7]

In general, the concepts and ideas presented in this chapter and throughout the book are appropriate no matter where in the organization key account management is being developed. We use the generic terms "firm" and "top management" in our discussions; the reader should make the appropriate identification for his or her situation.

Types of Key Account Relationships

The firm may enjoy one of several types of key account relationship with another organization. We consider five types of relationship—direct customer, indirect customer, complementary product supplier, other organizations with significant firm relationships, and internal divisions or business units.

Direct Customers. For most supplier firms, direct customers make up the bulk of their key accounts. After all, these firms are those from which the supplier receives cash (or goods) in exchange for its products and services.

Indirect Customers. Direct customers are important, but to restrict the definition of customer solely to these entities is to adopt too narrow a perspective. A fuller definition of customer embraces any person or organization in the channel of distribution and decision (other than competitors) whose actions can affect the purchase of the firm's products and services.

Thus, a key account customer may also include a firm further down the manufacturing and distribution channel. For example, for plastic chip manufacturers selling to molders, major automobile companies and appliance manufacturers may represent important key accounts.[8] However, particularly tricky issues arise if such a key account asks the supplier firm for recommendations regarding various potential suppliers from its set of direct customers. More seriously, this type of key account may request a direct supplier-firm/customer relationship, bypassing the firm's current direct customers.

Complementary Product Suppliers. The sales of many products are closely tied to the sales of complementary products, for example, cameras and film, chemical apparatus, and reagent chemicals, personal computers and peripherals, computer hardware and software, laundry machines and detergents, automobiles and fuel. In such cases, each supplier firm should consider its major complementary product suppliers (complementers) as key accounts.

EXAMPLE: Ford and General Motors have long-term partnerships with oil companies to develop new and potentially cleaner fuels.[9]

Although the two types of supplier firm rarely purchase significant product volumes *from* each other, they influence high volumes of product sales *for* each other. Use of the two product types requires them to interface seamlessly and problem-free at minimal inconvenience and maximum benefit to customers.

Other Organizations with Significant Firm Relationships. Organizations that may have a major impact on the firm's success or failure include many noncustomer groups such as major product suppliers, joint venture partners, certification agencies such as the Food and Drug Association (FDA) for drug and medical device companies, shareholders, and human resource suppliers.[10] Furthermore, third party entities playing a substantial role in the purchase process, such as designers, systems integrators in the computer industry, or consultants should also be considered for key account status.

Although complementary firm suppliers and other organizations with significant firm relationships should be considered for a form of key account status, in this book we focus on those key accounts that are direct and indirect customers (current and potential) for the firm's products and services.

Internal Divisions or Business Units. Whereas the thrust of key account management focuses on organizations in the firm's external environment, the principles of key account management are also valid for intraorganizational relationships. For example, internal service organizations threatened with being outsourced may improve their performance by adopting a customer orientation that includes a focus on "key accounts."

EXAMPLE: Chase Manhattan Bank's E-Tech is an internal department responsible for providing technology services to the bank's various lines of business. To improve its levels of support, flexibility, responsiveness, and innovation, top management is holding E-Tech to the same free market discipline as external providers. E-Tech's response to this challenge has been to develop a key account management system including key account managers responsible for strategic customers within the bank.[11]

Degree of Closeness of Key-Account/ Supplier-Firm Relationships

Although those customers designated as key accounts are strategically important to the firm, the nature of the relationship between supplier and key account may vary widely on a "degree of closeness of relationship" continuum. This continuum ranges from *vendor* (buyer/seller of commodity items) through *quality supplier* (deliver superior value) to *partnership* (supplier firm makes significant contributions to the key account) (Figure 2.2).[12]

VENDOR

On the left of the scale, the supplier-firm/key-account relationship is weak. It represents the traditional adversarial type of buyer/seller relationship. The supplier firm's need to reduce uncertainty drives the relationship but it tends to be narrowly focused around standard products and services, and concerned mainly with improving communication both interorganizationally and within the supplier firm. Notwithstanding its designation as a key account, the buyer tends to have arms-length relationships with a large vendor base, short-term contracts with frequent rebidding, chooses suppliers largely on the basis of price, and is likely to shift suppliers for small price reductions, better delivery terms, and so forth. Dominant relationships are between sales and purchasing; information

FIGURE 2.2: The Supplier-Firm/Key-Account Relationship

flow is restricted since shared knowledge is perceived as eroding negotiating positions; quality control processes are individual firm centered, and productivity improvement initiatives are unilateral. As a result, the supplier-firm/key-account relationship is likely to be spasmodic as first one supplier, then another, offers better terms and secures the business.

This type of relationship may also occur when the key account is ambivalent about having close relationships with its suppliers. This ambivalence clearly limits supplier-firm/key-account activities but does not necessarily invalidate key account selection. Regardless of the relative lack of closeness in the relationship, if the customer satisfies the firm's criteria for key account status it should be treated as such, even though managing such an account may be fraught with difficulty.

QUALITY SUPPLIER

The scale midpoint represents a relationship that moves beyond a predominantly internal, uncertainty reduction focus to one of mutual commitment. Both supplier firm and key account recognize that a closer long-term relationship, in which switching costs are raised for both parties as the two firms commit to each other, may have significant value. Each organization understands the importance of the interorganizational interface for producing high-quality final products, each plans for continuous quality improvement, and the supplier firm secures differential advantage by delivering products and services that supply real customer value better than competitors. Price is a matter for negotiation rather than being driven solely by market forces. Supplier and key account plan together but focus on tactical rather than strategic issues. The supplier firm's challenge is continually to enhance value to maintain its edge over competitors, just as competitors attempt to remove that advantage.

PARTNER

At the right of the scale, the relationship moves beyond a concern for quality supplies to a long-run partnership in which the two firms share (or jointly develop) future strategies, technologies, and resources; both firms are concerned with decisions along the entire industry value chain. The customer's supplier base is reduced to a handful (possibly single source)[13] and critical buying decisions tend to be made on value rather than on price. Each firm is involved early in the other's product development cycle and significant quantities of both routine and sensitive information flow between the organizations as the supplier firm moves beyond its basic business to solve important problems for the key account. Partnership relationships involve multilevel interactions across the two organizations including joint quality control processes and bi-company project teams that share information and expertise to secure benefits for both parties. When the core rationale for serving the key account is broadened to embrace assisting the account in achieving its objectives, many activities that would not be considered under a narrower definition of the key account relationship become possibilities.[14]

EXAMPLE: Armstrong World Industries operates a management development program for its key accounts. This program is not a sales pitch for Armstrong's products and services; rather, the focus is to improve the skills of its key accounts' mid-level and senior managers. To the extent that management skill is improved, key accounts perform better and Armstrong's prospects or business are enhanced.[15]

EXAMPLE: A major manufacturer, Cedar Products Inc.*, noting that its key distributor frequently called for rush orders yet later "discovered" lost inventory, installed a new inventory control system for this key account. Similarly, Baxter Healthcare Corporation develops optimal inventory levels for its hospital customers.

EXAMPLE: Dogwood Corporation* had significant experience with several vendors in outsourcing its data system. As a supplier firm, it was able to provide valuable advice in helping its key account develop a process for outsourcing its own data system.

In each of these examples, the supplier firm was able to deepen its relationship with the key account. As a result of adding value to the account, competitive pressure for the supplier firm's business is mitigated and price pressure eased. (Because of the increasing importance of partnership relationships, we devote Chapter 9 to discussing critical issues in forming supplier-customer partnerships.)

In developing its portfolio of key accounts, the supplier firm must make some tough strategic decisions regarding the distribution of these three relationship types across its key account base. From vendor through quality supplier to partner, both the level of mutual dependency and the cost of coverage increase. Other resource commitments necessary to maintain each type of relationship increase in a similar fashion. A critical decision for the supplier is the number of each type of relationship it wishes to maintain.

Furthermore, the supplier firm's choices are typically constrained by history. For example, a firm with little key account management experience is unlikely to be able to develop a large number of successful supplier-firm/key-account partnerships overnight. And at the individual level, not all of these options may represent viable choices for a particular supplier-firm/key-account relationship, since both parties must together decide the type of relationship they wish to form. The specific relationship deemed most desirable by the supplier firm will not be achieved unless the key account also desires a similar relationship. The most crucial area concerns partner relationships, simply because the resource requirements are most extensive. Making the partnership bet with the "wrong" key account can be very costly. (We pick up these issues in Chapter 9.)

SELECTING KEY ACCOUNTS[16]

Because a key account program requires the firm to make exceptional efforts at its major accounts, it is extremely important that it select as key accounts only those organizations that are truly important for long-run organizational health. Indeed, key account selection should be ruthless, for if the "wrong" organizations are chosen, not only will critical scarce resources be wasted, but some "right" organizations, denied key account status, will not fulfill their long-run potential. In this section, we address three issues—candidate criteria, using the criteria for key account selection, and other general issues in selecting key accounts.

Criteria for Selecting Key Accounts

Potentially useful criteria that can be used in the key account selection process are grouped into three major categories—direct sales revenue and profit, organizational interrelationships, and indirect potential volume and profit.[17]

DIRECT SALES REVENUE AND PROFIT

Two of the most important criteria for key account selection are current sales volume and current profits. In addition, we consider future sales volume and profits, financial security, and acquisition potential.

Current Sales Revenue. Current sales revenue is the criterion most frequently used by companies to select key accounts. Clearly, the loss of an account meeting this criterion is serious since sales revenue and associated profits decline immediately.

> **EXAMPLE:** In November 2000, DaimlerChrysler decided to consolidate its $1.8 billion advertising account with a single supplier, the Omnicom Group. The impact on True North, the losing agency, was about 9% of total revenues ($140 million) and as much as 15% of total profits.[18]

This criterion may even be valid if specific products purchased by the key account return a bottom-line loss, inasmuch as high-volume products typically carry a significant share of the overhead burden. Loss of "unprofitable" volume would require this burden to be carried by other products in the product line, thus reducing overall firm profits.

In spite of the many positive features of high-volume accounts, this criterion should not be applied automatically. Some high-volume accounts may be truly unprofitable regardless of burden-sharing advantages; indeed, firms that institute customer profitability systems not infrequently discover that, because of a combination of excessive price discounting and high support costs, high-volume customers are unprofitable. Finally, some accounts may be so difficult to deal with—for example, make excessive demands or have poor business practices—that regardless of the high volume involved, it may not be worth the firm's trouble to assign them key account status.[19]

Current Profits. Just as some customers may be responsible for significant product volumes but provide relatively little profit (yet still warrant key account status), other customers may provide relatively low volumes but significant profits. Frequently this situation occurs in markets where large customers have significant bargaining power and are able to force prices down to levels that return little gross profit to suppliers.[20] By contrast, somewhat smaller customers may be less price sensitive, perhaps because they are more concerned with receiving additional services from the supplier that larger customers can provide internally. As a result, mid-size customers may be highly profitable and so warrant key account status.[21]

However, in order to apply this criterion, supplier firms must have systems that measure profitability by account. Unfortunately, because of poor information and antiquated cost accounting systems, many firms do not know the profitability of their key accounts. For key accounts whose purchases span several businesses or countries, the firm may not even know its sales revenues at those accounts! In addition, product costs may not be known because activity-based costing (ABC) systems have not been implemented for operations, and marketing costs such as sales force, order processing, field service, technical assistance, and delivery are not well assigned by account.[22] Although implementation difficulties are significant, increasing numbers of companies are grappling with this issue.

EXAMPLE: Boise Cascade Office Products (BCOP) measures return-on-sales for all key accounts using an ABC system. Unprofitable key accounts are either returned to profitability or are dropped.[23] BCOP creates added value by making this system available to its key accounts to help them understand and control their own costs and drive out unnecessary processes.

EXAMPLE: American Electric Power (AEP) has developed a software package that projects account profitability. In addition to use in account selection, the tool helps AEP to justify investments in key accounts.[24]

(See Appendix 6.1 for a worked example of measuring key account profitability using ABC methods.)

Future Sales Volume and Profit. Unfortunately, many organizations incorrectly use high current sales volume as a key account criterion to the exclusion of all others. In particular, they often fail to use *potential sales volume*. In relying exclusively on current sales volume, they are guilty of mortgaging the firm's future by ignoring significant opportunities for increased sales and profits. Future sales and profits are typically available from several different sources. These include important current customers targeting growth markets, small growing customers, customers currently purchasing similar products from competitors, customers in new market segments being targeted by the firm, and potential customers for new products emerging from R&D.

Of course, this criterion should be applied with care since some customers may represent significant but unattainable potential. For example, a competitor's customer may purchase large product volumes yet be unworthy of significant effort because a close long-term relationship between the two organizations makes it unlikely that significant business could be secured.[25] On the other hand, demonstrated requirements for a particular product type may spur the supplier firm to develop competitive advantage that can surpass the associated switching costs and, of course, some close relationships do atrophy over time.[26]

In some cases, doing business with one firm in an industry forecloses the possibility of doing business with others. The supplier may have to decide which customer is the most appropriate for key account status.

EXAMPLE: Prophet, the fast-growing, San Francisco–based brand strategy consultant, worked closely with credit card organization, Visa. However, when Visa was unwilling to increase its commitment, Prophet resigned the Visa account and took on MasterCard which, it believed, offered greater potential.

Financial Security. Supplier firm management must ensure that its key accounts are financially secure. Not only does the supplier firm wish to be paid for products/services delivered, long-run investment in developing relationships with key accounts that fail will be wasted.

Acquisition Potential. As we indicated in Chapter 1, the pace of mergers and acquisitions increased substantially during the 1990s. When two organizations, each with its own procurement organization, are merged, or one acquires the other, it is likely that supply will be rationalized and procurement placed in a single organization. All things equal, the supplier to the stronger of the two original organizations is more likely to become the major supplier to the new organization. Thus, key account effort on firms likely to be acquired may be wasted if the acquiring organization is given the dominant procurement responsibility. By the same token, selecting potential acquirees as key accounts may bring long-run benefits.

ORGANIZATIONAL INTERRELATIONSHIPS

Criteria in this category include coherence with firm strategy, the extent to which the supplier is valued by the customer, and cultural fit.

Coherence with Firm Strategy. Key account management programs do not exist in isolation from overall firm strategy. Regardless of where critical choices are being made, for example, at corporate or the business-unit level, key account selection is a strategy implementation decision. At its core, each higher level strategy has a well-formulated marketing strategy or strategies with which key account selection must be coherent. For example, if marketing strategy involves a broad product line, the supplier firm may require its key accounts to purchase multiple firm products; if innovation were critical, only accounts with a bias for creativity (perhaps measured by R&D expenditures) might be selected. In addition, distribution coverage may be an important criterion, even though potential volume may not be particularly high:

> **EXAMPLE:** In Germany, the Spar organization operates a large number of small retail stores. Because of its distribution coverage, Spar is a key account for several cigarette and other consumer goods manufacturers.

Supplier Valued by the Customer. In addition to coherence with the firm's overall strategy, a selected key account should also value, currently or potentially, the firm's offer. Unless the customer believes, or can be persuaded, that the supplier firm can meet its needs over the long run, the firm is better off allocating its scarce resources to other accounts. The firm should also be concerned with any "legacy" issues that might affect selection as a key account.[27]

Cultural Fit. Any firm may find that while some organizations are easy to do business with, others are very difficult. For example, at some customers, organizational personnel act as gatekeepers and will not allow suppliers to talk to important decision makers; other customers may operate with a set of ethical principles different from those of the supplier firm. A key account should be able to embrace the firm's key account process, and those firms seeking partnership relationships require assurance that the prospective key account is open to, and/or has experience with supplier partnership relationships. A useful term for describing these interface issues is degree of cultural fit. If this fit is poor, the supplier firm may wish to exclude a potential key account from consideration, regardless of its attractiveness on other dimensions.

INDIRECT POTENTIAL VOLUME AND PROFITS

In this section, we focus on opinion leadership.

Opinion Leadership. In many industries, certain firms are well known for product testing competence and the care they exercise in selecting suppliers. Frequently, these firms are industry leaders in sales volume and so may qualify for key account status under either the current or future sales volume criteria. However, smaller firms that would never be considered as key accounts under any of the direct revenue and profit criteria sometimes play this role because of the influence they exercise on other firms in their industries, and the resulting potential volume they impact. In addition, they may serve as development (beta) sites for the supplier firm's new technology, as, for example, teaching hospitals in the medical industry. Because of their high standards of excellence and their encouragement of maximum performance from the supplier firm, they function as a launch platform for the supplier, allowing it to take a market leadership position.

> **EXAMPLE:** Leading financial services group ICICI was the first Indian company listed on the New York Stock Exchange. One of ICICI's key accounts is Infosys, India's fastest growing software company, well-known for its commercial success, product quality, and high ethical standards, and the first Indian company listed on NASDAQ. Although ICICI transacts little business with Infosys, it regards Infosys as a key account because of its exemplary reputation.

> **EXAMPLE:** In Florida, Tampa Electric Company (TECO) is a very successful, well-managed, and highly respected organization that invests in long-term solutions. Although it is a relatively small organization, many suppliers treat TECO as a key account because of its *resume* value.

Furthermore, selecting an innovative smaller customer as a key account may be appropriate if a larger potential account is unwilling to adopt the supplier firm's new product. Adoption by the smaller account may be key to securing business at the larger account.

> **EXAMPLE:** A Hong Kong distributor of food products, Elderberry Inc.*, was unable to secure distribution for a new line of frozen chicken from either of the two major supermarket chains that together control 75% of food distribution in Hong Kong. As a result, Elderberry focused on two smaller chains, secured agreement for distribution, then launched a highly visible promotional campaign for its new product. Shortly thereafter, the major chains wanted both to carry the product and to cooperate in promotional efforts.

Using the Criteria for Selecting Key Accounts

As we indicated above, the supplier firm must select those criteria that it believes are most appropriate for identifying its key accounts. Clearly, a variety of different methods are available for combining these criteria to make key account choices. In general, these methods rely on developing a series of attractiveness scores for the firm's customers, then selecting as key accounts those that exceed some minimum score, subject to resource availability. We illustrate the *compensatory* approach in which lesser attractiveness on one criterion may be balanced (compensated for) by greater attractiveness on another.[28] In this approach, the account attractiveness score for an individual account is developed from responses to three statement completion tasks.

Responses to the first two statements are general for the firm across the entire set of customers being considered for key account status; responses to the third statement are specific to individual customers. (See Figure 2.3 for an example.)

GENERAL STATEMENTS

Step 1: Factor Identification. "We like key accounts that . . ."

This statement identifies the set of criteria (drawn from the previous section) for discriminating between attractive and unattractive candidates (Figure 2.3, column 1).

Step 2: Factor Weighting. "What importance weights do you assign for each criterion from step 1, such that the total sums to 100?"

This statement weighs the relative importance of the key account criteria (Figure 2.3, column 2).

SPECIFIC STATEMENT

Step 3: Account Opportunity Rating. "Considering customer X, the candidate key account, what rating best represents its position on each criterion (1 = low and 10 = high)?"

This statement rates the candidate account on each of the criteria (Figure 2.3, column 3).

Two steps remain to complete the analysis:

Step 4: Develop Factor Scores. Multiply the entries in Figure 2.3 column 2 by the corresponding entries in column 3 to produce the figures in column 4.

Step 5: Develop the Account Attractiveness Score. Sum the figures in column 4.

The final figure secured from step 5 should fall between 100 and 1,000. Clearly, the higher the number, the more attractive the customer for key account status.

All of the supplier firm's potential key accounts receive an attractiveness score. Typically, the firm accepts as key accounts a specified number of high-scoring customers that exceed some minimum attractiveness score.[29] Notwithstanding the quantitative value of this analysis in ranking potential key accounts, use of this approach has qualitative value in the issues raised as groups of executives attempt to come to grips with selecting this important group of customers. We develop a more complex key account selection approach below when we address managing the key account portfolio.

FIGURE 2.3: Illustration of the Compensatory Approach for Calculating Key Account Attractiveness

1. Attractiveness Criteria for Key Accounts	2. Importance Weights for Criteria	3. Customer X's Score on This Criterion	4. Col. 2 × Col. 3
"We like key accounts that . . ."			
a. Are a good cultural fit with our firm	25	4	100
b. Provide us high volume	20	5	100
c. Provide us high gross margins	15	7	105
d. Offer good potential for future growth	15	8	120
e. Are technologically sophisticated	15	3	45
f. Act as opinion leaders in their industry	10	4	40
Total	100		510

General Issues in Selecting Key Accounts

Regardless of the specific criteria employed for choosing key accounts and the method of combining customer performance on those criteria, the firm must address several key account selection issues: Should it develop key accounts or account tiers? How should it treat non-key (tier I) accounts? When should it disengage from key (tier I) accounts? These and other questions demand continuous evaluation of key accounts and key account criteria.

Key Accounts or Account Tiers? Rather than place customers into one of two categories, key accounts and others, increasingly firms prefer to place their key accounts in tiers. In each tier, customers are eligible for a certain type and level of resources:

> **EXAMPLE:** The Travelers insurance company developed three categories of agency: Category 1 agencies were eligible to sell a particular range of products for which they received a certain degree of support from Travelers; category 2 and 3 agencies were eligible for progressively more sophisticated products for which they received increasing levels of support.[30]

> **EXAMPLE:** Moore's Business Forms & Systems Division used a three-phase key account selection system. Successful phase 1 accounts had high potential incremental volume and placed a high value on support services. Successful phase 2 accounts, in addition, required high levels of support services and accepted Moore's standardized offerings. Successful phase 3 accounts also provided high gross margins (realized price less cost of goods sold) and had high order sizes. (Order size was a critical cost driver for Moore's.) In addition, Moore's labeled its top seven customers "Enterprise" accounts because of their high core volume and complexity of support needs.

> **EXAMPLE:** Because a small number of high-value customers were monopolizing DHL's account management resources, other critical accounts were receiving insufficient attention. DHL developed a four-tier structure based on customer need to better serve all its global accounts.[31]

The tiering issue interfaces with the question of degree of closeness of the supplier-firm/key-account relationship discussed earlier—vendor, quality supplier, partnership. In general, higher-tiered accounts are more likely to have quality supplier or partnership relationships; lower tiered accounts may tend toward vendor relationships. Indeed, just as any introductory marketing student knows that markets must be segmented, so the key account base should also be segmented. Typically, key account segments differ one from another on the type and degree of resources required to serve them well; correspondingly, the firm's coverage model should differ across key account segments. All things equal, for those accounts receiving the most resources, the firm will have higher break-even points. As a result, high-tiered accounts should have sufficiently high revenue potential and/or be prepared to offer commitments to the supplier so that break-even can be exceeded.

Multinational firms committed to key account management may have key accounts both at the global level and the individual country level. The key account management process should allow for strategy development at each level. For national key accounts, the country manager typically has a large degree of control over the manner in which the account is addressed. However, for global key accounts, where strategy is developed at a broader level, although individual country level executives may have significant input into the key account strategy development process, their basic task is largely one of implementation. Difficult resource allocations often arise when a global key account is not particularly important for an individual country. We address this issue in Chapter 10.

Non-Key (Tier I) Accounts. To the extent that some firms are designated key (or tier 1) accounts and thus receive firm resources equivalent to their status, those customers that are not so designated receive proportionately fewer resources. In other words, from the supplier firm's perspective, they are treated as somewhat less than first-class citizens. Nonetheless, many of these customers are extremely important to the supplier firm's future. In developing a key account system, the firm must deal sensitively with these important yet non-key or tier 1 accounts. It must, for example, be prepared to counter the competitor that offers key account or tier 1 status, with well-defined benefits, as a competitive weapon to secure business.

EXAMPLE: Both IBM and Hewlett-Packard (HP) operate key account tiering systems. In Mexico, the Sun Microsystems subsidiary makes a point of targeting as its key accounts those customers whose status with IBM or HP is either a low-tiered key account or not a key account at all. It approaches these accounts with the argument, "You will be tier 1 with us."

Disengagement from Key (Tier 1) Accounts. The issues involved in assigning key account or higher tier status are different from those rescinding key account or lowering tier status. In general, customers view key account status positively and are pleased to receive it; conversely, they do not like to lose it. As a result, reducing a customer's key account status is often a difficult issue and many pressures, from both key account and supplier firm personnel, may act to undermine such action. Clear criteria should be developed for key account deselection and uniformly applied in these situations. Unacceptable reasons to retain key account status are altruism, personal relationships, personal benefit to firm personnel such as visits to sites in attractive locations, and lethargy.

Once the decision has been made to deselect a key account, the firm should implement a well-thought-through key account deselection strategy. For some accounts, this may involve a reduction in service, for others it may mean severing the supplier-customer relationship altogether. Regardless of how the disengagement process proceeds, it should be conducted sensitively with the recognition that the customer may need to develop alternative supply sources to maintain its operations.

Necessity for Specific Criteria. Regardless of the particular set of criteria used to define key account status, the firm should strive to develop specific quantitative levels for each selected criterion. This allows a consistent set of decisions to be made across the entire customer base, as illustrated earlier.

If hard and fast rules are not developed, the award of key account status may become a political issue as nonqualifying customers seek key account status, and supplier firm executives seek advantage in accessing scarce resources for their favored customers. Such internally based, politically motivated allocations are likely to be suboptimal for the firm as a whole. (Of course, clear criteria should also be set for removal of key account status [see above].) Notwithstanding the foregoing, although the supplier firm may strive for objective quantitative criteria, some level of managerial judgment in the selection process may be unavoidable.

Continuous Evaluation of Key Accounts and Key Account Criteria. Regardless of the set of criteria employed at a particular point in time, such changes as business cycle stage, technological evolution, customer and competitor actions, and supplier firm strategic initiatives are likely to impact the firm's set of key accounts.

First, the firm's key and near-key accounts should be evaluated periodically to assess whether certain accounts should be upgraded or downgraded. Second, less frequently, but also periodically, the firm's criteria for selecting key accounts should also be reevaluated. Reevaluation may also be triggered by such unforeseeable events as significant volume loss.

As a result of these reevaluations, customers that today warrant key account status may not warrant such status tomorrow. Conversely, today's non-key or tier 2 accounts may grow sufficiently, in current and/or potential business, to warrant upgrading in the future. To the extent that the firm's key account assignments remain frozen in place too long without evaluation, critical scarce resources will be misallocated.

DEVELOPING AND MANAGING THE FIRM'S KEY ACCOUNT PORTFOLIO

Earlier, we discussed the development of customer attractiveness measures for selecting key accounts. Some supplier firms like to use more complex selection methods or, in any event, to array customers already selected as key accounts on two dimensions rather than use just a single attractiveness measure. In this section, we present two alternative methods for arraying the firm's current and/ or potential key accounts—the key-account-attractiveness/business-strengths portfolio, and the key-account-attractiveness/account-vulnerability portfolio.[32] In each case, the key account attractiveness measure is developed as discussed above.

No matter which of these (or other) approaches are used to gain insight into the firm's candidate key accounts, following the tiering discussion above, they should be grouped into segments based on the extent and type of resources required. These groupings will permit the firm to develop alternative coverage models in terms of those resources it decides are appropriate for the various key account segments.

The Key Account Attractiveness/Business Strengths Portfolio

The business strengths measure is developed in a similar manner to the key account attractiveness measure discussed earlier. As with the attractiveness measure, it employs a *compensatory* approach in which lesser strength on one crite-rion may be balanced (compensated for) by greater strength on another crite-rion. The business strengths score for an individual account is developed from responses to three statement completion tasks, each of which is specific to the candidate key account.

> *Step 1:* Factor Identification. "What business strengths (skills, resources, ca-pabilities and relationship) must any supplier possess to be successful with this candidate key account?"

This question highlights success factors (typically six to ten) at the account (Figure 2.4: column 1).

> *Step 2:* Factor Weighting. "What importance weights do you assign for each business strength identified in step 1, such that the total sums to 100?"

This statement weights the relative importance of the business strengths cri-teria at the particular account (Figure 2.4: column 2).

> *Step 3:* Supplier Firm Rating. "How does the supplier firm rate on possession of each business strength, where 1 = low possession and 10 = high posses-sion?"

This statement rates the supplier firm on each business strength (Figure 2.4: column 3).

Two steps remain to complete the analysis:

> *Step 4:* Develop Factor Scores. Multiply the entries in Figure 2.4 column 2 by the corresponding entries in column 3 to produce the figures in column 4.
> *Step 5:* Develop the Business Strengths Score. Sum the figures in column 4.

The final figure secured from step 5 should fall between 100 and 1,000. Clearly, the higher the number, the stronger the firm's business strengths at this key account.

Although the analytic framework is robust, typically the supplier firm uses a separate analysis for each candidate key account.

FIGURE 2.4: Illustration of the Compensating Approach for Calculating the Supplier Firm's Business Strengths at the Key Account

1. Business Strengths Criteria	2. Importance Weights for Business Strengths Criteria	3. Supplier Firm's Rating on This Criterion	4. Col. 2 × Col. 3
What business strengths must any supplier possess to be successful with this key account?			
a. Good R&D	25	7	175
b. Well-trained local sales force	15	9	135
c. Low-cost operations	10	4	40
d. High-quality service	15	6	90
e. Deep pockets	10	9	90
f. In-place distribution	20	5	100
g. Fast-moving organization	5	3	15
Total	100		645

Placing Entries in the Matrix.[33] The result of applying this analysis to the supplier firm's set of candidate key accounts is a portfolio matrix of the form shown in Figure 2.5. Several points should be noted:

- This simple framework displays the entire set of the firm's candidate key accounts.
- Each candidate key account is positioned in the matrix based on its key account attractiveness and business strengths scores.
- The size of the circle represents the supplier firm's current revenues from the account; the larger the revenues, the greater the area of the circle.
- The supplier firm may be able to improve its business strengths score by allocating resources appropriately.

Decisions on which customers to select as key accounts, and on the relative level of resources provided to each selected key account, are informed by the position of the account in the matrix. All things equal, candidate accounts in the high/high, high/medium, and medium/high key account attractiveness/business strengths cells are good candidates for key account status. Those in the low/low, low/medium, and medium/low cells are poor candidates. Entries on the diagonal—low/high, medium/medium, and high/low—suggest that the firm should proceed with caution or at least undertake further analysis.

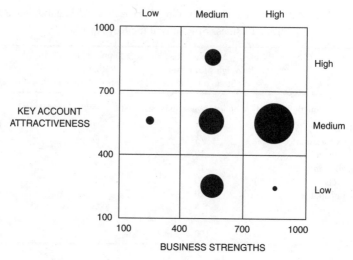

FIGURE 2.5: The Key Account Attractiveness/Business Strengths Portfolio Matrix

The Key Account Attractiveness/ Account Vulnerability Portfolio

A second portfolio approach is especially useful for already selected key accounts with which the supplier firm has significant current business. These accounts are arrayed on an attractiveness/vulnerability matrix. This matrix can be a valuable supplement to the key-account-attractiveness/business-strengths portfolio just discussed. The key account attractiveness measure is developed as before.

The key account vulnerability scale is developed by focusing on the potential loss of business to competitors. Three broad types of factor underpin this scale. Individual key account scores are based via differential diagnosis by comparing the supplier firm to its competitors. These factors embrace:

- **Relative performance.** The focus here is on benefits required by key accounts. These include both "hard" product performance benefits and "soft" service type benefits, increasingly important in markets trending toward commoditization.
- **Prices.** How the supplier firm's prices compare to those of its competitors. Price includes not only list price, or even invoice price, but credit terms, quantity discounts, buy back arrangements, and so forth.

- **Switching costs.** Several factors may make it difficult for the key account to switch to a competitor, regardless of relative benefits and price performance. These include in-place contracts, incompatibility of competitor delivery and account receiving systems, and close supplier-firm/key-account personal relationships.

Based on these factors a subjective vulnerability assessment of each key account is made on a 1 to 10 scale: A typical scale might embrace the following scale points:

1 = Highly vulnerable to losing a substantial proportion of volume at this account. For example, the firm's performance is less than account expectations and/or a major competitor meets specifications at lower price, and switching costs are low.

5 = The account seriously considers switching a portion of the supplier firm's business to competition but the competitor evaluation is incomplete; there is sufficient time for a strengthening of position and switching costs are moderate.

10 = Extremely secure account relationship; competitor activity is minor, the product/service position is very strong and switching costs are high.

Combining these two scales produces the nine-cell matrix shown in Figure 2.6. Each entry represents one of the firm's key accounts; as before, circle size is proportional to the supplier firm's sales revenues at the account such that larger circles represent greater current sales revenues. In this example, the supplier firm has a portfolio of ten key accounts, two smallish accounts (a,b) in the dangerous high-vulnerability/high-attractiveness cell and a single small account (c) that is highly attractive but not particularly vulnerable.

The data in this chart are important input into the supplier firm's decision regarding the type of resources that should be allocated to each of its key accounts. For example, in Figure 2.6, the supplier might decide to place major effort on the six accounts in the four high/medium attractiveness, high/medium vulnerability cells (a,b,d,e,f,g). It might further decide to invest to maintain its position with the high attractiveness/low vulnerability account (c), but to disinvest in the low attractiveness accounts (j,k,l) and deselect them as key accounts.

Insight into each key account's trajectory over time can be secured from an extension of this chart (Figure 2.7). The circles once again define the key account's current position. The directional arrows indicate the trajectory; the

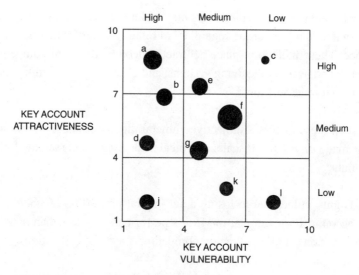

FIGURE 2.6: The Key Account Attractiveness/Account Vulnerability Portfolio
Note: The attractiveness score has been divided by 100 to correspond to the vulnerability scale.

end of the arrow indicates the key account's position at the previous measurement point. This example illustrates that the two high-vulnerability/high-attractiveness accounts (a,b) secured their positions slowly, by different routes, and that the low vulnerability/high attractiveness (c) account only recently secured its current solid position. A more sophisticated resource allocation analysis might also consider these historic account movements.

Current versus Developmental Key Accounts

An important strategic key account decision concerns the distinction between resource allocation for current versus developmental business. Some firms are chosen as key accounts because of their importance to the firm's current sales and profits; others are selected because of anticipated future sales and profits; still others are selected for some combination of current and future performance.

It is important that the supplier firm make an affirmative decision regarding the degree to which resources for key account management should be divided between maintaining current business and developing new business. In part because of the pressure for current performance, not only may smaller customers

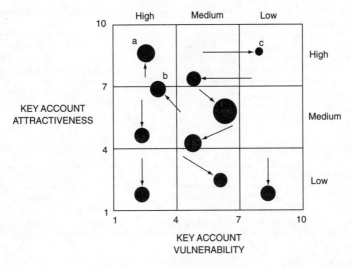

FIGURE 2.7: The Key Account Attractiveness/Account Vulnerability Portfolio: Current Business Trajectory

with attractive sales and profit potential be overlooked in the key account assignment process, developmental projects with current key accounts may also be underfunded.

To ensure that potential high-volume accounts are neither overlooked nor dealt with inappropriately, the supplier firm may chose to develop two related key account budgeting systems—one based on current business, the second based on anticipated future business. The benefit of such a process is that the allocation of resources for potential high-volume accounts becomes a strategic matter rather than a more tactical account-by-account issue. Senior management decides how much of the firm's scarce resources should support current business at its key accounts versus how much should support anticipated future sales and profits. In such a system, potential high-volume accounts are less likely to be underfunded when budgets tighten.

One way of deciding which accounts should receive developmental investment is to identify the various opportunities for increased business at each candidate key account. The supplier should broadly assess the resources required to pursue each opportunity, forecast potential revenues and profits over both the short run and long run, and assess the probability that the firm will be successful (Figure 2.8).

Multiplying the feasible result for a particular opportunity by the probability that the firm will be successful leads to an "expected value" for each opporttu-

Account A: Short-Term Analysis				
Opportunities for Increased Business	Resources Required	1. Feasible Short-Term Result ($ Revenues, profits)	2. Success Probability	3. Expected Value (Col. 1 × Col. 2) ($ Revenues, profits)
Opportunity A				
Opportunity B				
Opportunity C				
Etc.				
Total				
Account A: Long-Term Analysis				
Opportunities for Increased Business	Resources Required	Feasible Long-Term Result ($ Revenues, profits)	Success Probability	Expected Value (Col. 1 × Col. 2) ($ Revenues, profits)
Opportunity A				
Opportunity B				
Opportunity C				
Etc.				
Total				

FIGURE 2.8: Developmental Key Account Analysis

nity. The sum of all the "expected values" for all of the opportunities provides an overall "expected value" for each developmental key account that can be used as the basis for allocating resources by account. This analysis may be elaborated by considering the likelihood of success over various time horizons, using discounted cash flow techniques, and by sensitivity analysis.[34]

The allocation of resources between current and future business is a particularly crucial issue when one considers the developing information economy, and the number of currently significant firms that a few years ago were no more than a gleam in an entrepreneur's eye. Indeed, as "new" economy firms increasingly compete with "old" economy firms, those suppliers focused solely on the old economy risk being left behind as new firms and new methods of doing business proliferate.

Of course, investing in potential new business may be a riskier proposition than supporting current business. As a result, care should be given to constructing a developmental key account portfolio with full recognition that some investments will produce no returns, just operating losses. No matter, as long as some of the investments produce big wins.

SUMMARY

Because of the increasing importance of key accounts to long-run firm success, the firm must make critical recourse allocation decisions around key account management. At a fundamental level, it must decide on the level of corporate commitment to key accounts in general, on a vision for the key account program as a whole, and on the types of key account relationships it wishes to develop. More specifically, it must identify specific criteria and selection processes for choosing key accounts, considering both current and potential revenue and profit streams, and other important issues. Both in making critical key account selection decisions and for allocating resources among its key accounts, a variety of portfolio approaches may provide significant managerial guidance.

CHAPTER THREE

Organizing for
Key Account Management

In Chapter 2, we indicated that, across firms, the breadth and depth of commitment to key accounts differs widely. Furthermore, in the case studies in Appendix 2.1, we showed that an individual firm's commitment to key accounts changes over time. The critical issue regarding organizing for key account management is congruence; the organization structure and processes must be appropriate for whatever overall key account strategy is adopted by the firm at a particular point in time. Furthermore, since commitment to key accounts evolves over time, we expect the organization for key account management to evolve similarly.

For firms adopting key account management for the first time, a transformation must be made from the traditional sales force system of interfacing with customers to a new key account management system. For firms with a key account management system already in place, significant change may be required to shift to a new method of addressing key accounts, for example, from a national or multinational regional organization to a global organization.

Typically, introduction of a key account management program cuts across existing lines of responsibility and authority, and various organizational systems and processes. Power bases are affected and, as a result, turf wars and individual political agendas may get in the way of successful key account program introduction. As we note later in the chapter, strong committed support from the top of the organization can ease the introduction of key account management but, nonetheless, considerable skill is required to get a key account management program up and running.[1]

In this chapter, we demonstrate how particular organizational approaches to key account management reflect two factors—the firm's commitment to key accounts, and the complexity of the relationships between supplier firm and customer. In particular, we discuss both the type and location of key account programs, the macrostructure organization, and issues involved in the transition from one type of key account organization to another. In the second part of the chapter, we discuss the roles and responsibilities of key actors in the key account management process, in particular, top management, the key account director, and key account managers.

DESIGNING THE KEY ACCOUNT MANAGEMENT STRUCTURE[2]

In Chapter 2, we discussed the firm's commitment to key account strategy using the matrix reproduced as Figure 3.1. The organizational approach to key account management should be closely related to the level of strategy commitment as indicated by the supplier firm's position in the matrix.

We commence by exploring the implications of the firm's commitment to key accounts for key account management structure. We then turn to discuss the

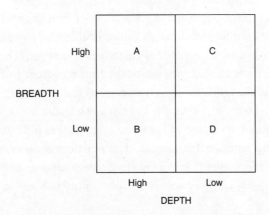

FIGURE 3.1: Firm Commitment to Key Accounts

issue of supplier firm and customer complexity for those organizations making high levels of commitment to key accounts.

Organizational Approaches for Low Depth of Commitment to Key Accounts

LOW DEPTH/LOW BREADTH

In the low-breadth/low-depth cell (D), the supplier firm has minimal commitment to a key account strategy. To the extent that it addresses some customers as key accounts at all, this effort is most likely localized and occurs through the efforts of individual salespeople and local sales managers.

For example, in the traditional sales force system, individual salespeople, in addition to handling small and mid-sized customers, are often responsible for a small number of large accounts—current or potential. The salesperson merely treats these customers somewhat differently from, and better than, her other accounts, making available those organizational resources to which she has access. Alternatively, an individual district or regional sales manager may decide that some customers in his district or region should be designated as key accounts. The manager may deal with these accounts on a part-time basis, or assign one or more salespeople to focus exclusively on those accounts.[3]

LOW DEPTH/HIGH BREADTH

In the high-breadth/low-depth cell (C), the supplier firm has made the judgment that key accounts are important to its future health, and has assigned key account status to a significant number of customers. However, it has not made the concomitant decision to allocate significant firm resources to these accounts. Rather than make the major changes necessary to really make key account management work, it essentially attempts to graft key account management onto existing organizational structures and processes, and makes little extra effort in the way of providing additional resources. The most common organizational approaches involve formalizing localized key account representatives, supporting the sales force, and giving key account responsibility to a senior executive.

Formalizing Localized Key Account Representatives. As noted above, district or regional sales managers may independently appoint individual salespeople as key account representatives in their districts/regions. However, this approach may be formalized by appointing key account managers, reporting at the regional or district level, throughout the entire sales organization. Appointing key account managers within the regional sales force system has the significant benefit of drawing on the supplier firm's experience base. In addition, it reduces the potential for sales force morale problems resulting from nonpromotion of successful salespeople, by developing a nonmanagerial career track in the sales force.

Alternatively, the firm may place responsibility for individual key accounts with senior executives, for example, with a district/regional sales manager or the national sales manager on a part-time basis, or with a specially designated manager of key accounts. This approach has the benefit of placing responsibility for key accounts with seasoned executives. However, when key accounts become the responsibility of sales managers, they may distract from the performance of other managerial functions.[4] In addition, assigning key accounts to sales managers may cause morale problems among individual salespeople who feel "robbed" both of the opportunity to be responsible for large accounts, and the related possibilities of increased compensation.

Sales Force Support. This approach involves appointing a general key account manager in a sales force support role with coordination and information processing responsibilities. This individual has little line authority and the traditional sales force system continues more or less in place. This manager's major function is to make certain that the various salespeople responsible for individual key account locations, for example, branches or factory sites, have access to relevant information concerning activities at the key account in locations for which they have no responsibility. Periodically, the key account manager may be required to take a broad customer view and to offer advice regarding the manner in which the account should be handled.

Senior Executive Responsibility. Sometimes the firm believes that, in addition to relationships managed through the sales force(s), it needs a top-level relationship with its key accounts, perhaps at the corporate level. Such a "diplomacy" type relationship is often the responsibility of a senior executive, either as a full-time job or as one of several responsibilities. This individual's major responsibility is to develop and cement personal relationships, and to be involved as necessary in contract negotiations.

Organizational Approaches for
High Depth of Commitment to Key Accounts

In each of the high-depth cells (A and B), the firm is committed to in-depth management of its key accounts. The difference between the cells is mainly a question of how many accounts are involved in the key account program. Two basic approaches are available to addressing key accounts with high depth—matrixed key account managers and a self-contained key account unit.

Matrixed Key Account Managers. In matrix approaches, the majority of day-to-day customer contact remains with local representatives, frequently the traditional sales force. Individual salespeople report to first-line sales managers on a "solid-line" basis, and to key account managers on a "dotted-line" basis, in a matrix fashion. Key account managers have overall responsibility for their accounts, including managing major interpersonal relationships. They are typically charged with developing the key account strategy, maintaining existing sales and profit streams, and identifying new opportunities.

These key account managers typically have little formal authority; rather, they achieve their goals by exercising leadership skills and marshaling organizational resources. In particular, their key account teams typically comprise individuals with a variety of functional expertise, for example, logistics, information systems, sales engineering, and customer service, sometimes as direct reports, but more likely as members of virtual teams whose main reporting lines are to their own functional organizations.

Self-Contained Key Account Unit. In the self-contained key account unit, a single key account manager is responsible for customer contact; she does not work through a geographically deployed sales force. Management of key account relationships is placed within a self-contained key account unit staffed by several key account managers. Such units are typically provided with significant levels of dedicated resources. These resources are frequently specific to individual key accounts—for example, sales engineers or customer service—but may also be available in a pool from which key account managers may draw. Although key account managers may be located within sales regions for geographical convenience, they often report to a key account director through a structure that operates in parallel with the regular sales force.[5]

Key account managers assume total responsibility for their accounts including all types of selling activity, complaint resolution, and so forth, and for concomitant coordination within the supplier firm. They are not necessarily expected to be technically competent in all aspects of the firm's products and applications, but are expected to be able to find and deliver the appropriate technical and other expertise when and where it is required.[6]

ORGANIZATIONAL IMPLICATIONS OF SUPPLIER FIRM AND KEY ACCOUNT COMPLEXITY

Whether a matrix system or a self-contained key account unit is the critical organizational device depends largely on the level and type of key account and supplier firm complexity. These are integrated in Figure 3.2.

Key Account Complexity. Key account complexity is a multidimensional construct comprising mainly structural considerations. If the account has many purchase-decision points, influence points, and/or usage points, especially if these are geographically dispersed, coordination demands may be substantial and costly to satisfy.[7]

Supplier Firm Complexity. The greater the number of product lines, services, applications, and/or distribution points offered to the key account, the higher the supplier firm complexity. When the supplier firm offers a single product, service, application and/or distribution point, little internal coordination is required. However, as the number of products, applications and/or distribution

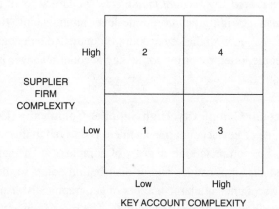

FIGURE 3.2: Supplier Firm and Key Account Complexity

points increases, internal coordination can be a severe challenge for the supplier firm.[8]

Low Key Account Complexity, Low Supplier Complexity (Cell 1). This cell captures the most straightforward set of interactions between the supplier firm and its key account customers. These key accounts are critically important sources of sales revenue but are not particularly complex to deal with. Little complexity exists on the supplier's side either. Both responsibility for, and action at, the key account can be largely handled by a single account manager in a *self-contained key account unit,* backed up by appropriate support units.[9]

Low Key Account Complexity, High Supplier Complexity (Cell 2). Here key account complexity remains low, but supplier complexity is high. The firm offers many products, applications, and/or distribution points to the key account, possibly from different organizational units. Once again, an individual key account manager in a *self-contained key account unit* may be the appropriate organizational device. However, because of the higher degree of supplier complexity, not only do key account managers require broader skill sets, the nature of the support units is likely to be more varied.

High Key Account Complexity, Low Supplier Complexity (Cell 3). In this cell, customer complexity is high, the key account has large numbers of geographically dispersed purchase-decision points, influence points, and/or usage points. By contrast, supplier complexity is low—the firm offers relatively few products, services, applications, and/or distribution points. The most appropriate system is *matrixed key account managers.* The key account manager plans strategy and manages important corporate-level relationships. However, much day-to-day interaction with the key account is conducted by geographically dispersed salespeople, often reporting to the key account manager in a dotted-line relationship.

High Key Account Complexity, High Supplier Complexity (Cell 4). Perhaps the greatest value of key account management is derived in this cell. Both sides of the relationship comprise high degrees of complexity. The supplier firm offers many products, applications and/or distribution points to the key account. In turn, the key account has a large number of geographically dispersed decision points, influence points, and/or usage points. The most frequently used system for this situation is *matrixed key account managers.*

Locating Key Account Management

Strategy for individual key accounts may be developed at different levels within the firm. The supplier firm may develop key account strategy within one or more of its divisions or business units, but strategy may also be developed at the corporate level. Furthermore, on a geographic axis, the supplier may develop key account strategy on a within-country regional, national, multicountry regional, or global basis.

The line organization for key account management should reflect the manner in which strategy is developed. Essentially, the location question has two dimensions: organizational unit and organizational level.

ORGANIZATIONAL UNIT

Regardless of the structure developed for managing individual key accounts— matrixed key account managers or a self-contained key account unit—the organizational unit where key account management is placed is a critical decision.

For single business firms operating in a single national economy, the location decision is trivial; in-depth key account management for national customers is most likely placed at the national level. By contrast, for more complex corporations such as the global multimarket multibusiness firm, key account management may reside within individual divisions or business units, in individual countries, and/or in regional groups and/or globally, and/or at corporate. Furthermore, since commitment to key account strategy may vary across the firm, from business unit to business unit, and from one geographic area to another, the firm may simultaneously operate with several types of key account management organization.

Thus, for its major multinational customers, the firm may implement global account management via matrixed global account managers. In individual countries, the local operations of these global accounts, and major national accounts, may be managed through a combination of self-contained key account units and matrixed key account managers. For smaller customers that qualify for key account status at a sales district or regional level, some form of key account management may operate within sales districts or regions.[10]

Corporate Account Management. If a particular key account purchases from several business units, strong arguments can be made for locating key account responsibility both within the business units *and* at the corporate level. The business unit level becomes the focus for product/market strategy, but overall enterprise-to-enterprise relationships are developed and maintained at corporate. Furthermore, if individual business units offer competing and/or complementary or potentially complementary products to similar key accounts, more active corporate-level key account management may be required.

EXAMPLE: 3M is a highly innovative company with over fifty operating units run by general managers with bottom-line responsibility. In addition to key account programs at the business level, its corporate accounts program was developed with the aim of leveraging its core competencies and technologies across business units in ways that would be mutually beneficial to both 3M and its key accounts.[11] (See Appendix 3.1 for a description of 3M's program.) Shell has a similar program in which its "value creation directors" are charged with identifying opportunities to serve its key accounts that might not be surfaced from regular business-level relationships.[12]

A corporate key accounts program may be called for if the customer deals with several firm divisions, especially if significant cross-selling opportunities are believed to exist but are not currently being exploited. Indeed, in some cases it may be appropriate to scrap selling efforts by individual business units in favor of a corporate accounts program.

EXAMPLE: Previously, the corporate and project finance group of ICICI, the leading Indian financial services group, operated with twelve product divisions, each responsible for its own sales force effort. Customer analysis revealed that 100 key accounts were responsible for a large proportion of the group's revenues. In a major reorganization, selling responsibility was removed from the product divisions and placed with a group of key account managers reporting to a key account director who was equivalent in status to the product division heads.[13]

However, if customer business is predominantly with one business unit and less so, or only sporadically, with other units, a corporate accounts program probably cannot be justified. In these circumstances, other mechanisms must be developed to ensure that important customers of one division are appropriately treated by sister divisions, for which they may be quite unimportant customers.

EXAMPLE: John Deere sells heavy equipment into the farm and construction industries through separate business units. Although customers for its farm products generally do not purchase construction equipment (and vice versa), occasionally a construction industry key account requires products from the farm division. Management in Deere's construction division uses informal mechanisms involving personal contacts to ensure that the key account is appropriately served by the farm division.

In some cases, one business unit is given formal responsibility for the entire corporate relationship. These relationships are more likely to be successfully managed to the extent that the firm has a team-oriented culture, reinforced by appropriate measurement systems.

EXAMPLE: Milliken business-level global account managers are charged to be on the lookout for opportunities for other business units. The Milliken culture, a salary-based compensation system, and rigorous annual evaluations reinforce these efforts.

A particular problem arises when two supplier organizations with considerable customer overlap are either merged, or one acquires the other. In order to present a unified front to the customer, critical decisions must be made regarding account responsibility.

EXAMPLE: The formation of Citigroup posed significant problems of key account responsibility. Both Citibank relationship managers and Salomon Smith Barney investment bankers each had close relationships with major accounts. Although Salomon bankers wanted to form independent relationships with Citibank's 1,700 multinational customers, Citibank relationship managers reportedly assumed the lead responsibility.[14] As the result of this arrangement, Salomon Smith Barney investment bankers secured significant business from customers with which they had previously enjoyed only minimal relationships.

Relationships among Key Accounts. Particularly tricky issues arise when the supplier's individual key accounts are themselves direct competitors and especially if they are both seeking a piece of business for which the supplier firm offers a critical input. In such cases, the supplier firm must demonstrate to each key account that it is acting fairly and has implemented organizational processes that prohibit transfer of privileged information from one key account to the other. This may be achieved through separate organizational locations of the key account managers, total non-overlapping membership of the teams supporting them, and *firewall* protections for key account specific data.

A second issue concerns the treatment of key accounts when one key account is the customer of the other. As noted earlier, extreme sensitivities may be involved at the direct customer if potential forward integration by the supplier firm is a concern. Regardless, if both direct and indirect customers are key accounts, the supplier firm can play a useful role in improving information flow between the two key accounts and by encouraging progress on critical initiatives. In these situations, use of the same or a different key account manager is a critical decision. If the supplier-firm/direct-customer key relationship is strong, appointing the same key account manager to both accounts may offer significant benefits.

EXAMPLE: 3M has a longstanding successful key account relationship with Lucent Technologies. In 2000, it enhanced the responsibilities of the Lucent corporate account manager to include AT&T, Lucent's largest customer.

ORGANIZATIONAL LEVEL

Related to the decision of where to place key account management is the question of organizational level. A key account management system placed deep in the organization, far from the centers of power, will have little organizational clout and senior key account management will find it difficult to secure required resources. If top management is truly serious about a key account strategy, key account management must be placed at a high organizational level.

EXAMPLE: In Betz and Dearborne, the senior manager of the key accounts group reported to the national sales manager. Resources to serve key accounts were difficult to secure and candidates attracted to key account management positions were lower caliber than desired. In a reorganization, the key account group was moved out from the national sales manager's jurisdiction and the newly appointed key account director reported at the same high level as the national sales director. Immediately, resources flowed more freely and the quality of candidates for key account manager positions rose dramatically.

Organizational Macrostructure

In the prior discussion we focused on individual supplier-firm/key-account relationships. Because, in general, supplier firms have relationships with multiple key accounts, the complete set of supplier-firm/key-account relationships should be managed as a coherent whole. To accomplish this, the supplier firm should appoint a manager/director of key accounts to whom key account managers report. We discuss the roles and responsibilities of this position later in the chapter.

Managing the Transition

Regardless of what form of key account management structure is selected, the supplier firm must manage the transition from pre-existing arrangements to the new organization. As with all organizational transitions, key account management transitions should be made *very carefully*. Attention should be focused on two major areas: the "hard" financial areas of revenues and profits, and "soft" areas such as relationships and information provision.

Before the transition, the supplier firm should have good information on both the revenue history and the true costs of serving its key accounts. In addition to direct product costs, the firm should identify support costs such as sales, service, and administration at the individual key account level. For example, it should measure sales force effort spent on external matters such as shipments and invoices, and on internal administrative issues such as meetings and presentations to management. This sort of analysis, using activity-based costing, should produce *real* profitability numbers for its key accounts under the preexisting organizational system so that the effectiveness of the new system can be readily assessed. (See Appendix 6.1 for an illustration of determining key account profitability.)

Second, the supplier firm should take care that the individuals affected by the organizational change are provided both with the rationale for, and the likely impact of, the change. This would include, of course, both individuals at the key account and those supplier firm personnel whose roles, responsibilities, and behavior at the key account will have to be modified for the new organization.

ROLES AND RESPONSIBILITIES IN KEY ACCOUNT MANAGEMENT

It is one thing to develop the appropriate line organization for key account management, it is quite another to identify the roles and responsibilities of critical players in the supplier firm's key account program. We focus on three critical roles—top management, the key account director, and key account managers.

Top Management

For a key account strategy to realize its potential, senior management must fully and openly support the key account program in a tangible manner. This support must be multifaceted and may be evidenced in a key account program champion, a top manager who openly and consistently supports the program.[15]

> **EXAMPLE:** At IBM, the program champion/executive sponsor of the global customer management program is a senior vice-president and group executive of sales and distribution who reports directly to CEO Lou Gerstner and runs IBM's sales organization worldwide.

COMMIT TO THE KEY ACCOUNT STRATEGY

Top management must be comfortable with making the tough choices that require a disproportionate amount of firm resources to be allocated to key accounts at the expense of other customers. For those personnel involved in key account management, such allocation makes eminent sense and is consistent with the designation of important customers as key accounts. However, these allocations do not always occur. One key account manager in a major U.S. health care firm complained that "Our top managers tell us they support the key account program but they are just not prepared to make the tough decisions on resource allocation. Instead of giving priority to our key accounts and providing them with excellent service, as befits their importance to us, we just give the same *lousy* service to all our customers."

PROVIDE A POSITIVE INTERNAL ENVIRONMENT
FOR SECURING HIGH-QUALITY HUMAN RESOURCES

Top management must play its part in ensuring that the appropriate type and quantity of high-quality human resources can be secured to play critical roles in the key account management process. Among the most critical decisions is the reporting level for the key account director. As discussed in the previous section, the organizational location of this executive carries a powerful message regarding top management's commitment to key account management. It plays an important role in the ability to secure key account resources in general, and to make high-quality appointments for key account managers and other team members in particular. Another important decision is the individual appointed to be key account director; much care should be taken to select an experienced, committed executive for this position.

FUND THE DEVELOPMENT AND/OR PURCHASE OF
SYSTEMS AND PROCESSES

Regardless of how good a job top management does in promoting the appointment of high-quality human resources to key account positions, key account management will not be successful unless the appropriate organizational systems and processes are put in place. As we discuss in later chapters, for key account management to function at a high level on a day-by-day basis, the resources required for these systems and process are significant. Top management must be prepared to make these resources available.

SUPPORT THE DEVELOPMENT OF A KEY ACCOUNT CULTURE

Top management must support development of a key account culture in the organization. The ultimate goal of key account management is to secure revenues and profits by building long-term relationships for the mutual benefit of both the supplier firm and its key accounts. Relationship building is essential for any supplier-firm/key-account dyad, but particularly so in those cases where the firm is seeking *quality supplier* and *partnership* relationships (Chapter 2).

A critical factor in nurturing key-account/supplier-firm relationships is the behavior of individuals in the support functions interfacing with key accounts. Not only must they be competent to do their jobs; they must be imbued with a customer-focused culture that pervades the supplier firm organization. Although key account management and sales force personnel are typically highly customer focused, support personnel may relate more to their functional departments and/or professions than to serving customers. This problem can be exacerbated both by the nature of the job and by status differences between key account management and support personnel, leading to resentment, envy, and lack of cooperation. For example, much of the work of *information* and *administration* specialists is mundane compared to the "exciting" travel and freedom of movement of key account managers and salespeople.

Notwithstanding a compelling logic for key account management, the organization's history, culture, and reward systems may militate against the key account managers' ability to be effective.

> **EXAMPLE:** One global bank, ABN AMRO, instituted a key account management program in its equity division. However, because of the individualistic culture of sales and trading personnel and a similarly based compensation system, not only did key account managers find it difficult to secure buy-in, key account information was not shared.[16]

It is top management's responsibility to ensure that all personnel truly understand the importance of key accounts to the firm's future. By their words and deeds, the firm's top managers must demonstrate, on a continuous basis, that they are committed to the key account strategy and are prepared to make the tough decisions that are required to serve customers effectively.

The corollary of securing top management support is that because of the significant costs associated with key account programs, their directors and managers must earn this support by demonstrating the true value of key account management.

ENSURE LACK OF CONFLICT AMONG INDIVIDUAL KEY ACCOUNT PROGRAMS

We noted earlier that key account management might operate in various businesses (divisions) and/or at the corporate level. Typically, senior management in each business decides whether or not to introduce a key account program, and determines the type of program and the nature of the leadership role. If key account management at a higher level is also relevant—for example, corporate versus business, global versus national—senior management must ensure that, at the least, the different ways of addressing key accounts are not in conflict.

BE DIRECTLY INVOLVED WITH KEY ACCOUNTS

Regardless of the key account manager's skills in developing and leading the key account team, senior management must be engaged with the key account from time to time, if only to demonstrate the importance the supplier firm places on the relationship.

> **EXAMPLE:** While attending an executive program in key account management, the key account director for Holly Corp.*, an equipment manufacturer, received a phone call from his divisional president. A key account was having trouble with a replaceable part. Holly's president wanted this problem fixed immediately!

> **EXAMPLE:** Fir Inc.*, a major supplier to the pharmaceutical industry, engages an independent marketing research company to conduct periodic customer satisfaction studies of influencers and decision makers in each of its global accounts. Fir's CEO insists on receiving, immediately, any data that suggests a current or potential problem with one of the accounts. He then acts on this data right away.[17]

Furthermore, only senior management can make the kinds of major commitments that key accounts periodically require.[18] In particular, strong support for an *executive partner* program (see below) is a tangible demonstration of commitment to key account management.

The Key Account Director

The key account director is the quarterback of the entire key account management process.[19] The person in this position must be an experienced executive who has the complete support of top management to fulfill the mission of the job. The key account director must assure congruence among the four elements of key account strategy: organization, human resources, and systems and processes. In addition, as the environment changes, the key account director should not only seek opportunities to gain senior management agreement to modify the key account strategy, but should then modify the congruence elements as appropriate.

The following discussion addresses the role of the key account director at the business (divisional) level. Many of the issues raised may also be relevant at the corporate level, depending upon the degree of independence/interdependence of the various organizational subunits. The key account director's ability to fulfill her roles and responsibilities is considerably enhanced by having a key account program champion at the highest organizational level. Ideally, this person is the CEO, but it may also be the senior sales or marketing executive. Depending on the organization, the program champion and key account director may be the same person.

INFLUENCE DEVELOPMENT AND IMPLEMENTATION OF THE KEY ACCOUNT STRATEGY

The key account director is the organizational "cheerleader" for key account management and the major influence on top management in regard to key accounts. In particular, the director should actively manage various elements of developing strategy for the firm's customers by spearheading evolution and change as appropriate. Specific areas of responsibility include fixing the appropriate breadth and depth of the firm's key account program, choosing the distribution of key accounts along the vendor—valued supplier—partner continuum, developing and modifying the criteria for selecting key accounts, selecting those accounts, deselecting accounts that no longer meet the firm's criteria, and generally managing the firm's key account portfolio.

ENSURE ORGANIZATIONAL CONGRUENCE

The firm's organization, human resources, and systems and processes for key account management must be congruent with its strategy:

Organization. The key account director has the responsibility for designing, gaining approval for, and implementing the appropriate *organizational structure*. This structure is expected to evolve both as the result of environmental change and the firm's changing commitment to key account management.

Human Resources. The key account director is responsible for developing and implementing processes for recruitment and selection, training, managing, retaining, and rewarding key account managers. In addition, the director is responsible for ensuring that other resources necessary to optimize performance at key accounts are in place.

Systems and Processes. The key account director should develop and/or purchase, and manage the appropriate systems to enable key account management to function appropriately. In particular, he should manage the key account database and ensure that appropriate coordination occurs among various key account systems within the firm—for example, global, regional (multicountry), and national key account management.

The director should develop (and continually update) a process and format for key account planning, set planning timetables, seek efficiencies in required common data and analyses across key accounts (for example, industry and competitor analyses), approve the plans, and ensure they are implemented. The key account director should see that individual key account plans are coherent with marketing plans, and should also compare and contrast individual account plans for customers within a given industry to ensure consistency.

EXAMPLE: An Asea Brown Boveri (ABB) spokesman opined: "A deciding factor for success is to compare the account plans of different customers in an industry. Why should we have different positions for similarly structured customers? With the help of this benchmarking, it is important to recognize even better the potential of ABB."[20]

The key account director should also manage the aggregation process for rationalizing the allocation of resources across key accounts.

A particularly important issue for the key account director concerns organizational goal alignment. Whereas key account manager goals are typically related to measures of key account performance, other elements of the organization may have conflicting goals. For example, difficulties may ensue when a regional sales manager, measured on regional performance, supervises a national (key) account manager located in her region. Similarly, a key account manager matrixed with the sales force may find individual salespeople resistant to implementing the key account strategy when goals are not well aligned.

The key account director must work to ensure that goal setting in such related areas is congruent with measures of key account manager performance. Management by objectives (MBO) systems may be very useful in this regard.

SECURE ACCEPTANCE OF KEY ACCOUNT MANAGEMENT BY BUILDING A KEY ACCOUNT CULTURE

Securing acceptance is always an issue, but particularly so when key account management is first introduced or if the firm has strong functional and/or business silos. These internal barriers must be reduced for key account management to work effectively.[21] Furthermore, regardless of apparent top-level commitment to key account management, the harsh reality is that CEOs have many other concerns as well. Furthermore, sometimes the depth of CEO support is rather shallow and the key account program is just one of several major initiatives undertaken by the supplier firm.

In these situations, a critical challenge for the key account director is to secure and maintain internal commitment to the key account management program. Many members of the organization, ranging from executive committee members such as the CFO and CIO, geographic and functional heads, and customer contact personnel around the company, must be "brought on board." Many methods may be used to secure acceptance of key account management, but ultimately these boil down to high levels of communication. Of course, because of personnel changes, this job is never really completed.

When any new corporate initiative is introduced, organizational members will develop expectations about that initiative. The key account director's job is to set expectations, develop a measurement system, and establish objectives for the key account program that are realistic and attainable. Of course, individual managers will likely require different types of information before they are fully supportive of the program.

> **EXAMPLE:** At Abbott Laboratories, a division president was skeptical about the value of key account management; he viewed it as unnecessary overhead. To be convinced he needed to see numbers. Key account personnel developed several methods of packaging data to demonstrate the revenue generating performance of the key account program.[22]

> **EXAMPLE:** At Boise Cascade Office Products, the newly appointed key account director spent his first nine months on the job working with internal contacts including field managers, field sales, sales support, and senior managers to secure agreement on what the key account program should be before taking it on the road.[23]

Some companies develop a "brand" for their key account programs to demonstrate to customers and organizational members that the firm is going to market in a different way. For example, Marriott introduced "Alliance Accounts" and developed a brochure explaining the nature of the program. Some firms have developed logos and printed T-shirts to make their key account programs tangible; others have developed web sites, updated on a continuous basis with information about the program, success stories, and so forth.

An important related issue is to ensure that other functional groups do not negatively impact the key account management program. Unless other departments are "in the loop," they may take actions that seem reasonable from their perspectives but that may severely hamper development of the interorganizational relationship

> **EXAMPLE:** Redwood Inc.'s* largest account was having cash flow problems. With the help of the marketing department, the key account manager was putting in enormous effort to help the account. Unaware of this effort, at sixty days, the accounts receivable clerk initiated the process that cut off delivery and sent a dunning letter to the account. The customer paid the invoice and never did business with the supplier again!

> **EXAMPLE:** In the midst of a radical downsizing, Redbud* put pressure on its personnel to generate incremental revenue. The accounting department examined the ten-year history of invoices to the firm's largest accounts. It found numerous errors and sent "corrected" invoices. The strategic account manager was not advised of this action and customers were furious.[24]

Whereas top management is responsible for introducing and sustaining a key account culture, the key account director undertakes most of the day-by-day activity. For example, the director should make all support personnel feel they are part of the teams serving key accounts. Various mechanisms can be used to achieve this goal, such as by supporting managers in key account meetings, and arranging for support personnel to visit their "customers" in the key account. Such visits might include logistics personnel visiting the key account's receiving group, or administrative personnel visiting the key account's finance group, to better understand their objectives, the nature of their jobs, and the constraints under which they operate.

In addition, the key account director must manage upward to secure top management commitment both to a customer-oriented key account philosophy throughout the firm, and provision of sufficient resources to achieve organizational congruence.[25] An important device used by several key account directors is the pipeline report. Issued monthly or quarterly, this report details the status of projects with all key accounts and estimates future associated revenue streams. By keeping senior management aware of key account activities, the report has the additional benefit of ensuring that operations personnel are aware of upcoming implementation needs.

Developing a key account culture is also aided by seeking explicit feedback from a group of key accounts. The key account director should contemplate developing advisory boards comprising nondirectly competing key accounts (see below).

INITIATE AND MANAGE AN EXECUTIVE PARTNER PROGRAM[26]

An executive partner program is a particularly valuable device for both demonstrating senior executive commitment to key account management in general, and providing significant value-added to supplier-firm/key-account relationships in particular. Executive partner programs tend to be idiosyncratic both to supplier firms and executives, but generally take the form of members of the top management cadre being "assigned" to one of the firm's key accounts. In a very real sense, the executive partner "works for" the key account manager and is part of the key account team engaged in developing and implementing strategy. This last item is an important issue, for key-account/executive-partner meetings should be held when the key account manager deems it appropriate, and not simply because it happens to fit the executive's schedule.

The executive partner can be a valuable resource for the key account manager in developing strong relationships with the key account. Typically, he can engage in conversations at a higher level than the key account manager and is able to gain entree that may be otherwise denied. The executive partner should be available for firm/key-account meetings when senior corporate presence is required, and able to cut through the supplier firm's bureaucracy to get things done when roadblocks prevent customer-related actions from occurring. Depending upon the nature of the supplier-firm/key-account relationship, and the predisposition of the executive partner, the level of interaction with the account may range from weekly meetings to biannual firm/key-account executive steering committee sessions. These latter meetings deal with critical issues, focus on potential opportunities, and help develop the interorganizational relationship. In addition, the executive partner may host critical supplier-firm/key-account events such as contract signings or new product announcements.

EXAMPLE: Hewlett-Packard's (HP) "assigned executive" program,[27] outlined several responsibilities:
- Foster personal rapport with key customer executives
- Develop and champion HP sales opportunities
- Resolve issues top-down for the sales process
- Participate in account planning and review meetings
- Mentor and coach the HP account manager and sales team

The key account director's role is to make the executive partner program work, if necessary by calling on the CEO to support the initiative and even to act as the executive partner for at least one key account. A "suggestion" from the CEO that each member of the managerial elite participate in several of these relationships is apt to find top managers scrambling to associate themselves with key accounts. Typically, executive partner programs carry no compensation, but recognition programs based on well-documented key account manager recommendations have proven useful.

The key account director must match top executives to key accounts based on data secured by interviewing the top management cadre. These matches, which may be based on any current interpersonal or other type of relationship between senior executives and key account personnel, are made without regard for current job responsibilities. Indeed, the underlying philosophy of executive partner programs is that top-manager/key-account relationships should be very long term and overarch any particular job responsibility. Of course, the key account director must exercise some degree of selectivity when matching senior executives to key accounts. And some senior executives may be totally unsuited for this role! The key account director must institute a control system to ascertain how individual relationships are performing and make the tough reassignment decisions, including "firing" executive sponsors when necessary.

For a firm that embarks on an executive partner program, the number of key accounts to which an individual executive is "assigned" is an important issue. Clearly, this decision is a function of the number of executives available (and appropriate) for the position, and the number of key accounts designated for an executive partner. Given the pressures of organizational life, it is unlikely that any single executive can effectively act as partner for more than a handful of key accounts. Certainly, one industry leader whose executives average thirty to forty executive partner relationships is probably not receiving the full potential from its program.

In recent years, executive partner programs have become widespread in firms committed to key account management.

EXAMPLES: Hewlett Packard, IBM, Xerox, and 3M have had executive partner programs for several years. One of C. Michael Armstrong's first actions as AT&T's incoming CEO was to initiate an executive partner program.[28]

In addition to the specific value afforded the supplier-firm/key-account relationship, executive partner programs ensure that senior managers, whose different functional responsibilities do not involve interaction with customers, play a part in nurturing the firm's most important assets, its key accounts.

FORM A CUSTOMER ADVISORY BOARD

A number of companies have developed customer advisory boards in which key accounts are the major participants. Typically, boards comprise five to ten members, with fifteen as a recommended maximum number; they meet at least twice a year, sometimes quarterly, and may rotate membership. Members may include senior management of key accounts or critical functional executives, and appropriate supplier firm personnel.

Customer advisory boards may focus on specific business issues related to product/service delivery from the supplier and/or provide a forum for discussion of more general issues of concern to all members. They can supplement key account manager and executive partner programs and may provide an additional valuable tool for managing supplier-firm/key-account interfaces.

Some boards may be industry specific; others may deliberately avoid having direct competitors as members so that the information flow between key accounts may be enhanced. Clearly, suppliers that form customer advisory boards run some risk in dealing with problems in an open forum; conversely, the openness involved in creating such a board may bring such invaluable benefits as feedback and relationship building, and may act as a subtle way of raising customer-switching costs.

EXAMPLES: Hewlett Packard has a twenty-member board, focused on R&D, that meets annually; Sun Microsystems has a similar twelve-member board.

Microsoft has multiple twenty-member boards organized by geographic region plus a fifty-member global executive roundtable focused on business development that meets biannually. Other major organizations with customer advisory boards are IBM and Merck.

MAKE KEY ACCOUNT MANAGEMENT THE BEST IT CAN BE

Continuous improvement should be a goal in any key account program. Several methods are available to the key account director.

Benchmarking. Senior key account personnel should avoid "reinventing the wheel." Many corporations have significant experience with key account programs. The key account director should benchmark practices from leading firms and incorporate this learning into the firm's congruent elements. By developing an understanding of processes other companies have used, highlighting what worked, what didn't work, and why, the firm may avoid pitfalls and move expeditiously to operate a successful key account management program. Indeed, to the extent that the firm understands the processes employed by key competitors, it can employ its own key account management system as a powerful competitive weapon.

This activity should not be a "one-time-deal"; rather, the firm should benchmark its own practices periodically. Another possibility is to form loose relationships with noncompetitor organizations to exchange information on key account practice.[29]

Problem Diagnosis. The key account director should be on the lookout for system-wide problems and introduce appropriate organizational modifications to ensure smoother operations.

> **EXAMPLE:** The Fritz Companies, providers of global integrated logistic services, identified several problems of implementation slippage between decisions made by key account management and the operational level. To address this problem, several implementation managers were appointed to manage this interface.

Best Key Account Practice. The supplier firm should develop procedures for exchanging "best practices" in key account management across the firm on an ongoing basis. Individual key account managers may develop creative solutions to specific problems that have broad applicability across the firm's key accounts. Making this expertise generally available to all relevant key account personnel raises the entire system to higher performance levels.[30]

MANAGE POTENTIAL CONFLICT IN DEALING WITH KEY ACCOUNTS

As noted earlier, quite frequently a supplier firm's key accounts are not independent. For example, a supplier of plastic chip may have as key accounts both its direct customers (molders) and their customers (end users such as automobile manufacturers). Or two key accounts may be direct competitors, such as General Motors and Ford. The key account director should be proactive in identifying potential conflicts in dealing with these key accounts and making the necessary structural arrangements discussed earlier.

Key Account Managers

Regardless of the particular organizational structure and set of systems and processes the supplier firm employs for implementing its key account strategy and managing the key account portfolio, primary responsibility for individual accounts typically rests with a single person in the role of key account manager. Typically, this is a formally appointed position but, as indicated in Chapter 2, a salesperson or senior executive may assume the key account manager role in addition to other responsibilities. Regardless, the key account manager is the lynchpin around which the entire interorganizational relationship revolves. (See Appendix 3.2 for a series of key account manager objectives developed for a major U.S. manufacturer.)

Of course, the roles and responsibilities of key account managers differ from relationship to relationship, in particular across the complexity dimensions introduced earlier in this chapter. As we indicated, key account complexity is related to the number and geographic dispersion of purchase-decision points, influence points, and/or usage points. The supplier's complexity depends on the number of product lines, services, applications, and distribution points. When we consider the two polar extremes, low account complexity and low supplier complexity (LAC/LSC), versus high account complexity and high supplier complexity (HAC/HSC), we can see that the roles and responsibilities of the key account manager differ markedly.

Compared to LAC/LSC relationships, HAC/HSC relationships are much more complex. Typically heavily matrixed, the key account manager has an enormous job coordinating the many players in both the key account and the supplier firm. By contrast, although key account managers with LAC/LSC relationships have an important coordination role, they often reside in specialized key account units and have considerably simpler coordination tasks.

The types of supplier-firm/key-account relationships are also important in determining the number of key account relationships that an individual account manager can handle. For simple relationships, in which the manager interfaces with few key account and supplier personnel, several accounts per manager are probably reasonable. However, for complex relationships, where the manager must interface with multiple personnel in both the key account and supplier firm, a single account assignment is more likely to be appropriate.[31]

From the simplest to the most complex organizational arrangements for addressing key accounts, the key account manager must manage a human resource system. This system includes the key account team, and comprises various sets of relationships both within the key account, and across the supplier-firm/key-account interface. These relationships involve personnel at several organizational levels and from many functional areas. These individuals frequently have different values, stakes, assumptions, goals, and perceptions about the supplier-firm/key-account relationship, and are rewarded through vastly different systems. The difficulty of managing this human resource system, and dealing with a myriad of actual and potential conflicts, makes the key account manager's job one of the most difficult and challenging within the firm.

In particular, because the key account manager occupies a boundary role between the supplier organization and the key account, she must balance conflicting demands from both sides.[32] On the one hand, the key account manager must resist "unreasonable" demands from key account personnel that would adversely affect the supplier firm's profitability. On the other hand, she may have to rein in supplier firm personnel wishing to take actions that might benefit the supplier firm in the short run but which would adversely affect the long-run relationship.

The key account manager will be successful to the extent that he is sensitive to the needs and perspectives of all relevant personnel on both sides of the interorganizational relationship, and is able to build trust, establish rapport, in-

FIGURE 3.3: Key Account Manager's Time Allocation (%)[34]

	Task	Time Allocation (%)
Within Supplier Firm	Reps and other sales channels	15
	Marketing department	9
	Production and operations	5
	Other internal departments	6
	Subtotal	35
Customers	Upper-level decision makers	11
	Purchasing department	5
	Production and operations	5
	Customer's sales channels and marketing departments	4
	Subtotal	25
Other	Other/administrative	21
	Travel	19
	Subtotal	40

spire respect, and create a sense of excitement.[33] Notwithstanding the importance of developing and managing personal relationships, a central goal of the key account manager should be to institutionalize the interorganizational relationship. A survey (Figure 3.3) provides some indication of the complexity of the key account manager's job.

In order to optimize supplier firm performance at the key account, the key account manager must successfully undertake several quite different roles and responsibilities. Included are securing supplier firm objectives at the key account, developing strategy and action programs, ensuring that they are implemented as planned, developing and managing key account relationships, building and managing the key account team, managing relationships with the sales force, and managing the information system.[35] Of course, we expect the effort placed on these different roles and responsibilities to relate to the complexity of the interorganizational relationship, and to vary over the exploration, establishment, maintenance, and disengagement phases of the key account manager's life cycle.

SECURE SUPPLIER FIRM OBJECTIVES AT THE KEY ACCOUNT

The most important responsibility for the key account manager is to secure the supplier's objectives at the key account. In most cases, suppliers seek profits from their key accounts although, in the absence of systems for measuring profits by customer, objectives may be stated in terms of levels and growth of sales revenues.

Perhaps the most important dimension across which supplier firm objectives differ is the timing of revenue and profit flows. For some key account managers, the crucial objective is securing sales and profits today, from products that are fairly well specified for well-defined customer needs. Other key account managers may be identifying future opportunities for which the supplier is able to use its current and/or developing technology. Still other key account manager jobs have goals that contain components of both types of objective.

Regardless of the complexion of supplier firm objectives at the key account, the key account manager's success will be highly dependent upon how well she fulfills her other roles and responsibilities.

DEVELOP STRATEGY AND ACTION PROGRAMS

Top management bears the responsibility for making macro-level strategic decisions concerning the supplier firm's entire key account strategy. By contrast, the key account manager develops a plan and lays out the firm's goals, strategy, and action programs for a single key account. Each key account strategy is focused on satisfying critical customer needs in the face of competitors' actions.

The key account manager has ultimate responsibility for plan development, and must exhibit total commitment to the strategy and action programs. However, he does not typically conduct all the required planning activities personally; much data collection and analysis may be performed by others. Nonetheless, by tapping the creative human potential of both the key account team and personnel at the key account, not only is the quality of strategy development enhanced, the probability that the key account strategy and action programs will be implemented as planned is also improved. During the planning process, the key account manager should be open to influence, but should strive to avoid the strategy and action programs becoming a political compromise between powerful organizational subunits.

ENSURE IMPLEMENTATION OF STRATEGY AND
ACTION PROGRAMS

Objectives developed in the key account planning process will only be achieved if the relevant strategy and action programs are implemented as planned. However, it is one thing to develop a plan, it is quite another to achieve successful implementation of the strategy and action programs. The major difficulty, of course, is that in many cases, the key account manager has no direct line authority over specific individuals performing the implementation tasks, nor direct access to required organizational resources. Indeed, some of the relevant individuals and resources may have to come from the key account.

Of course, as noted above, if the key account manager has done a good job of managing plan development by involving key players in the process, the probability of successful implementation is considerably enhanced. However, notwithstanding this involvement, many required resources are scarce and the manager must often exercise considerable skill to ensure that promised resources are in fact made available.

The key account manager's ability to secure resources can have a far-reaching long-run impact. Note how a senior finance executive with a major drug company, Warner Lambert, described his experience with Wachovia Bank.

> We've worked with First Wachovia since 1979, beginning with a number of accounts, and now we have 55 to 60. . . . The number one reason is service, and the number one key to that service is the account officer. Tom Patton . . . understands our company because he's worked hard at understanding it. He functions as the liaison between us and the bank . . . there is an exceptional degree of communication and give-and-take by both parties. We appreciate that. [Early on] when we were shifting some operations to the Charlotte lockbox center . . . Tom . . . brought in a team of cash management and operations specialists. . . . I was flabbergasted at the amount of advance preparation that had been done. . . . We like the continuity Tom has provided over the years. . . . It's so much more efficient than being called on by separate specialists from the same bank, with each giving priority to the area of the organization he or she represents."[36]

Of course, during the operating cycle, the key account manager should monitor progress against plan—both the implementation of planned actions and desired results. When "actuals" differ from "plans," the manager should take the necessary steps for "course corrections," possibly involving changes in the key account strategy and action programs, in a "steering" control (plan-do-check-act) sense.

DEVELOP AND MANAGE RELATIONSHIPS
WITH THE KEY ACCOUNT

In the context of a relationship strategy developed during the planning process, the key account manager must develop and manage a host of relationships with key account personnel. These may range far and wide across many functions and organizational levels. Some relationships may require frequent contact; others are more episodic and based on situational contingencies. In any event, the number of relationships can be extraordinarily large; for example, IBM's key account manager at Citibank maintains relationships with over three hundred Citibank personnel!

In addition, a variety of relationships among supplier firm and key account personnel have to be developed and managed. These also may involve various functions and managerial levels. Each individual contact between supplier firm and key account personnel is, in Jan Carlzon's terms, "a moment of truth" that can enhance or detract from the overall interorganizational relationship.[37]

Through such mechanisms as meetings, presentations, social activities, firm visits, and the like, the key account manager may orchestrate interactions ranging from CEO to CEO, to those involving supplier firm shipping personnel and key account receiving personnel who may spend time together at both shipping and receiving locations. If these relationships are to develop effectively, the key account manager may have to play the roles of teacher, coach, and facilitator with members of the key account team. In this context, it is important that the key account manager and executives at the key account agree about the nature and frequency of regular interorganizational contacts.

EXAMPLE: In 3M's corporate accounts' system, expectations are set for the time commitments of corporate account managers. They are supposed to spend 20% of their time making connections with 3M personnel in its fifty different operating units and 20% in making linkages between customer personnel and 3M personnel for specific identifiable application possibilities. The bulk of their time (60%) is spent in developing the 3M customer relationship and understanding where 3M technologies might be applied.

Finally, the key account manager should attempt the difficult task of managing relationships within the key account. These relationships are particularly important, because how important personnel at the key account interact and form judgments about the supplier firm and its competitors has a major impact on the supplier firm's success. Key account managers should use meetings and other forms of information provision to achieve their communication goals. They should also recognize, though, that persuasive information about the supplier's superior offer is more effective coming from a respected source at the key account than from a supplier firm representative.

A particularly critical issue for the key account manager is to ensure that the supplier firm is responsive to the customer's concerns. There are many ways to demonstrate such responsiveness, ranging from swift reply to telephone calls to following through expeditiously on actions agreed on at supplier-firm/key-account meetings. Managing day-to-day execution can be critical in forming the key account's judgment of the key account manager, the key account team, and hence of the supplier firm in total.

BUILD AND MANAGE THE KEY ACCOUNT TEAM

> A team is . . . a small number of people with complementary skills who are committed to a common purpose, set of performance goals, and approach for which they hold themselves mutually accountable.[38]

In most cases, the key account manager achieves supplier firm objectives not by his or her own actions but through the efforts of an account team whose members are characterized by diversity and interdependence. The size and scope of team effort increases the greater the degree of customer and supplier firm complexity and typically includes some combination of personnel from such functions as administration, applications engineering, customer service, finance, logistics, operations, marketing, R&D and technical service. In some cases, team members report directly to the key account manager; in other cases, the key account manager has no line authority over these personnel who thus operate as a "virtual" team. For ongoing key account management, key account teams (direct or virtual) are permanent features of the interorganizational relationship between the supplier firm and key account. However, for individual projects key account teams may be formed on an *ad-hoc* basis for the life of the project.[39]

Regardless of team structure, the key account manager must assemble the necessary human resources to form the team. She must ensure that team members are both involved in the development of, and fully conversant with, the objectives, strategy, and action programs for the key account relationship. She must also ensure that the team presents a coordinated approach at the key account. This is accomplished by significant day-by-day information flow and regular team meetings so that all members are up to date with key account-related activities. An annual team review should set the stage for developing the strategy and action programs for the following year.

However, because of the realities of organizational life, individual team members and their various functional "homes" will have their own goals, priorities, and constraints. These differences, which are greater for virtual than directly managed teams, can lead to duplication of effort, disagreement, and internal conflict.[40] When these negative consequences directly impact the key account, the result may be lack of clear understanding of account needs, inferior service, lower product quality, higher costs, and disenchantment with the supplier.

The key account manager leads the supplier firm's efforts at the key account. He must resolve internal conflicts and coordinate the actions of team members across functional areas and managerial levels so that the supplier firm presents itself as a seamless organization.[41] This may be a particularly difficult task when the team is convened on a temporary *ad-hoc* basis to develop a proposal for an individual project.

The difficulties involved in managing virtual teams should not be taken to imply that directly managed key account teams are necessarily superior. Indeed, Ginkgo Inc.*, a major U.S. manufacturing firm with significant key account experience switched from a directly managed to virtual team structure when it was discovered that key account managers' focus on their accounts was being diluted by day-to-day line management responsibilities.

Key account managers must see that team members have a realistic understanding of their roles and responsibilities. These include:

- effective collaboration
- sharing information, perceptions, and feedback
- demonstrating leadership
- making team goals a priority
- expending effort as needed
- confronting important issues

Key account managers should also encourage the taking of responsibility by providing sufficient autonomy and presenting challenging opportunities. Team members should be measured against goals, and superior performance should be recognized. However, while being fair and impartial, key account managers should also be prepared to confront and deal with inadequate performance.[42]

The team-building task is best approached by considering the manager–team member relationship as an alliance based on trust and reciprocity from which each may secure benefits. As we discuss in the next chapter, the sorts of currencies that may be exchanged include:

- *Inspiration:* providing meaning to the other's work
- *Task:* assistance in getting the job done
- *Position:* enhancing the other's organizational position
- *Relationship:* strengthening the other's social relationships
- *Personal:* enhancing the other's sense of self

Key account managers need to understand and address team member needs, and take into account each team member's many inter- and intraorganizational relationships. Depending on the quality of these relationships, at any point in time, it might be necessary to maintain, improve, repair, or terminate a member's relationship with the team.

MANAGE RELATIONSHIPS WITH THE SALES FORCE

Of all organizational personnel that develop relationships with the key account, other than the key account manager, perhaps the most critical are members of the sales force. The supplier firm must set clear policies outlining the roles and responsibilities of both the key account manager and the sales force. This is especially true in those situations where the supplier firm implements a matrixed management system in which key account managers have overall responsibility for key accounts, yet much day-to-day contact is the responsibility of a traditional, geographically dispersed sales force. Unless there is absolute clarity regarding roles and responsibilities of both key account manager and salespeople, unintended, negative consequences for the supplier firm may occur.

The problem is often most acute in times of change; for example, when key account management is introduced, or during transition from one key account management system to another. Unless these changes are made sensitively, such disruptions of the status quo may lead to bad feelings and dysfunctional behavior resulting from a sense of loss. A number of problem situations may arise:

- The sales force sees key account management as encroaching upon its territory.

- The sales force "passes the buck" when problems occur with important customers.
- The sales force is made to feel like second-class citizens, merely implementing at a local level what has been *decided* by the key account manager.
- Poorly planned allocation of sales credit between local salespeople and the key account management leads to bad feelings regarding financial compensation.

Key account managers can minimize the potential for conflict with salespeople by being generous with recognition for their role in securing revenue. In addition, an important role of the key account director is to make sure that organizational processes do not get in the way of key account manager/salesperson collaboration. Sales credit and compensation is frequently an important issue.

EXAMPLE: In Honeywell's Fire & Security business unit, the national account program produces over 30% of annual revenues. Local sales representatives receive sales credit both for "incoming" revenues developed by national account managers and for locally developed accounts whose revenue is earned in another territory.[43]

Furthermore, unless the key account manager and salesperson roles are clearly defined, salespeople are likely to complain of unfair penalties when sales are lost through no fault of their own. Correspondingly, key account managers are likely to complain that they receive insufficient sales force support.

As discussed above, an important part of the key account manager's role is planning and strategy development. Salespeople should be part of the team providing information and insight to assist in this task. More importantly, field sales personnel can both implement strategy at the local level by selling and servicing locally controlled opportunities, and develop and maintain ongoing local relationships. To the extent that the key account manger secures a broad-scale contract with the key account, the sales force is provided with a "hunting license." Its job is to maximize sales within the contract.

In some organizations, key account managers have other sales-related responsibilities as well. For example, in addition to serving as key account manager for one account, an individual may also function as the local sales representative for another key account. Such dual responsibility provides the individual with significant insight into both types of role and may provide for greater teamwork and superior implementation.

It is important to ensure that key account manager and salesperson objectives do not seriously conflict. If conflicts are present, they should be identified early and worked through with the salesperson and his first-line sales manager.

MANAGE THE KEY ACCOUNT INFORMATION SYSTEM

The key account manager is the central figure in the communication process between the supplier firm and the key account. In the context of the firm's generic information systems and those developed specifically for key account management, the key account manager must ensure that the appropriate information is being collected, analyzed, and disseminated to the appropriate personnel. Of course, it is not necessary for the key account manager to be aware of every item of information, but it is his responsibility to ensure that information flows effectively and efficiently.

In addition to managing day-to-day information flow, the key account manager should plan periodic communication events. For example, she may organize a review of the contracting process once a contract is signed (or lost), and conduct periodic executive-level reviews of the supplier-firm/key-account relationship. In addition, the manager should ensure that information about the supplier's progress and/or successes is made known to the appropriate people, possibly via a newsletter focused on the supplier-firm/key-account relationship.

> EXAMPLE: Milliken and Co. is a major supplier of carpet to Citigroup. Periodically, the Milliken Carpet division's global account director for Citigroup produces a newsletter for customer personnel that details current information on the relationship. This includes information on major projects, benchmarking,[44] customer visits, on-time delivery record, and other ways in which Citigroup has been aided in achieving its critical success factors.

SUMMARY

Supplier firm management must make critical organizational decisions based on the level of commitment to key accounts that it deems appropriate. Whereas modest commitment to key accounts dictates a modest organizational response, high levels of commitment require major organizational changes, typically through the development of some form of matrix structure or a self-contained key account unit. Important related decisions concern the location of key account management, for example, in the business unit and/or at corporate, the organizational level at which key account management is placed, and the organizational macrostructure for key account management overall.

For key account management to be successful, several sets of roles and responsibilities must be clearly articulated. Most important are the various aspects of top management's supportive role; those of the person charged with making the entire key account program function effectively, the key account director; and the quarterback of the relationship between the supplier firm and its key accounts, the individual key account managers.

CHAPTER FOUR

The Key Account Manager

The third major building block of the congruence model for key account management is human resources. Clearly, when the supplier firm adopts some form of key account management program, many supplier firm personnel are involved. However, the critical role in the interorganizational relationship is the key account manager.

The increasingly important yet difficult role played by key account managers makes it imperative that individuals of the highest caliber staff this position. The supplier firm must be very clear about the particular set of knowledge, skills, and abilities that it requires in its key account managers. Then, it must put in place appropriate procedures for recruitment, selection, and training to generate key account managers who can effectively carry out their several roles and responsibilities.

Because effective key account managers are an extremely valuable organizational resource, and should be treated as an asset rather than as an expense, the supplier firm must develop ways of retaining them. In particular, reward systems must be carefully thought through. Clearly, financial compensation is an important issue but the firm must also consider several other types of reward mechanisms.

In this chapter, we address all of these issues. We commence with a discussion of skill sets, then turn our attention to recruitment, selection, training, and retaining key account managers. We conclude with a section on rewarding the key account manager.

SKILL SETS

The key account manager's job is one of the more difficult and demanding in organizational life. As noted previously, similar to many sales jobs, the key account manager occupies a boundary role and must make difficult trade-off decisions between the requirements of the key account and those of the supplier firm. However, the main feature that distinguishes key account managers from traditional salespeople is the level of responsibility involved.

As we discussed earlier, the supplier firm should exercise great care in deciding which customers are worthy of key account status. Those selected to be key accounts are critically important to the supplier firm's future and typically represent a substantial fraction of the firm's current and/or potential revenues. Clearly, individuals selected as key account mangers must be able to handle that level of responsibility. Firms considering key account management programs should complete a thorough assessment of skill requirements for their key account manager positions. This assessment should relate directly to the roles and responsibilities of the key account manager discussed in Chapter 3.

In assessing skill requirements for its key account managers, the supplier firm should be very clear about the results these managers are expected to achieve. For example, the skills necessary to ensure that current sales levels for a set of mature products are maintained and increased may be quite different from those required to identify opportunities for the firm's emerging technologies. Furthermore, the skills necessary to coordinate a complex key-account/supplier-firm relationship in a matrix organization may be quite different from those in a more straightforward relationship handled within a special key account unit.

In this section, we discuss a series of general requirements for effective key account management under several headings—business management skills, boundary spanning and relationship building skills, and leadership and team building skills. We conclude by reporting the results of recent studies of key account managers.[1]

Business Management Skills

To a very large extent, the job of the key account manager is to run a business; that business is the key account. Depending on the sizes of key account and supplier firm, and the nature of the products involved, this business may represent annual revenues of hundreds of millions of dollars. Furthermore, in well-run key account programs, the key account manager not only has top-line (sales revenue) responsibility, but is also measured on bottom-line profit (or, at least, profit contribution).

Significant skill is necessary to run a multimillion-dollar business. The key account manager plays the central role in articulating the strategy and action programs for the key account. Not only is substantial data gathering required to accomplish these tasks successfully, the key account manager must possess a strong market and customer focus and significant conceptual, analytic, and planning skills, based on such abilities as mental agility, critical thinking, quantitative reasoning, and divergent (out-of-the-box) thinking. For example, he must be able to diagnose the key account's procurement systems to understand the various actors and decision processes involved. He must be able to make difficult trade-off decisions, often involving complex economic factors requiring a level of sophistication in marketing and financial analysis not normally found in the sales force. In part because of the growth of Internet technology, key account managers must also become increasingly computer literate.

But, planning and strategy development skills alone are not sufficient; action programs flowing from the planning process must be implemented both at the key account and within the supplier firm. Managing the key account requires skills in running and facilitating meetings, consultative selling, and in negotiation, presentation, and communication, often with executives at high organizational levels. Furthermore, the key account manager must also be an entrepreneur, always on the lookout for opportunities to add value to the supplier-firm/key-account relationship through creative identification and solution of key account problems, regardless of whether personnel at the key account have yet recognized them as problems.

Boundary Spanning and Relationship Building Skills

To fulfill her many roles and responsibilities, the key account manager must work across multiple organizational boundaries. These include functional barriers and hierarchical levels within the key account, but also within the supplier firm. At the key account, the key account manager must promote the supplier firm's position and secure business. In the supplier firm, the key account manager must secure the required types and amounts of resources for satisfying key account needs.[2] Access to critical networks of individuals and good working relationships with personnel in both the supplier firm and key account are invaluable assets for the key account manager.

In conducting these boundary-spanning activities, the key account manager must manage many complex sets of relationships. When supplier and key account are substantial organizations, literally hundreds of individual relationships among, and between, key account and supplier personnel may be involved. The key account manager must have extensive information system knowledge to ensure appropriate levels of communication among key players. He must also be sensitive to the organizational structures, processes, procedures, and cultures of both the key account and the supplier firm. A deep understanding of organizational behavior and sensitivity to the political realities of organizational life is necessary to navigate both organizations effectively. These skills may be sorely tested in merger and acquisition situations when the key account manager assumes responsibility for relationships between the firm's new units and the key account, some of which may have been troubled.

In general, the key account manager's focus is on business relationships *per se* and on social activities that support these relationships. However, from time to time, she may have to deal with difficult personal relationships between supplier firm and key account personnel.

> **EXAMPLE:** One key account manager was responsible for a team of sixty twenty-eight- to thirty-five-year-olds that interfaced with personnel of similar ages from the firm's largest accounts. He observed that interorganizational business relationships often developed into personal relationships. He lamented the fact that termination of such personal relationships tended to have negative effects on interorganizational business relationships.

Leadership and Team-Building Skills

In most cases, key account managers do not operate as individuals but are leaders of key account teams. However, in general, they do not get things done through direct line authority associated with a formal organizational position. Rather, they must rely on the exercise of personal influence via leadership and team-building skills. Team leadership "requires a complementary mix of skills, a purpose that goes beyond individual tasks, goals that define joint work-products, and an approach that blends individual skills into a unique collective skill—all of which produces strong *mutual* accountability."[3] To successfully lead a key account team, the key account manager should possess strong interpersonal skills that engender trust, resolve conflict, and bring about the required behavior. In addition, such personal traits as assertiveness, attractiveness, charisma, energy, flexibility, integrity, persistence, personal discipline, reflectiveness, and toughness improve the chances for success. The key account manager should be prepared to challenge current organizational practices, inspire a shared vision, develop intelligent agendas for action, communicate these well, and motivate key account and supplier firm personnel—both persons at a comparable organizational level and senior management, in part by recognizing contributions and celebrating accomplishments. He must have the ability to set a positive example and to extract promises of deliverables from both supplier firm and key account personnel, and the requisite organizational clout to ensure that these promises are kept.[4]

Among the characteristics of successful teams are:[5]

- High levels of skill and/or skill potential
- High levels of mutual trust among team members
- Mutual support among team members in keeping promises
- Flexibility and adaptability of the team and individual members
- High standards of excellence in behavior and performance
- Openness to feedback
- Facilitative and principled leadership
- A clear elevating goal for the team as a whole
- A unified commitment to results
- Effective communication structures

If the key account manager is effective, the team performs at a high level. The key account is well served and hears the supplier firm speak with a single voice. If not, the key account hears inconsistent messages from uncoordinated company representatives to the detriment of the supplier-firm/key-account relationship.

In the remainder of this section, we discuss the social styles/leadership practices framework, developed into a leadership model by William Klepper. This approach has proved to be particularly successful with key account managers.[6] We follow by suggesting a variety of organizational currencies that the key account manager can trade to secure required behavior.

THE KLEPPER LEADERSHIP MODEL

Klepper's model is based on fifteen years of working with the Social Styles theory developed by TRACOM Corporation.[7] The popular TRACOM framework focuses on social styles, "the most persistent, socially evident, pattern[s] of behavior that a person demonstrate[s] to others."[8] TRACOM's Social Style Profile is a description of how others see a person position himself within the available actions on two key dimensions: assertiveness and responsiveness.

- assertiveness is concerned with how the person interacts with others and the degree to which he sees himself as:
  - tending to ask—ask assertive
  - tending to tell—tell assertive
- responsiveness focuses on how the person deals with her feelings and emotions:
  - tending to keep feelings and emotions inside—control
  - tending to display feelings and emotions to others—emote

Combining these dimensions produces the four Social Style archetypes in Figure 4.1.

- analytical—ask assertive/control
- amiable—ask assertive/emote
- expressive—tell assertive/emote
- driving—tell assertive/control

All social styles have value, but people interact differently with one another based on these observable, repetitive patterns of behavior. The *analytical* person tends to ask questions, gather facts, and study data seriously. The *amiable* displays feelings openly, but is less assertive and more interested in being agreeable and cooperative. The *expressive* is more willing to make his feelings public and is decisive and forceful. The *driver* is primarily assertive, serious, and makes an effort to tell people what she thinks and requires.

A key account manager's social style has implications for how she relates to others, her use of time, and how she makes decisions. The key account manager must read a group situation and apply the appropriate behaviors in her interactions with others. Each manager's own social style will determine her preference for which behaviors to employ, but she can learn those behaviors that will gain her endorsement from those she must work with to be successful.[9]

Leadership Behavior. In linking the social style behaviors with leadership practices research, Klepper has identified specific types of leadership behavior associated with each social style, and with a team leader role that applies to all four social styles.[10] Individual key account managers may employ any of these leadership styles.

- *Analyticals* set examples for others by behaving in ways consistent with their stated values; they plan small wins that prompt consistent progress and build commitment.
- *Aimiables* foster collaboration by promoting cooperative goals and building trust; they strengthen others by sharing information and power, and by increasing their discretion and visibility.
- *Drivers* search for challenging opportunities to change, grow, innovate, and improve; they experiment, take risks, and learn from their mistakes.
- *Expressives* envision an uplifting and ennobling future; they enlist others in a common vision by appealing to their values, interests, hopes, and dreams.
- *Team Leaders* recognize individual contributions to the success of every project and celebrate team accomplishments regularly.

The key account manager's team leadership behavior has a direct effect on the motivational needs of team members. The work of motivation theorists reinforces the importance of recognition and celebration of team members' results as a means to motivate and build the team.[11] It is the team's sense of belonging that is reinforced, motivating members continually to seek superior performance as a group.

The leadership behaviors of the analytical, amiable, expressive, and driver are appropriately applied in support of the team's needs. Specifically, Klepper suggests that some leadership behaviors are likely to be more appropriate than others at different stages in the life of a team. In infancy, the team needs a challenging opportunity from the *driver*. To overcome social inertia, the *expressive* must engage the values, interests, hopes, and dreams of the team with the vision this opportunity offers. To grow into a collective effort, the *amiable* fosters collaborative effort among team members by promoting cooperative goals and

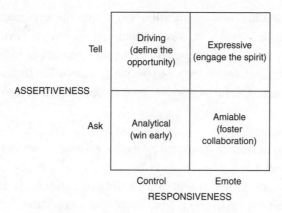

FIGURE 4.1: The Klepper Leadership Model

building trust. Finally, as traction is gained, the *analytical* shows the way, setting examples for others through small wins that prompt continuous progress toward team goals.

To secure his objectives, the key account manager must rely on the exercise of personal influence via leadership and team-building skills. Personal influence is the direct result of gaining the endorsement of those with whom the key account manager interfaces in carrying out his role—both team members and executives at the key account. All things equal, successful exercise of personal influence leads to winning endorsement, then winning and continuing to win the account. Unsuccessful exercise of personal influence leads to losing endorsement, and losing the account!

The starting point for the key account manager is to be aware of her own individual social style and leadership practices. Then she should understand the styles and practices of others. The successful key account manager adjusts her behaviors to complement the behaviors of those from whom she is seeking endorsement. The critical success factor is to exhibit to others the social style behaviors and leadership practices that contribute to a mutually productive relationship. Building the supplier-firm/key-account relationship, like leading team members in the supplier firm, is a team-building effort that is strengthened by a synergy of skills and abilities.

ORGANIZATIONAL CURRENCIES

Currencies are resources that can be exchanged and are the basis for exerting influence. They are extremely important for key account managers to get things done, both within his own organization and within the key account. The language of currencies enables the key account manager to see beyond a specific situation and to understand the variety of possible sources of influence that he possesses. Currencies are important to people and are willingly traded for other currencies or for goods and services. They may be categorized into five separate types:

- Inspiration: reflect inspirational goals that provide meaning to individuals in organizations
- Task: directly related to a person's ability to perform his assigned tasks and achieve the satisfactions from successful completion
- Position: enhance the person's position in the organization and indirectly her ability for career advancement
- Relationship: strengthening a relationship with someone
- Personal: related to the individual's sense of self

Each of these categories contains several related currencies; examples from each group are shown in Figure 4.2. Of course, different people put different values on individual currencies, so that what is important to one may be unimportant to another. The job for the key account manager is to understand the "currency" needs of the individuals he wishes to influence, then offer the appropriate currency for the behavior he wants to secure. For example, he might gain support from a team member by offering the opportunity to work on an exciting new project (task-related). Or he might move an application test along by providing an engineer at a key account visibility to her senior management (position-related). Of course, in some cases, the manager will not possess sufficient currency and will have to secure it from an ally. For example, recognition that may be important to an executive at the key account could be provided by a visit from the key account director or executive partner (position-related).

Research Findings

In recent years researchers have investigated the requirements for successful key account managers. An early-1990s study categorized these requirements into personal traits, skill requirements, and areas of knowledge and experience (Figure 4.3).

FIGURE 4.2: Commonly Traded Organizational Currencies[12]

Currency Category	Currency Type	Currency Description
Inspiration-related	Vision	Providing involvement in a task with larger significance for the unit, organization, customers, or society
	Excellence	A chance to do important things well
	Moral/ethical correctness	Offering the chance to do what is right by a higher standard than efficiency
Task-related	Resources	Lending or giving money, budget increases, personnel, space, and so forth
	Assistance	Helping with existing projects or undertaking unwanted tasks
	Cooperation	Giving task support, providing quicker response time, approving a project, or aiding implementation
	Information	Providing organizational as well as technical knowledge
Position-related	Advancement	Giving a task or assignment that can aid in promotion
	Recognition	Acknowledging effort, accomplishment, or abilities
	Visibility	Providing a chance to be known by higher-ups or significant others in the organization
	Reputation	Enhancing the way a person is seen
	Importance/ insiderness	Offering a sense of importance, of "belonging"
	Network/contacts	Providing opportunities for linking with others
Relationship-related	Acceptance/ inclusion	Providing closeness and friendship
	Personal support	Giving personal and emotional backing
	Understanding	Listening to others' concerns and issues
Personal-related	Self-concept	Offering the opportunity to affirm one's own values, self-esteem, and identity
	Challenge/learning	Sharing tasks that increase skills and abilities
	Ownership/ involvement	Letting others have ownership and influence
	Gratitude	Expressing appreciation or indebtedness

A more recent study of national account managers and their superiors identified five critical success factors[13]:

- managing key account relationships
- understanding the account's business
- ensuring action and responsiveness to customers
- involving others with the account
- ensuring commitment to the key account program

This research showed that in general key account managers spent appropriate effort in two areas—managing key account relationships and ensuring action

FIGURE 4.3: Personal Traits, Skill Requirements, and Required Knowledge and Experience (in order) for Successful Key Account Managers[14]

Personal Traits	Skill Requirements	Knowledge and Experience
Tact	Relationship building	Customer's personnel and personalities
Integrity	Negotiation	Company products/services
Concern for ethics	Communication	Company procedures
Self-motivation	Leadership	Customer's industry
Creativity	Human relations	Customer's products and/or services
Responsibility	Presentation skills	Experience in handling large accounts and in planning and goal setting
Achievement orientation	Diagnosing customer problems	Knowledge/experience of customer's company procedures
Ambition	Conflict resolution	Pricing and terms of sale
	Coordination	Customer company's operating strengths and weaknesses
	Generating viability and reputation	
	Closing	

and responsiveness to customers. They did less well in understanding the account's business, involving others with the account, and ensuring commitment to the key account program.

A further study identified a set of competencies whose frequency of use discriminated statistically between more and less effective account managers[15]:

- aligning account and supplier firm strategic objectives
- listening beyond product needs
- understanding the financial impact of decisions
- consultative problem solving
- orchestrating organizational resources
- establishing a vision of the customer/supplier relationship
- engaging in self-appraisal and continuous learning
- building strategic plans
- utilizing basic selling skills[16]

RECRUITMENT AND SELECTION

The shift from a traditional sales force system to key account management represents a major organizational change. As a result, the recruitment and selection process is often most difficult when key account management is first being introduced into the organization. At that time, the supplier firm faces the very real danger of appointing personnel without the appropriate knowledge, skills, abilities, experience, and/or organizational influence.

Essentially, there are two sources of key account manager candidates—internal and external.

Internal Candidates

Perhaps the most obvious candidate for a new key account manager position is a salesperson who has been selling to a division or single location of the newly designated key account. However, whereas the salesperson may have been extremely successful in a fairly straightforward situation (perhaps spending most time with purchasing agents), the shift to broader responsibility and key account management may be too large a jump. The capability profile of successful key account managers is quite different from that of successful salespeople; not all successful salespeople are able to make the transition.

Certainly, the firm should avoid appointing unqualified salespeople to be key account managers. However, the key account manager position may represent an important career move for individual salespeople. It is not at all unusual for companies to promote their best salespeople to sales managers, only to see them fail because they are unable to manage a group of salespeople in a formal structure. The key account manager position may provide an alternative career track for those superior salespeople able to make the difficult transition to key account manager, without saddling them with the day-to-day responsibilities of managing a sales district or region.

Of course, the sales force is not the only internal source for key account managers. The most attractive sources of candidates depend on the specific set of key account manager roles and responsibilities. As a result, candidates may emerge from many different functional areas in the firm; for example, one of 3M's successful corporate account managers formerly ran an R&D laboratory.

Key account manager may be a terminal position for those organizational personnel a few years from retirement. Such employees may be especially effective because of their extensive experience and relationships both within the supplier firm and the key account. A second source of internal key account manager candidates is rising stars in the organization; such personnel may originate from one of several functional areas. Both they and senior corporate personnel may view the key account manager role as an important experience builder; indeed the firm may even build in several years' key account manager experience as a necessary condition for higher level appointments. After all, key account managers have responsibility for managing some of the firm's most valuable assets and in doing so gain significant experience that may equip them well for general management responsibility.

Regardless of the fast-track potential of individual key account managers, the supplier firm should do what it can to avoid too frequent turnover of key account managers. Since relationship building is such a critical factor in key account management, the organization's needs for high-caliber managers in other positions must be carefully weighed against both the key account manager's personal development goals, and the requirements of the supplier-firm/key-account relationship.

External Candidates

The second source of key account manager candidates is executives working for other organizations. Such candidates may have significant key account management experience and/or considerable knowledge, experience, and relationships at the key account, developed with a competitor, a noncompetitive supplier, or as an employee. Such candidates may lack intimate knowledge of the supplier firm, but balance this deficit with powerful key account credentials.

EXAMPLE: Faced with appointing a new key account manager for a state government customer, Holly Inc.*, a major computer company recruited strongly from state government employees. Holly executives reasoned that it would be easier to train such an individual in computer issues than it would be to have a current employee learn the intricacies of selling to state government.

Issues in Recruitment and Selection

Many issues surround the inside/outside hiring decision. Benefits of hiring internal candidates are an intimate knowledge of firm processes and procedures, and the positive morale boost of providing exciting opportunities to firm employees. However, if sufficient key account management expertise and/or potential is not available within the firm, outside hires may be the only method for placing key account management on a solid organizational footing.

Regardless of the particular source of candidate key account managers, those firms adopting key account management should consider developing systems that produce an "inventory" of potential managers, in effect, a talent pool of key account managers in waiting. Because key accounts are so important to the supplier firm, it cannot afford to have key account manager positions unfilled or to fill them with inappropriate personnel.[17]

For internal candidates, such systems involve identifying potential key account managers and ensuring they receive opportunities to gain the relevant skills and experience via training programs and job assignments. For external candidates, a continual process of recruiting and interviewing potential hires should provide a ready source of candidates for whenever a position becomes available.

The selection process for key account manager positions should conform to the same rigorous standards that the firm employs for other critical managerial positions. Typically, such systems involve multiple interviews with a panel of senior executives experienced in key account management. These interviews focus on the roles and responsibilities of the position and the skill sets required. Oftentimes, firms employ psychological testing instruments to aid in the selection process.

One variation of the typical senior executive selection processes is the involvement of the key account. Some firms experienced in key account management ask personnel at the key account to interview a short list of acceptable candidates and provide input into the selection process. In some situations, the key account makes the selection from the short list developed by the supplier firm!

TRAINING

The key account manager position is pivotal in the supplier firm's relationships with its key accounts. For this reason, the particular human resources occupying these positions should be the best the supplier firm can provide. The role of training is to take the human resources appointed through the recruitment and selection process, and mold these into effective key account managers. Training is particularly crucial in those organizations where key account managers are promoted internally from traditional sales force positions. The substantial shift in perspective from short-term transaction-based selling to developing long-run relationships requires a significant training intervention.

The specific training required by newly appointed key account managers is in part a function of the supplier firm, its key accounts, and the nature of desired firm/key-account relationships. It also depends on the knowledge, skills, abilities, and experience of those executives appointed to be key account managers. For example, an existing key account manager given responsibility for a more important key account, or an experienced key account manager who previously served the key account for a competitor, might require one type of training. A newly appointed rising organizational star who has just spent three years developing the firm's new procurement system will likely require a very different training experience.

> **EXAMPLE:** In Motorola's Land Mobile Products Sector (LMPS), sales representatives assigned to key accounts previously focused their efforts on broadening the customer base. As a result, a total cultural realignment was required. LMPS developed computer simulations in which trainees worked in teams and simulated all activities involved in managing a key account including phone calls, negotiations, and resource allocation. The productivity of these new strategic account managers tripled.[18]

Some key account managers may require training in developing key account plans; others may benefit from improving their negotiation, proposal and contract development, time management, leadership, and/or team building skills. Regardless, one approach to training is for the supplier firm's human resources department to prepare individualized training programs for key account managers based on their specific requirements. An alternative, but more expensive, approach is to develop a standardized training program that all new key account managers must complete. Of course, training should not be a one-time event, and periodic educational and training programs should be considered.

In particular, since key account managers represent the firm to its customers, they should be well briefed as the firm evolves to interface with its changing environment. Furthermore, since these managers typically operate at higher organizational levels than regular salespeople, they are expected to know more about both their own companies and their key accounts. Various methods, including corporate videos, seminars, and web-based methodologies, are available to ensure that managers are kept up to date.

> EXAMPLE: Once a quarter, Boise Cascade Office Products provides a two-and-a-half-day session on the company for all of its national account managers. The group is addressed by vice presidents from each department.[19]

In addition to developing recruitment, selection, and training processes to ensure that key account managers are competent to handle the requirements of their positions, the supplier firm should also consider the training needs of the various members of the key account team. In supplier firms committed to a key account strategy, these team members must interact outside their functional specialties and deal both with colleagues from other functions at multiple levels, and with a variety of personnel from the key account. Since this multifunctional, multilevel, interorganizational environment is very different from the work environment of the traditional functional specialist, appropriate training to be a fully contributing member of a key account team may be a critical requirement.

> EXAMPLE: To ensure that its regular sales representatives fully understand the nature of the key account program, Abbott Laboratories appoints a regional/national key account manager to keep a focus on key accounts within the region and to train new salespeople to operate in a national account context.[20]

Nor should the training necessarily be offered by firm personnel and independent experts. For those firms truly committed to a key account focus, customers may become involved in the training process.

> EXAMPLE: The training program at Owens Corning Composites (OCC) embraces both key account managers and participants from other functions. A critical feature is its focus on the processes, products, and needs of its strate-

gic accounts and the ways in which OCC can anticipate future needs and develop customized solutions. Customers are regular presenters at these training sessions.[21]

In some cases, it may be advantageous for the entire key account team to undergo training together in an action learning environment.[22] For example, one particularly powerful device is the 2 + 1 + 1 approach developed by the author for training in key account planning and strategy development. In addition to learning a creative yet robust methodology for developing key account plans, each of several account teams both develops a key account plan and enjoys the secondary benefit of integrating and solidifying key account team membership through participation in a focused activity.

The details of this methodology are:

- Day 1: Instructor provides rationale for, and discusses key issues in, key account management, and lays out the key account planning methodology.
- Day 2 (day following): Each key account team conducts several key account planning exercises; each team reports its findings to the large group of several key account teams; presentations are critiqued by the instructor and peers.
- Day 3 (plus one month): Each team presents a mostly completed situation analysis including planning assumptions, and opportunities and threats, plus a draft key account strategy; the instructor, peers, and management critique presentations.
- Day 4 (plus one month): Each team presents situation analysis highlights, planning assumptions, and opportunities and threats, key account strategy and action programs; the instructor, peers, and management critique the presentations.

This action learning approach has been employed in several major companies with considerable success.

RETAINING

Because of the importance of key accounts to ongoing corporate success, well-trained effective key account managers are an extremely valuable corporate resource. To executives in the key account, key account managers often *are* the supplier firm.

When a successful in-place key account manager leaves his or her position, the potential exists for the value residing in the scores of individual manager/key-account personnel relationships to disappear overnight. Even under the best of circumstances as, for example, when the key account manager receives an internal assignment, succession planning is well developed, and sufficient time is built in for a measured hand-over, still the personnel change may be fraught with difficulties. By contrast, when a successful key account manager leaves unexpectedly (in the worst case for a key account manager position with a competitor at the same account) and succession planning is nonexistent, disaster may ensue.

Notwithstanding the value many executives place on job stability (especially in this era of downsizing and reengineering), successful key account managers are often highly marketable and vulnerable to poaching from competitors (and other firms) seeking to upgrade their own management processes. Although individual key account managers may face significant switching costs and high risks in moving from known long-term employers to new organizations, firms that lag the market in rewarding key account managers will surely lose critical personnel. Certainly, firms should maintain a database on the destination of departing employees to ascertain where noncompetitive situations exist.

EXAMPLE: In the mid-1990s, Varityper, a $120 million manufacturer of desktop publishing equipment, lost several successful key account managers to new PC competitors offering higher salaries and commissions.

In addition to financial compensation, supplier firms must consider the full range of available reward systems—promotions, other formal rewards, and intangible personal rewards—discussed below, so as to preempt unexpected key account manager resignations. Management should also consider processes such as identifying role models and developing mentoring relationships, as well as assisting the key account manager in balancing personal and family life with work responsibilities.

As a subset of retaining, the firm must also consider key account manager *redeployment*. Promotions for successful key account managers are considered later. However, not all key account managers will succeed. Of course, the more effective the firm's recruitment, selection, and training processes, the higher the probability of success. Nonetheless, as their roles become ever more complex, some key account managers will certainly have to be replaced. These individuals may be valuable employees who simply ended up in the wrong job. The firm should deal sensitively with these situations and identify more appropriate positions rather than losing these employees to competitors and other organizations out of frustration at their unsatisfactory performance.

REWARDING

The starting point for developing a reward system is clarity on the requirements of the job. In particular the firm must be clear about the appropriate performance metrics. We commence this section with a discussion on performance measurement before turning to reward systems.

Performance Measurement

Key account manager responsibilities can be conceptualized as varying on two related dimensions:

- *Scope of the job:* Responsibility at regional, national, or global level, and at the business or corporate level
- *Nature of the job:* From a short-term sales focus based on individual achievement to long-run relationship development involving management of a key account team

As the scope of the job expands, and as the nature of the job shifts from short- to long-term, the measurement system has to change. For key account managers whose major responsibility is short-term sales, sales volume (or, possibly, profit contribution) in the current period is a typical metric. As the time horizon becomes longer, revenue and profit in the current period are still important, but maintaining or putting the key-account/supplier-firm relationship on a sound footing for the long run typically has increased significance. In addition to sales revenue, such measures as sales growth, share of relevant business (frequently termed "wallet share"), profit contribution, product mix, new business development, pipeline measures, designation as a preferred supplier, and customer satisfaction may be warranted. Clearly, developing metrics to measure long-run performance is more complicated than focusing solely on current sales volume.

Some firms have started to use the "balanced scorecard" approach for evaluating the performance of key account managers.[23] In this method, performance measures are developed in several different areas that may include:

- *Financial performance* including sales revenues and profit contribution
- *Growth* including new applications developed and sales to previously unsold customer divisions
- *Customer* including customer satisfaction
- *Internal* including the quality of internal firm relationships, inventory management, and team leadership

The balance among short-term and long-term success measures is likely to vary across the type of supplier-firm/key-account relationship—vendor, preferred supplier, and partner (see Chapter 2). In addition, performance measures for a key account manager operating at the corporate level for a multibusiness supplier firm are likely to load more heavily on the long run. By contrast, performance measures for a key account manager role occupied by a salesperson reporting to a regional sales manager are likely to be more short-run oriented.

EXAMPLE: Pharmacia & Upjohn employs four groups of measures for key account teams encompassing nine measures in total: *financial*—sales by account, market share, responsibility earnings; *operational efficiency*—budget, process improvement; *innovation/creativity*—learning, resource utilization; *customer/team satisfaction*—customer and 360° team survey.[24]

EXAMPLE: Mobil Oil developed a systematic process for identifying goals for a key account relationship, measures to meet the goals, and a balanced scorecard to monitor progress in meeting the goals.[25]

In measuring key account manager performance, management should select metrics that meet four often-competing objectives:

- Alignment with the vision, mission, strategy, and objectives at the key account
- Controllable by the key account manager
- Trackable by the firm's reporting systems
- Focused, meaning avoiding too many measures

FIGURE 4.4: Performance Measures for Key Account Managers

Number of Plan Measures	1	2	3	4	5 and over
Percent of Sample	19%	19%	26%	12%	24%

Focus is especially important, because an excessive number of measures is confusing and may divert the manager from the central objective. Figure 4.4 shows study results indicating the actual number of performance measures used for key account managers.[26]

Having identified the appropriate performance metrics for key account managers, supplier firm management and individual key account managers should jointly agree on required performance levels at individual key accounts. These performance levels should be linked as directly as possible to objectives developed in the key account plan. In turn, they should also be closely linked to the key account manager's reward structure.

Structuring the Reward System

An appropriately designed reward structure should be highly motivating for key account managers and, as a result, should generate high levels of effort. Those efforts, by well-recruited, selected, and trained key account managers, should in turn lead to high levels of organizational performance. As noted in an earlier section, the supplier firm must ensure that its reward system is competitive in the labor market so that it retains, rather than loses, its high-performing key account managers.

Successful key account managers may be rewarded in several different ways. We commence with a focus on financial compensation, then turn our attention to promotions, other formal reward mechanisms, and intangible personal rewards. See Figure 4.5 for conceptual development of the reward system for key account managers.

FINANCIAL COMPENSATION

For most key account managers, financial compensation is a significant motivator. In order to arrive at a compensation plan that appropriately rewards key account managers, significant attention should be paid to the process of devel-

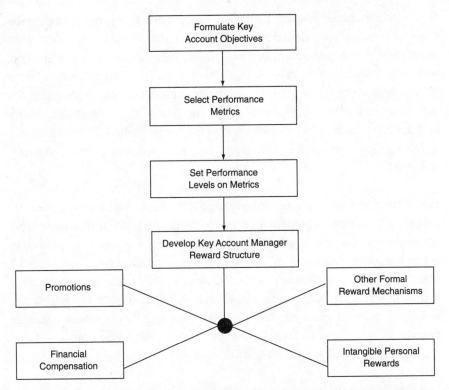

FIGURE 4.5: Conceptual Development of Reward System for Key Account Managers

oping the compensation system. In particular, an early discussion should be held at senior corporate levels to be clear about compensation expectations before detailed analysis is undertaken. The special nature of the key account manager position should be recognized by making the design process a multi-functional effort that, at a minimum, includes representatives from key account management and human resources. Such a process should ensure that key account compensation is handled separately from regular sales force compensation.

Part of the development process should involve discussing with in-place key account managers their perspectives on the current system and what they would like to see changed or retained. In addition, conversations with customers may reveal important information. For example, key accounts with which long-run partnership relationships are being developed may object to compensation packages heavily based on current sales revenues.

Any new compensation plan should be simulated forward and backward.

Backward simulation involves taking key account manager performance for the previous two or three years, demonstrating what the payouts would have been under the new compensation plan, and making comparisons with actuals. Forward simulation involves calculating compensation based on a series of "what if" questions about future performance. Each analysis has value both to individual managers and to compensation system designers, and ensures that neither group will be surprised when the new system is implemented.[27]

During the compensation plan design process, a series of questions must be answered:

How Much Should Key Account Managers Be Paid? Management must decide on a target total compensation level for its key account managers. This amount consists of either salary or salary plus target incentive compensation, depending on the structure of the compensation system (discussed below).[28] Many firms develop target key account compensation by reference to the compensation levels for sales manager positions—first-line (district) manager, second-line (regional) manager, and so forth. Total target compensation can be thought of as varying on two dimensions—amount of revenue impacted and time horizon of results. Thus, in general,

- The greater the amount of revenue the key account manager can impact, the greater should be his or her financial compensation.
- The more importance given to current sales revenues as the key account manager's objective versus long-run development, the greater should be cash compensation.[29]

Across the scope of key account manager responsibilities, for example, from regional through national to global account manager, compensation generally increases: from equivalent to the first-line manager at the low end, to greater than second-line manager at the top end. Earnings of the most well-compensated key account managers are in the top 10% of all field sales personnel. Actual financial compensation levels for key account managers are shown in Figure 4.6.

Regardless of the particular levels and mix of compensation variables employed, the supplier firm must ensure that the entire financial compensation package is marketplace competitive. If not, it may lose valuable key account managers to competitors or other firms seeking qualified key account managers. (Recall the experience of Varityper, cited above.)

Other important issues concern the relationship of key account manager

FIGURE 4.6: Financial Compensation for Key Account Managers[30]

	1995	1997	2000
Annual Salary			
Median	$75,000	$78,000	$82,000
Range	$38,000 to $225,000	$27,000 to $220,00	$45,000 to $160,000
Variable Compensation (avg.)	20.6%	22%	17%
Total Cash Compensation			
Median	$95,000	$100,000	$120,000
Range	$43,000 to $425,000	$27,000 to $281,000	$56,000 to $327,000

compensation to other organizational positions.[31] For example, if compensation levels are too low, the supplier firm may be unable to attract sufficiently qualified personnel to key account manager positions. In addition, in matrixed organizations, significant selling effort is typically conducted by locally based salespeople. Often their function is to identify and address specific sales opportunities within a framework developed by the key account manager operating largely at the corporate level. Not only must the key account manager be appropriately compensated, so also must individual salespeople.

How Should the Compensation System Be Structured? Options for developing key account management compensation mostly involve three principal variables:

- *Salary*—fixed annual amount
- *Commission*—variable pay typically based on volume/revenues
- *Bonus*—lump sum payment based on reaching performance standards

As within any sales-oriented compensation system, design efforts should focus on stimulating behavior that achieves objectives by implementing the chosen strategy. Clearly, since both the responsibilities of key account managers and the range of potential key account objectives and strategies vary broadly, so too does the range of potential compensation systems.

For key account managers who focus on short-term sales volume, target incentive compensation (commission and/or bonus) may exceed 50% of total compensation. For managers whose focus is long-run account development, target incentive compensation may be as little as 10%. (Of course, some firms

FIGURE 4.7: Incentive Compensation for Key Account Managers by Decile Groups[32]

	Smallest Amount of Incentive Compensation							Largest Amount of Incentive Compensation		
Incentive Mix Percentile	10%	20%	30%	40%	50%	60%	70%	80%	90%	100%
Mean Percent Incentive Compensation	6%	10%	16%	18%	24%	25%	29%	33%	40%	83%

have salary-only policies.) Actual incentive compensation data for key account managers are shown in Figure 4.7.

How Much Should Incentive Pay Be Leveraged? This question refers to the upside potential of target incentive compensation. In principle, as the key account manager's personal influence in achieving key account objectives increases so, too, the leverage should increase, and may include accelerators. Frequently, payouts commence at well below 100% of the key account manager's goal (or quota) and are paid quarterly. Clearly, there is no right answer to leverage structure, but a good rule of thumb is that potential upside earnings should be around 1.5 times the compensation at risk.[33]

Regardless of the particular compensation structure, compensation *caps* are often an emotional topic for key account managers, as for all salespeople. Regrettably, they appear to be fairly widespread. Our basic position is that, in general, compensation caps are demotivating and should be avoided if at all possible. Indeed, if the compensation system is well designed, caps should not be necessary. Frequently, they are imposed because management has not done its homework in simulating the compensation system during the planning stage.[34]

Who Should Receive Credit for Key Account Sales? Unless appropriate compensation frameworks have been put in place, sales force members are likely to complain that they expend significant effort on making important sales yet receive little credit. The supplier firm must be careful to avoid these demotivating situations in which sales force members, including salespeople and district managers, believe their efforts enrich the key account manager but not themselves. In order to ensure fairness, many firms employ a "double credit" system for incentive compensation; successful performance at key accounts is compensated twice, once for the key account manager and once for the local sales force.[35]

When the supplier-firm/key-account relationship develops into a partnership, the key account manager typically leads a team dedicated to that account. In such situations, it may no longer be appropriate to provide incentives just to the manager. Rather, the entire key account team should be rewarded for superior performance. Regardless of management's desire to implement a fairness doctrine, it is not at all unusual for organizational rigidities to prevent incentive compensation being paid to key account team members in such functions as logistics, technical service, and merchandising. Faced with this problem, a commercial manager in one fast-growing division of a *Fortune* 500 company has a "pot of money" at her disposal to pay performance bonuses outside the regular compensation system.

When Should the Key Account Compensation Plan Be Reviewed. The Alexander Group has identified several symptoms that suggest that the compensation plan should be reviewed.[36]

- The key account manager job design is unclear or has been changed without a compensation system review.
- In plans designed for incentive compensation, a high proportion of key account managers receives little or no incentive compensation.
- The variance of key account manager performance is much greater than the variance in key account manager pay.
- The compensation plan has four or more performance measures; some have little effect on pay.
- Payout calculations contain surprises to the key account manager and/or the firm.
- Frequent major changes are made to the incentive compensation system.
- It is difficult to recruit qualified key account managers and/or to retain high performers.

If management identifies any of these conditions, it should contemplate redesign of the financial compensation system.

Promotions

We noted earlier that the key account manager might be a senior salesperson, or an appointee from another functional area, for whom the job is a terminal organizational position. Alternatively, the key account manager may be a rising organizational star for whom the key account manager position is one stop on a more extensive career journey.

Clearly, for these two polar career situations, organizational promotions have very different meanings. In the first case, promotion possibilities are few. Indeed, they may be limited to assuming key account manager responsibility for a larger or more complex key account. For these managers, promotions will probably pay a relatively minor role in their reward structures.

On the other hand, for key account managers whose aspirations lie in broader and more extensive managerial responsibility, promotion possibilities may be highly motivating. Indeed, senior managers may view successful performance in running "the key account business" as an important stepping stone to general management. The set of talents that can successfully grow revenues and revenue share and repel stiff competition while managing a disparate group of loosely linked organizational resources are similar to those required for general management.

Other Formal Reward Mechanisms

Other formal reward mechanisms for key account managers include extra job assignments, job modification, and recognition. Offering a high-performing key account manager a time-limited extra job assignment can be a powerful motivator inasmuch as it demonstrates, in a tangible way, the organization's recognition of his performance and abilities. These extra assignments may include such responsibilities as acting as the "shadow" for a major competitor, being the firm's representative to an industry association, or having responsibility for developing specific elements of market research data and analysis.

Job modification is distinguished from extra assignments as being more closely related to current responsibilities and having an air of permanency. For example, the manager for the division of a major key account might assume similar responsibilities for an additional division; alternatively, a key account manager with European responsibility might assume responsibility for that account worldwide.

Finally, as any sales manager knows, recognition can be an extremely powerful motivator. Recognition has the important organizational benefit of being inexpensive to provide. However, if thoughtfully administered, it may stimulate exceptional levels of key account manager performance. Recognition is an important element of the supplier firm's motivational arsenal.

> **EXAMPLE:** Betz and Dearborne developed a program in which key account managers were evaluated on several dimensions such as revenue increase, new business opportunities, and customer satisfaction. Annually, the best performer on each dimension both received a CEO award for meritorious performance and made a presentation on the reasons for his/her success. In addition to the highly motivating effect of being recognized by the CEO, this event was a useful way of exchanging best practice.

Intangible Personal Rewards

These more subtle forms of reward rely on the key account manager rewarding herself by succeeding in a particular assignment. For example, some key account managers get a tremendous "charge" out of turning around losing situations. Whereas most key account managers might be distressed to be moved from a stable key account relationship to a highly volatile situation where the firm is losing business, others might view this as a tremendous challenge. To the extent that such managers succeed in these assignments, their significant intangible personal reward will be well deserved feelings of accomplishment.

From the perspective of the supplier firm, this element of the reward system is less concerned with providing specific rewards to the key account manager, contingent on a defined performance level, than it is with designing an environment in which the key account manager can reward himself.

SUMMARY

In order to fulfill the roles and responsibilities of the key account manager, to formulate and implement a key account plan, and to achieve supplier firm objectives at the key account, personnel with the appropriate knowledge, skills, abilities, and experience must fill key account manager positions. In particular they must be skilled in business management, boundary spanning and relationship building, and have significant leadership and team-building abilities.

Such individuals may be secured from within an organization or brought in from the outside. To ensure that they function effectively on the job, key account managers must be given appropriate training so that they can meet or exceed well-thought-through job criteria. In addition, the organization's reward system should both motivate them to perform at high levels and ensure that they are retained by the supplier firm.

III. SYSTEMS AND

PROCESSES

In this chapter and the three that follow, we address systems and processes for key account management. In Section II, we discussed the first three elements of the congruence model—strategy (Chapter 2), organization (Chapter 3), and human resources (Chapter 4). This final element of the congruence model includes systems and processes for planning, managing information flows, identifying opportunities, measuring customer satisfaction, and many others. These systems and processes enable key account managers effectively to develop and implement strategies and plans for individual accounts.

To the greatest extent possible, this wide variety of human- and information-technology-based systems and processes should be common across all key accounts. Common systems not only reduce development costs, they promote an organizational coherence that is impossible to achieve if individual managers develop and use idiosyncratic processes. Of course, these systems and processes should not "straitjacket" the key account manager. But within a framework of common systems and processes, the key account director should identify best practice that can increment key account management overall to a higher level of performance.[1]

Chapters 5 through 7 focus on perhaps the most important managerial process undertaken by key account managers—planning. In firms with well-developed key account management systems, the key account plan is the crucial document that drives the supplier-firm/key-account relationship. In Chapter 8, we turn to a series of other systems and process for enhancing key account management.

PLANNING AND STRATEGY MAKING FOR KEY ACCOUNTS

Key account planning and strategy should be closely related to a broader level of planning and strategy—typically by market or market segment, possibly by customer industry—that logically precedes planning for individual key accounts. However, if a few key accounts together comprise the vast majority of the available market, this broader level of strategy making effectively coalesces with key account planning and strategy. Regardless of the order of strategy development, the key account strategy must be consistent with strategy developed at the higher level.

As part of developing the broader level of planning and strategy making, marketing personnel should collect the appropriate data and conduct various strategic analyses of the market and market segments, competition, and the supplier firm. Key account managers should be able to access this data so that they don't have to reinvent the wheel for each of their own key account plans. As information is used and reused, the supplier firm benefits from scale economies in data collection and analysis. Since all key account plans in a particular industry are based on a common understanding of critical market and competitive imperatives, individual readers should identify areas where their own organizations might benefit from such centralized data gathering and analysis.

The Key Account Plan

Essentially, the key account plan comprises two elements, the situation analysis and the key account strategy.[2] It should, however, also include an executive summary that can serve as a briefing document for senior executives who may interface with the key account. The process for developing the plan is embedded in a broader managerial system that includes plan implementation, and a coordination and control process by which the plan is updated over time (Figure III.1). Later, we offer a series of planning exercises to aid in conducting the situation analysis and formulating a key account strategy.

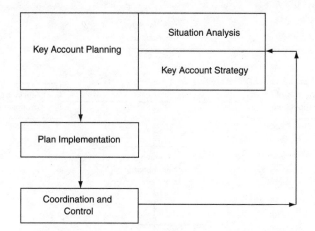

FIGURE III.1: Managing the Key Account

SITUATION ANALYSIS

The situation analysis is the fundamental underpinning of the supplier firm's key account strategy. If competently performed, the situation analysis provides a solid foundation for strategy development. Conversely, if the situation analysis is not well done, the foundation for the strategy will be weak, suboptimal decisions will be made, and scarce resources allocated ineffectively.[3] For these reasons, the situation analysis must be comprehensive; as a result, the discussion here and in Chapter 6 is dense. I make no apologies for this, because effective key account strategy is a direct consequence of solid situation analysis (Figure III.2).

Still, we fully recognize that the level of analytic detail suggested may not be appropriate for all supplier-firm/key-account relationships. For example, it is one thing to supply products based on technology critical to the key account's survival and growth; it is quite another to be a secondary supplier of a noncritical raw material. The appropriate level of information gathering and analysis may well differ in these two cases. Furthermore, many key account managers have responsibility for multiple accounts and just do not have the resources for as extensive an approach as we suggest. For these reasons, the key account manager must decide the appropriate planning approach for his or her situation. That said, better strategy emerges from more thorough planning.

For each of three basic sets of analyses—key account, competition, and supplier firm—three related steps must be conducted:

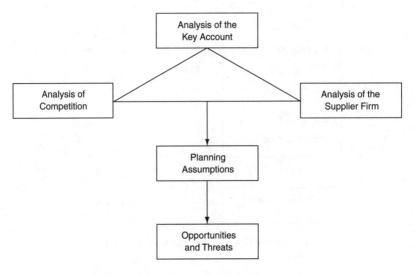

FIGURE III.2: The Situation Analysis

- Significant amounts of data, some primary and some secondary, some qualitative and some quantitative, some anecdotal and some formal, must be collected to form the raw material for the various analyses.
- From this data, fundamental trends must be separated from random fluctuations and projected into the future.
- For each fundamental trend, two questions must be asked:
  - What are the implications of this particular trend for the key account?
  - What are the resulting implications for the supplier firm?

Such questioning provides insight that leads both to the development of planning assumptions, and the identification of a set of opportunities and threats for the key account manager to address in developing the key account strategy.

KEY ACCOUNT STRATEGY

The key account strategy is concerned with resource allocation. It is developed in the context of a broad overall focus on the key account relationship comprising a vision and mission that set broad parameters for the resource allocation process. As we shall see in Chapter 7, the key account strategy encompasses several interrelated elements that must both be internally consistent and follow logically from the situation analysis.

CHAPTER FIVE

Key Account Planning
Analysis of the Key Account

THE PURPOSE OF
KEY ACCOUNT ANALYSIS

Successful completion of the key account analysis provides the key account manager with various possible means of assisting the key account in achieving its several corporate, business, financial, and market objectives. The analysis helps the key account manager identify the full scope of potential opportunities and threats at the key account. This identification, together with analyses of competitors and the supplier firm itself (Chapter 6), leads to a series of decisions regarding which opportunities to pursue (and which to avoid), which threats to combat, and the particular strategic approaches to pursue (Chapter 7).

To achieve the level of insight necessary to become so well positioned, the key account manager must seek information and conduct analyses in four related areas. In this chapter, we discuss key account fundamentals, strategic key account analysis, identifying and addressing key account needs and delivering customer value, and the buying analysis. We conclude by identifying potential information sources. (See Exercise 1 for a planning document to conduct an analysis of the key account.)

KEY ACCOUNT FUNDAMENTALS

Key account fundamentals represent what an educated observer of the key account, much less a key account manager, should know about the account. For the key account manager, it frames the account and helps provide perspective when a particular subunit of the organization is addressed. Of course, the supplier firm may seek business only in a restricted domain, for example, in an individual business unit. Nonetheless, a broad knowledge of the organization can be invaluable in understanding the internal reality faced by those key account executives with whom the manager and other supplier firm personnel must deal.

In addition, good understanding of the fundamentals demonstrates to key account executives a significant personal commitment by the key account manager. The ability to speak knowledgeably about the organization enhances the manager's credibility with key account personnel. This is especially true if the key account manager can show himself as better acquainted with the key account than its own employees! Conversely, if the key account manager does not possess this information, it may result in a real credibility problem at the account.

Finally, in those organizations with complex interlocking shareholdings and directorships, understanding the overall corporate dynamics may provide invaluable insight into the location of critical sources of power in the key account.[1]

Among the sorts of fundamental data the key account manager should assemble are:

- **Ownership.** How does the overall organization fit together in terms of parent companies, subsidiaries, ownership interests, and so forth? Who are the directors, principal owners? What roles do they play in the corporation? Do they rubber stamp the CEO's decisions or are they more active? Where are corporate offices located? Is the key account a public company; if so, where are its shares listed?
- **Organization.** Is the organization centralized with significant power at corporate headquarters or do individual subsidiaries operate more or less autonomously? If the key account is a global organization, does it operate with a domestic U.S. division and a separate international division, with geographic area divisions, with global product divisions, or some other kind of structure? How are developments in telecommunications, com-

puter technology, and the Internet affecting the key account's organization structure and processes?

- **Top Management Cadre.** Who is the CEO and who are other members of the top management group? Are they successful? Do they have the confidence of the board of directors or is there a difficult relationship? What is known about their business and management philosophies? What type of corporate culture are they trying to instill? In particular, have they articulated a vision and/or values for the corporation:
  - *Vision* is the description of an ideal future state, a statement meant to inspire employees over the long haul.
  - *Values* are a set of beliefs that serve to guide behavior. Values may either be "hard," such as profitability and market share, or "soft," such as integrity, respect for others, trust, and preeminence of customers.
- **Locations.** Where are the account's fixed assets located? Where are its plant and distribution center locations? What are its production capacities? How many employees does the account have? How are they distributed across locations?
- **Corporate Actions.** What important actions has the key account taken recently as regards major resource shifts, significant capital spending, mergers, acquisitions, divestitures, strategic alliances, joint ventures, R&D initiatives, vertical integration and disintegration (outsourcing), new product introductions, increased internationalization, new market entry, use of the Internet, participation in B2B exchanges, and the like? How successful have these been?
- **Financial Performance.** What has been the key account's revenue and profit history both overall and for relevant business units? What is its trend in return on assets? What is the trend in its stock price? What is the trend in earnings per share? What is its debt/equity ratio? How is its debt rated? What ratios are important to the account? How does its performance compare to major competitors?
- **Future Prospects.** What is the long-run outlook for the key account? Does it face any significant legal or regulatory problems? How is it perceived by the financial community? Do the majority of financial analysts recommend sell, hold, or buy? Why?
- **Timing.** What are the time cycles for the key account—for example, the budgeting cycle? What are important dates, such as the fiscal year and annual meetings. Is there a regularity to important announcements, for example, CEO meetings with financial analysts.[2]

STRATEGIC KEY ACCOUNT ANALYSIS

Strategic account analysis is especially important for those firms that wish to become quality suppliers to, or partners with, their key accounts. In order to make sensible decisions on how to help the key account achieve its objectives, the key account manager must both understand the key account's objectives and strategy, and also assess its ability to be successful. To develop the appropriate depth and breadth of data to conduct these analyses, the manager should attempt to become intimately involved with the key account's strategic planning process. She should strive to secure a seat at the table as the key account's senior executives plan their firm's future directions. The manager should not be just a passive recipient of information about the key account. Rather, by working closely together, supplier firm and key account personnel may together engage in creative problem solving that improves the competitiveness of both parties.

Clearly, to achieve this level of intimacy with key accounts is not a simple matter. However, over the years, I have been impressed with the number of key account managers who claim to enjoy this sort of relationship with their major clients. Such a level of mutual commitment only results from feelings of trust that may take many years to develop. But, once achieved, if carefully nurtured, these relationships can provide enormous payoffs to both the supplier firm and its key accounts.

One method successfully used by leading companies is to schedule a two-day account planning workshop early in the planning process. Attendees include the key account manager, members of the key account team, and other support personnel such as marketing and business development. For the first half day, executives from the key account are invited to share their goals, strategies, critical issues, and so forth. This input plays an important role in subsequent situation analysis and the strategy development process.[3]

The strategic key account analysis comprises four major elements (Figure 5.1): identification of mission, external analysis, internal analysis, and an analysis of strategic coherence.

Mission

The key account's mission statement specifies the broad terrain in which it will search for opportunity. The mission, often termed the "market-product" scope,

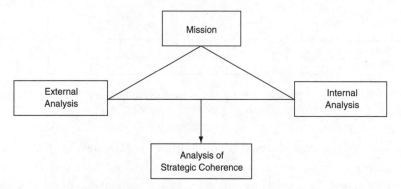

FIGURE 5.1: Strategic Key Account Analysis

should include a clear and concise description of the key account's current and potential business. Knowing the key account's mission, the key account manager should be able to predict, broadly, those markets where the key account will seek sales revenues, the types of products it will offer, and those domains where it will not seek business. Of course, the key account may not have a well-articulated mission. Nonetheless, the key account manager should endeavor to develop a usable version as a guide in approaching the account, from data supplied by senior key account management. For example, a key account mission may state:

> "Our mission is to provide a broad array of financial products and services . . . competitive in quality and value . . . to middle and up-per-middle income households and small businesses with five principals or less and fewer than 100 employees."

This clearly defines the key account's target markets and product scope. But, by omission, the key account manager would also know that the key account will not seek as customers either medium or large-size companies; nor will it court upper or low-income consumers. Furthermore, it may offer many types of financial products and services, but no others.

In some industries, a crucial element of mission concerns the degree of vertical integration pursued by the key account. For example, suppose Figure 5.2 captures the essence of value development in the supplier-firm/key-account's industry. The supplier firm produces and sells *subassemblies* to the key account; the key account in turn produces *modules*. Clearly, forward integration to produce *module groups* would represent an important mission change for the key

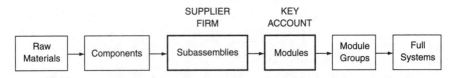

SUPPLIER   KEY
FIRM   ACCOUNT

| Raw Materials | → | Components | → | Subassemblies | → | Modules | → | Module Groups | → | Full Systems |

FIGURE 5.2: Building Value in the Industry

account. Such a change would have significant implications for the account's objectives, strategy, and organization, each of which would impact the supplier firm. Of course, backward integration by the key account into the production of subassemblies would have an even more critical impact!

Many multibusiness firms have individual business unit (division) missions nested within overarching corporate missions. These various missions form the broad framework within which the key account's business units set objectives, formulate strategies, and design action programs. The key account manager should make a point of identifying these missions.

Of course, for any individual key account, some business unit missions may suggest potential opportunities for the supplier firm; others may not. Potential opportunities typically arise from directions already being pursued by the key account, but some may result from the supplier firm's own efforts, alone or working with the key account, in exploring the limits of, and possibly helping to expand, the key account's mission.

Since the supplier firm's own opportunities are constrained by those of the key account, a clear understanding of both today's various key account missions and their evolution over time is extremely important.

External Analysis

The external analysis sets the stage for identifying opportunities and threats for the supplier firm at the key account. The key account manager must strive to understand both the account's current reality and major trends that may affect its actions both in the short and long term. The external analysis comprises five elements: market analysis, environmental analysis, competitive structure analysis, competitor analysis, and customer analysis.[4]

As noted earlier, in this analytic area, the key account manager should secure considerable assistance from a centralized marketing group, particularly if the supplier firm has targeted several key accounts in a particular industry. In such circumstances, each key account likely faces similar industry dynamics—for example, regulation and technology—and has common customers and common competitors. Rather than having several key account teams perform essentially the same analysis, the key account director should seek scale economies.

MARKET ANALYSIS

Market analysis requires an understanding of the size, growth, and composition of the current and future markets that could be addressed by the key account, given its mission(s). The key account manager should be aware of the products and services currently offered by the key account to those markets and their full potential for the key account (Figure 5.3). Markets can be categorized as follows:

- Served Available Market (SAM). That portion of the market currently addressed by the key account.
- Technically Available Market (TAM). That portion of the market technologically available to the key account:
  - Currently addressed opportunities; the served available market (SAM), and
  - Current Technological Possibilities (CTP); that portion of the market that the key account could address, given its technology, but has elected not to do so.[5]
- Future Technological Possibilities (FTP). That portion of the market currently unavailable to the key account because of technological limitations. This area could form the basis of R&D efforts by the key account and/or the supplier firm. (FTP is represented in Figure 5.3 as PAM less TAM.)

The key account manager should know how the account segments its various markets and should be aware of those segments the key account is currently addressing, those it plans to address, and those it may exit if competition becomes fierce. The manager should be able to answer the following questions:

- How large are the markets the key account could address given its mission?
- How does the key account segment its chosen markets?
- Which market segments is it currently addressing?

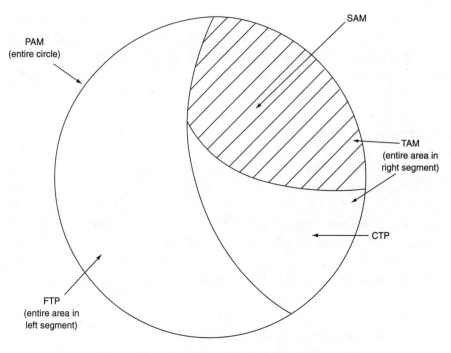

FIGURE 5.3: Analysis of the Key Account's Market

- Which segments is it planning to address in the future?
- What are the long-run market growth rates in the targeted segments?
- What are the critical success factors in these targeted segments?
- What are the key account's market shares? What are the recent trends?
- How secure are the key account's market shares? Are its market shares likely to improve? If so, why? If not, why not?

ENVIRONMENTAL ANALYSIS

This analysis involves understanding the various economic, technological, demographic, legal, regulatory, political, and sociocultural forces affecting both the key account and its competitors. (Some of these forces may also impact the supplier firm.) For example, how is the key account likely to be impacted by such considerations as:

- The presidency of George W. Bush
- The increasing penetration of PCs into households?

- Various possible outcomes of Justice Department action against Microsoft?
- The balance of power shift in the U.S. Congress?
- The increasing Hispanic population?
- Abolition of the Glass-Steagall Act?
- The Asian economic recovery?
- Policies developed by the World Trade Organization?
- Growth in the Internet and electronic commerce?

In some cases, environmental analysis results in understanding long-term trends, for example, demographics. In other cases the analysis provides a window on the probabilities that particular events will or will not occur. In the latter case, the key account manager may gain superior insight regarding these events and be able to cause her firm to take action earlier than its competitors, thus gaining first mover advantage.[6]

COMPETITIVE STRUCTURE ANALYSIS

The competitive structure (or industry) analysis isolates changes taking place within the industry and identifies likely threats to the key account's current and potential business as the result of these changes. In particular, the key account manager should identify the direct and indirect, current and potential competitive threats to the key account as well as any supply chain competition, such as suppliers (the supplier firm, competitors, or other firms) integrating forward or buyers integrating backwards.

COMPETITOR ANALYSIS

In the competitive structure analysis, the key account manager identifies the major competitive threats faced by the account. In the competitor analysis, he conducts a more in-depth analysis of these threats, seeking to understand the current and likely future strategies of those competitors. Note that some of these firms may also be current or potential customers for the supplier firm.[7]

CUSTOMER ANALYSIS

The key account manager must gain a solid understanding about the key account's customers in those markets relevant to the supplier firm's products and services. In certain markets, an understanding of the key account's customers' customers is also helpful. Of course, some of these organizations may also be the supplier firm's key accounts. The sorts of questions the key account manager should ask include:

- Which are the key account's major customers? Is its customer base changing?
- Is there a significant change in industry concentration for the key account's customers?
- Are any of the key account's customers integrating backwards to engage in operations similar to those of the key account and its direct competitors?
- Are the key account's customers' needs changing? In what ways?
- Are the key account's customers changing their buying practices?
- What are the critical demand-sensitive elements for the key account's products and services?

It is absolutely imperative that the key account management understands the nature of these customer relationships right down the channel.

EXAMPLE: Pratt and Whitney was originally the exclusive engine supplier for the Boeing 737. However, it failed to understand the growing popularity of this aircraft among Boeing's customers, the airlines. As a result, it abandoned work on the 737, developing instead a new engine for the 757. Subsequently, it lost all of the growing 737 engine business to General Electric.[8]

Internal Analysis

In addition to having a good understanding of the key account's external reality, the key account manager must identify both the key account's strategic thrust—how it intends to address its external environment—and its competence levels. These analyses lead directly to the analysis of strategic coherence—examining the likelihood that the key account will be successful.

STRATEGIC THRUST

The strategic thrust analysis embraces an understanding of the key account's objectives, strategy, and action programs. (Of course, if the key account operates with many product and process technologies, in many product and national markets, it may have several strategic thrusts.)

Objectives. A good understanding of the key account's objectives commences with an analysis of its business portfolio. Many firms set broad qualitative strategic objectives for their various business units, such as growth, market share, profits, or cash flow. In addition, some units may be divestiture candidates. The key account manager should gain insight into the strategic objectives for those specific divisions or business units with which it currently has business, or may do business in the future. Furthermore, she should understand the specific short-run and long-run performance requirements in terms of quantitative targets such as sales revenues, profits, and market share, together with time lines.

Understanding the key account's objectives is important for three quite separate reasons.

- Since the supplier firm's goal is to help the key account secure its objectives, it needs to know what these objectives are.
- Since key account decision making, including procurement, may vary with strategic objective (e.g., market share versus cash flow), the key account manager must assess the appropriate way of interfacing with the key account's decision system.
- A translation of objectives into required resource inputs allows the account manager to predict potential demand in advance of firm orders being placed.

Strategy. The key account manager should know how, broadly, the key account intends to compete in its chosen markets. For those market segment(s) the manager should answer the following sorts of questions:

- What specific opportunities and threats has the key account identified in its target markets? (Of course, the key account manager may aid in identifying these opportunities and threats.)
- Which of these opportunities and threats does the key account intend to address?
- How is the key account positioned in each target market segment?
  - What are its customer targets?
  - What are its competitor targets?
  - What is its core strategy or value proposition?

- How do other elements of the key account's business strategy support its marketing strategy? In particular, what are its resource commitments in such areas as finance, operations, human resources, and R&D?
- What other significant strategic moves has the key account made, or is likely to make. For example, are any acquisitions, divestitures and/or strategic alliances planned?
- What are the key strategic issues with which the key account is struggling at the present time?

A particularly important strategic issue concerns the key account's approach to outsourcing. In order to increase shareholder value, many firms are outsourcing activities previously conducted within the firm. Significant opportunities may be available for key account managers that identify outsourcing possibilities and act accordingly.

Action Programs. Finally, the key account manager must know what specific action steps the key account will take to implement its strategy. Action steps may occur in several domains:

- **In the marketplace:** e.g., relaunching old products, launching new products, opening up new distribution channels
- **Adding value to the key account's products and services:** e.g., by improving raw material quality or upgrading the customer service department
- **Reducing costs:** e.g., by purchasing new production equipment, outsourcing database management, or introducing a new inventory control system

To the extent that the key account manager gains a solid understanding of the key account's objectives, strategy, and action programs, the supplier firm is well positioned to identify opportunities for helping the key account achieve its objectives. If the supplier firm is successful, the key-account/supplier-firm relationship is enhanced to the benefit of both organizations. Conversely, if the key account manager has a poor sense of the key account's future direction, the supplier firm can do little more than act in a reactive manner.

KEY ACCOUNT COMPETENCE

Assessment of key account competence requires analyses of both its strengths and weaknesses, and its past performance.

Strengths and Weaknesses. The key account manager should conduct a dispassionate analysis of the key account's strengths and weaknesses versus its competitors in the various market segments it has targeted for effort. He needs to understand whether or not the account is satisfying, or is likely to satisfy, customer needs better than competitors—in other words, to secure a differential advantage. This analysis forms the strengths and weaknesses part of a traditional SWOT (strengths, weaknesses, opportunities, threats) analysis.

The key account manager needs to know where in the resource-conversion process—encompassing technology, product design, raw materials, operations, marketing, physical distribution, and customer service—the key account adds value, where it incurs costs, and how it compares with its principal competitors. The manager should be aware of any changes or initiatives the key account is contemplating via the incorporation of such innovations as quality management systems, outsourcing, and business process reengineering. In particular, she should identify implications for the supplier firm.

Value chain analysis (see, also, Chapter 6) is a powerful tool for assessing the key account's competitive position and identifying where the supplier firm can assist the key account to increase value and/or reduce costs. Of course, reducing key account costs is not just a matter of offering lower priced products. Rather, the key account must have a clear understanding of how the supplier firm's product/technology fits with the account's business functions and how these functions might be reengineered to take advantage of the supplier's offerings to reduce costs and/or add value.

EXAMPLE: In spring 1995, Chrysler's purchasing chief, Thomas Stallcamp, reported that since 1993, Magna, an automotive supply company, had given Chrysler 148 different proposals for cutting costs, that could save over $93 million per annum. By 1995, Magna was Chrysler's No. 1 supplier!

Indeed, the key account manager should complete a detailed analysis of the key account's processes as they relate to the supplier firm's offerings. Only through such an analysis will the manager identify methods of reducing the account's costs without necessarily reducing its own prices (see below). When the key account manager identifies process changes that would benefit its customer, he should be clear who are the process owners, who would be affected if the identified solutions were implemented, and what possible steps might be taken to alleviate any problems.

Analysis of Past Performance. A second means of assessing key account competence is to learn about the key account's financial and market performance. In particular, the key account manager should analyze such data as trends in sales volumes, shares in targeted market segments, and profitability for the key account as a whole. She should also conduct these analyses for major business units (divisions), product groups and user locations that are relevant to the supplier firm's current and potential business.

In addition, the key account manager should have a good understanding of product lines that are now, and in the future are expected to be, the account's major revenue and profit generators. He should know if the key account achieved objectives set for prior periods. If the key account was unsuccessful, the key account manager should know if the cause was:

- A poorly planned yet well-implemented strategy
- A well-planned strategy that was improperly implemented
- A strategy that would not have succeeded and which was not implemented anyway

Answers to these questions better enable the key account manager to assess the likelihood that the key account will be successful in the future.

Analysis of Strategic Coherence

The two fundamental underpinnings of the analysis of strategic coherence were just discussed. First, the strategic thrust analysis represents the key account manager's best understanding of the key account's approach to dealing with its external reality. Second, analysis of key account competence provides the key building block for assessing the key account's ability to be successful.

In the analysis of strategic coherence, the key account manager determines whether or not the strategic thrust is reasonable in light of the key account's competence:

- Are the key account's objectives, strategy, and action programs feasible in light of its external reality and internal capabilities?
- Are the major challenges faced by the key account well addressed?

If the key account manager believes the key account has planned effectively and positively assesses its ability to achieve the desired objectives with its strategies and action programs, she can move ahead to put in place resources to support the key account. However, this assessment should not be taken for granted. Supplier firms often make considerable investments in their key accounts but they only make profits if the key accounts are successful. If the account manager believes that the account's objectives are unreasonable and/or its strategies untenable, then she should advise the key account of her concerns. If necessary, she should take appropriate action to protect the supplier firm's interests. Indeed, many supplier firms might fare better in key account bankruptcy situations had they previously developed a better understanding of their key accounts' strategies and the business environments they faced.

The basic purpose of the strategic coherence analysis is to assess the key account's strategic thrust in the absence of new supplier firm initiatives. However, one result of a thorough key account analysis may be the identification of options for modifying the key account's strategic agenda. For example, the supplier firm may develop a new technology that leads the key account to redefine its mission and to offer new products to new markets. More modestly, the supplier firm may institute an action program that enables the key account to cut costs for a particular work process.

IDENTIFYING AND ADDRESSING KEY ACCOUNT NEEDS, AND DELIVERING CUSTOMER VALUE

The strategic key account analysis provides the overall framework within which the key account manger can seek opportunities for satisfying key account needs. If this analysis is competently accomplished, it provides the fundamental underpinning for allowing the supplier-firm/key-account relationship to develop and grow. However, to truly satisfy customer needs, the key account manager must understand the key account at a very deep level and identify ways to maximize the value that the supplier firm can bring to the account.[9] We provide four related frameworks for identifying key account needs and delivering customer value—type of customer value, the return-on-investment (ROI) equation, meta-level relationship needs, and depth of key account needs and customer value. Finally, we raise some issues in addressing key account needs.

Type of Customer Value

Broadly speaking, key account needs can be satisfied by the provision of three types of value—functional, economic, and psychological[10]:

Functional values relate to the solution of some tangible problem for the customer. For example, the supplier firm's raw materials enable the key account to manufacture its products; automobile tires offer such functional values as cornering ability, tread life, skid resistance, and displacement of water on the road.

Economic values concern the economic cost to the key account including the price paid by the key account, credit arrangements, and cost savings related to doing business with the supplier firm.

Psychological values encompass such values as risk reduction, peace of mind, status, and comfort with a relationship that do not fulfill a specific functional or economic need.

EXAMPLE: BOC, the British multinational liquefied gas supplier, hosted a potential Korean key account that was considering Britain as a site for a new European factory. When the Korean delegation arrived at the supplier's offices, its members were surprised and gratified to see the Korean flag flying to welcome them. The thoughtfulness and attention to detail that this small gesture exemplified played a major role in their decision to build in Britain.

Another example illustrates the flip side of the coin.

EXAMPLE: Joshua Inc.*, a U.S. technology firm, was well placed to win a major contract from a potential Chinese key account. However, at a banquet given by the Chinese company, one of Joshua's senior managers started eating before the host, a cultural no-no. The contract was finally given to a French firm, whose technology was inferior but with whom the Chinese felt more comfortable.[11]

In many cases, of course, the key account is already being supplied with some combination of functional, economic, and psychological values to satisfy its needs, either by the supplier firm or by a competitor. The key account manager should be very clear about which needs are being satisfied and what values are being delivered, how well, by which supplying organization, and what gaps remain.

In the following section, we concentrate mainly on functional and economic values.

The Return-on-Investment (ROI) Equation

For most companies, improving long-run return on investment (ROI) is a satisfactory proxy for maximizing shareholder value. Analysis of the ROI equation, therefore, may provide insight for the key account manager to aid the account in improving its shareholder value.

ROI = Profit/Investment
ROI = (Sales Revenues − Costs)/Investment
ROI = ([Unit Sales × Prices] − Costs)/Investment

This decomposition of the ROI equation reveals four broad options for improving the key account's ROI. In addition, the supplier firm may be able to reduce its customer's risk.

INCREASE UNIT SALES

In this option, the supplier firm helps the key account to improve its unit sales. A variety of means are available:

- *Raw materials.* Provide higher quality raw materials to the key account. In turn, the key account produces higher quality products that generate increased demand.
- *Product features.* Add features to the product that are desired by the key account's customers.
- *New products.* Provide new products that, in turn, enable the key account to produce new products that surpass competitor offerings or tap new market segments.

- *Market research.* Engage in research to better enable the key account to understand its markets and hence increase its unit volumes.

EXAMPLE: In 1987, Denko, a Japanese manufacturer of tape and adhesive products, hired the Boston Consulting Group to conduct a study of the U.S. disposable diaper industry. As a result of this study, Denko was able to provide one of its major customers, UniCharm (Japan's largest disposable diaper maker) with "outstanding intelligence for improving and defending their home markets while establishing a small beachhead in the United States. Unicharm was *astonished and ecstatic* with the free results."[12] (Emphasis added.)

- *Consulting assistance.* The supplier firm offers its expertise to the key account to help it increase unit volumes.

- *Promotional assistance.* Provide direct promotional assistance, for example, in the form of cooperative advertising allowances. Relatedly, the supplier provides sales training and other assistance to key account personnel.

EXAMPLE: Manulife, a Canadian life insurance firm, sells variable annuities to its key accounts, retail brokers. Manulife has strong relationships with brokers' corporate offices and their geographically dispersed branch offices. Frequently, branch offices are mandated to sell a specific proportion of internally managed brokerage house funds in their variable annuities. Local Manulife representatives assist branch office representatives in meeting their quotas of internally managed funds and are rewarded with sales of Manulife funds when internally managed funds are not appropriate.

- *Demand generation.* Develop demand further down the marketing channel via sales force effort, and/or advertising and other promotional means.

EXAMPLE: In third-world countries, Nortel works with new companies setting up cellular telephone systems in fierce competition with governments seeking to deregulate existing telephone operations. Nortel gives advice on marketing, ways to sign up customers, customer service, and so forth to improve these firms' revenues.

EXAMPLE: IBM funded market research for one of its bank customers to leverage the bank's sales force to sell PCs and banking-related software.

EXAMPLE: When it raises prices of its syrup to bottlers, Coca-Cola increases consumer advertising in an attempt to increase demand for its products.

EXAMPLE: American Express's (AMEX) exclusive credit card partnership with Costco provides Costco with both new customers and increased purchases per customer. AMEX develops and executes direct mail and mass media campaigns to secure new co-branded Costco cardholders, and provides Costco with access to its current customers. Costco's customers earn "Costco dollars" through AMEX's Rewards program and may take advantage of discounts from market leaders such as IBM, Federal Express, Hilton, and Hertz.

INCREASE PRICES

In this option, the supplier firm takes actions that allow the key account to raise prices to its customers. Among actions the supplier can take are:

- *Increasing demand.* By and large, actions that the supplier firm can take are similar to those just discussed except that the key account may decide to raise prices and accept a smaller unit volume increase.
- *Product mix changes.* The supplier may enhance its product mix such that its key account's products command higher prices in its marketplace.

EXAMPLE: The Lighting Division of Philips, the Dutch-based multinational, attempts to increase profitability for its retail key accounts by developing systems to increase sales of higher-price, higher-margin, longer-life light bulbs.

REDUCE COSTS

Broadly speaking there are six types of opportunity for the supplier firm to help the key account reduce its costs. Some of these require actions within the supplier firm, some within the key account, and others across the supplier-firm/key-account interface[13]:

- *Reduce prices.* This may be accomplished by the supplier firm initiating an across-the-board price reduction, or introducing various forms of discount schedule.

- *Reduce other financial expenses.* For example, the supplier firm may modify its terms for accounts receivable. In addition, more favorable arrangements may be offered for returns, inventory stored at the key account, and so forth.
- *Reduce direct operating costs.* By modifying its products and processes, the supplier firm may be able to reduce costs for the key account. Improving product quality for example, may eliminate resource duplication, reduce the costs of rework and delay at the key account, and cut the key account's costs of after-sales service. Product inspection at the supplier may reduce the need for inspection at the key account. A slightly modified product and/or providing assemblies rather than subassemblies may allow the key account to cut out production steps. In addition, the supplier may conduct R&D for its key account.[14]
- *Reduce direct administrative costs.* Doing business with the supplier firm may be costly for the key account. For example, key account personnel may receive sales calls from several supplier salespeople, and have to pay multiple invoices. Simplification of the supplier-firm/key-account interface offers the potential for considerable cost savings. Many firms are now using the Internet to reduce interorganizational administrative costs.
- *Reduce indirect operating costs.* In the course of working with the key account, the key account manager and other team members may identify opportunities for cost savings that are only indirectly related to the supplier firm's products. For example, the supplier firm may use its expertise and buying power to source raw materials for the key account, or team members visiting the key account's factories may identify ways to cut costs.
- *Reduce indirect administrative costs.* In a similar fashion, the key account manager and other team members may identify ways of saving administrative costs that only indirectly relate to the supplier firm. For example, the key account may benefit from adopting the supplier firm's key account planning system or inventory control system. (See the Milliken example, Figures 5.5 and 5.6, for an example of reducing customers' administrative costs.)

EXAMPLE: Holland Hitch (HH) was under severe price pressure from large fleet owners for its premium truck and trailer components. HH gathered in-depth operational data from customers and developed a software tool that enables it to conduct detailed analysis of customer costs. As a result, working in real time and using the customer's own data, HH can identify specific realizable cost savings for customers using its products.[15]

EXAMPLE: Traditionally, oil companies delivered products when they received orders from customers. Shell Chemicals (SC) realized that, administratively, it could function as a "water company," delivering product when required by the customer but without the necessity of an order. SC installed a vendor-managed inventory system at its key accounts giving it full responsibility for managing the key accounts' fuel inventories. By sharing information, customers were able to reduce administrative costs and Shell was better able to forecast customer requirements.

EXAMPLE: Boise Cascade Office Products (BCOP) used its knowledge of activity-based costing (ABC) to measure customer-related costs more effectively so as to capture key account profitability.[16] The success of this program led BCOP's own key accounts, in turn, to request assistance in measuring profitability for their key accounts. Unwilling to enter the process consulting business, BCOP developed a software program, *SAVE,* to analyze its customers' process costs. Trained BCOP representatives assist their accounts to secure better information on requisitioning, order placing, receiving and distributing, and accounts payable, then use "what if" modeling to explore cost reduction possibilities. Successful cost reduction has even encouraged some of BCOP's key accounts to use *SAVE* to help their own customers reduce their process costs.[17]

Some customers actively challenge suppliers to provide cost savings ideas.

EXAMPLE: In the 1990s Chrysler's Supplier Cost Reduction Effort, SCORE, motivated its supply base to meet annual 5% cost reduction targets by agreeing to split savings equally with suppliers.[18]

REDUCE INVESTMENT

The focus here is on the key account's fixed and current investment.[19]

- *Reduction in fixed investment.* To the extent that the key account outsources some of its activities to the supplier firm, it can reduce its investment. For example, the supplier may offer assemblies rather than subassemblies, or otherwise offer processed raw materials that save production steps and the associated fixed investment.

- *Reduction in inventory investment.* The supplier firm may cut the key account's inventory investment via just-in-time (JIT) delivery systems.

EXAMPLE: Typically, to prepare for the winter season, plumbing supply wholesalers have to order and take delivery of supplies in summer at significant cost in terms of inventory investment and warehouse space. For each of its five key accounts, Emerson-Swan, a regional plumbing supply distributor, offered to self-inventory 25% of forecast volume for 25 high-volume items. (The cost of inventory and warehouse space assumed by Emerson-Swan was more than compensated for by additional volume.)

- *Financing packages.* Attractive financial arrangements may ease the strain on the key account's capital. They may even make it possible for the account to purchase supplier firm products that it would otherwise have forgone.

EXAMPLE: The airline customer of Gum Company*, an equipment supplier, was unable to purchase the products it required because of a severe capital shortage. Gum devised a financing plan in which the airline paid per flight mile, thus removing the requirement for its investment capital.

Marketers would argue that customers don't really want the supplier's capital equipment; they want the benefits that the capital equipment provides. Thus, the supplier is able to price based on the benefits received—flight mile in the example above. In addition to improving its customer's ROI, by not selling the capital equipment, the supplier firm provides the important additional benefit of reducing the key account's risk.

Meta-Level Relationship Needs

In the process of delivering value to satisfy the key account's core needs, the supplier firm must establish a framework for how it wishes to be perceived by the key account in its everyday business relationships. Although many of these meta-level needs are functional and/or economic in nature, others relate directly to the provision of psychological values [20]:

Accessibility. Is there a functioning key account manager providing a single point of contact for the key account? Is it easy for the key account to identify and reach the people it needs to work with? Not infrequently, accessibility is most effectively provided by the supplier firm's physical presence at the key account. Often, key accounts are willing to provide space for an important supplier—for example, an administrative or factory office—as insurance and to facilitate the relationship. In addition, staffing an in-key-account physical presence is an important statement of the supplier firm's commitment to the key account.

Responsiveness. How quickly does the supplier firm deal with issues that arise in the course of business, such as delivering a specially requested raw material?[21] Other areas where response speed may be important include fixing an incorrect invoice, setting up a technical meeting, and delivering a price. For example, a pricing system that provides consistent prices and fast response may allow the key account's business to run more smoothly. Several years ago Shapiro and Moriarty reported that Dow Chemical's pricing system was consistently praised: "We get a price from Dow in much less time than from its competitors"; and "Dow doesn't take forever to come back with a price." More recently, the Internet and company intranets have helped push the envelope on responsiveness.

> EXAMPLE: Air Products' engineers working in three separate offices—Allentown, London, and Singapore—pioneered an intranet-based publishing and review process to achieve twenty-four-hour turnaround on proposals that previously would have taken weeks.[22]

In addition, *customized products, packaging, and/or services* are a frequent requirement for key accounts; indeed, many large organizations such as Sears Roebuck and the U.S. government set their own product specifications. Because standardized processes and procedures for interfacing with key accounts are typically insufficient, customization generally requires additional costs for inventory (raw materials, work-in-process, finished goods), product changeovers, and special engineering and equipment. However, customization may increase supplier-firm/key-account interdependence, and be a point of competitive differentiation.

Keeping Promises. When the key account and key account manager agree on a particular course of action, does the supplier firm keep its promises? A particularly crucial area is timing. Regardless of whether the concern is delivery of product, services, technological development, or information, overall quality depends not only on the individual item *per se,* but *when* that item is received by the key account. Of course, even in the best-run supplier organizations, delays sometimes occur. When this happens, the customer must be given prompt and accurate information regarding when delivery will be made, and the reasons for the problem.[23]

> **EXAMPLE:** Lime Inc.*, a Connecticut-based provider of limestone, was in a fierce competitive battle with a Canadian producer for an important contract requiring delivery in Connecticut. The Canadian producer's product was higher quality and CIF[24] prices were comparable. However, Lime won the contract by showing that rail transportation from Canada was sufficiently complex that there was a high likelihood that the Canadian firm would be unable to keep its delivery promises.

For many customers, early delivery is a positive experience, exceeding their expectations. However, for those organizations operating JIT inventory systems, early delivery may pose significant problems and act as a negative. The supplier firm must understand each key account's preferences in this regard.

Understanding Critical Customer Issues. Does the supplier firm expend effort actively to assist the key account in achieving its goals and objectives? This effort might take the form of strategic account analysis (see above).

> **Example:** Maple*, a commodity chemical firm, secured preferred supplier status because the customer viewed it as a real partner in developing its business plan! Maple designed factory floors, secured technical help, benchmarked other factories globally to identify best manufacturing techniques, and advised its customer which markets to enter and which to avoid.[25]

A deep understanding of the key account may allow the supplier firm to offer many types of needed services. Product availability is a particularly crucial area, made more difficult both by a requirement to reduce working capital—perhaps by inventory reductions and just-in-time (JIT) systems—and greater uncertainties resulting from complex and fast changing environments. Plant location, flexible manufacturing, delivery speed, delivery reliability, and special logistics requirements such as field and/or consignment inventory[26] all relate to product delivery. The key account manager must understand the account's logistics and inventory systems and develop creative methods that meet account delivery needs satisfactorily.[27]

Communications. Does the key account manager ensure that personnel at the key account are well informed about relevant matters concerning the supplier firm. Is this information timely and in a language they can understand? Indeed, information needs, often considered the "glue" binding the supplier firm and key account, are many.

- *Routine information* includes such areas as ordering, availability, shipping, receiving, and billing. Typically the responsibility of low-level employees, inadequate and/or incompatible systems for dealing with these information flows can cause much key account dissatisfaction.
- *Urgent information* is unusual and time-sensitive. Examples include an emergency caused by a competitor's inability to deliver a critical product, or failure of the supplier firm's product. The key account manager's ability to recognize this information and respond effectively can enhance the supplier firm's reputation for responsiveness and allow it to gain competitive advantage.

Information needs may concern the past, the present or the future. *Historic data* may be in the form of reports on account purchases or supplier firm actions, perhaps as part of a relationship audit.

EXAMPLE: The Norton Company provided individual key accounts with detailed analyses of product usage on twenty-four-hours notice. These reports led to improved purchasing efficiency since local orders could be combined and/or order specifications revised.[28]

Present data relates to current operations and key-account/supplier-firm interfaces necessary to keep the relationship functioning. The manager may also provide information relating to the account, gathered from many individual supplier-firm/key-account relationships, with which individual key account personnel are unaware!

Information about the future may range from supplier firm estimates of delivery to planning assumptions developed in the key account planning process. Information may also be characterized as simple versus complex.

Easy to do business with. Does the supplier firm operate with inflexible rules and procedures for managing the supplier-firm/key-account interface, or does it strive to be easy to do business with? Such areas as administration, and documentation required for ordering and billing purposes, are typically handled by low-level personnel yet may cause major ruptures in the interorganizational relationship if badly managed. Of course, the supplier firm must realize that, from the key account's perspective, its own internal procedures may be considered as irrelevant.

Competence. Are supplier firm personnel who interface with the key account competent to do their jobs? In addition to the key account manager, many supplier firm employees can affect the firm's relationship with a key account favorably or unfavorably. They include:

- applications engineers who adapt products to key account's requirements
- field service personnel, including maintenance, repair, and technical, who enhance the account's ability to use the product
- engineering and development personnel who customize the firm's products
- promotional experts who support the key account's marketing efforts
- legal staff who address product liability and government compliance concerns

A recent study identified a series of relationship-related issues that both "bother" and "impress" buyers (Figure 5.4). As we can see, the items generated in the study partially map with the list of meta-level relationship needs. Supplier firm performance on these items may be secured from a customer satisfaction survey.

This set of meta-level needs overarches fundamental-product/service-related needs discussed earlier. In recent years, as many firms have embraced the quality movement and improved their products and services, the competitive bar for satisfying these types of needs has been raised. Increasingly, supplier firms will secure and retain key accounts by exemplary performance on these meta-relationship needs.

Clearly, the meta-level needs of an individual key account may range broadly

FIGURE 5.4: Behaviors That "Bother" and "Impress" Buyers

Bother		Impress	
Behavior	Percent	Behavior	Percent
Lack of follow-up	28%	Thoroughness, follow-through	78%
Lack of preparation for meetings	15%	Willingness to fight for customer in own firm	59%
"Cold calls"	15%	Market knowledge/willingness to share	40%
Too pushy/bad attitude	15%	Knowledge of own products	40%
Lack of product knowledge	11%	Imagination in applying products to needs	29%
Dishonesty	7%	Knowledge of your product line	28%
Lack of knowledge of company's operations	6%	Preparation for sales calls	20%
Lack of market knowledge	5%	Diplomacy in dealing with operating departments	15%
Not adhering to appointment times	5%	Regularity of sales calls	9%
		Technical education	9%

across these categories. As part of the planning process, the key account manager must isolate those that are critical to the key account and identify ways of providing the appropriate value. Furthermore, whereas satisfaction of some needs may be necessary to maintain the business, satisfaction of other needs is required for relationship development. Maintenance needs, for example, relate to solving problems caused by product failure, extended delivery promises, late deliveries, poor technical service follow-up, and insufficient product availability. By contrast, developmental needs include delivering new product samples for testing, implementing a new ordering system, and joint marketing research studies of end-use markets.[29]

Depth of Key Account Need and Customer Value

In the previous sections we focused on different types of account needs and related values that the supplier might offer to satisfy those needs. Here we focus on the depth of value for the key account. We discuss meeting or exceeding customer expectations, developing solutions to existing problems, and solving new and/or unrecognized problems.[30]

Meeting or Exceeding Key Account Expectations. Customer satisfaction is directly related to the supplier firm's ability to meet or exceed expectations. Typically, these expectations are set in the context of the current set of products and services purchased by the key account and may include product quality levels, prices, delivery time, and after-sales service. Frequently, these sorts of expectations are established in formal meetings between key account and supplier firm teams. Meeting or exceeding these expectations is crucial to maintaining the supplier-firm/key-account relationship, but they are the easiest for competitors to copy.

Developing Solutions to Existing Problems. If the key account manager can orchestrate a new solution to an existing problem, he has a greater ability to differentiate the supplier firm from competition than by simply meeting expectations. The supplier firm's ability to develop such solutions depends in large part on its key account manager's ability to fully diagnose the problem.

Solving New and/or Unrecognized Problems. This represents the greatest depth of potential key account satisfaction. Here, the manager delivers the solution to a problem of which the key account is not yet aware. The supplier firm may offer services that cut costs significantly in an area the key account believed was cost efficient; or it may demonstrate that outsourcing a particular process will improve the key account's capital utilization; or it may develop a new product that allows the key account to address new market segments. Quite often, the expectation that the supplier firm will solve such problems in the future functions as a significant switching cost for the key account.

Addressing Key Account Needs

Regardless of the type of need, the key account manager should seek the key account's assistance in prioritizing its requirements, considering both the absolute importance of the required value and its timing. Typically, some needs are immediate; others may be important yet their timing is less critical. In some cases, customers present sets of requirements, *all* of which are "critically" important, such as meeting tough specifications and short time frames with low prices and extended credit terms; often supplier firms are unable to satisfy all requirements. In such situations, the key account manager must probe beneath the surface to ascertain the nature of the tradeoffs the key account is prepared to make, and may have to be prepared to walk away from the business if necessary. Some needs may be absolute "givens"; others may be negotiable. (See Appendix 5.1 for a discussion of *conjoint analysis,* a formal method for estimating customer tradeoffs.)

In this context, the key account manager should do the groundwork that will ultimately lead to action programs to satisfy these needs. Here we consider several actions that the key account manager should take.

Make Careful Judgments About Which Needs to Satisfy. The key account manager must make a series of decisions regarding which key account needs the firm is prepared to satisfy. Of course, the greatest profit leverage is secured by offering services that are highly valued by customers but cost the supplier firm little to deliver.

Identify Alternative Solutions and Costs. For each significant unsatisfied key account need, several potential solutions should be developed in an acceptable time frame, together with the associated costs. This process may be accomplished in brainstorming sessions involving the key account team and, possibly, key account representation. Note that some key accounts insist that their suppliers regularly submit cost reduction ideas.

In general, supplier firms attempt to use their core competencies to satisfy key account needs. However, it is quite possible that the twin portfolios of key account needs and firm abilities may not be congruent. Consider specialty chemical manufacturer Clariant Corporation:

EXAMPLE: Clariant was working with a key account that wished to simplify its purchasing operations; in particular, it wanted to consolidate the procurement of a range of specialty and commodity chemicals. Although Clariant could manufacture the entire range, it believed it would be uncompetitive overall inasmuch as its own specialty chemical focus would lead to high costs for the required commodity chemicals. Clariant decided to bid on the basis of in-house manufactured specialty chemicals but outsourced commodity chemicals. It searched globally for the lowest-price commodity chemicals with security of supply, bid on that basis, and won the contract. Secondary benefits for Clariant of pursuing this contract were the development of global sourcing skills and new ways of dealing with a key account that could be used in dealing with other customers.

A related example also concerns an extension of the firm's competence while offering simplification value for the customer:

> **EXAMPLE:** In its new fourteen-story Minneapolis office building, Dayton Hudson confronted the time-consuming task of dealing with multiple consultants and multiple sales reps to select products and suppliers for its communications infrastructure (voice, video, data). The U.S. West account manager developed a bundled solution and won the bid to design and develop the infrastructure.[31] Successful completion positioned U.S. West for similar future business; one significant win—also in Minneapolis—was a Dayton Hudson building twice as large.[32]

Determine the Most Attractive Options. An analysis of the various potential solutions and costs for each key account requirement leads to a determination of preferred solutions. The ability to identify the most attractive options is enhanced if the firm has knowledge of the key account's profitability model and understands the profit build-up.

Identify Switching Costs. Oftentimes, a supplier firm may develop a preferred option for a key account but be unable to secure adoption because of "switching costs." The costs that must be incurred by the customer in changing from one supplier to another may outweigh the benefits of the new alternative. Two important types of switching costs are hard dollar costs and perceived risk. Hard dollar costs include, for example, the cost of required new equipment to use the supplier firm's product. Perceived risk comprises performance risk (the new product may not perform as promised), financial risk (the customer absorbs out-of-pocket losses from using the new product), and personal risk (the decision maker faces intraorganizational retribution for making a poor purchase decision).[33] Of course, hard dollar costs may be mitigated by the supplier firm assuming all or part of the new equipment cost; perceived risk is more difficult to address, but may be ameliorated via such devices as warrantees and guarantees.

Decide Whether, How Much and How to Charge for Solutions. Depending on the particular key account need to be satisfied, the supplier firm's options range from setting a high price to no charge or even subsidization. Items such as customized products may carry a high price; others, for example, improving delivery, may be considered as enhancing the supplier-firm/key-account relationship. A further issue is whether a particular service is charged for separately, or bundled into the price for the core product.

Ultimately, the key account manager must conduct a cost/benefit analysis for the various requirements and preferred solutions. Here, the key account director has an important role in assessing whether or not individual key account solutions can be joined to gain economies in satisfying the needs of several key accounts.

In competitive bidding situations, the supplier firm should develop flexibility in satisfying key account needs. It should prepare its bidding documents on the basis of its best understanding of these needs, but build in the ability to submit a revised bid very quickly, based on tradeoffs the key account is prepared to make if it learns its price is too high.

EXAMPLE: When it bids on major projects in China, Siemens develops multiple options for the various project components. It submits an initial bid based on its best analysis of customer requirements but can submit a revised bid within twenty-four hours if it believes it is likely to lose the business on price. As a result, it gains considerable advantage over competitor European firms that have to work with their head offices for revisions and whose turnaround time for revised bidding documents is two to three weeks.

BUYING ANALYSIS

The purpose of the buying analysis is to understand how the key account buys. This requires a detailed understanding of the key account's procurement system. Although the various types of information gathered in the strategic key account analysis provide the key account manager with excellent material for identifying business opportunities and hence making overall resource allocation decisions, a solid understanding of the procurement system is critical for making sales. The key account's procurement system is a complex undertaking of which many questions should be asked. We identify four key elements: the procurement process, decision-making players, procurement specifics, and the nature of the purchase.

The Procurement Process

Purchase decisions by key accounts are rarely unitary events that occur at a single point in time. Rather, procurement occurs over time and may involve different individuals, occupying different roles, at different managerial levels, in different functional areas, in different geographic locations, with different interests and perspectives. A single key account may employ a variety of different procurement processes depending upon the nature of the purchase. For purchases that involve new product development by the supplier firm it is likely that technical personnel from the key account will be highly involved. However, for repeat purchases (straight rebuys, see below) the process is likely to be heavily influenced by procurement personnel.[34]

In some firms, procurement personnel dominate the process, often acting as "gatekeepers" of information and access to individuals in specialized functional areas. In other organizations, procurement decisions are made by cross-functional supply teams comprising representatives from, for example, product engineering, quality engineering, receiving, purchasing, materials management, operations, design, and product development.

An often complicating procurement issue is the degree of centralization or decentralization for multilocation key accounts. In many of these organizations, advanced telecommunications technology, the Internet, and a desire for reduced costs and other efficiencies have led to increased centralization, often on a global scale. These systems do not always meet the expectations of individual key account locations, where local personnel sometimes generate complex "rogue" or "maverick" processes to "beat the system." The key account manager must understand these process shifts. If a key account is moving to globalized procurement with a national or multicountry/regional model, clearly the organizational disconnect is fraught with danger.

EXAMPLE: Ikea has several relatively independent buying offices around the world, each of which is in part judged on its success in writing global supply contracts. Two of these buying offices are in the PRC. When the Philips Lighting Division was working closely with the Shanghai office, it did not realize that the other China office was writing a global supply contract with Osram for OEM lamp sales. As a result, Philips was shut out of OEM business for a considerable period.

Two important features of the move to centralized buying should be monitored by key account managers—the products and services involved, and the level of pressure on the decentralized buying units. First, shifting to centralized buying is a complex process and procurement organizations tend to proceed deliberately and incrementally. If a product is not currently being procured centrally, it may have a scheduled date for centralized buying, or it may never be purchased centrally. Either way the supplier firm should understand the situation. Second, the firm should be aware of the extent to which centralized procurement is mandated by the buying organization. For example, Caterpillar mandates sticking to centrally negotiated supply arrangements. On the other hand, Johnson & Johnson uses a voluntary system but, because of extensive internal consultation and coordination, anticipates at least 80% compliance with its supplier agreements by individual purchasing entities.

In order to maximize leverage on the key account's procurement processes and so raise the probability of securing any particular piece of business, the supplier firm must have a clear knowledge of critical elements in the key account's organization structure. In addition, constructing flow charts of the procurement process(es), paying close attention to who does what, and when, can facilitiate this understanding.

In recent years a central feature of corporate cost reduction efforts has been business process reengineering, a principal tool of which is process mapping.[35] The firm charts out the entire sequence of process elements, and the process map serves as the vehicle by which random occurrences are driven out, non-value added steps eliminated, related steps combined, and others streamlined. The process is standardized, and is adjusted over time in a relentless search for continual improvement in reliability and predictability. For each step in the existing process, several questions should be asked:

- Why is this step necessary?
- Where is it done?
- Why is it done there?
- When is it done?
- Why is it done then?
- Who does it?
- Why do they do it?
- How is it done?
- Why is it done this way?

In key account buying analysis, the supplier firm also undertakes process mapping, but for the procurement processes at its key account. The goal is to understand the process and help improve its efficiency and effectiveness by analyzing opportunities to reduce cycle times, remove waste and redundancy, and offer suggestions and recommendations. (Other areas for process mapping investigation are the RFP/proposal cycle, order entry, and product defects/claims.) A successful mapping exercise may be an eye-opener for the key account and enhance the supplier-firm/key-account relationship.[36] For example, Milliken Carpet maps out its key accounts' procurement processes and provides system improvement recommendations that earn its key accounts considerable savings. See Figures 5.5 and 5.6 for illustrations of a before-and-after customer procurement processes.[37]

Of course implementation of a new process requires education and training

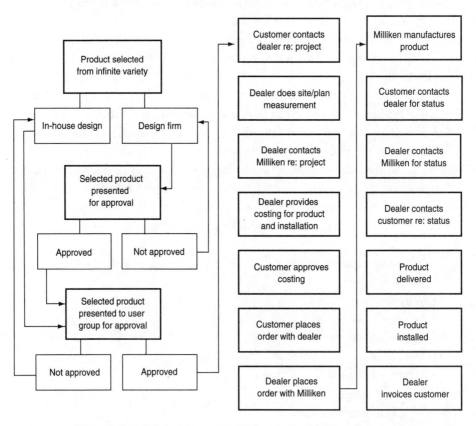

FIGURE 5.5: Original Procurement Process by Milliken Customer

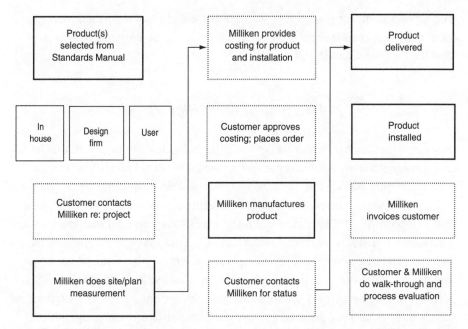

FIGURE 5.6: Revised Procurement Process by Milliken Customer
Note: Activities in the boxes with dotted lines can be accomplished electronically.

of interface individuals at both the supplier and the key account. However, successful implementation eases price pressure and enhances customer satisfaction by developing the lowest total process cost and making it easier to do business. At a minimum, a thorough understanding of the key account's procurement processes allows the supplier to husband its resources to exert leverage at the appropriate times, in the appropriate places, for maximum payoff.

EXAMPLE: For one major customer, analysis of its design and procurement process allowed Milliken Carpet to demonstrate savings in excess of 30% of the carpet price.

In some organizations, and for some types of purchase, the procurement process evolves as the purchase decision proceeds. For example, although the purchase process is in principle defined in many Chinese enterprises, as decision time approaches, competing suppliers often attempt to gain influence at increasingly high levels in the buying organization, even involving important political figures in government ministries. Unwilling to be caught in the crossfire among competing suppliers well connected to their superiors, managers nominally responsible for the procurement decision are only too willing to allow the decision locus to shift upwards.

Decision-Making Players

Because procurement decisions are made by individuals in organizations, and not by organizations *per se,* key account managers should identify who are the important "players" at their key accounts. Key account managers need to understand these players' roles, their "power" to get things done, their willingness to use that power, and their functional allegiances.[38] Key account managers must be aware of the relevant formal and informal relationships within the account, and the extent to which the important players are in conflict with, or work harmoniously with, other individuals or groups. Finally, key account managers need to know the players' motivations and perceptions of the key account's needs and its various product and supplier alternatives, their geographic locations, and the manner in which they might behave in a particular purchase context.

POSITIONAL POWER AND PERSONAL POWER

For those personnel involved in the procurement process, the key account manager must be able to distinguish between positional power and personal power (Figure 5.7). Clearly, the key account manager should focus significant attention on persons with high positional power and high personal power (Cell A), but may need assistance from senior management to be fully effective. However, he should be careful not to "waste" time by focusing excessive effort on persons who may have high organizational position but little influence on the buying process (Cell B). Persons who may have relatively lowly organizational positions should not be overlooked, for they may have significant influence on the buying process (Cell C).[39]

ROLE RELATIONSHIPS

A starting point for analysis of decision-making players is to understand their role relationships by asking and answering a number of questions.[40] This

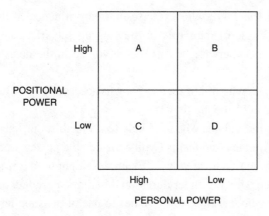

FIGURE 5.7: Positional Power and Personal Power

process will suggest ways the supplier firm can influence the key account's decisions by identifying the key players, the power relationships among them, and how they frame purchase decisions?[41]

- Who are the actual *decision makers,* the individuals that control the release of funds for purchase?

EXAMPLE: Goldenchain Inc.*, a major New York investment bank, lost a critical piece of business—to become the lead underwriter for an initial public offering (IPO) by a fast growing consumer goods company. In its meetings with the account, Goldenchain regularly worked with both the CEO and CFO. It made little effort to identify or address the chief stockholder, failing to realize that he was the ultimate decision maker.

- Who are the *influencers?* What is their relative degree of influence? What role, if any, do the key account's customers play in the procurement process?
- Do the *users,* e.g., shop floor personnel, have any role in the purchase process?
- What members of senior management are likely to become involved in specific purchase decisions?
- Should we be concerned about unions or other organizations, internal or external to the key account, for example, consultants or third party specifiers, whose actions may impact the key account's purchase of our products?

- Are there internal *specifiers* who exercise indirect influence in the purchase process by virtue of their role in drawing up specifications, even though they may not otherwise be formally involved in the decision *per se?* Who are they?
- Are there *gatekeepers* who might seek to deny us access to key influencers or the decision maker? Who are they?
- Are there *spoilers,* individuals who are likely to act against our interests at the key account? Are they *opponents* (with considerable power) or *detractors* (with weak power)? Who are they? (Examples might be, a former supplier firm employee who left under duress and harbors a grudge, or a key account employee who has close positive ties to one of the supplier firm's competitors.)

EXAMPLE: A Henkel subsidiary in China shipped to a key account what it believed to be test quantities of high-quality raw materials for detergent manufacture. Tests on the raw materials showed them to be substandard. On investigation, Henkel determined that an employee of the customer, whose cousin worked for a competitive supplier, had added water to Henkel's product, causing it to fail the tests!

- Are there *champions* who will promote our interests at the key account? Do they have considerable power *(backers)* or weak power *(supporters)*? Who are they?

EXAMPLE: Many former employees of the McKinsey consulting company reach senior levels in their former clients' companies. Frequently they act as McKinsey champions when high-level consulting services are required.

- Are there *information providers* who will keep us advised about the state of our action programs (and competitors' action programs) at the key account—procurement processes, competitive bids, relationship quality (ours and competitors') and so forth? Who are they? In addition to a variety of people within the account (including secretaries and administrative assistants), useful information may also be secured from the key account's customers and from former "players" who have moved to other organizational positions, and now feel more free to discuss purchase-related issues.

EXAMPLE: A Swedish manufacturer was a key account for John Bright, a major British cotton weaver. John Bright's key account manager had such excellent relationships with senior executives in Sweden that they would routinely advise him of competitive offers so that John Bright might decide whether or not to make a lower bid.

UNDERSTANDING THE KEY PLAYERS

Beyond becoming familiar with the relevant roles and persons filling those roles, the key account manager should gain a sense of the motivations, perceptions, and potential behavior of key players in a given procurement situation. For example, it should identify such information as:

- Career history including former employers, organizational positions
- Current organizational position, including nature of responsibilities and limitations on decision-making authority
- Reporting relationships, including subordinate and superordinate personnel
- Organizational future and potential career track, in particular the likely next career position
- Social styles and informal and cross-functional relationships within the key account
- Key drivers that influence the individual's attitude in specific purchase decisions. Is the individual driven to achieve particular organizational goals or, more selfishly, individual personal goals?

EXAMPLE: Orange Inc.*, a *Fortune* 500 firm, was surprised to learn it failed to win a big order from a key account even though it knew its final price was slightly below that of the winning competitor. Orange management later discovered that procurement personnel earned bonuses based on the percent reduction from the initial bid price they were able to secure from suppliers. Knowing this feature of the compensation system, the competitor had initially made a high bid that was significantly discounted for the final offer. By contrast, the losing firm had made a low initial bid that was reduced only marginally for the final offer. Procurement personnel acted to maximize their personal well being and, since the final price differences were relatively small, were able to justify the procurement decision to senior management.[42]

The key account manager may also ask other questions about key people in the decision-making system:

- What are their perceptions of the key account's needs as regards product or services of the type the firm could supply?
- What are their perceptions of, and relationships with, the supplier firm and its competitors (actual and potential)? In a particular buying situation, which supplier(s) do they currently favor?
- What are their reputations regarding business judgment, trustworthiness, integrity? What are their interests, hobbies, affectations?
- What are their specific "hot buttons"?

Of course, answers to these questions typically differ across type of purchase, and in different parts of the key account organization. Furthermore, in addition to answering these questions for near-term purchase decisions, the key account manager should also attempt to understand the roles and individuals likely to be involved in purchase decisions in the medium-term future. The importance of this cannot be overstated. Organization structures change and individuals are promoted, reassigned or leave altogether. The key account manager needs to be familiar with the key account's succession planning and pay the appropriate attention to those individuals who may move into influential and decision-making responsibilities. Witness the experience of a division of a major *Fortune* 500 company recounted by a senior executive:

> The manager for a major account was a person who focused his attention on the key influencers and decision makers and who liked to maintain tight control over his colleagues' access to the account. He was extremely effective in what he did and we experienced substantial volume growth over a number of years. Our major competitor meanwhile focused attention on the more junior people at the account, as their people found it impossible to make a dent in the relationships our key account manager had made.
>
> However, in a fairly short time frame, our key account manager's major contacts retired and ultimately he retired also. Because of his practices, we no longer had secure relationships with the key influencers and decision makers once the personnel had changed. Almost overnight we lost virtually all our business to the competitor.[43]

Finally, the key account manager should keep sharply aware about the quality of interpersonal relationships among members of the key account team and critical individuals at the key account. Even when a key account plan is first developed, the manager is not writing on a blank slate. The key account has probably already purchased from the supplier. Many relationships may exist or may once have existed among supplier firm and key account personnel, and the history of the interorganizational relationship is dotted with events (purchase and otherwise) that may, in some way or other, influence the future relationship trajectory. The key account manager must capture these elements in the planning process; she must make herself familiar not only with the quality of these relationships but how they differ from those of key competitors. Because this sort of information is extremely important to the supplier firm's success, it should be placed in a database that can be easily accessed and updated.

The key account manager is most likely well versed in those aspects of the key account's organization most closely related to current purchases, but he probably has far less information regarding potential business. If the key account's strategy involves business and/or geographic diversification, keeping on top of the developing organization and relevant personnel may be a tall order. However, it is just such key account knowledge that may be critical for gaining leverage both to expand current business and identify totally new potential revenue sources.

THE BUYING INFLUENCES CHART

For major purchases, the supplier firm should complete a buying influences chart (Figure 5.8). Consider a fictional example: the proposed purchase of a major piece of telecommunications equipment by Alpha Corporation* from Gamma*, rather than from its long-time supplier, Beta*. Here all key players are Alpha employees. If a purchase involved influence from other organizations, such as the key account's customer, distributor, retailer, consultant, or a third-party standards body, the chart should also reflect their influence.

Procurement Specifics

Four specific aspects of the key account's procurement process—supplier-rating programs, purchase methods, its philosophy on sharing business, and the

FIGURE 5.8: Example of a Buying Influences Chart

Influencers	Perceived Influence in Purchase Process (%)	Main Criteria for Deciding Between Beta and Gamma	Comments
Able, Group VP, Staff Operations	5%	1. Tendency to stick with the *status quo*	1. Mainly a rubber stamp
Baker, Head, Information Systems Division	40%	1. Opportunity to show major telecommunications supplier, Beta, that it should treat Alpha more like a valued customer	1. Gives formal approval for purchasing decisions 2. History of upsetting established procurement relationships 3. Very aggressive; moving upward in the firm
Charlie, Manager, Communications Division	20%	1. Neutral to Beta; will select best solution for firm	1. Reports to Baker 2. Major influencer in upgrading voice networks 3. Very knowledgeable about communications products
Desmond, Dallas Communications Manager	20%	1. Seeks best way to solve telecommunications problem resulting from division's fast growth 2. Demonstrates his innovativeness to senior management	1. Neutral to Beta; likely to switch if convinced 2. Aggressive risk taker
Ethan, Denver Procurement Manager	5%	1. Technology oriented; likely to advocate supplier with technological edge 2. Aware of how all business units function; interested in full systems integration	1. Mainly a bystander but critically interested because of his upcoming RFP for a new telecommunications system

nature of the purchase—can have an important bearing on the success of the supplier-firm/key-account relationship.

SUPPLIER RATING PROGRAMS

Many corporate procurement departments operate supplier-rating programs for choosing suppliers and/or allocating business among potential vendors. These programs typically assess suppliers by allocating points on various criteria. A variety of different models are currently being used and others have been proposed. The most common are based on weighted factors.[44]

In a popular five-step version of this model

- the key account identifies critical purchasing criteria such as quality, price, delivery, credit terms and responsiveness.
- The criteria are then weighted according to their perceived importance such that the weights sum to 100.
- Then, each supplier is rated on a 1 to 10 scale for its perceived performance on each criterion.
- The weights are multiplied by the ratings and
- the weighted criteria summed for each supplier to provide a series of supplier performance scores.
- These scores are used in both supplier selection and allocation of business among suppliers.

In Figure 5.9, supplier C outperforms suppliers A and B.

If the key account is using a supplier-rating model, the key account manager should find out what type of model is being employed, the various procurement criteria, the importance weights, and the scores on each criterion for both her firm and its various competitors. Frequently, key accounts provide this information on request, both at account-organized "supplier days," and at training and improvement forums, since they wish to improve supplier performance. For the key account manager, this information may provide the basis for developing action programs to improve its position at the account.

In addition, the key account manager should become aware of actions taken by the account to reduce its supply costs. These may include cost targeting, early supplier involvement in product design, use of experience curves to gauge

FIGURE 5.9: Illustration of the Weighted Supplier Selection Model

Supplier Selection Criteria	Importance Weights (a)	Supplier A		Supplier B		Supplier C	
		Rating (b)	a × b	Rating (b)	a × b	Rating (b)	a × b
Product quality	30	5	150	6	180	8	240
Customer service	20	6	120	7	140	9	180
Technical skills	15	7	105	8	120	7	105
Credit terms	5	4	20	7	35	6	30
Responsiveness	15	3	45	6	90	9	135
Reject levels	10	6	60	5	50	7	70
Industry knowledge	5	5	25	8	40	8	40
	100		525		655		800

productivity improvements, technology grouping, and part number reductions. Other potential methods embrace tighter specifications, value engineering,[45] idea incentives for suppliers, financial incentives/penalties for quality, delivery, performance, and inventory cost reduction, and extension of supplier management techniques to subsuppliers and sub-subsuppliers.[46] Only by understanding key account actions can the key account manager determine the appropriate supplier firm response.

PURCHASE METHODS

The types of contractual agreements that key accounts make for their purchases vary widely across firms. The key account manager must know answers to such questions as:

- Does the account negotiate annual contracts, or purchase as needed (spot purchases)?
- Does the account develop rigid specifications, or is it flexible in receiving proposals?
- Are purchase contracts drawn up centrally by head office personnel, or by personnel in individual divisions or branches?
- If contracts are drawn up centrally, do they clearly specify amounts, prices, and delivery schedules; or are they more loosely written, specifying only maximum quantities that can be purchased, with agreements on amounts, prices, and delivery to be made later in decentralized locations?
- What is the key account's budget cycle? How does this impact its purchase decisions?
- Is the key account moving any of its purchases into B2B exchanges via the Internet? If so, for what product categories?

SHARING BUSINESS

In practice, corporations have very different procurement practices regarding numbers of suppliers. Traditionally, many purchasing departments sent RFPs (requests for proposals) to multiple suppliers, then share the business around to keep suppliers "honest" and their own options open. At the other extreme, some firms offer single source contracts, believing that sole sourcing provides greater access to supplier technical resources and reduces administrative costs. Other firms seek two or more sources, both for such benefits as security of supply, price competition, and increased design options, and because they believe technological developments may occur in one of several suppliers. These firms believe that only by spreading business around will they have superior access to the appropriate supplier if a breakthrough occurs.[47]

On a different dimension, some firms favor internal sourcing because it allows them to capture a greater percent of the value added. Others believe that internal groups, protected from the market, will deliver less value over the long run and affirmatively prefer outside suppliers.

Several questions should be asked concerning the account's policy regarding multiple suppliers:

- Does the key account pursue a policy of actively seeking many potential bids? Or does it prefer to select a limited number of suppliers with which it can develop close relationships? What criteria does it use for sharing business?
- Does the account have policies that prohibit sole suppliers? If the firm is currently sole supplier, what might cause the account to share its business with competitors?
- Does the account have policies regarding its dealing with supplier firms for which it would represent a large percent of their capacity?
- Does the key account follow a policy of working closely with one supplier to develop product specifications, then shop the specifications to seek the cheapest source of supply, regardless of the initial supplier's efforts?[48] Or does the account provide some reward for specification development in the form of guaranteed purchase volume?
- What is the key account's policy regarding internal sourcing? If the supplier firm puts in extensive development efforts, does it risk losing this business to an internal division?
- How dependent is the key account on the supplier firm? If supply were unexpectedly cut off, would this cause a significant problem for the key account? Or, could it easily secure its requirements from another supplier?

The Nature of the Purchase

One useful framework for evaluating purchase decisions classifies them into three broad categories—straight rebuy, modified rebuy, and new buy—based on the level of complexity. We describe each of these three types of purchase and suggest the sorts of action required of the key account manager.

Straight Rebuy. This type of purchase is also known as routinized response behavior. For such purchases the product need is well established. Features and benefits of the various alternatives have been rigorously evaluated and the account has purchased many times before. As a result, the account has well-developed purchase criteria. It is well informed about, and has well-formed attitudes toward, potential suppliers that may be important in allocating business.

Consequently, these purchases are fairly routine and are frequently made by mid- and low-level purchasing staff. Purchase criteria typically include such variables as price, credit terms, and delivery. The task for the key account manager is to demonstrate superiority of its overall offer versus competition by promoting the "net competitive advantage" and building the supplier-firm/key-account relationship through frequent "value-added" interaction.

Modified Rebuy. These purchases, also known as limited problem solving, represent greater uncertainty for the key account than straight rebuys. The product need is well established and purchase criteria are well developed. However, the set of purchase alternatives and some potential suppliers are less well known. Modified rebuy purchases are exemplified whenever a new material replaces the traditional choice—for example, substitution of plastics for metal. The key account typically chooses from among a variety of different types of product and from a set of better or less well-known suppliers.

Whenever a new product form is introduced, especially if the supplier is relatively unknown to the account, a full-scale evaluation of the new product (and supplier) is typically undertaken before any large scale purchases are made. The selling task for the key account manager is to make the key account comfortable with its new product (and possibly with the supplier) in the context of the account's purchase criteria, and to address specific concerns.

New Buy. Also known as extended problem solving, in new-buy purchases the key account generally has little knowledge of either the alternatives or potential suppliers. Purchase criteria are poorly developed and, in the extreme case, the account may not, initially at least, even recognize a product need. Great uncertainty surrounds the purchase which, if consummated, may change the account's operational and/or management systems, and affect several departments and many personnel. An excellent example is the decision to outsource important activities. For example, purchase of long-distance telephone service is probably best represented as a straight rebuy for many firms; however, the choice of supplier to run the firm's entire telecommunications operations is perhaps best characterized as a new buy.

Because many dimensions of the purchase decision are new to the key account, it may lack a procurement process. As a result, potential suppliers may advance their positions by helping the account decide how to buy.

EXAMPLE: In the mid-1990s, Morgan Stanley (MS) was successful in winning the lucrative contract to broker the sale of Hughes Aircraft from its trustees. Observers believed MS's success was due in large part to partner Robert Greenhill's presentation focusing on the problems of being a trustee and developing his vision of both the way in which they should make the decision and their goals and alternatives.

In new buys, the key account manager should endeavor to address the needs of the many different individuals that may be affected. Among the key influentials, he should encourage the enthusiastic advocates, attempt to neutralize the opponents, and persuade the fence sitters to the supplier firm's perspective.

INFORMATION SOURCES

Data demands for a full-blown key account analysis are significant, but numerous supplier firm, key account, and other information sources are available, some primary and some secondary. Regardless of source, data collection should not be just an annual chore conducted at planning time, but a continuous activity whereby knowledge is provided to, and received from, members of the key account team.

Supplier Firm. Data from previous account plans, internal memos, call reports, and the like provide valuable background data on the key account. In addition, team members secure data on a day-by-day basis while interacting with key account personnel. One potentially important information source, generally little used by key account managers, is the supplier firm's own procurement department. Procurement practices are changing markedly and managers may gain important insights into their key account's procurement behavior from their own procurement departments whose personnel may be facing similar challenges.

Key Account. In the normal course of business, key accounts publish a variety of material on themselves such as annual and quarterly reports, 10Ks, proxy statements, press releases and newsletters, internal company magazines, product and applications literature, promotional brochures, press kits, web sites, and speeches by senior executives. These may all provide valuable information, especially for understanding key account fundamentals.

Key account personnel can provide a host of insightful information on the account's plans, organizational functioning, roles and responsibilities, performance and so forth. Indeed, as we discussed, the key account may share its strategic plan with a valued supplier or, better still, it may invite the supplier's personnel into strategic planning meetings. Here, the key account manager may probe the customer's goals, objectives and emerging strategy, and help influence the direction the key account ultimately takes.

Notwithstanding the degree to which valuable data can be secured from senior management, the key account manager should not ignore lower levels in the organization. In particular, invaluable data may be obtained from those shop floor personnel that use the supplier firm's and/or competitor products on a day-by-day basis. Information gathering "by walking around" may produce data that does not typically filter upward to regular contacts in the key account. Finally, where appropriate, supplier firms or their key account managers may become key account customers. In this role, they may gain a deeper understanding of the key account's products and services, and learn first hand how it deals with its customers!

Other Sources. These include trade associations, industry reports, the business press, financial analysts reports, credit reports (for example, Dun and Bradstreet), directories such as Value Line, the Internet, various business-oriented computerized data bases such as Lexus/Nexus, industry experts, consultants, and other organizations facing similar data-gathering problems.

SUMMARY

Effective key account strategy will result only from a thorough situation analysis. The core element of such an analysis is understanding the key account. A comprehensive key account analysis commences with account fundamentals, information that frames the account and provides perspective for the key account manager. Then, the manager should focus on the key account's strategic reality, including the environmental imperatives it faces, its objectives and strategy in the face of these imperatives, its strengths, weaknesses and prior performance, and the key account manager's assessment of the likelihood that the account can implement the strategy and achieve its objectives.

Perhaps the most critical area of the key account analysis is identifying and addressing customer needs. Here, the manager must probe the key account to identify places where the supplier firm can add real value to the relationship. He should focus not only on areas related directly to its products and services but also on meta-level relationship needs. The manager must develop an understanding of the level of importance of the various potential values the supplier firm might offer, and the various tradeoffs from both supplier and key account perspectives. Finally, the key account manager must develop a detailed understanding of the key account's procurement process, including a good knowledge of those individuals involved in the buying process and their role relationships.

Completion of a full-blown key account analysis, and keeping it updated, represents a large amount of work. However, since the various elements of this analysis are critical to successful development of the supplier-firm/key-account relationship, the key account manager cannot afford to ignore them. The key account analysis is a fundamental cornerstone of the entire situation analysis upon which the manager develops the supplier firm's strategy. Anything less than a major effort places the supplier firm's success at the key account in jeopardy.

That said, for the firm contemplating installation of a key account planning system, the critical issue is not that it follow the specific analytic framework presented in this chapter, but rather that it develop some systematic and comprehensive method for both collecting and analyzing data on its key accounts. Those firms that develop both workable frameworks for key account analysis, and systems and procedures for keeping them updated as new information becomes available, will find themselves far ahead of those competitors that rely upon hit-and-miss practices for understanding their key accounts.

CHAPTER SIX

Key Account Planning

Analysis of Competition and the Supplier Firm, Planning Assumptions, and Opportunities and Threats

In this chapter we continue with the situation analysis by turning our attention first to the analysis of competition, then to analysis of the supplier firm. These analyses pave the way for a discussion of planning assumptions, and the identification of opportunities and threats for the supplier firm. In Chapter 7 we turn to key account strategy.

Thus, we switch direction in the situation analysis away from the key account (Chapter 5) to focus on the key account's suppliers—the supplier firm's competitors and the supplier firm itself. Regardless of how thoroughly a key account analysis is completed, the supplier firm will only secure, maintain, and increase business at the key account if it satisfies the account's needs better than its competitors and delivers superior value.

These efforts will be enhanced both by a solid understanding of major competitors at the account, and by being clear about the supplier firm's own competencies. Only then will the key account manager be able to project competitor actions and so preempt or otherwise neutralize them.

ANALYSIS OF COMPETITION

This section comprises two elements, competitive structure analysis, which identifies the supplier firm's key competitive challenges, and analysis of the supplier firm's major competitors. We should reinforce the fact that although these analyses must be completed by the account manager, a competitive analysis group should undertake much of the background effort. Such an arrangement has the dual benefit of securing economies of scale across multiple key accounts, and allowing the key account manager to focus on competitive issues idiosyncratic to his or her account.[1] (See Exercise 2 for a planning document to conduct an analysis of competition.)

Competitive Structure Analysis

Competitive structure analysis allows the key account manager to identify the supplier firm's major competitive challenges at the key account. If the account represents significant current business, competitors represent threats to that business. If the key account represents significant potential business, competitors represent barriers to successfully exploiting opportunities.

Competitive structure analysis was touched on briefly in the key account analysis (Chapter 5) where we were attempting to understand the competitive challenges faced by the key account. In this section, the analytic format is expanded to focus on competitive challenges to the supplier firm. These challenges are conveniently arrayed along two dimensions—direct versus indirect, and current versus potential, thus forming four types of competitors (Figure 6.1). In addition, we discuss supply-chain competition. Furthermore, in identifying competitors, the key account manager should take a global view of com-

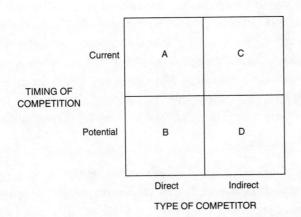

FIGURE 6.1: Competitive Structure Analysis

petition, rather than a narrow domestic perspective. Too many corporations have been surprised by the "sudden" entry of foreign competitors when a broader approach to competitor identification would have yielded significant early insight.

Current Direct Competitors (Cell A). These firms compete against the supplier firm with similar products using similar technologies. Typically, supplier firms know a lot about these competitors. Over time they observe their actions, results, successes and failures, and have a reasonably good idea of their strengths, weaknesses, likely future strategic moves, barriers to exit, and so forth. Indeed, supplier firm managers may have been employed by direct competitors, and vice versa. Notwithstanding their competitive positions, the supplier firm may enjoy close relationships with direct competitors, such as belonging to the same trade associations and competing according to "established rules of the game."[2]

Regardless, the supplier firm's assumptions about direct competitors may evaporate when an ownership change occurs, for example by acquisition, and the acquirer's purpose for acquisition is worked out through reformulated goals, strategies, and action programs of the acquiree. However, even though the acquired entity may enjoy greater access to resources, and represent a potentially more serious competitive threat to the supplier firm, cultural and other mismatches may cause this potential to be unrealized. In any event, pre-acquisition assumptions must be reexamined when competitor ownership changes. Divestiture may also change the competitive landscape when an established business, now freed from corporate strictures, is able to chart its own course.

Relatedly, a direct competitor may form a strategic alliance and similarly gain access to capital, skills, technology, production capacity, R&D capabilities, and/or other previously lacking resources. Once again assumptions must be reexamined but, as with acquisitions, although the new entity may represent a potentially tougher competitor, the harsh reality is that many strategic alliances are unsuccessful. Finally, the supplier firm should be aware of the potential for competitive exit; exit barriers change over time and the supplier may be able to help ease the transition!

Potential Direct Competitors (Cell B). This type of competition is similarly direct, but is potential rather than current. Perhaps these competitors are active in related markets but have yet to focus on markets represented by the key account. The most vivid recent examples are expansions by globalizing firms using strong positions in domestic markets to enter new geographic markets.

Although these competitive threats may be difficult to identify, it should be possible to develop an early warning system by understanding those actions that a new direct competitor would have to take prior to seeking key account business. At the very least, low-key approaches are typically made in advance of serious penetration efforts. The key account manager should understand the entry barriers faced by these competitors and the likely basis of their strategies. Watchfulness at the key account, supplemented by competent efforts in the competitive analysis group, should enable the supplier firm to keep abreast of these competitive developments.

Current Indirect Competitors (Cell C). Indirect competitors offer similar customer benefits to the supplier firm, but their products differ in form and possibly in the underlying product and/or process technology, for example, digital imaging for chemical-based film. Because of these differences, such competitors may prove to be a difficult challenge. Sometimes these firms' use of different products and technologies makes them difficult to identify as competitors. Regardless, the key account manager must identify their actions, understanding trends in their product forms (e.g., technology, costs, competitive structure), and secure good information.

Potential Indirect Competitors (Cell D). These competitive threats are the most difficult to identify. Such firms have little sales activity at the account and their products or technologies are dissimilar to those of the supplier firm. Their current action ranges from development efforts in the laboratory to products sold in other markets or to the key account's competitors. Once again, a good corporate competitive analysis group, aided by astute key account managers, should be able to monitor these forms of competition.

Supply-Chain Competition. In addition to these four competitive types, the key account itself may be an internal supplier of direct or indirectly competitive products, or may be considering backward integration to produce, in-house, products similar to those offered by the supplier firm. In this regard, the behavior exhibited by corporations varies dramatically and tends to shift over time.

On the one hand, some firms protect internal suppliers and seek to capture increased amounts of value-added by undertaking self-manufacture of specific parts or raw materials. At the other extreme, procurement staffs may source parts and raw materials from the least expensive source, even if this means a sister division may lose substantial business. Still other firms engage in self-manufacture but restrict the scope for a particular product by developing facilities that run at or close to capacity, purchasing in the slack when demand improves.[3]

Even if key account policy favors internal suppliers, substantial opportunities may still be available for an adept supplier firm. All too frequently, the internal supplying entity treats its sister division as the captive customer it is by exhibiting all the negative behaviors of a monopolist. In such cases, a disconnect often exists between company policy and the desires of executives in operating units for multiple sources of supply. The enterprising key account manager can exploit these disconnects to the supplier firm's benefit.

Relatedly, the supplier firm's own suppliers may currently sell directly competitive products to the key account, or be contemplating forward integration to become direct competitors.

The key account manager should pay close attention to both current and potential supply-chain competition. Depending on the situation, it may represent a substantial opportunity for increased volume, or a threat to current business.

We have seen that competition for business at the key account may come from many different sources. Clearly, resource limitations prohibit a thorough analysis from being conducted on all competitors. Regardless, such an analysis must be conducted on the most serious challenges to the supplier firms' current and potential business. Competitor identification is the process by which the most serious current and potential challenges are selected for concentration of analytic efforts.

Analysis of Specific Competitors

Having identified the most serious competitive threats, the key account manager must analyze individual competitors. The appropriate questions can be loosely organized around competitor position at the key account, competitor performance and strategy, and projecting competitor actions.

COMPETITOR POSITION AT THE KEY ACCOUNT

We offer three approaches to assessing the competitor's position at the key account. First is a set of general questions about the competitor's capabilities and weaknesses at the key account. Second, we introduce value chain analysis, and third, we present the competitor analysis matrix.

Capabilities and Weaknesses. The supplier firm should answer the following questions:

- What major competitor strengths can be brought to bear against us at the key account—such as product line breadth, excess capacity, applications engineering, and/or customer service operations?
- What are the competitor's vulnerabilities at the key account? For example, has it sufficient capacity to serve key account needs?
- What are its operating procedures? How good a job does the competitor do in product quality, service quality, new product development, delivery, payment terms, pricing, and so forth?
- How does the competitor organize to address the key account? Who are the key players at the competitor? What do we know about their decision-making styles and the personal relationships they have with key account personnel?
- What is the competitor's overall relationship at the key account? Upon what factors is this assessment based—long-term high quality service, long-standing personal relationships, brand name, and/or ability to react quickly to problem situations?

Two more formal analytic methods—value chain analysis and the competitor analysis matrix—can build on the foregoing to provide powerful insight about competitors.

Value Chain Analysis. Answers to the sorts of questions noted above can be formalized into a value chain analysis for identifying those areas where the competitor adds value and those where it incurs costs. This analysis identifies various elements of the resource conversion process (value chain), such as technology, product design, raw materials, operations, marketing, physical distribution, and customer service and compares the competitor to the supplier firm. Specifically, several questions should be asked.[4]

Compared to the supplier firm:

- Where does the competitor have a cost advantage?
- Where does the competitor have a cost disadvantage?
- Where does the competitor have a value advantage?
- Where does the competitor have a value disadvantage?

Answers to these questions lead directly to a more action-oriented question:

- What options does the competitor have to reduce costs and increase value to be better positioned at the key account?

Competitor Analysis Matrix. In this five-step analysis, the supplier firm is compared directly with its chief competitors. First the key account manager should ask three critical questions:

- Step 1: Factor Identification. What business strengths (skills, resources, capabilities, and relationships) would any firm have to possess to become the favored supplier at the key account?
- Step 2: Factor Weighing. What importance weights do you assign for each business strength identified in step 1, such the total sums to 100?
- Step 3: Competitor Firm Ratings. How do the several competitors at the key account (supplier firm and major competitors) rate on possession of each business strength, where 1 = low possession and 10 = high possession?

Of course, the best judges to make each of these three types of assessment are critical personnel at the key account. Their responses may prove to be highly insightful and lead directly to specific strategies and action programs to improve the supplier firm's position at the account. In addition, significant insight into the supplier's competitive position may be gained from the interaction of team members working through the analysis.

Two steps remain to complete the analysis:

- Step 4: Develop Factor Scores. Multiply the entries in Figure 6.2 column 2 by the corresponding entries in column 3 to produce the figures in column 4, for the supplier firm and its competitors.
- Step 5: Develop the Business Strengths Scores. Sum the figures in each column 4.

The final figure secured from Step 5 should fall between 100 and 1000.

In the illustration in Figure 6.2, although the supplier firm secures the highest overall score, significant dangers are present. For example, the supplier firm rates lowest on quality of products and largely succeeds by offering low prices; clearly, it is vulnerable to a competitor that competes on price. However, effort spent on upgrading product quality, improved after-sales service, and greater flexibility on credit terms represent opportunities to improve position at the account. Equally, this analysis suggests actions that competitor firms may take.[5]

COMPETITOR PERFORMANCE AND STRATEGY

The competitor's history at the key account may provide telling clues as to its likely future behavior. To the extent that the competitor has previously taken actions that were successful, it is likely to take similar actions in the future. Equally, it is perhaps less likely to make future moves similar to those that previously failed. The key account manager should answer such questions as:

- How much key account business does this competitor do? What is the competitor's share of business at the account? What are the trends? Is it profitable business for the competitor?
- Does the competitor have any existing contracts with the key account? When are these up for rebid/renewal?

As a starting point for projecting likely competitor strategies and resource allocations, the key account manager should attempt to unearth the competitor's objectives at the key account. In addition:

- What strategies
  - has the competitor employed in the past?
  - is the competitor employing now?
  - could the competitor employ in the future?
- What action programs is the competitor currently conducting at the key account?

The danger in not developing this level of competitor understanding is illustrated by an example from the advertising industry.

FIGURE 6.2: Illustration of the Competitive Analysis Matrix

1) Business Strengths Criteria — What business strengths must any supplier possess to be successful at this key account?	2) Importance Weights for Business Strengths Criteria	Supplier Firm Rating		Competitor A Rating		Competitor B Rating	
		3) Supplier Firm	4) Col. 2 × Col. 3	3) Competitor A	4) Col. 2 × Col. 3	3) Competitor B	4) Col. 2 × Col. 3
Quality of products	15	5	75	6	90	7	105
After-sales service	5	7	35	5	25	6	30
Prices	15	9	135	7	105	5	75
Flexibility on credit terms	5	6	30	10	50	8	40
Strength of brand name	10	8	80	5	50	7	70
Applications engineering support	10	9	90	7	70	6	60
Delivery reputation	20	10	200	9	180	9	180
Close relationships with senior executives	20	7	140	7	140	5	100
Total	100		785		710		660

EXAMPLE: Major advertising agency Leo Burnett lost several major clients (e.g., Miller Lite, United Airlines) to a small regional agency, Fallon McElligott. Interviewed by *Fortune,* Burnett's CEO said of Fallon McElligott, *"I can't name* Fallon's clients, except United and Miller. Whatever Fallon is doing right, *I have no idea* how their organization works or how they do things."[6] (Emphasis added.)

Answers to the sets of questions described here should lead to a summary conclusion regarding the true nature of the competitive challenge at the account, and issues that the supplier firm should be most concerned about.

PROJECTING COMPETITOR ACTIONS

The foregoing identification and analysis of major competitors at the key account puts the account manager in a good position to project future competitor strategic moves. These projections should act as an important input into the supplier firm's own strategy making. The analysis also allows the key account manager to assess long-run competitor commitment to the account: Will it seek business with the key account over the long run and/or will it withdraw if the going gets tough? Specific questions for which the key account manager should seek answers include:

- What will the competitor do to reduce its own costs and better position itself for price reductions at the key account?
- What will the competitor do to increase the value it offers the key account to better position itself?
- What objectives will the competitor set at the key account?
- What strategies will the competitor employ at the key account?
- What specific action programs is the competitor likely to implement?
- What other specific resource allocations will the competitor make at the key account?

and, when the key account manager is formulating his own strategy and designing his own action programs:

- How will the competitor view our proposed initiatives?
- How is the competitor likely to respond to these initiatives?

INFORMATION SOURCES FOR COMPETITOR ANALYSIS

Clearly, a thorough competitor analysis requires a significant amount of data. However, since business organizations tend to be very leaky, rarely is an inability to access required data the cause of failure in competitor information gathering. Rather, failure typically results from lack of a plan (comprising objectives, strategy, action programs, and organization) to secure the required data. These data may be partitioned into two types: generalized data about individual competitors and information specific to the key account. This partitioning should drive the information gathering function, which should be continuous.

Generalized Data. As we noted previously, the key focus here is to avoid a waste of resources by having several account managers spending time collecting essentially similar data. In the most common method, a centralized competitive intelligence group (possibly located in the marketing department) collects information about competitors on an ongoing basis and feeds this information to those in the organization who need it, including key account managers. In practice, many forms of this type of system can be found ranging from low commitment methods involving passive acceptance, sorting, and dispatch of data, to more proactive resource intensive in-depth analyses of individual competitors.

Unfortunately, many corporations spend little effort on competitive intelligence. In such circumstances a "shadow system" may be worthwhile. In this system, the key account director might assign individual key account managers to "shadow" individual competitors. The key account managers develop their own information sources for their competitor responsibilities and periodically brief their peers on the firms they are "shadowing."

Specific Data. Notwithstanding the value of "generalized" systems, much information regarding competitor activities at the key account must, of necessity, come from the key account. For these data, it is the key account manager's role to develop a competitive information gathering agenda, then assign responsibilities to members of the key account team for collecting, monitoring, and delivering information on competitor activities.

ANALYSIS OF THE SUPPLIER FIRM

The purpose of this analysis is to assess the supplier firm's ability to increase (secure) business at the key account, given its understanding of the key account and the competitive challenges. The supplier firm analysis completes the analytic trilogy—analysis of the key account, analysis of competition, and analysis of the supplier firm. With these three analyses in hand, the key account manager can develop a set of planning assumptions, and identify the opportunities and threats for the supplier firm.

The supplier firm analysis comprises four major elements—historical performance, relationship assessment, assessment of firm behavior, and resource availability. (Of course, some elements of the firm analysis are also contained in the analysis of competition.) (See Exercise 3 for a planning document to conduct an analysis of the supplier firm.)

Historical Performance

The key account manager should secure considerable data regarding the supplier firm's performance at the key account, both in terms of its own unit sales and revenues, and profitability. It should also be clear how this performance compares to competition.

SALES AND PROFIT PERFORMANCE

As the basis for understanding the supplier firm's position at the key account, the key account manager should be very clear about its levels and trends in sales (units and revenues). This information should be secured from the order entry/sales information system whose raw data should be updated on a continuous basis. These data should be collected and coded in disaggregated form for in-depth trend analyses of revenue sources.

Breakdowns that should be analyzed include product and product line, key account business unit, delivery location, application, geography (e.g., international, domestic regions), and supplier firm sales regions (and/or territories). Some data sequences, for example, by specific end-use application may require insight from key account personnel.

These data should be compared both with prior years' performance and with the supplier firm's objectives at the key account. Unfortunately, in many companies this information is not readily available because of limitations in internal accounting systems.

> **EXAMPLE:** The CEO of Plane Inc.*, one of the United States' major information systems companies, asked the relevant direct report, "How much business do we do annually with Sycamore* around the world?" Sycamore* was one of the firm's five biggest accounts. The answer, "Give me a couple of days and I'll get back to you!"

We do not suggest that this information is necessarily easy to secure. Indeed, if much of the supplier firm's sales volume reaches the key account through distributors, unless the supplier has good agreements with distributors on sharing information, it may be extremely difficult to track. Furthermore, corporations often conduct business under different names, making it very difficult to track the corporate end user. For example, prior to its merger with Lockheed, Martin Marietta used over fifty different company names in the United States.

Notwithstanding these problems, good unit and revenue information is a prerequisite for developing profitability data, and the key account manager should have a good understanding of the financial implications of the supplier firm's business at the key account. She should have ready access to prices for all purchased products, individual product contribution margins, mean contribution margin of all products purchased, and gross contribution. She should know the net margin for the key account, as this figure should not be the result of some arbitrarily allocated overhead subtracted from gross contribution, but a realistic number secured from an activity-based costing system (ABC).

> **EXAMPLE:** Boise Cascade Office Products (BCOP), a distributor for Boise Cascade Corp., employed ABC methods to determine key account profitability. BCOP identified seventy-eight processes such as bin order pulling, bulk order pulling, order entry, and collections used in conducting its business. These processes were costed-out at some forty BCOP distribution centers and each of the seventy-eight processes was standardized on the most cost-efficient method. Key account profitability is determined by rolling up the account's gross margin at all relevant BCOP locations for that account and subtracting the costs to serve.[7]

EXAMPLE: Historically, American Electric Power (AEP) executives were often uncertain how to justify significant expenditures for key accounts. Introduction of a customer profitability measurement system has had numerous benefits: enhanced quality of key account planning, permitted financial evaluations of account relationships and individual initiatives, and increased individual accountability. The system has demonstrated to company personnel the short- and long-term profitability of individual account relationships, and justified the marketing function in an organization more used to regulation than competition.[8]

Unfortunately, these sorts of benefits are not realized in many organizations because such profit-oriented information cannot be secured. On the one hand, internal accounting systems are often limited; on the other hand, accurate cost information by customer is simply not available. See Appendix 6.1 for a worked-out example of key account profitability analysis using ABC methods.

PERFORMANCE VERSUS COMPETITION

In addition to the supplier firm's unit, revenue, and profitability data, the key account manager should have a clear idea about how the firm stacks up against competition. For each of the major product groups that it supplies to the key account, two questions should be answered:

- What are our various market shares at the key account?
- What are the trends in the supplier firm's market share(s) versus competitors?

These data allow the key account manager to size up the supplier firm's opportunities and to assess the threats to current business. The manager should also be clear about the dynamics of the revenue base. In particular, his analyses should highlight:

- What major sales has the supplier firm secured at the account in the past two to three years?
- Who were the competitors and why was the firm able to defeat them?
- What major sales has the firm lost to competition at the account in the past two to three years?
- Why did the supplier firm lose this business?

EXAMPLE: When laboratory supplier Richard Allan Scientific lost a piece of business, it conducted a side-by-side comparison with the competitor, carefully tracking accuracy and performance. It won back the client and now uses "side-by-side" as a marketing approach to better quantify the value offered to customers.[9]

In addition to the questions cited above, answers to the following questions can help the key account manager compare her firm's performance to that of the competition:

- What is the status of current contracts?
- What key account purchases are in progress?
- How is the firm positioned versus its competitors?
- To the extent that supplier firm has any partnership, joint venture, or strategic alliance relationships with the key account: How have they performed? What is the status of these relationships?

Relationship Assessment

In addition to "hard" performance measures, the key account manager should assess the current strength of the supplier-firm/key-account relationship, including the security of current business and the likelihood of achieving new business. All things equal, a healthy relationship should allow the supplier firm to retain current business and grow new business. In contrast, an unhealthy relationship will lead to loss of business.

Perhaps the most common approach to assessing the supplier-firm/key-account relationship is measurement of customer satisfaction.[10] Increasingly, suppliers with key account programs are putting these measurement systems in place. (We discuss customer satisfaction measurement in more detail in Chapter 8.) Although these systems have great merit, it is important to recognize that when supplier firms lose business, typically the key account is not unsatisfied with the supplier firm! The conceptual explanation is shown in Figure 6.3.

The figure depicts the change from uncompetitive (AA') to competitive (BB') markets.[11] Along the AA' line, customer loyalty rises quickly even though customer satisfaction remains low; the absence of alternatives prohibits customers from readily switching suppliers. As competition increases (represented by the arrow) to curve BB', a different situation is depicted. At low customer satisfac-

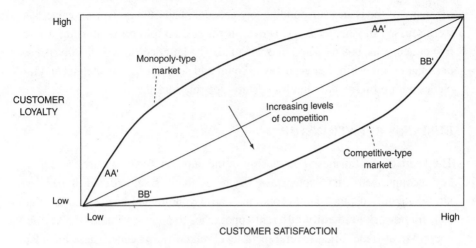

FIGURE 6.3: A Customer Satisfaction/Loyalty Chart

tion there is little customer loyalty; however, when satisfaction rises loyalty still remains low. The reason: customers have many alternatives and will switch from "good" suppliers if a better deal is offered. Nonetheless, very high levels of satisfaction pay off in high loyalty.

Furthermore, strong relationships have been documented between level of customer satisfaction and other important measures. Thus, the data in Figure 6.4 demonstrate that "totally satisfied" customers outperform "somewhat satisfied" customers on first mentions (top-of-mind recall), recommendations, and repurchases. These results translate into significant revenue relationships. "Totally satisfied" customers spend more than "somewhat satisfied" customers.

The important issue for the key account manager to address: What is driving the key account's level of satisfaction with the supplier firm? The supplier-firm/key-account relationship is a complex multidimensional construct involv-

FIGURE 6.4: Relationships to Customer Satisfaction

Measure	Totally Satisfied	Somewhat Satisfied	Ratio
First mention	58%	13%	4×
Recommendation	62%	17%	3.5×
Repurchase	45%	22%	2×
Revenue	$1.00	38 cents	2.6×

(Based on 37,000 data points from respondents to key account customer satisfaction surveys conducted by Development II, Inc., Woodbury, Connecticut.)

ing many of the issues surrounding key account needs and delivering value that we discussed in Chapter 5.[12] However, it may be simplified by parsing it into two dimensions, business and interpersonal. The latter consists of the myriad of personal relationships between key account and supplier firm personnel and includes both professional- and friendship-type relationships

BUSINESS RELATIONSHIPS

The heart of the business relationship is the supplier firm's ability to address key account needs. In Chapter 5, we discussed these in some detail. In particular, we identified functional, economic, and psychological needs, and used an ROI framework to identify different approaches to adding value to the key account. We also identified several meta-level relationship needs. These included accessibility, responsiveness, keeping promises, understanding critical customer issues, communications, ease of doing business with, and competence. All things equal, the greater the value delivered to the key account to satisfy the needs, the greater key account satisfaction and the stronger the supplier-firm/key-account business relationship.

Furthermore, we identified three levels of depth of key account need and customer value—meeting or exceeding key account expectations, developing solutions to existing problems, and solving new and/or unrecognized problems. In general, each successive level is more difficult to accomplish. As a result, the supplier-firm/key-account relationship is likely to be stronger, the greater the average depth of key account need satisfied and customer value delivered.[13]

To address these areas, the key account manager may draw up a chart such as that shown in Figure 6.5. Here, supplier firm performance is measured against the key account's most important business issues. The better the supplier firm's performance in addressing these issues, the stronger will be the interorganizational business relationship.

INTERPERSONAL RELATIONSHIPS

Over and above the interorganizational business relationship, the key account manager must assess the quality of the interpersonal relationships among supplier firm and key account personnel. Certainly, exemplary performance on business relationship dimensions may be counteracted by poor interpersonal relationships.

A useful way to analyze the sum quality of the myriad of interorganizational

FIGURE 6.5: Illustration of Supplier Firm Performance versus Important Key Account Issues

Key Account Issue	Supplier Firm Participation	Supplier Firm's Impact
Cost of procurement	In consultation	None yet
Penetrating X market	End-use customer advertising	Market share increased by 3 points since advertising commenced
Inventory control system in shambles	Project team assisting customer	None yet
Unacceptable product quality in key raw material	Designing our own quality improvement process	None yet
Sales force expertise in supplier firm	Continual training	55% of salespeople now certified
Haphazard receipt of invoices from supplier firm	Working out new procedures with our accounting department	None yet

interpersonal relationships is to construct an interpersonal relationship chart (Figure 6.6). The entries under key account personnel are those believed to play an important role in the purchase decision process (see Chapter 5). In each case, these individuals are matched with supplier firm personnel and the nature of the relationship identified. Note that both professional- and friendship-type relationships are included in the table. After all, friendship relationships may be extremely powerful in securing business. Not only may such emotional commitments create bonds that are difficult to break, the trust they engender may help secure business when objective supplier selection criteria are difficult to identify.[14]

EXAMPLE: Jack Grubman is the lead telecom analyst for Salomon Smith Barney. His friendship with WorldCom chairman Bernard C. Ebbers helped his firm secure the role of lead investment banker in the $35 billion World-Com-MCI merger.[15]

This analysis is even more powerful if a companion table can be developed for the supplier's major competitors at the key account, and a differential diagnosis performed for each of the important key account personnel.

FIGURE 6.6: Illustration of an Interpersonal Relationship Chart

Key Account Personnel (Name, Organizational Position)	Supplier Firm Personnel (Name, Organizational Position)	Nature of the Relationship
Tony Jackson, CEO	Mike Smith, Vice-Chairman	Acquainted – annual golf game
Tony Jackson, CEO	Alasdair MacLean, Head R&D Executive Partner	Close friendship, college room mates, play tennis monthly
Anthony Benton, COO	David Lankester, Key Account Manager	Good professional relationship, working on projects
Peter Wilson, Head of Procurement	David Lankester, Key Account Manager	Satisfactory professional relationship, but increasing tension due to reduction in Wilson's decision-making authority
Winston Harris, Procurement Officer in Dallas	Gay Crossman, Local Sales Representative	Good professional relationship
Edward Windsor, Research Scientist	Madge Wallace, Research Scientist	Close relationship in joint research project—developing into friendship
George Hanover, Inventory Manager	Ellen Reed, Logistics Manager	Difficult working relationship becoming negative personal relationship
William Orange, Quality Manager	No supplier firm contact appointed	None, but must be addressed

CONSIDERING THE ENTIRE SUPPLIER-FIRM/ KEY-ACCOUNT RELATIONSHIP

A useful broad-based approach to integrating the firm's business and interpersonal relationships is provided by a business relationship versus interpersonal relationship-quality matrix (Figure 6.7).[16] The entries relate to the several different areas in which the supplier firm and key account interface. This analysis is competitively focused and paves the way for the development of alternative courses of action by examining the entries in each matrix cell.

In particular, the matrix suggests that if the supplier firm performs better than or equal to competition on both business and interpersonal relationships (cell A), all things equal, it should continue the previous sets of action that seem to have been most successful. Better than or equal business relationships but worse interpersonal relationships (cell C) suggests that the firm is vulnerable to a competitor that improves its business performance. On the other hand, if in-

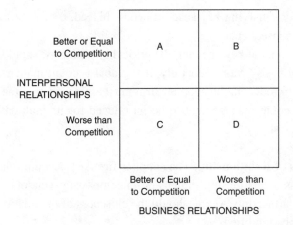

FIGURE 6.7: Business Relationships versus Interpersonal Relationships Matrix

terpersonal relationships are better than or equal, but business relationships are worse (cell B), the firm should develop an agenda to improve its business performance. If the supplier firm finds itself in cell D, worse than competition on both business and interpersonal relationships, it clearly has a lot of work to do.

CHANGE IN RELATIONSHIP STATUS

A specific issue that should be examined periodically is whether the time is right for a change in the status of the supplier-firm/key-account relationship. We noted in Chapter 2 that, at a broad level, key account relationships can vary on several important dimensions—including organizational level, degree of closeness of relationship, and adherence to a tier system.

Organizational level. An individual business unit at a supplier firm may have multiple key account relationships with a customer's several business units. Equally, various business units of the supplier firm may each have independent relationships with a single key account business. In either of these cases, a critical issue is whether or not to augment (or replace) these multiple business level relationships with a higher level key account relationship. A special case concerns the geographic dimension of key accounts.

Many supplier firms have "national" account programs in which key accounts are managed at the country level. However, in the face of increased globalization and developing global structures in their key accounts, such interfaces may be inadequate for satisfying key account needs. Indeed, they may lead to unintended negative consequences.

For a particular individual key account, the critical questions is: should it be managed on a global basis? More generally, if a global account management system has not been introduced, the supplier firm must assess whether the time is right for global account management to be introduced for its multinational key accounts.

Degree of Closeness of Relationship. The supplier-firm/key-account relationship may vary across a relationship dimension encompassing vendor, value-added supplier, and partnership. Again, should the closeness of the relationship with the key account be modified?

Tier System or Not? The supplier firm may operate a system in which individual key accounts are assigned to specific tiers based on previously formulated criteria. Accounts in one tier are treated differently from those in another as regards access to resources and other benefits. Depending on the results of the relationship assessment, an individual key account may be ready for "promotion" to a higher tier (more resources) or for "relegation" to a lower tier (fewer resources) or displacement from the key account program altogether.

Assessment of Firm Behavior

The key account management process does not occur in a vacuum. Rather, key account managers operate in an environment in which executives make a variety of strategic and organizational decisions—at the corporate level, in the various business units, and in related functional areas. Strategic decisions include major resource shifts such as acquisitions, divestitures, joint ventures, R&D initiatives, new product introductions, increased internationalization, and new market entry.[17] Organizational decisions comprise geographic location, the line organization, reporting responsibilities, information systems, compensation systems, and so forth.

As one element in the supplier firm analysis, the key account manager should assess his firm's strategic and organizational decisions, and derive implications for the supplier-firm/key-account relationship. Of course, this analysis should be conducted in real time during the operating cycle and appropriate actions taken. Nonetheless, in the key account planning process, the key account manager should formally review critical actions that have occurred since the previous planning cycle.

However, it is not sufficient merely to analyze past firm behavior. The key account plan must be developed in the context of the supplier firm's current and future actions. For many firms, key account plans are one element in a planning process that may include a corporate plan, several business-unit plans, and a series of related functional plans—for example, marketing, operations, and human resources. Furthermore, whereas many corporate plans comprise a set of individual business plans plus some degree of corporate value-added, if the key account is a customer of several business units, the key account plan must be matrixed with those business unit plans.

The significance for the key account manager is that she must develop a good understanding of the corporate, business unit, and related functional plans, especially the marketing plans. Of course, if these plans are developed simultaneously with the key account plan, the key account manager must take measures to stay abreast of developing thinking at corporate level and in the business units. Conversely, as the key account plan is developed, important insight should be provided for the developing business unit and corporate plans.

If key account management is practiced at the business unit level, the key account manager must be concerned about the relationships of sister business units with the key account. It may be possible to positively leverage these relationships in dealing with the account. Alternatively, less than stellar performance by a sister division may negatively impact the key account manager's relationship. In any event, the key account manager should explore the nature of these other key account relationships so as to access their impact on his key account relationship.

Resource Availability

The supplier firm secures business at the key account through the allocation of various types of resources. The key account manager must develop a solid assessment of the supplier firm's ability to meet key account requirements, both absolutely and compared to critical competitive challenges. Understanding relevant business-unit and component functional plans may be very helpful in this process. The key account manager should attempt to complete the critical-for-success/supplier-firm-competence matrix for relevant resources (Figure 6.8).

Different sorts of action are suggested by different positions in the matrix:

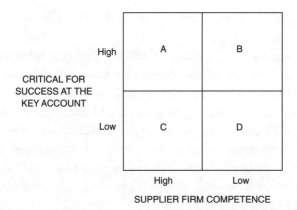

FIGURE 6.8: Critical-for-Success/Supplier-Firm-Competence Matrix

Critical for success at the key account-high, current competence-high (cell A). This cell represents the supplier firm's core competence; the key account manager should ensure that it continues to excel on these dimensions.

Critical for success at the key account-high, current competence-low (cell B). This cell identifies critical dimensions for the key account manager to push for improvement and greater resource allocation by the supplier firm.

Critical for success at the key account-low, current competence-high (cell C). This cell suggests inadequate resource distribution and a focus on areas that are not important from the key account's perspective. The relevant resources might be better redeployed elsewhere.

Critical for success at the key account-low, current competence-low (cell D). This cell comprises a series of irritants. Although items in this cell are not critical for success at the key account at the present time, at a minimum should be closely monitored by the key account manager so that their importance to the key account does not grow unheeded.

More specifically, the sorts of questions the key account manager should address include:

- How do the supplier firm's capabilities and limitations relate to key account needs? What is the supplier firm's most critical weakness that could limit its ability to maintain/increase business with the key account?
- Is the allocation of required resources to the key account consistent with the supplier firm's overall marketing strategy?

- What action programs has the supplier firm planned for this key account in the past? Were they fully implemented? What results were achieved?
- Does the supplier firm possess the production capacity to satisfy key account requirements? Where are the bottlenecks?
- What new supplier firm products can impact its business at the key account? Are any supplier firm system changes such as product delivery and customer service likely to impact the key account?

This section completes the analytic portion of the situation analysis for the key account. Analysis of the key account, analysis of competition, and analysis of the supplier firm have paved the way for identification of critical planning assumptions, and an assessment of opportunities and threats for the supplier firm at the key account. These opportunities and threats in turn set the direction for the key account strategy, which we discuss in Chapter 7.

PLANNING ASSUMPTIONS

Planning assumptions are predictions about the future that flow from the situation analysis. They represent a key synthesis of critical issues that form the building blocks upon which the entire key account strategy is based. In particular, planning assumptions are concerned with future conditions or events over which the key account manager and her team have no control. The occurrence or nonoccurrence of these conditions or events could have a significant effect upon the supplier firm's performance at the key account.

Planning assumptions may concern any of the three analytic areas upon which the situation analysis is based—the key account, competitors, or the supplier firm. For example:

Key Account Assumptions
- The key account will increase its market share in X market from 25% to 35% during the next two years.
- Critical personnel with whom we have good relationships will remain in their current positions for at least the next two years.
- The key account will commence a major strategic sourcing initiative within the next eighteen months.

Competitor Assumptions
- The major competitor's key account manager will retire by the end of the first quarter next year.
- None of the three major competitors will be able to reach our product quality levels for at least one year.
- The major competitor will not increase the authority of its key account group.

Supplier Firm Assumptions
- Our new technology will be available by the end of the second quarter next year.
- The planned merger with firm Y will finally occur and provide us access to an integrated order/delivery system that surpasses competition.

(See Exercise 4 for a planning document for identifying Key Account Planning Assumptions.)

OPPORTUNITIES AND THREATS

Opportunities and threats are the basis for formulating the key account strategy for, in general, strategy is designed to exploit opportunities and repel threats. In our lexicon, opportunities refer to potential business that might be gained; threats refer to current business that could be lost.

Sources of revenues at a key account can usefully be identified in terms of product, application, and organizational locus.[18] For analytic purposes, it is useful to distinguish between current and potential business. Current business is earned from the supplier firm's current products sold to the key account for use in current applications at current organization units. For potential new business, one or more of the products, applications, and organization units is new.

The full set of opportunities and threats is represented by means of an eight-cell matrix that maps products, applications, and organization units as either existing or new (Figure 6.9). Current business is captured in Cell 1; the remaining seven cells capture different types of potential new business. Revenues in the next operating period are secured by protecting current business from competitors, expanding current business, and/or securing new business.

PRODUCTS

ORGANIZATIONAL UNIT	Existing		New	
	Existing	New	Existing	New
APPLICATION Existing	1	2	3	4
New	5	6	7	8

FIGURE 6.9: Identification of Opportunities and Threats

Protecting and Expanding Current Business

The possibilities for protecting and expanding current business are reserved for Cell 1 in Figure 6.9: Existing Products/Existing Applications/Existing Organization Units. Two major external factors influence the extent to which the supplier firm secures current business in the next operating period—trends in key account requirements and competitor activity.

- *Trends in key account requirements.* Key account requirements are ultimately related to conditions in its target markets. These conditions are affected by the underlying demand for the key account's products, perhaps related to efforts by the key account and its competitors in targeted markets, and by the key account's success versus competitors in those markets. As a result of these conditions, the derived demand for products sold by the supplier firm to the key account may increase, be stable, or decline.
- *Competitive threat at the key account.* The anticipated level of competition for the supplier firm's current products used in the key account's current applications in current organization units may vary from weak through moderate to strong.

Insight into the opportunities and threats faced by the supplier firm for current business is gained from a business-trend/competitive-strength matrix (Figure 6.10). This matrix visually comprises solid circles contained in open circles:

- The horizontal axis represents the trend in demand for the products of the supplier firm and its competitors, for a particular application, in a particular organizational unit.
- The vertical axis represents the key account manager's assessment of the supplier firm's competitive strength at the key account.
- Each open circle represents the key account's purchases (larger circles imply greater purchases) of a particular product type, for a particular application, at a particular organization unit (PAO).
- Each solid entry represents the supplier firm's PAO sales.
- The fraction of the open circle filled by the solid entry represents the supplier firm's market share.
- The net difference between the open and solid circles represents sales by competitors.
- Independent solid circles imply that the supplier firm is securing all of the key account's PAO business.

Addressing Threats to Current Business. The supplier firm's current business is represented by the solid circles in Figure 6.10.[19] Since the matrix provides in-

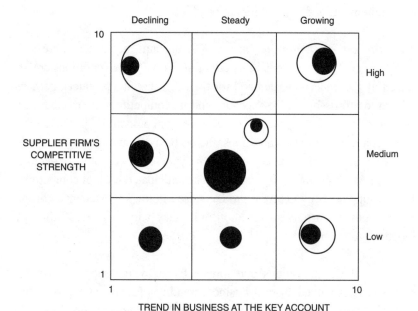

FIGURE 6.10: Current Business: Opportunities and Threats Matrix

formation regarding current sales, likely future trends in demand, and competitive strength, it can be very helpful in deciding which threats to address, and the level of resources that should be allocated to each.

Expanding Current Business. The supplier firm can expand current business in two ways. First, it can hold its share position in PAOs whose sales are growing (represented by the horizontal dimension). Second, it can take sales from competitors (represented by the differences between open and solid circles).

Securing New Business

New business is defined such that one or more of the following is new—the supplier firm's products or the key account's application or the organization unit. Of course, although business may be new to the supplier firm, the key account may currently be served by either a direct or indirect competitor. New business options are represented by the following cells in Figure 6.11:

- *Existing Product/Existing Application/New Organization Unit (Cell 2).* The opportunity is to expand the product/application use within the key account. Sales to companies often occur in a sequential fashion. The solution to an application problem in one organizational subunit leads to sales in another organizational subunit facing a similar application problem.
- *Existing Product/New Application/Existing and New Organization Units (Cells 5 and 6).* In solving one application problem for the key account, the supplier firm becomes aware of a different application problem it can solve. The opportunity is to find new applications for existing products both in organization units currently purchasing the product and others with which it is currently not doing business.
- *New Product/Existing Application/Existing and New Organization Unit (Cells 3 and 4).* The task for Cell 3 entries is to replace a current product as a way to strengthen position at the key account.[20] Cell 4 entries represent a similar application in another organization unit for which the supplier firm's current products are less than fully satisfactory.
- *New Product/New Application/Existing and New Organization Unit (Cells 7 and 8).* The opportunity is to expand business at the key account by of-

fering new products for new applications in either currently served or new organization units.

The foregoing set of options identifies the extent of opportunities for new sales revenues at the key account and the extent of competitive threats for current business.[21] The key account manager must decide which opportunities and threats to address, and which to eschew.

As an aid in making these decisions, the key account manager should prepare a table summarizing revenue potential and probability of success in the next operating period, based on an "average" level of effort. Together, these data produce the "expected value" of business at the key account (Figure 6.11). This information is a valuable diagnostic for investigating the value of assigning different levels of resources to the various opportunities and threats at the key account. As the key account manager moves towards strategy formulation, he assigns a priority to each of the threats and opportunities at the key account.

A useful addendum to this analysis is to draw on the *buying analysis* (Chapter 5) to identify the locus of responsibility for the purchase decision for each identified opportunity and threat.

The analysis presented in this section serves as an excellent input for strategy formulation. In addition, it is a useful device for assuring top management that priorities decided at the key account level are consistent with a broader set of priorities for the supplier firm as a whole. (See Exercise 5 for a planning document to assist in identification of Opportunities and Threats.)

SUMMARY

A solid key account strategy must exploit opportunities for the supplier firm and repel competitive threats at the key account. However, before a key account strategy can be put in place, the key account manager must develop a very real sense of the variety of options that might be available and for which resources could be allocated. To reach this stage, she must assemble a variety of analyses. Most critical are an analysis of the key account (Chapter 5) and analyses of both competitors at the key account and the supplier firm. These analyses lead in turn to a set of planning assumptions on which the key account strategy will be based (Chapter 6).

FIGURE 6.11: Illustration of Identification of Key Account Potential

	Actual Revenues 200X	Potential Revenues 200X + 1	Success Probability	Expected Value of Revenues 200X + 1	Supplier Firm Priority[a]
Current business (cell 1): Continuation	$15.5 million	$13.3 million	0.9	$11.97	10
less					
Current business: Potential loss	—	($1.5 million)	0.5	($0.75)	9
plus					
Current business: Potential expansion	—	$4.5 million	0.8	$3.60	9
New business (cell 2): Existing products/existing applications/new organization units	—	$2.3 million	0.3	$0.69	2
New business (cells 5, 6): Existing products/new applications/existing and new organization units	—	$1.2 million	0.2	$0.24	5
New business (cells 3, 4): New products/existing applications/existing and new organization units	—	$2.2 million	0.3	$0.66	4
New business (cells 7, 8): New products/new applications/existing and new organization units	—	$4.2 million	0.4	$1.68	1
Total	$15.5 million	$26.2 million		$18.09	

[a]10-point scales: 1=low priority; 10 = high priority

The material presented in Chapters 5 and 6 is extensive, even overwhelming, in scope. The reader may be tempted to ask: "Is it necessary to do all of this work for a single customer?"

The answer to this question takes us back to the 80/20 rule and the value of key accounts. If it would really hurt the supplier firm to lose a current key account, or be of immense value to gain a potential key account, then performing a full-blown situation analysis, isolating planning assumptions, and carefully identifying opportunities and threats is surely worth the effort.

The problem for the key account manager is that securing business with a key account depends both on setting a clear course of action, and getting a whole lot of details right. Missing any one of a variety of details can defeat all the firm's other efforts. For example, the key account manager may fail to identify a major influencer, or not understand an important trend in the key account's market. Or, she may not realize that a competitor is working on a new product to obsolete the firm's best seller, nor be aware that the supplier firm's billing system is playing havoc in the key account's accounting department. Without in-depth analysis, the key account manager may have little idea where the critical items may lie.

CHAPTER SEVEN

The Key Account Strategy

In developing strategy for his key accounts, the key account manager should be concerned with the long-run future of the customer organization. Since key accounts represent the 20% of companies that currently (and in the future will) account for 80% of the firm's business, a myopic short-term view may spell disaster. Key account strategy should be made for the long run. Whether the long run is more appropriately chosen to be two years, three years, or five years is of less importance than that the strategic perspective be unconstrained by short-term thinking.

In this chapter, the strategy for a key account is developed in the context of an overall focus on the key account relationship comprising a vision and mission. Vision and mission set the broad parameters within which resource allocation for the key account occurs. The key account strategy *per se* comprises several interrelated elements—performance objectives, strategic focus, positioning, action programs, agreements on resource commitments, and budgets and forecasts. Although each element is discussed separately in this chapter, in strategy development an iterative process must be put in place to ensure that all elements are both internally consistent, and follow logically from the situation analysis.

In addition to developing individual key account strategies, in this chapter we address several other issues in the key account planning process—internal consistency in the key account plan, communicating the plan, identifying information gaps in the situation analysis, and aggregation issues across individual key account plans.

THE KEY ACCOUNT VISION

The key account vision (or charter) is an overarching statement of how the supplier firm wishes to interface with the key account over the long haul. Vision is loftier in tone than mission (see below), and acts as a guide on how the supplier firm will conduct itself with the key account. As discussed earlier, sometimes vision statements are developed for the entire set of key accounts. They may also be developed for individual key accounts.

The British multinational, BOC, developed a vision statement for one of its global accounts:

> We shall offer Balsam Inc. access to our extensive market development/sales resources, technology development programs, and developing capability in total solution packages to help expand its interface with the iron and steel industry, enhance its market penetration, and strengthen its ability to be more responsive to its customers' needs.

To be truly effective, the vision must be actively embraced by all members of the key account team. Indeed, an important team-building exercise for the key account manager is to engage key account team members in developing a vision for the key account.

THE KEY ACCOUNT MISSION

Compared to the broad-brush nature of vision, mission is more specific in terms of areas of the key account to be served, and products/technologies to be offered. In particular, the key account manager must clearly delineate those business units or divisions (addressable entities) of the key account it will target for revenues, and those that it will forego.

Typically, some areas of the key account are preferred for current business, and others for potential business. Still others areas may exhibit little potential or interest for the supplier firm. For example, a supplier to General Electric may currently do business with its plastics and home appliance divisions, and target the entertainment division for new business. However, it may also decide to forgo effort in jet engines, electricity generation, and locomotives.

Furthermore, a multibusiness supplier firm may wish to address different areas of the key account with different technologies or product lines, leading to a multifaceted and quite complex key account mission.

EXAMPLE: To serve divisions Alpha and Beta with our various innovative plastic technologies; and to serve divisions Gamma and Delta with our traditional lines of synthetic fibers.

The mission defines the *field of play* at the key account. It is both inclusive, defining where the key account manager will seek business and, implicitly at least, exclusionary, defining areas where he will not seek business.

The mission can be expected to vary over time, but typically has a longer life than the key account strategy (see below). For example, in recent years, enhanced product quality has led to quality parity among competitor firms in many industries. As a result, several firms have sought competitive advantage by broadening their missions and increasing customer value-added by incorporating service elements into their offers.

A COMPLETE KEY ACCOUNT STRATEGY

As we indicated earlier, the key account strategy is only as good as the situation analysis on which it is based. A sloppy situation analysis, developed with incomplete data and/or inadequate analysis, will likely lead to the development of a key account strategy whose implementation delivers inadequate results. Similarly, a failure to work through the several key building blocks of the key account strategy (Figure 7.1) in a thoughtful manner, and to make the appropriate set of decisions, will also lead to poor performance.

Typically, a key account strategy has multiple components, each relating to a different part of the key account mission. In the example above, at least two components of key account strategy would be required, one for innovative plastic technologies at divisions Alpha and Beta, and one for traditional synthetic fibers at divisions Gamma and Delta.[1] The remainder of this chapter focuses on development of a single component of a key account strategy.

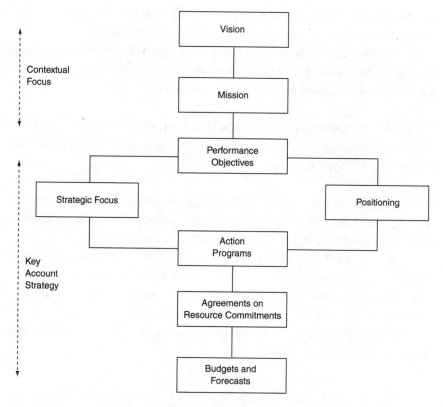

FIGURE 7.1: A Complete Key Account Strategy

Performance Objectives

Performance objectives specify the business results that the supplier firm intends to achieve. Three key issues are involved in setting these objectives. First, *performance objectives are not unidimensional.* Frequently, they are simply stated in terms of levels or percent increases in sales volume. Objectives set in this fashion beg the question of whether or not sales volume itself is the critical performance dimension at the present time. Depending upon circumstances, other dimensions such as profit margins, gross profit, or share of related business at the key account may be more important.

Second, *performance objectives may conflict with one another.* If key account managers have to deal with multiple objectives, most likely they will conflict. For example, success in achieving increased sales volume will most likely come at the cost of allocating resources to the account, thus decreasing profit margins.

As part of the objective-setting process, key account managers must set priorities for attaining conflicting objectives. If the environment at the key account is supportive, and the supplier firm's action programs are successful, perhaps seemingly conflicting objectives—such as sales growth and increased profit margins—may each be attained. However, a judgment must be made regarding primary objectives that must be achieved, and secondary objectives that are desired but are of lesser importance.

Third, *performance objectives have two distinct dimensions—strategic and operational.* Two unfortunate generalizations can be made regarding the setting of performance objectives in business life. First, they are frequently set from the top. Second, they are generally quantitative in nature. The receipt of quantitative objectives from senior management frequently begs the question as to whether the appropriate performance dimension has been selected. For example, although top management may set a performance objective of increasing sales revenues from a particular account by 15% over the next year, volume increase *per se* may be a less appropriate performance objective than increased profit margins. The problem arises because of a failure to make a clear distinction between strategic objectives and operational objectives.

Strategic objectives set the direction for the relationship with the key account. They are qualitative and directional in nature, and typically focus on such dimensions as volume or volume growth, share of business at the account, and profitability.

Operational objectives, by contrast, are quantitative and time dependent, and are logically developed subsequent to the setting of strategic objectives. For example, alternative strategic objectives for two particular key accounts may be stated as:

- Our primary objective at Johnson Controls is to *increase sales volume.*
- Our primary objective at Howard Machining is to *increase profitability.*

Operational objectives follow from the setting of strategic objectives and have the form:

- Our primary objective at Johnson Controls is to increase sales volume from $2.5 million to $3.5 million by 200X.
- Our primary objective at Howard Machining is to increase profit margins from 25% to 30% by 200Y.

These objectives should, of course, be realistic, attainable, and consistent with the various elements of the situation analysis.[2] For example, for those key accounts that provide high current volume but little growth potential, objectives should be set consistent with a focus on revenue protection—defensive strategy. Conversely, for key accounts with low current volume but high growth potential, objectives should be set consistent with account investment—offensive strategy. Objectives for key accounts with both high volume and high potential should reflect both revenue protection and account investment.

The important clarifying principle is that strategic objectives are free of both numbers and a time dimension. Questions of "how much," and "by when" are the province of operational objectives. It is very important to be clear about the strategic objective before asking the "how much," and "by when" questions. Precisely determined quantitative objectives are positively harmful if the performance dimensions upon which they are based have been incorrectly selected.

Strategic Focus

The strategic focus comprises a set of broad courses of action from which the key account manager may choose to achieve her performance objectives (Figure 7.2). These actions fall into two categories, those designed to maintain and increase sales volume, and those that improve key account profitability.

MAINTAIN AND INCREASE SALES VOLUME

In Chapter 6, we presented an eight-cell matrix for conceptualizing the supplier firm's opportunities and threats at the key account. These comprised existing and new products offered by the supplier firm, for existing and new applications at the key account, to organizational units with which it currently does business, and to new organizational units. Somewhat more simply, revenue maintenance and improvement may be achieved in just four ways:

Maintain current uses. The supplier focuses on its current business at the key account and repels competitor attempts to secure revenues at its expense. For any particular set of objectives, the greater the firm's ability to maintain existing business, the less pressure to secure a new business.

Expand current uses. Essentially, the key account manager focuses on current key account applications but seeks to enhance revenues in current and/or new key account organizational units. For example, if the key account were using the supplier firm's software in a limited number of departments, the strategic focus might concentrate on broadening use of this software to other departments.

Displace competitors' products. The key account manager seeks to persuade the key account to switch suppliers, and hence displace competitor products from applications that the supplier firm can serve.

Open up new applications. The key account manager puts his efforts into finding new uses for the supplier's product(s) and/or technologies at the key account. The applications, which may be found in any organization unit, are new to the key account and may or may not be new to the supplier firm.

These four options represent the broad courses of action that can be taken by the supplier firm to maintain and increase sales volume. Of course, the supplier firm can take many different actions that fall into these four categories. These must be worked out as specific programs for supplier firm implementation.

IMPROVE ACCOUNT PROFITABILITY

Four separate broad courses of action may be taken to improve account profitability. Two options focus on improving revenues while holding current volume constant—raise prices and improve product mix. The other two options focus on reducing costs—operating costs and financing costs.

Raise prices. This action is conceptually the most simple option for increasing profitability. However, it is typically one of the most difficult to put into effect as key accounts tend to resist price increases. Careful planning is needed to avoid a negative impact on the supplier-firm/key-account relationship.

Improve product mix. Trading the key account up to more profitable products and/or adding service elements is an important means of improving profitability. A deep understanding of key account needs may allow the firm to increase profits while simultaneously offering improved value. Although total volume may remain constant, profitability is increased.

Reduce operating costs. In serving key accounts, supplier firms incur both variable and fixed costs. Raw materials, direct labor, and freight are some of the variable costs. After-sales support, technical service, and adminis-

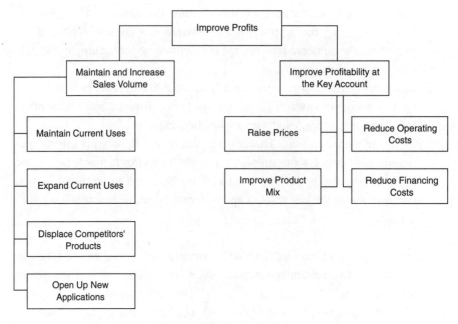

FIGURE 7.2: Strategic Focus

trative support are fixed-cost activities that frequently require considerable resource outlays. The key account manager's challenge is to reduce those costs that she controls without reducing value to the customer.[3]

Reduce financing costs. The supplier firm incurs two major types of financing costs in serving key accounts—inventory carrying costs and accounts receivable costs. Inventory costs can be reduced by streamlining production and delivery systems, and by using such devices as just-in-time inventory management. Tightening up on credit terms can reduce accounts receivable costs.

These four options represent broad courses of action for improving profitability. As with increasing sales volume, the supplier firm can take many different actions that fall into these four categories. These must be worked out as specific programs for supplier firm implementation.

RELATING STRATEGIC FOCUS TO PERFORMANCE OBJECTIVES

Combining the two foci of maintaining and increasing sales volume, and improving profitability at the key account, performance objectives can be achieved from the eight—and only eight—quite different courses of action just cited. A cursory examination of these action courses demonstrates that, in general, some are incompatible with others. For example, the supplier firm may find it difficult to displace competitor's products while simultaneously raising prices and cutting costs by reducing technical support. The core question is: On which broad courses of action should the supplier firm focus? To answer this question requires an examination of performance objectives at the key account.

If the supplier firm's primary objective is to increase sales volume, increase its share of business, and the like, it should focus its efforts on the four growth actions—maintain and expand current uses, displace competitor's products and open up new applications. The key account manager will be less concerned with the four profitability options.

Conversely, if the supplier firm is attempting to increase profitability from its business with the key account it will take such steps as raising prices, improving the product mix, and cutting operating and financing costs. The key account manager will be less concerned with the options designed to increase sales volume. If profits are the key objective, the key account manager must balance carefully these eight possible strategic foci.[4]

Clearly, the statement of strategic focus must closely relate to performance objectives set for the key account. For example:

Performance objective: Increase sales volume at Johnson Controls from $2.5 million to $3.5 million by 200X.

Strategic focus: Displace competitor's product in the Jackson application; secure acceptance of our specification for the new Lehmann application.

Performance objective: Increase our profit margin at Howard Machining from 25% to 30% by 200Y.

Strategic focus: Raise prices 5% by year-end. Replace selected low margin products with higher margin products.

Positioning

In the strategic focus, the key account manager selects broad courses of action to take at the key account. By contrast, positioning specifies more precisely how the firm will retain and/or secure business. Elements of positioning include positioning objectives, target contacts, competitor targets, and the key persuasive argument.

POSITIONING OBJECTIVES

The positioning statement should clarify how the key account manager will attempt to influence the key account's behavior such that it benefits the supplier firm. Depending on the specific situation, the key account manager may set one of several different objectives. Two objectives seek a favorable conclusion to the purchase decision; two other objectives seek to modify the key account's purchase decision.

Seek a Favorable Conclusion to the Purchase Process. Two methods can be used for seeking a favorable conclusion to the key account's purchase process— influence the decision-making criteria, and influence the key account's perception of its various options:

> *Influence the decision-making criteria:* The focus here is to influence the basis on which the key account makes its purchase decisions. This approach is most frequently used in new buy (extended problem-solving) situations (Chapter 5), where purchase criteria are often unclear. The supplier firm can be of real service to the key account by assisting with criteria development. Of course, these criteria may also benefit the supplier firm and improve the probability that it will eventually win the business.[5] In addition, influencing the cast of characters involved in the decision-making process (see below) may also lead to modified procurement criteria.

EXAMPLE: Pine Inc.*, a technologically advanced *Fortune* 500 firm, poured significant resources into a successful product development effort with a key account. During the development process, Pine personnel worked mainly with the key account's development engineers. When the time came for production orders, the project was handed over to procurement. Procurement personnel focused on price, and were unconcerned with the supplier firm's time and resource commitment to develop the new product. However, the specifications were written in such a way that they strongly favored Pine. It ultimately won the business.

Influence the key account's perception of its various purchase options: This is perhaps the most frequently found objective for positioning statements. The key account manager attempts to demonstrate to the key account that, given its purchase criteria, the supplier firm's offer is superior to those of competitors.

Only a thorough familiarity with customer needs and priorities, and competitive offers, will enable the key account manager to make wise decisions about where to focus efforts. Of course, many methods are available for convincing key account personnel of supplier firm superiority for delivering benefits that satisfy key account needs. These include examination of performance data, product and field testing, and so forth.

Modify the Purchase Decision. The purchase decision may be modified by influencing the scope and timing of the decision, and the set of personnel involved in the decision:

Influence the scope and timing of the decision: Suppose the key account is developing plans for a specific purchase decision. The supplier firm may put itself in a more advantageous decision by convincing the key account to expand or contract the scope, and hence the timing, of this purchase.

EXAMPLE: The key account customer of Palm PLC*, a European telecommunications company, was planning to purchase a new telephone system for one of its divisions. Fearing that its current products were less sophisticated than those of its chief competitor for this application, Palm's key account manager attempted to convince the customer that it should only make this decision in the context of improving the firm's total system-wide capability. Palm anticipated that its new products would be available within a year, and that these would leapfrog the competitor. Thus, pushing the decision into the future would be advantageous. By contrast, Palm's chief competitor sought to narrow the customer's decision scope.

Influence the set of personnel involved in the decision: Many procurement decisions take place over time and involve a variety of different players from both the key account and supplier firm. The key account manager may be able to influence the cast of characters by requesting the involvement of certain key account, key account customer, and/or supplier firm personnel in the decision process. As a refinement, the juncture at which key executives become involved may be crucial; the key account manager may be able to influence the "when."

EXAMPLE: A key account manager at Evodia Inc.*, a major U.S. chemical company, believed it might fail to secure renewal of an important contract with a key account. The new procurement director seemed enamored of a strong competitor with which he had a close relationship in his previous position. To combat this threat, Evodia's key account manager involved his senior management and the key account's CEO in the decision. He also raised the ante by successfully linking the renewal contract with others that were shortly coming due, in such a way as to reflect favorably on the procurement director.[6]

TARGET CONTACTS

Target contacts are those individuals at the key account whom it is important to convince of the supplier firm's superiority. These individuals are selected from the set of decision makers and major influencers identified in the situation analysis. The key account manager must take great care to identify not only who these individuals are, but also their functions, organizational positions, when influence attempts would be most appropriate, and so forth.

EXAMPLE: Our major efforts will be focused on convincing the key account's technical director and her direct reports of the value of our new technology.

COMPETITOR TARGETS

From the full set of competitor firms at a key account, for any particular purchase decision, typically one or two are major targets for the key account manager. These organizations and the relevant individuals must be clearly specified because they help determine how the supplier firm should approach the key account.

EXAMPLE: Our central thrust will be directed against our primary domestic competitors of alternative forms of nucleobenzide, specifically Dow,

DuPont, and Union Carbide. Secondarily, we shall build a defensive position against Hoescht and Bayer, who, we anticipate, will enter the market with new technology within the next three years.

KEY PERSUASIVE ARGUMENT

The key persuasive argument is the core reason the key account manager offers the key account for behaving in the manner specified in the positioning objective. When the manager is attempting to secure a purchase, the major reason for the key account to purchase from the supplier firm rather than competitors is typically called the *key buying incentive* or *value proposition*. For example, a typical statement of key buying incentive might be:

EXAMPLE: Our key persuasive argument to the key account's technical director and her direct reports will be that using Tanide increases throughput. Specifically, we shall show that by using Tanide, rather than Corfide (major competition), molding time is reduced, cleaning time is reduced because of fewer deposits in the mold, and the need to clean flashing from the part is eliminated.

The key buying incentive should represent the core contribution the purchase makes to the key account's ability to attain its objectives. Of course, for any particular purchase situation, several individuals occupying different roles may represent key target contacts, and yet have different (yet related) objectives. As such it may be necessary to offer different buying incentives for each of these target contacts, based on their particular needs. For example:

Target Contact, Chief Engineer: "The key account's new product will exhibit superior performance characteristics when powered with our device versus Alpha Inc.'s."

Target Contact, Operations VP: "Use of our component versus Beta Inc.'s increases production line speed by 10%."

Target Contact, Marketing VP: "Use of our brand name via co-branding will significantly increase the key account's sales volume."

Target Contact, CEO: "The exceptionally high level of service commitment and performance improvement in our products will continue to reduce the key account's production costs."

FIGURE 7.3: Formulating Positioning Statements

Customer Benefits	Relative Importance	Competitor I		Competitor II		Competitor III	
		Benefit	Rank	Benefit	Rank	Benefit	Rank
A	1	A	1	A	2	A	3
B	2			B	1		
C	3			C	1	C	2
D	4	D	2			D	1

POSITIONING ILLUSTRATION

Figure 7.3 will help to explain positioning.[7] Three competitors (I, II, III) are seeking a particular piece of business from a customer. The customer has identified four required benefits (A, B, C, D) that are important to its purchase decision. These benefits decline in importance as A>B>C>D.

Note that as regards the most important benefit, A, competitor I is superior to competitor II, which in turn is superior to competitor III. Competitor II is the only firm that offers benefit B (e.g., a warranty). Competitor II offers the best benefit C, followed by competitor III; competitor I does not offer this benefit. Competitor III offers the best benefit D, followed by competitor I; competitor II does not offer this benefit.

Competitor II's Dilemma. Suppose the customer is the key account of competitor II. How should competitor II position itself at the key account?

Competitor II dominates competitor III on benefits A, B, and C, and is only inferior on benefit D. Since this is the least important benefit we can probably infer that the major problem for competitor II comes from competitor I. Competitor I should thus be the competitor target. The basis for competitor II's problem is that competitor I is superior on A, the most important benefit.

Options for Competitor II. Possible methods of positioning competitor II are:

- Persuade the key account that its ranking of competitors I and II on benefit A is incorrect. In fact, competitor II is superior to competitor I!
- Persuade the key account that its criteria are inappropriate for its underlying needs. The correct order of required benefits should be B>A>C>D.

With this ordering, competitor II now dominates competitor I on the three most important benefits.

- Persuade the key account that rather than focus on individual benefits, its criteria should be formulated on the basis of securing a set of benefits. Competitor II provides the account's three most important benefits, A, B and C. Although competitor I has superior performance on benefit A and also provides benefit D, it offers neither benefit B nor C. As a result, when considering the entire benefit set, competitor II's offer is superior to that of competitor I.

Competitor III? A final issue with this simple example concerns competitor III. What hope is there for this competitor to secure the business at this customer? The correct answer is not much! A more important question is: Given its inferior performance in offering benefits that the customer requires, why is competitor III attempting to secure business at this customer? Perhaps this account represents one of the 80% of competitor III's customers that provide 20% of its revenues yet are extremely costly to serve. If so, it should probably stop trying to gain business at this customer and focus on more attractive opportunities.

Action Programs

Two types of action program should be developed: strategic action programs that follow directly from the supplier firm's performance objectives, strategic focus, and positioning, and relationship action programs concerned with supplier-firm/key-account interpersonal relationships.

STRATEGIC ACTION PROGRAMS

Whereas the development of performance objectives, strategic focus, and positioning is largely conceptual in nature, action programs identify the supplier firm's specific implementation steps. In designing action programs, the key account manager must decide whether the goal is to meet account expectations, exceed those expectations, develop solutions to existing problems, and/or solve new and unrecognized problems.[8]

Action programs have two major elements—objectives and action steps. Action steps in turn comprise both actions that must be completed, and clearly specified time lines indicating when they should be completed. The key account manager will probably need to develop action programs in various functional areas—for example, communications, human resources, marketing, operations, logistics, sales force, and R&D—to implement the strategy fully.

Of course, these action programs should not be developed in a vacuum. In general, customers should be involved in their formulation and agree on the expected performance from each set of action steps.

> **EXAMPLE:** Boise Cascade Office Products (BCOP) jointly develops implementation plans with each of its key accounts. BCOP's standard implementation plan is a minimum of thirty-four pages of instructions for every account.[9]

Action programs may be focused on achieving sales revenues and profits in the near or medium term. They may also be concerned with longer-term objectives such as developing the supplier-firm/key-account relationship by improving personal relationships, and laying the groundwork for joint-technology development.

Of course, key account strategies are typically not developed from scratch but build on previously developed strategies and related action programs. While the new key account strategy is being developed, it is likely that action programs are being pursued to implement an earlier strategy. In light of the new strategy, it is important that existing action programs be rigorously examined, and if necessary curtailed to avoid wasting resources.

Action Program Objectives. Action program objectives are the key linkage between the strategic focus and positioning statements, and actual actions carried out by the supplier firm. However, for the various elements of strategic focus and positioning that the key account manager elects to pursue, several possible action program objectives may be developed. Thus it is necessary to identify priorities and intermediate objectives.

Priorities. Because of resource limitations, the key account manager must assign priorities to each objective based on a rigorous analysis of requirements for achieving performance objectives at the key account. It is useful to categorize objectives into three types:

- *High-priority objectives: Must-accomplish* objectives that are vital to the success of the team at the key account such as achieving product acceptance for a strategic application

- *Medium-priority objectives:* Important but less critical objectives, such as replacing a competitor for a moderately important application
- *Low-priority objectives:* Less important objectives that are worth achieving but which will have a minor effect if not accomplished

Intermediate Objectives. In many cases, achieving an action program objective does not immediately lead to sales revenues or profits. However, unless the supplier firm is successful in achieving these objectives, sales revenues and profits will not follow. Frequently, such action program objectives are termed "intermediate" to recognize their role as lying between supplier firm actions and eventual purchasing behavior by the key account. They may include, for example, reduced field inventory, improved customer service, agreement for new product trials, and merchandising programs accepted. Achieving action program objectives is always more powerful if the key account has to take some serious action. For example, compare these two statements of objective:

STATEMENT A: The key account will conduct tests on our new device. On the basis of our superior performance characteristics, the chief engineer will recommend that our device, rather than Alpha Inc.'s, be used to power the key account's new product.

STATEMENT B: We shall conduct tests on our new device. The results will demonstrate to the key account's chief engineer that the key account's new product has superior performance characteristics when powered by our device versus Alpha Inc.'s.

Statement A conveys a more powerful action program objective than Statement B inasmuch as it requires recommendation behavior from the chief engineer.

Action Steps. The specific action steps (or tasks) developed by the key account manager are designed both to achieve program objectives, and address various obstacles. For each action program objective, the key account team should develop several alternative steps to ensure the full range of opportunities has been considered. Each alternative should be tested for reasonableness and required resources. The selected alternative should be that which best satisfies the key account's requirements, while simultaneously minimizing use of the supplier firm's resources.

When a specific action step has been agreed, the various tasks should be scheduled, with start and finish dates clearly specified, and responsibility assigned for each task. Such scheduling gains commitment from key actors at both the supplier firm and the key account. For example:

Objective: The key account will conduct tests on our new device. On the basis of our superior performance characteristics, the chief engineer will recommend that our device, rather than Alpha Inc.'s, be used to power the key account's new product.

   Action Steps:
   Quarter 1: Secure agreement to test our product against Alpha's
   Quarter 2: Formulate agreement on test criteria
   Quarter 3: Run test
   Quarter 4: Evaluate results; discuss with key account; secure initial order

Objective: The key account's marketing VP will agree that co-branding with our firm will significantly increase the key account's sales volume.

   Action Steps:
   Quarter 1: Design consumer survey to test brand name combination
   Quarter 2: Formulate agreement on test criteria
   Quarter 3: Administer survey; analyze results
   Quarter 4: Present results; secure commitment

It is critical that relevant supplier firm personnel are kept fully apprised of details of the various action programs. It is also important that these be fully communicated to, and agreed by, relevant key account executives. Such communication helps set the key account's expectations regarding supplier firm activities. In addition, it clarifies those actions the key account must take, and when they must be taken, so that the programs can be successfully completed.

However, it not sufficient just to develop the action programs. The key account manager and key account executives must together establish measurement and monitoring methods. These methods should focus on both supplier firm and key account performance in implementing action steps and achieving action program objectives.

Activating and Resisting Forces. In order to enhance the probability that an individual action program will be implemented successfully, the key account manager should complete a "force field" analysis. In this analysis, the manager identifies those forces that may enhance the program's chances of being implemented—activating forces, and those that may act as obstacles—resisting forces, any of which may be more closely related to the key account or the supplier firm. The key account manager should seek to enhance activating forces, convert resisting forces to activating forces or, at least, attempt to diminish resisting forces.

Activating forces may include such items as a senior executive at the key account who is especially keen to see the action program succeed and may act as a program champion (or an unexpected budget surplus at the supplier firm that will help free up needed resources). Although the action program is planned for success, these forces can play an important role if implementation is getting bogged down.

Resisting forces or obstacles can frustrate the successful implementation of an action program. They should be clearly spelled out in a cause-and-effect format. For example:

- Anticipated high demand for the key account's products in 200X may make it difficult for our new raw material to be fully tested;
- Unless our new key account team is fully in place, we shall be unable to approach the key account with our new strategic thrust.
- Because the new procurement director previously had an excellent relationship with our major competitor, we shall have to make extraordinary efforts to be able to bid on the new project.

INTERPERSONAL RELATIONSHIP-BUILDING ACTION PROGRAMS

An important aspect of the situation analysis (Chapters 5 and 6) is to identify critical key account personnel, and assess the quality of their individual relationships with supplier firm personnel. Based on this analysis, the key account manager should develop action program objectives, and put in place a series of steps to improve the set of professional- and friendship-type interpersonal relationships. These may include designing special events to promote interaction among supplier firm and key account personnel. As with other action programs, the results of these relationship-building action programs should be monitored over time.

From time to time, it may be necessary to replace supplier firm personnel in critical positions with others more congenial to the key account. In addition, it may prove advantageous to develop new relationships with key account personnel, for example, when an executive partner is appointed.

The interpersonal relationship building plan may be developed by extending the interpersonal relationship chart (Figure 6.7). We illustrate this extension in Figure 7.4.

Agreements on Resource Commitments

The supplier firm must allocate resources to the key account both to complete the various required action steps in the strategic and interpersonal relationship-building action programs, and to maintain the ongoing supplier-firm/key-account relationship. Some of these resources relate to activities conducted by, or specifically directed by, the key account manager. These might include visits to key account contacts for information gathering, identifying key influencers, initiating and cementing interpersonal relationships, and social calls for such extra-work activities as golf and entertainment.

ELEMENTS OF SUPPORT SYSTEMS

Many required resources do not reside in the sales force or key account management, but with the supplier firm's support system(s).[10] This system comprises many elements:

- *Information system:* Including routine data such as orders, invoices and bills; reports, such as summary of purchase orders placed and user installations; and special reports, such as a census of supplier firm equipment at key account locations
- *Administration:* related to information systems, and including billing and accounts receivable
- *Field and technical service:* Repairing and maintaining capital equipment, and helping customers use capital equipment, raw materials, and components
- *Logistics:* Transferring the product to the direct customer in a timely and reliable manner, typically including both inventory control and handling and transportation

FIGURE 7.4: The Interpersonal Relationship Building Plan

Key Account Personnel (Name, Organizational Position)	Supplier Firm Personnel (Name, Organizational Position)	Nature of the Relationship	Action Program Objective	Action Steps
Tony Jackson, CEO	Mike Smith, Vice-Chairman	Acquainted – annual golf game	Move toward friendship	Invite Tony Jackson to Mike Smith's CEO forum
Tony Jackson, CEO	Alasdair MacLean, Head R&D, Executive Partner	Close friendship, college roommates, play tennis monthly	Maintain relationship	No corporate action required
Anthony Benton, COO	David Lankester, Key Account Manager	Good professional relationship, working on projects	Maintain relationship	No corporate action required
Peter Wilson, Head of Procurement	David Lankester, Key Account Manager	Satisfactory professional relationship, but increasing tension due to reduction in Wilson's decision-making authority	Fully understand shifts in decision making at the key account	Take appropriate action based on full analysis. Involve Executive Partner Alasdair MacLean in next steps
Winston Harris, Procurement Officer in Dallas	Gay Crossman, Local Sales Representative	Good professional relationship	Move toward friendship relationship	Crossman to invite Harris to Dallas Cowboys games
Edward Windsor, Research Scientist	Madge Wallace, Research Scientist	Close relationship in joint research project—developing into friendship	Develop friendship	Monitor; fund Madge Wallace for family dinners
George Hanover, Inventory Manager	Ellen Reed, Logistics Manager	Difficult working relationship becoming negative personal relationship	Improve relationship	Identify and appoint replacement for Ellen Reed
William Orange, Quality Manager	No supplier firm contact appointed	None, but must be addressed	Develop relationship	Appoint new contact

- *Manufacturing/operations management:* Responsible for product and service quality, and (with logistics) for delivery speed and reliability;
- *Applications engineering:* Typically a mixture of pre-sales and post-sales activities. Applications engineers work with customers' custom design engineers, production/process engineers, procurement specialists, and/or manufacturing and operations managers
- *Development, design, and product engineering:* Often called upon to develop special products for the key account, or for customers of the key account that incorporate the supplier firm's products
- *Finance:* Responsible for financial arrangements such as contract management, leasing, datings and credit terms, and approvals
- *Legal:* May ensure legality, especially in pricing matters, and develops programs involving legal restraints such as product liability and licensing
- *Control:* Responsible for analyzing key account profitability
- *Sales development:* Producing sales tools including video tapes, samples, presentation aids, and the like
- *Marketing research:* For data gathering and analysis to monitor customer satisfaction levels
- *Senior management:* Available for meeting with parallel-level key account executives for reasons such as demonstrating supplier firm commitment and involvement in complex negotiations.
- Director of key accounts/key account policy group/marketing: Coordinates strategies and action programs across key accounts, and provides support to individual account teams on such matters as specific price and promotion decisions, and developing creative pricing approaches.
- *The supplier firm's suppliers:* To solve specific problems, to investigate cost saving potential and/or to strengthen supply chain relationships; three-way meetings including the supplier firm's supplier(s) may be important

The key account manager must secure commitments from the various support groups to provide the necessary resources, at the appropriate times. In some cases, the key account manager may know exactly what resources are required. In other cases, she may be able to specify an outcome but must work with her key account team to determine the exact nature of the required resources.

EXAMPLE: From extensive discussion with his customer, the Nortel key account manager for Corning's Component Product business unit knew that a significant yet incremental technological innovation was required within two years. This knowledge became the basis for discussions with the technical development department to define the specific requirements and allocate resources to ensure a successful effort.

Regardless of who decides on the specific required resources, critical personnel should be identified by name and agreement obtained about their roles and responsibilities, regardless of whether the key account assignment is full-time or periodic. This element of the key account manager's job is often fraught with controversy. It is difficult enough to secure resources in outward-oriented organizations truly focused on satisfying customer needs. It can be excruciatingly difficult in those more inward-oriented organizations where the central role of the customer has yet to be fully accepted.

In the international arena, when the key account is a foreign government, the supplier firm's support system may extend far outside the organization into various arms of government. For example, in the first Clinton Administration, the Department of Commerce led by Secretary Ron Brown played an extremely active role in assisting U.S. corporations to secure major contracts abroad. In 1995, President Clinton helped Boeing conclude a $6 billion sale of sixty-one aircraft to Saudi Arabia. In 1997, Vice President Gore appeared at a signing ceremony in Beijing to aid Boeing and General Motors in concluding Chinese contracts worth almost $2 billion.[11]

SUPPORT SYSTEM DESIGN

A particularly difficult issue regarding support systems is the extent to which they should be tailored to individual key accounts, versus providing similar service to all key accounts at a particular tier level. Support systems are expensive *per se;* those designed for individual accounts are even more expensive— for example, dedicated technical service or special delivery arrangements. However, if a tailored support system for a demanding customer can ultimately become part of a standard package and raise the firm's overall competitiveness, it should be viewed as a long-term investment rather than a short-term cost. Clearly, decisions regarding customization must be made on an account-by-account basis, and should be related to current and potential sales revenues and profits.

Design and operation of support systems can have an important impact on profitability. Support systems are costly to maintain and operate, but directly impact sales revenues. Effective and responsive support may provide competitive advantage possibilities, and lead to securing preferred supplier status. Higher sales resulting from preferred supplier status imply greater efficiency of sales force effort, an enhanced ability to manage the product mix by avoiding the "cherry-picking" syndrome faced by less favored suppliers, and possibly better prices.[12]

Support systems are especially important for the key account manager as they directly affect his ability to make and keep commitments. When commitments are kept, the manager earns credibility and respect at the key account, tightening the interfirm relationship and leading to increased sales and profits. Simultaneously, his respect and power at the supplier firm increase, leading to higher key account service levels and increased purchases in a self-reinforcing, virtuous, spiral. Conversely, an inability to make and keep commitments leads to a self-reinforcing spiral in the opposite direction!

Mismanaged support systems can be very costly for the supplier firm. For instance, if price-setting mechanisms are ineffective, key account buyers may exert monopsony power and force prices down. Or, lax controls may allow successful key account managers to secure service support levels that bring inadequate returns for supplier firm efforts.

Because of the profitability impact of resource spending to serve key accounts, both in general and for support services in particular, the supplier firm should not provide key account managers with a license to use whatever resources they may believe they require. Not only are resources costly, uncritical provision to key account managers should not function as a substitute for their own development of critical knowledge and expertise. Richard Snelshire, manager of corporate banking administration at Wachovia Bank explained how that institution dealt with this potential problem in product management support:

> We staff this function [product management support] only to the level that is required to deal with really difficult and complex issues. In general, we expect the account managers to learn about our products. Indeed, we force this by providing few product management resources. The product managers learn to allocate their time where the reward potential is high. They will not waste their time with more elementary matters for an account manager who hasn't done his homework.[13]

Budgets and Forecasts

Budgets and forecasts represent the detailed performance requirements and expense levels set for the key account. These include absolute levels and trends in such measures as sales revenue, share of key account business, gross profit and/or profit contribution, expenses, and sales-to-expense ratios, both in total and broken out by product or product line, organization unit, and application, where appropriate. Budgets and forecasts relate directly to performance objectives set in the key account strategy, but are much more detailed. Indeed, they function as a managerial tool to track performance through the operating period. Typically, annual forecast and budget items are disaggregated and specified by quarter or by month.

ISSUES IN THE KEY ACCOUNT PLANNING PROCESS

The foregoing material presented elements in the key account strategy; now we address several other matters concerning the key account planning process.

Internal Consistency in the Key Account Plan

When the key account manager develops a key account plan, she should conduct a series of consistency tests to ensure that the various elements of the strategy hang together. If inconsistencies are found, revisions must be made. The questions that follow can help to reveal those inconsistencies.

- Based on the situation analysis, is the key account mission appropriately defined?
- Based on the situation analysis, do the performance objectives make sense?
- Is the supplier firm's strategic thrust consistent with the performance objectives?
- Are the strategies we developed appropriate to address the opportunities and threats identified in the situation analysis?

- Are the target contacts consistent with the knowledge developed in the situation analysis?
- Do the action programs appropriately implement the strategy?
- Have we secured the required resources to conduct the action programs?
- Have the budgets and forecasts been developed with the appropriate level of detail? Are they consistent with the performance objectives?

Of course, these sorts of questions should be asked right through the strategy development process, but they should be asked one final time when the key account plan is approaching completion. (Appendix 7.1 presents an outline of the key account plan.)

Communicating the Key Account Plan

It is one thing for the key account manager to complete the key account plan. It is quite another to ensure that relevant personnel in both the supplier firm and key account are familiar with those elements of the key account strategy and action programs that they need to know. As a result, the key account manager must develop a strategy for communicating this information. He must decide who should receive key account strategy information and what they should receive, as well as when and in what form. The key account manager should then make sure that his communication plan is carried out. With the development of the Internet, companies are starting to put key account plans on-line, with various levels of access, so that the plan truly becomes a living document.

Identifying Information Gaps in the Situation Analysis

Significant amounts of information are required to complete the key account planning process successfully. Indeed, as the process proceeds, the key account manager should both identify and allocate responsibility for securing the required information. However, no matter how thorough a job of information gathering she directs, it is likely that, at plan completion, several information gaps will have surfaced. For this reason, at the conclusion of the planning process the manager should formally identify these information gaps, and put in place a process for ensuring that they are filled for the next key account planning iteration.

Aggregation Issues across Individual Key Account Plans

In this chapter, we focused on key account strategy for an individual key account. However, the supplier firm's customers comprise other key accounts together with numerous important but non-key accounts. This total customer set represents a variety of disparate claims on the supplier firm's human and other resources. As a result, the supplier firm's ability to implement successfully strategy for a particular key account is related to strategies both for other key accounts, the firm's non-key account customers, and to the total set of resources available to the firm.

In order for the supplier firm to make appropriate resource allocation decisions, each key account plan should be reviewed at a higher level, for example, by the director of key accounts. In addition, several types of aggregation analysis, involving the key account director and marketing and other relevant personnel, should be conducted to ensure compatibility of individual key account plans with overall supplier firm strategy and resources.

Among the types of aggregation that should be completed are:

- *Market and market segment objectives and strategies:* To ensure the entire set of key account plans is consistent with the firm's market and market segment strategies.
- *Sales volume:* To ensure that anticipated sales volume by product is consistent with production capacity expectations. Indeed, during periods of capacity shortage, allocating scarce capacity is a critical function. Typically, the supplier firm must make judgments regarding the amount of capacity available for each key account versus all other accounts.
- *Capital:* To ensure that capital (fixed and working) is available for various key account investments.
- *Research and development:* Especially in fast growth markets, where technology is changing, various individual key accounts will likely require development effort specific to their own development projects.
- *Technical assistance:* To ensure that sufficient manpower is available to provide appropriate levels of technical backup.

Of course, a first-cut aggregation analysis may reveal that insufficient resources are available to satisfy all requirements identified in the set of key account and marketing plans. Indeed, the key account director may have to "go to bat" for key accounts at the senior management level, and with functional heads such as R&D and production, to increase available resources. However, the key account director may also find it necessary to make tough decisions regarding what resources should be made available to which specific individual key accounts. Of course, it is possible that a single action item may satisfy requirements at more than one account, thus providing possibilities for scale economies.

The results of the aggregation analysis should be fed back to individual key account managers. It may be necessary for key account objectives, strategy, and action programs to be modified for consistency in the context of a resource-constrained environment.

CONCLUSION

Because managing key accounts is so critical to the supplier firm's future, and because key account planning is fundamental to key account management, we have devoted three entire chapters to developing the key account plan. In Chapters 5 and 6, we focused on the situation analysis; in Chapter 7 we turned to key account strategy.

The entire key account planning process should be driven from the top of the organization, notably by the key account director. He is responsible for planning the overall process and ensuring that each key account plan is developed systematically, according both to an agreed-upon framework and an established timetable. The director should also provide feedback, and manage the aggregation process for individual account plans.

A common framework is important for comparing, contrasting, and aggregating individual key account plans. The established timetable is important for the assessment of overall investment and other resource needs for the set of key accounts. Feedback both improves individual key account plans and educates key account managers. Aggregation of key account plans allows the supplier firm to make the difficult choices regarding increasing the levels of certain scarce resources, and allocating other scarce resources among the set of key and other accounts according to predetermined criteria.

The key account manager typically manages the process for his key account(s). He sets target dates, schedules meetings, manages agendas, and agrees on assignments with team members. Although he is responsible for gathering much key account material for the situation analysis, other critical information is prepared by a functional department or by key account team members based on their specific expertise. For example:

- Marketing—key account market, market segment and competitor data, and supplier firm's market segment strategies
- Finance—supplier firm data on contribution margins and gross dollar contribution
- Technical service—potential solutions to the key account's operational problems
- R&D—new products
- Operations—production capacity and quality levels
- Customer service—service delivery performance

Preparation of the situation analysis component of the key account plan is a valuable exercise in its own right. It requires gathering substantial information about the key account, competitors, and the supplier firm, but also requires identification of critical information gaps that must be filled before the key account strategy can be developed. In this process, all members of the team should become well informed about the key account, to the benefit of both the supplier firm and key account.

Deciding on a vision and mission, and formulating key account strategy provides a clear direction for the key account manager in directing the supplier-firm/key-account relationship over the planning period. This process also plays an important role in building a functioning key account team from a set of individuals with diverse backgrounds and expertise. Team building is enhanced to the extent that everyone on the team, led by the key account manager, participates in the entire planning process. When the key account strategy has been formulated and the action programs designed, team members should take responsibility for ensuring that required resources from their particular functional areas are made available to complete the action steps.

In addition to managing a process to ensure that all team members are committed to the key account plan, the manager should secure buy-in from the key account. In the most successful key account relationships, the supplier firm involves key account personnel in its planning process. At one extreme, personnel from both firms work together in both developing the situation analysis and formulating the account strategy and action programs. At the other extreme, key account personnel attend approval meetings at the conclusion of the process. Regardless of the method used, securing key account agreement to a set of actions aimed at improving the interorganizational relationship is clearly an important step.

In addition to acting as a guide to manage the key account relationship through time, the completed planning document is an invaluable resource for introducing new key account managers to their responsibilities. Over time, key account managers move on via promotions, transfers, or resignations, and new managers must be appointed. Unless a key account plan or similar document is available, most accumulated knowledge about the key account departs with the former account manager, and the new manager has to start from scratch. In addition, a well-developed key account plan is a valuable briefing book for an executive partner or other senior manager when key account visits are in order.

Lack of knowledge can be especially serious in the changeover period when the supplier-firm/key-account relationship is particularly vulnerable to competitive attack. It is not at all unusual for individual key account managers, maintaining little in the way of written account records, to be highly successful at an account on the basis of long-term relationships. When that key account manager leaves to join a competitor, the supplier firm is at a severe disadvantage in commencing an account-retention strategy.[14]

Finally, a simple but useful way of summarizing how an individual key account will be addressed is to identify a set of key questions that relate to vision, mission, and key account strategy.

- *Vision:* What do we want the supplier-firm/key-account relationship to become?
- *Mission:* In what divisions, business units, and/or departments of the key account shall we seek business, and with what products or technologies?
- *Performance objectives:* What results do we require?
- *Strategic thrust:* What broad courses of action shall we pursue?
- *Positioning:*
    What do we want to achieve?
    Who shall we persuade?
    Against whom shall we compete?
    Why should they buy from us rather than from competitors?
- *Action programs:* What specifically shall we do? When? Who will do it?
- *Resource commitments:* What resources are necessary to implement action programs, and to maintain and develop key account relationships?
- *Budgets and forecast:* To what specific detailed forecasts of results and expense budgets are we committing?

CHAPTER EIGHT

Managing the Key
Account Relationship

In this chapter, we discuss several managerial processes that are critical to developing and managing key account relationships through the operating cycle. We look initially at the key account team and discuss ways of ensuring that every member operates with a consistent focus. Next, we move to the supplier-firm/key-account interface and suggest processes to ensure that the interorganizational relationship develops appropriately through time. A section on the role of technology follows in which we discuss the impact of the Internet on key account management. Finally, we review various forms of performance measurement that act as control mechanisms either to reinforce, or trigger changes in, supplier firm and key account activities.

KEEPING THE KEY ACCOUNT TEAM FOCUSED

In a well-developed key account management system, team members either participate in, or are at least fully apprised of, the key account planning process. It is essential for them to stay focused on the agreed-upon actions and work continuously to develop and improve the supplier firm's relationship with the key account.

ONGOING INTERNAL COMMITMENT TO THE
KEY ACCOUNT PLAN

As we discussed in Chapter 7, all members of the key account team should be committed to the supplier firm's vision for the key account. More specifically, each member must be thoroughly familiar with, and committed to, the key account strategy and related action programs. Strategy, like the yoke on the team of oxen, may be heavy, but it should guide the day-by-day activities of supplier firm personnel. However, it is one thing for them to agree to a series of actions in the plan development stage. It is quite another for them to free required resources and take action during the operating period. It is the key account manager's responsibility to see that team members remain committed to the plan, and that agreed upon actions are being taken.

ONGOING INFORMATION ABOUT THE
INTERORGANIZATIONAL RELATIONSHIP

On a day-by-day basis, supplier firm and key account personnel interact about a myriad of items, from order, delivery, and billing issues to strategic planning and high-level meetings. For seamless management of the supplier-firm/key-account relationship, key account personnel must be kept up to date with these various issues, often in real time.

A well-developed information system should have multiple functions. U.S. multinational chemicals and machinery manufacturer FMC identifies three different functions for its *Magellan* information system.

- *Disseminating information*—reference (e.g., policy and procedures manuals, benefits guides) and news (industry, customer, competitor)[1]
- *Interacting*—tracking (sales management, customer service, project management, call reporting) and discussion (user groups, brainstorming, new product design)
- *Work flow*—forms routing (RFPs, pricing/contract approval, purchase orders, status reports) and messages (event driven, notifications)[2]

Some information is internal, concerned with supplier firm issues such as production scheduling or new product development. Other information is external, focused on the key account, the key account's business environment, competitors, and so forth. Both types of information must be gathered, analyzed, and appropriately disseminated.

In addition to receiving and disseminating descriptive data, key account managers should develop real-time systems for securing the perspectives of others on developing business and interpersonal relationships. This information, added to their own observations and insight, provides an important mechanism for keeping supplier-firm/key-account relationships on track.

A particularly critical information area concerns transactions data. The key account manager should have up-to-date information on order flow and shipments. When only a few products, order sources, and delivery locations are involved, this should not be difficult. However, when product lines are broad, and procurement and delivery locations many, this task becomes much more complex. It is even more difficult if the key account's purchases occur via an intermediary, especially if the firm's product is one component of the key account's purchases. Global accounts add another layer of complexity. Notwithstanding the difficulty of gathering and assembling this data, it is absolutely necessary for the key account manager if he is to truly lead and manage the supplier-firm/key-account relationship. Furthermore, since many key accounts do not have the systems to gather this information for themselves, this knowledge can be a valuable tool for key account managers.

Over and above real-time information for day-to-day management, significant amounts of external and internal data are required in the planning process to develop the key account plan. One important feature of the information system should be a methodology for gathering and storing data in an ongoing fashion. Then, when the new planning cycle commences, data collection is already partially completed.

FAST RESOLUTION OF INTERNAL CONFLICTS

Because many individuals from many different functions, with a myriad of responsibilities and reporting relationships, are likely involved in the interorganizational relationship, internal conflict is inevitable. When conflict occurs it should be recognized and dealt with openly and swiftly to avoid impeding the work of the entire account team. If key account members are not all "singing to the same tune," the potential for providing mixed messages to key account personnel is very high, and problems between the key account and supplier firm are likely to ensue. The responsibility for developing team agreement lies squarely with the key account manager. Like an orchestra conductor, she must work to ensure that all team members are playing together.

Of course, not all conflicts result from business related issues; interpersonal relationships may also be a serious matter. The key account manager must take responsibility for monitoring relationships among account team members to preempt serious problems from occurring, and take appropriate action.

REGULARLY SCHEDULED INTERNAL MEETINGS

Regardless of how well communications flow among the various members of the key account team, and how successfully conflicts are resolved, meetings of the full account team should be scheduled on a periodic basis. Members may discuss progress, follow up on action program items, share information and concerns, identify loose ends, decide on specific actions, and so forth. It is particularly important that progress on action step items be documented, probably on a monthly basis, then reviewed at a quarterly meeting.

Regular meetings have the additional benefit of providing the key account manager with the opportunity to exercise leadership. Meetings are most productive if meeting objectives are shared, and time limits and meeting norms made very clear to all participants. Where face-to-face meetings are difficult to arrange—for example, in global account management—they may be supplemented by telephone conference calls and/or Internet chat rooms. In any case, the discipline of regular review should be embedded in the key account management process.

STATUS ANALYSES

Two important types of analysis focus on securing business at the key account—win/loss analyses and pipeline analysis.

Win/Loss Analyses. During the operating cycle, the supplier firm may win some pieces of business at the key account and lose others. For each significant win or loss the key account manager should conduct an analysis to identify the root causes. Aggregated across all key accounts, win analysis might uncover *best practice* activities that can be repeated in new situations. Loss analysis might uncover problems that can be rectified for the future.

EXAMPLE: In its global accounts area, IBM makes a practice of assembling the various team members that worked on a major sale and asking them to relive the story. Team members are videotaped interrupting, correcting, supplementing, and reminding each other of what occurred and why. Analysis and editing of tapes from multiple deals results in many ideas that are shared as best practices. Other actions that led to less than successful conclusions are identified so they can be avoided in the future.[3]

Pipeline Analysis. In many purchase situations, the customer's process involves several stages—agreement on needs, development of specifications, qualifying suppliers, going out to bid, selecting the supplier, placing the order, purchasing product, going out for rebid, and so forth. Identifying the status of each potential piece of business in the "pipeline" provides the key account manager with valuable information regarding potential future resource requirements and sales revenues.

Furthermore, when similar data from the supplier firm's entire set of key accounts is aggregated, resource requirements and potential revenues are available at the organizational level. This moving "scorecard" is a powerful planning tool.

INTERFACES WITH THE SUPPLIER FIRM'S OTHER ORGANIZATIONAL UNITS

In any multibusiness organization that places key account responsibility at the business unit level, multiple business units may have relationships with a particular customer organization. For one business unit the organization may be a key account. For another, the organization may have some other form of customer relationship. For yet another business unit, the organization may be a supplier, competitor, or joint-venture partner. Furthermore, a key account relationship may also exist at the corporate level, either formally or via informal senior executive relationships.

From the perspective of the business-unit key account manager, each of these other relationships has the potential to impact the relationships of his team with the key account. At the very least, informal contact should be made with colleagues having customer responsibility in other business units (and at the corporate level). These contacts will be helpful in identifying synergies and potential trouble spots that may impact the supplier firm as a whole.

The key account manager should also be concerned when a sister organizational unit is not a supplier of the key account but could be. Consider the following situation that occurred in a high-technology company:

EXAMPLE: Chemical manufacturer Elm Inc.* supplied large quantities of product to its key account Oak*. Oak had a short-term requirement for a small quantity of a raw material that Elm manufactured in a separate business unit. Almost as an aside, the key account manager was asked if this unit could supply Oak's requirement. To be helpful, the key account manager provided information to Oak executives about whom to contact about the raw material in Elm's sister division. This division was having trouble fulfilling commitments to its current customers and declined to supply Oak. Oak then found an alternative supplier for its short-term requirement; this supplier used the opening to mount a major effort for the business Oak was giving to Elm.

The moral: the key account manager must stay on top of *all* relationships with the key account, whether or not they seem to involve the business under her responsibility. In the situation described above, the sister division could probably have been persuaded to supply the required limited quantity had it fully understood Elm's relationship with Oak, since it was important for the firm as a whole.

INTERFACING WITH THE KEY ACCOUNT

Supplier-firm/key-account interfaces can be grouped in three main areas—required activities in real time, problems and opportunities at the key account, and supplier-firm/key-account review processes.

Required Activities in Real Time

The key account manager and key account personnel must agree, at least in a general sense, on the frequency and type of contact between the two organizations. Direct contact may include visits by the key account manager, technical personnel, and senior managers to the key account, and key account personnel visits to the supplier firm.

Contact density is an especially important issue for those key accounts that purchase a range of products from the supplier firm. Indeed, in recent years, sophisticated procurement organizations, concerned with administrative expense, have demanded that suppliers reduce the numbers of salespeople assigned to them. Furthermore, some of these organizations have attempted to remove noneconomic bases for purchasing decisions by banning the acceptance of supplier-financed entertainment. Clearly, the key account manager must know the customer's policies and act accordingly.

In some cases, both the supplier firm and key account may gain from locating a supplier-firm employee on-site at the customer. As noted earlier, though costly, the supplier firm gains by increasing the depth of the interorganizational relationship.[4] From the key account's perspective, on-site physical presence may offer some level of insurance. Indeed, on-site personnel may be able to solve a problem before the customer realizes there is a problem!

PERSONNEL CHANGES

We already indicated that continuity in interpersonal relationships is an important factor in dealing with key accounts. However, as time passes, personnel change. They may leave, or assume new roles as the result of promotions, new assignments, or resignations. Since such changes can be potentially disruptive, relevant key account personnel need to be advised of these changes, and appropriate hand-over procedures designed and implemented. As noted in Chapter 4, in some supplier-firm/key-account relationships, key account personnel are involved in the selection process, often at the final approval stage.

PRE-MEETING PLANNING

Pre-meeting planning is a methodology to ensure that supplier firm and key account resources are well spent in meetings. Indeed, as indicated earlier, customer measures of supplier effectiveness now frequently include items concerning the use of key account personnel's time. The key account manager should also be effective in using supplier firm resources.

For every meeting concerning the key account, regardless of whether or not key account personnel will be present, the key account manager should see that a pre-meeting plan is developed. If the meeting involves key account personnel, the process of developing the pre-meeting plan fulfills several important functions. These include gathering new information on the account, ensuring that all supplier firm personnel at the meeting are up to date on the supplier-firm/key-account relationship, and creating a mind-set of how to approach the key account. For each meeting, the pre-meeting plan should specify objectives, strategy, execution, and next steps.

Objectives. The key account manager and relevant team members should know what they want to accomplish at the meeting. The key account manager may wish to gather background data for preparing the account plan, secure agreement to test a new product, or convey bad news about a shipping delay. Other objectives might be to demonstrate supplier firm commitment to the key account, identify the relative importance of various benefits required by the account, or surface issues whose resolution may enhance the supplier-customer relationship.

Not only should meeting objectives be well specified, supplier firm personnel should affirmatively decide the criteria for measuring success. For supplier-firm/key-account meetings, the best criteria typically require actions by the key account. For example:

- Key account agrees to a new product test by the end of August
- Key account provides importance weightings for the benefit set
- Key account agrees to actions specified in the key account plan

Strategy. In pre-meeting planning, strategy involves laying out how the meeting should proceed. It involves such elements as deciding who should or should not attend from the account team, and who should or should not be invited from the key account. Other elements include setting the agenda, deciding what information to prepare for attendees, what roles each supplier firm representative should play in the meeting, what the probing strategy should be (who asks what questions, in what order), what materials are needed (visuals, exhibits), and so forth.

Execution. The meeting should be managed effectively by the key account manager. In supplier-firm/key-account meetings, he should act as chair to the extent that key account executives are comfortable with him assuming that role. The manager should endeavor to ensure that the meeting strategy is implemented, and conclude the meeting by clarifying agreements on action items, including completion dates, for individuals in both organizations. He should also be open to dealing with unexpected issues raised by key account personnel during the meeting.

Debrief. Just as the pre-meeting plan lays the road map for the meeting, a debrief is necessary to evaluate the extent to which the objectives of the meeting were achieved. Individual supplier-firm personnel will probably have different views on what happened in the meeting. It is important to strive for collective understanding of what transpired so that additional actions (supplementary to those agreed at the meeting) may be formulated as necessary.

Next Steps. As the result of discussion in the meeting, typically some degree of follow-up is required. This follow-up should be clearly specified as action items for individual supplier firm and key account personnel, and should be confirmed in writing soon after the meeting.

The key account manager should be responsible for circulating meeting notes, including next steps, to all members of the key account team. A specially designed Web site is a convenient vehicle for accomplishing this purpose. Frequently, meetings with key account personnel do not involve all team members. Nonetheless, the entire team must be kept abreast of developments both at the key account and within the supplier firm, so as to enhance their own individual effectiveness.

Problems and Opportunities

No matter how well developed its quality processes, inevitably problems occur at the supplier firm. Delivery schedules may be missed, product quality may be below par or service less than optimal, or faulty invoices may be sent. In addition, customers create problems that they expect the supplier to address. Rather than be faced with surprises late in the game, customers (and suppliers) prefer to know about problems as early as possible, together with potential solutions. Sometimes, if sufficient notice is given, the two organizations can together reach a jointly acceptable solution.

EXAMPLE: China's Shangai Chlor-Alkali Chemical Company (SCAC) supplies PVC resin to several major customers in southern China. These accounts commit to purchasing agreed-upon quantities of PVC in the upcoming period. When supply shortages occur, SCAC attempts to identify accounts whose current requirements are below their commitments. It then "borrows" PVC from these accounts to supply customers whose current needs exceed their own commitments.[5]

Relatedly, if the key account manager is having difficulty implementing an agreed-upon action program because of problems at the key account, the matter should be raised at the appropriate time with key account personnel. Only through open acknowledgment of difficulties can program implementation move ahead as required.

FAST RESOLUTION OF CUSTOMER COMPLAINTS

Regardless of best efforts by the supplier firm to catch problems early, undoubtedly it will receive complaints. When complaints occur, they should be acknowledged and dealt with openly and swiftly to avoid souring the interorganizational relationship. Indeed, not only may swift action take care of the matter at hand, such occurrences provide the supplier firm with an opportunity to demonstrate its ability for fast response. Thus, a seemingly negative situation may allow the manager to enhance the supplier firm's reputation with key account personnel.

> **EXAMPLE:** IBM's customer complaint management system involves routing each complaint and suggestion for improvement to a specially designated complaint resolution owner who is responsible for resolving the issue. Ninety-four percent of these issues are dealt with in seven business days!

Complaint management systems require a well-thought-through process that involves conceptualizing the various areas in which complaints are received, identifying supplier firm personnel in each complaint area, matching complaints with these personnel, and following through to ensure that each complaint is handled expeditiously. In addition, an easily accessible database of resolved complaints speeds the resolution process. Overarching this process should be a system that identifies the causes of complaints and makes permanent changes in the supplier firm's processes to reduce the probability of reoccurrence.

Furthermore, the supplier firm should not simply be reactive to the key account. Its personnel, led by the key account manager, should seek out areas of less than stellar performance so that these areas and customer satisfaction can be improved

IDENTIFYING AND MANAGING OPPORTUNITIES AT THE KEY ACCOUNT

One of the key account manager's major responsibilities is to identify opportunities for the supplier firm to secure business at the key account. In most cases, the manager develops her information sources in the key account, and pursues this search on an ongoing basis. In other cases, a more formal process may offer benefits.

> **EXAMPLE:** At Orange Inc.*, the fifteen members of the key account team attempt to identify opportunities for the firm's products and technologies at their account. Using a semistructured questionnaire developed by a corporate support group, teams of two conduct upwards of fifty interviews with senior key account executives from various functional areas. After an initial set of interviews, the entire Orange team convenes to discuss findings and develop a questionnaire for a second round of interviews. Following this second round a priority list is drawn up of opportunities for further exploration.

In most supplier firms, the number of key account opportunities surfaced is greater than the firm's resources, especially when a high proportion of the key accounts are either developmental accounts, or accounts with significant upside potential. However, all too frequently, a retrospective analysis may discover that bids were not made on time, or were made when they should not have been (because of low success probabilities). Furthermore, proposals may have been poorly crafted, or excessively stubborn resistance made to price concessions, even though the potential volume would have more than offset the price reduction.

In order to make informed choices about which opportunities to pursue, the supplier firm should consider developing an opportunity management process. Such a process would employ a standard format for describing opportunities and comprise standard qualification, prioritization, and selection routines. Opportunities would be triaged, and the progress of those that were pursued could be easily tracked.

From time to time, once an opportunity has been identified, the team may not have the appropriate expertise to pursue it. Some companies conclude the opportunity selection routine by appointing an opportunity owner. This expert puts together a team to conduct RFP analysis, cost modeling, operational feasibility assessment, and proposal development to pursue the opportunity under the general direction of the key account manager.

Review Processes

REGULAR ACCOUNT/FIRM REVIEWS

Periodically, through the operating cycle, key members of the supplier firm account team should meet with their opposite numbers at the key account to review their relationship. This review should cover the gamut of such issues as product quality, delivery, service, and new product introductions, and should complement an ongoing customer feedback program (see below). Indeed, results from the feedback program should form a crucial input into these meetings.

Supplier firm personnel should also seek an honest and open discussion regarding the extent to which the interorganizational relationship is being moved forward, or retarded, by interpersonal relationships—between supplier firm and key account personnel, as well as among supplier firm personnel, and among members of the key account team. (Of course, as noted earlier, the key account manager should be paying attention to key account team dynamics on an ongoing basis.)

ANNUAL REVIEW OF ACHIEVEMENT[6]

In addition to these regular reviews, the supplier firm should conduct a complete review of the relationship with the key account on an annual basis. This review, which should include senior executives from both organizations, focuses on where the supplier has performed well, and where it has performed poorly: which objectives have been met, which have slid beyond target deadlines, and which are completely off target. It should also address such issues as technology development and raw material forecasts. From the perspective of the supplier firm, this review provides invaluable input into the situation analysis for the next planning cycle, and the development of key account strategy and action programs.

EXAMPLE: In 1995, Siemens called in representatives from key accounts Opel, Ford, and Sony to provide feedback on Siemens' performance. Sony blasted chip managers for rotten service and erratic delivery. "It was brutal," recalled a Siemens manager.[7]

Key accounts increasingly demand that supplier firms identify specific areas in which the key account relationship has benefited their operations. For example: Where has competitive advantage increased? What specific cost savings have been enjoyed? These data should be well documented, for executives at the key account may have short memories for value that the supplier firm has delivered.

Among the items that should be considered for inclusion in the annual review are:

- The accuracy of the supplier firm's perception of the key account's goals and strategy, especially as they impact the supplier firm
- The supplier firm's vision, mission, and strategy for addressing the key account
- Review of the key account's procurement history versus prior years (if appropriate) and plan
- Success stories, perhaps including such items as on-time delivery record, results of shared initiatives, customer visits, major supplier firm projects that impact the key account, and results of customer satisfaction studies[8]
- Review of resources focused on serving the key account, including key account team members
- Results from ongoing key account satisfaction surveys (see below)
- Identification of next steps. The generation of a discussion on ways in which the supplier firm can help the key account achieve its goals in the upcoming time period.

Such meetings are likely to raise the supplier firm's level of influence at the key account, and shift the nature of the interorganizational relationship from one of vendor/buyer in the direction of value-added supplier and partnership. As the relationship develops, it is increasingly likely that the account will show a greater willingness to act on the firm's recommendations. However, these meetings also tend to raise key account expectations that issues raised will be expeditiously addressed by the supplier.

If such meetings do not occur, seemingly unimportant issues such as minor time delays and administrative snafus may be not be addressed. Left to fester, they can become crucial issues to at least one important person at the key account. It may then be only be a matter of time until the supplier firm is displaced by a competitor. Only issues that are raised can be dealt with! The annual review is a powerful means of bringing up issues and discussing mutual problems.

EXAMPLE: Consumer products company Camphor Inc.'s* "rigid billing procedures" increasingly irritated, and caused it to lose Laburnum*, its principal retail client. Camphor had no mechanism for assessing Laburnum's perceptions of its billing practices.[9]

THE ROLE OF TECHNOLOGY [10]

We live in an era in which technology increasingly affects how work is conducted in organizations. Indeed, in recent years, the technological ante has been raised by the increasingly widespread use of the Internet. Internet and related technologies have the ability to impact key account management as much, or maybe more, than many other jobs in organizations. In general, value offered by the Internet relates to its ability to:

- provide lots of data inexpensively
- standardize information flows
- reduce intermediary data handling errors
- reduce time, effort, and money on corporate mechanics
- sort and disseminate data—quickly, everywhere, regardless of geography
- enhance communications possibilities
- allow users access to information at their convenience
- make revisions of data easy to manage and current
- allow universal access through a browser

The organizational challenge is to take this potential value and apply it to key account management, both within the supplier's organization and across the organizational boundary.

INSIDE THE SUPPLIER'S ORGANIZATION [11]

Technologically based solutions to organizational problems tend to be most appropriate when the following four conditions hold—large numbers of personnel are involved, these personnel are widely dispersed geographically, asynchronous delivery of information is required (when and where convenient), and knowledge must be captured and disseminated. Organizations with significant numbers of key account managers, each leading and managing a team, certainly meet this set of criteria. When these managers have global responsibility, the argument for Internet-based solutions is even stronger.

Several discrete areas are most appropriate for Internet-based solutions, frequently via firm-specific *intranets:*

Foundation knowledge is important data that the key account manager and team members should be able to access twenty-four/seven (whenever needed). It might include organization charts, the supplier firm's annual report, training materials, and background on the industry.

Tools help users to be more effective and efficient in their jobs, and tend to be stable over time. Examples of tools include forms, checklists, templates for preparing the key account plan and call reports, tools for preparing expense reports, and canned presentations that may be customized for individual key accounts.

> **EXAMPLE:** Milliken's carpet organization has an image bank consisting of before and after photographs of installations involving Milliken carpets. These images can be e-mailed to key accounts or downloaded from the Milliken web site.

Perhaps the most valuable Internet-based tool is e-mail, both the ability to copy and forward all messages directed to, and received from, the key account and continuously log all inter- (and intra-) organizational communications.

Information differs from *foundation knowledge* inasmuch as it is specifically needed to perform a job. Technology's role is to anchor information systems to enhance organizational effectiveness; frustration and search time are reduced when the information is easy to supply and can be accessed when and where needed. Of course, care should be taken regarding user preferences, and concerns about "data smog" should be sensitively addressed.

Examples are myriad but include internally developed data such as sales call reports, action steps from the key account plan, tracking orders through manufacturing, market and competitor analyses, access to corporate extranets, and best practice ideas.

EXAMPLE: Bain Consulting and other organizations develop knowledge libraries that might include solutions to key account problems. Key account managers can access these sites as a first step in trying to solve such a problem.

In addition, information may be accessed from web sites or via search engines that deliver particular types of required information.

Collaborative networks allow individuals to come together to create, capture, share, and use organizational knowledge. Collaboration may be either synchronous, for example, chat rooms, or asynchronous. In general, synchronous collaboration may be less valuable than asynchronous collaboration because it requires simultaneous availability and scheduling.[12]

EXAMPLE: The Asian division of Buckman, a $270 million specialty chemicals manufacturer, used the firm's collaborative network to enhance its prospects at an Indonesian pulp mill. Buckman's knowledge-sharing system unearthed several types of information: a master's thesis on paper mills using tropical hardwoods (Memphis); paper mill control problems in British Columbia (Canada), two current pulp mill programs (South Africa), and data on Buckman's newest paper processing chemicals (R&D team). The result, a $6 million contract. Even though only 20% of Buckman's personnel use on-line collaboration, the system is viewed as a huge success.[13]

ACROSS THE ORGANIZATIONAL BOUNDARY [14]

Supplier firms are increasingly developing web sites to improve interfaces with their key accounts. These web sites may either be publicly accessible though the Internet, or set up as individual *extranets* by integrating supplier firm and key account *intranets*.

In general, the supplier firm's web site interfaces with key accounts using one of three approaches—content-driven, transaction-driven, or relationship-driven.

Content-driven web sites provide information to customers. They take information that was previously available in some other form, such as basic organizational information, annual reports, product catalogs, and new product offerings and make it more easily available to customers. A good content-driven web site allows key account personnel to secure information directly, rather than from a member of the key account team, thus springing time savings for both supplier-firm and key-account personnel.

In addition, a web site may be designed to function as a supplementary communications medium like advertising, and as a means to build the firm's image. Indeed, a web site may enable the supplier firm to reach nontraditional areas of the key account, identify innovators within the key account, and function as a lead-generation device.

EXAMPLE: Under Dell Computer's traditional transactional model, 100,000 catalogs might lead to 10,000 calls and 2,000 (20%) orders. In Dell's Internet model, 100,000 online store visits lead directly to 500 electronic orders. However, the on-line store would also generate 5,000 calls leading to 1,750 (35%) orders.[15]

Transaction-driven web sites provide customers with the ability to place orders for products. These sites may function independent of, or in conjunction with, a key account management program. Because the key account manager is no longer involved in the transaction *per se,* time is freed up for other activities, including selling. The ability to transact business through the Internet is bringing about a change in firms' procurement activities; it enables cost reduction in procurement and by tracking purchases, the firm can secure greater employee compliance with corporate purchasing guidelines, especially for those items such as travel and PCs that are purchased widely throughout the organization.

EXAMPLE: Dell Computer's *Premier Pages* allows major accounts "Internet access to password-protected, customer-specific information about Dell's products and services. . . . Customers [can] configure, price, and buy systems at approved, discounted prices, track orders and inventory through detailed account purchasing reports, and access contact information for Dell account and service and support team members, including telephone numbers, e-mail addresses, and pager numbers"[16]

Dell observed that whereas in the traditional system account managers spent 15% of their time in active selling, 45% for operational, and 40% for travel, with *Premier Pages,* active selling increased to 45% and operational dropped to 15%.

Relationship-driven web sites include the attributes of content and transaction-driven sites but provide such extra value that customers are motivated to return. It is still early days in the development of relationship-driven sites, but they promise to become a valuable tool. One example is their ability to track the progress of an order through the supplier's production system. If these systems are well designed, they may both enhance customer value and reduce the supplier's costs—a true win-win.[17]

> **EXAMPLE:** SouthCo, manufacturers of latches and access hardware, has developed a web site that allows key accounts access to many years of purchasing history, tracks orders back to the shipper's site, has a "my parts" pull-down menu to reduce the number of key strokes, and provides real-time inventory information along with local currency and language support.[18]

> **EXAMPLE:** Federal Express's original package tracking system required customers to call an 800 number to talk to a customer service representative. More recently, FedEx has developed an Internet-based system so that customers can track the progress of their own packages through the FedEx system.

These web sites also have the ability to provide customer service to key accounts. SouthCo's customer service facility is available globally 24/7, using a template system to respond to customer inquires within five minutes in seven languages.

Customers can be given suggestions for future purchases based on previous purchases. For repeat customers, Amazon.com offers book suggestions based on customers' previous purchases.

Chat rooms allow key account personnel, possibly from several key accounts, and supplier personnel to meet to discuss issues of mutual interest. Johnson & Johnson Japan operates chat rooms for its key physician customers. Here geographically dispersed specialists can meet with their peers to discuss matters of mutual interest.

Of course, not every problem facing key account management can be solved by technology. The firm must sort through a myriad of impediments to high-performing key account management to identify those that seem most suited to a technological solution. However, before solutions are attempted, the organization needs to assess the extent to which it is ready to adopt technology-based solutions. For example, the firm may not have the required basic infrastructure, there may be cultural barriers to adopting technology-based solutions, or experience with the Internet may be insufficient to move forward. Unless the conditions are appropriate in at least some pocket of the organization, a technology-based solution is better deferred until the conditions generally become more favorable. Of course, when a technology solution is developed, it should be implemented on a small scale to iron out the bugs before moving to widespread deployment.

Finally, some key account management issues require budgets and significant involvement of IT professionals. However, if, for whatever reason, needed systems are not forthcoming, the individual manager may consider moving forward independently. A basic web site may be constructed for a small outlay, yet provide significant value for both key account personnel and team members.

PERFORMANCE MONITORING

The key account plan should be a living document that helps manage the supplier-firm/key-account relationship through time. For this to occur, the supplier firm must develop a planning control process or processes.

Control of the key account plan operates at four levels:

- Performance control focuses on whether or not performance objectives have been met.
- Implementation control is concerned with whether or not the key account strategy and action programs were implemented as planned.
- Strategy control is concerned with whether or not the results of implementing the key account strategy and action programs are perceived to be satisfactory, given that they were implemented.
- Control of the planning process focuses on quality of the planning process.

At each level, control is exercised through a feedback process based on a measure–inspect–problem-solve system.[19]

Performance Control

The set of budgets and forecasts developed during the key account planning process functions as the raw material for the supplier firm's performance control system. Forecast annual sales revenue, share of business, gross profit and/or profit contribution, expenses and sales-to-expense ratios, both in total and broken out by product or product line, organization unit, and application should be disaggregated into quarterly or monthly benchmarks where appropriate.

Throughout the operating period, actual performance should be tracked against these budgets and forecasts. In some cases, data required for performance monitoring is derived from the order entry system. In other cases, it comes from contact reports or action-planning guides related to action programs, and in still others from independently administered surveys. These "steering control" comparisons form the basis for a fine-grained performance analysis.

Furthermore, they spur the development of agenda items for both supplier-firm account team and key-account/supplier-firm meetings, and are the springboard for developing action programs to deal with variances. Negative variances typically require affirmative action by revisiting the planned key account action programs and/or strategy, and deciding on remedial action. Positive variances may require little action although, in such cases, unexpected opportunities may have surfaced that require the supplier firm to commit new resources and take previously unplanned actions to exploit them fully.

CUSTOMER FEEDBACK

In addition to the *hard* performance control measures just described, the supplier firm should track *soft* measures. Included are "trust indicators" such as sharing confidential information, providing access to key decision makers, sponsorship of important programs, and important "customer indicators" such as satisfaction and its determinants (e.g., responsiveness, communications).[20] In addition, the supplier should track the key account's intent to continue the business relationship and its perception of the value brought to the key account by the supplier.

All things equal, the supplier firm enhances its position at the key account to the extent that trust increases, customer satisfaction improves, and the supplier is delivering significant (and increasing) value. The fundamental underpinning for these measures is understanding customer needs, making promises to satisfy those needs, then delivering on those promises. Securing this understanding and deciding how to act is a critical element in the key account planning process.

Many supplier firms are putting in place systems to capture key account feedback. Various methodologies, including surveys and open-ended personal interviews, are available for this critical task. The supplier firm should select a system that provides it with the data it requires, including areas of, and suggestions for, improvement. In practice, those firms pushing the envelope of key account management practice use both surveys and open-ended personal interviews.

Surveys. Using a survey methodology, the supplier firm works with critical key account personnel in a comprehensive attempt to identify the core elements of customer satisfaction. Of course, these elements differ from key account to key account but, nonetheless, a similar process should be followed across all key accounts (Figure 8.1).[21] The key account manager and supplier firm personnel also identify those persons from whom satisfaction measures and other feedback elements should be received.

As a result of these efforts, one or more survey instruments may be developed, some of which may be specific to a set of potential respondents (e.g., procurement, receiving, accounts payable, key decision makers). In any event, even if a single questionnaire is used, the data should be analyzed in both an aggregated and disaggregated form. Each completed survey should be viewed as an individual case study requiring review and possible follow-up by the key account manager.

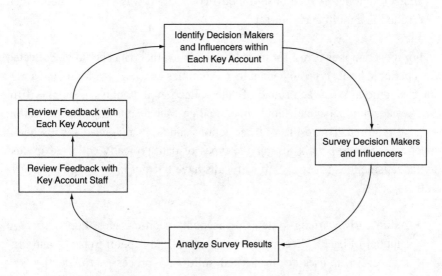

FIGURE 8.1: The Customer Feedback Loop

EXAMPLE: In one key account satisfaction study, the aggregated score was 3.9 (1 = highly unsatisfied, 7 = highly satisfied). However, the three respondents with most decision-making power rated the supplier, 1.0, 1.0, and 1.5![22]

The instruments should be sufficiently robust that they provide useful trend data, yet flexible enough to allow for questions on specific areas of interest as required. A variety of methods may be used for data collection including mail, telephone, in-person interview, and Internet based.[23] During the process, interviewees may identify other individuals who should be surveyed and who may turn out to be influencers or decision makers of whom the key account manager was not previously aware. In general, data is best collected by an independent organization that is also responsible for tabulation and developing preliminary conclusions. At all costs, the interviewers should be impartial. For example, using key account managers to conduct feedback interviews may well provide biased results, perhaps because those being interviewed are reluctant to provide negative feedback to personnel who may be the source of the key account's dissatisfaction.

EXAMPLE: At Cedar Inc.*, key account satisfaction studies were conducted by key account managers. When a consulting firm was brought in for validation purposes it found that Cedar's largest customer was actively seeking out another supplier. A relationship recovery program was then initiated which resulted in a multiyear contract.[24]

For most supplier firms, for most key accounts, this data should be collected on a periodic basis, typically annually (sometimes quarterly) or following a major transaction. After each round of data collection and analysis, supplier firm and key account personnel should meet to digest the results and agree on action steps as required. The results of these actions should be reviewed at subsequent meetings. (See Appendix 8.1 for the types of data typically collected in customer satisfaction surveys.) Survey results have been used by suppliers in several ways:[25]

- As an early warning system for account specific issues, Poplar Inc.*, a supplier of back-office processing, service, and support to banks and brokerage firms, uses feedback and follow-up processes to identify key account-specific and more general customer issues of which it was not previously aware. Frequently, the issues are minor and easily fixed, yet the process shows the key account that Poplar is responsive. In some cases, potentially significant issues have been identified prior to causing a key account problem.

- As an opportunity to up-sell and cross-sell, Hemlock*, a major chemical company, uses its feedback process to assess whether it can better meet key account needs with other products. Hemlock discovered that often when key accounts are dissatisfied with the firm in general, or with product quality in particular, they are either unaware that the firm offers more appropriate products, or they have been offered the wrong products.

- As a bargaining tool in negotiations with key accounts, Ash Inc.*, a major supplier to the pharmaceutical industry, surveys several different functions within each key account around the globe. Before annual contract reviews, Ash examines the survey data to gain insight into the key account's perspective of the state of each relationship. By stressing the high level of satisfaction and value provided to the key account, Ash leverages especially positive feedback.

- As a means of motivating and evaluating key account team members at Hawthorne*, a major financial institution, feedback is now directly related to each key account team's "at risk" compensation and keeps both senior management and team members focused on customer needs. Evaluation of team-specific results allows management to identify teams that are excelling, and those that require further training or replacement.

Open-ended Personal Interviews. Open-ended interviews, conducted by the executive partner (or similar-level manager) with senior executives at the key account, can be a vehicle for raising the contact level and for probing feedback secured from survey instruments. They may be particularly useful for assessing key account manager performance, and surfacing general areas of dissatisfaction. Although mostly focused on the key account, some interviews are also typically held with critical internal personnel (e.g., customer service, technical service, quality assurance).

EXAMPLE: On an annual basis, two senior Hewlett-Packard (HP) managers conduct interviews with executives at HP's key accounts to assess their degree of satisfaction with the performance of individual key account managers and their teams. These unstructured interviews provide a useful way of securing additional key account data, identifying opportunities not surfaced by the key account manager, and strengthening relationships.

Although lacking the rigor of well-conducted survey research, effective personal interview systems allow for more rapid response when problems are identified.

EXAMPLE: During a periodic interview at one of its more important key accounts, interviewers from Monkey Inc.*, a large hi-tech company, identified considerable dissatisfaction with its key account team. Within three business days, Monkey management replaced the entire team. The customer was amazed and delighted at Monkey's swift response.

Whereas collecting customer feedback is critical for the supplier, the process should be seen as a collaborative effort with the key account. In the best relationships, key accounts participate by agreeing on the areas to be surveyed, identifying potential respondents, and completing the survey. The supplier shares the results with senior executives and operating personnel at the key account, and the two organizations jointly develop plans to deal with dissatisfaction. Regardless of the methodology used, it is important to keep individual responses in perspective and to ensure that resources to solve perceived problems are not allocated simply on a "squeaky wheel" basis.

Implementation Control

Control of action programs should follow measurement and control procedures agreed to during program formulation and should include measuring completion of action steps, following up where necessary, and achievement of action program objectives.[26] If action programs are not being implemented appropriately, supplier firm and key account personnel must identify the source(s) of blockage. For example:

- Is the supplier firm delivering the required resources?
- Is the supplier firm's service department following agreed upon procedures at the account?
- Are personnel at the key account being uncooperative? For example, perhaps operations personnel are unwilling to provide production facilities for testing a new raw material.

These action program issues should be dealt with both at internal key account team meetings and at periodic key-account/supplier-firm meetings. Resolution of problems may involve securing promised but as yet undelivered resources.

Strategy Control

Even if strategy and action programs are implemented as planned, they may not yield the hoped-for results from the perspectives of either the key account or supplier firm. When performance falls short of requirements, the key account manager must be prepared to take the tough decisions to stop, or appropriately modify, the action programs. (Of course, such decisions should be made with clear understanding of the sunk cost principle: that considerable resources may have already been spent should not influence the decision of whether or not to continue. The resources are *sunk* and the decision to stop or continue should be made in the light of current information.)

Furthermore, although the supplier firm may develop strategy and programs on an annual basis, typically key accounts do not make decisions to match the supplier firm's planning schedule! It may be necessary to update or modify the key account strategy and action programs midway through the operating cycle.

In evaluating action programs, it is useful to classify ongoing performance as successful or unsuccessful from both key account and supplier firm perspectives (Figure 8.2).

Key Account: Successful/Supplier Firm: Successful (Cell A): If the action program falls into this cell, it should continue.

Key Account: Successful/Supplier Firm: Unsuccessful (Cell B): Perhaps, with the benefit of hindsight, the supplier firm believes that the action program objectives were inappropriate or the committed resources too high. Perhaps, the supplier's goals have changed and program objectives are no longer meaningful. The supplier firm must make some tough decisions. To cancel an ongoing program considered successful by the key account risks damaging the relationship. Yet, to continue the program does not otherwise serve the supplier firm's interests. The decision to discontinue the action program in its original or modified form must be taken very carefully.

Key Account: Unsuccessful/Supplier Firm: Successful (Cell C): Perhaps the key account's objectives and strategy have changed, and the action program objectives are no longer meaningful. Or, perhaps, successful pro-

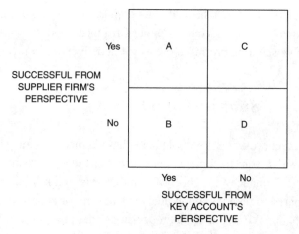

FIGURE 8.2: Analysis of Action Programs

gram completion would constrain the key account's actions. (A change in objectives may occur because important players at the key account were not fully consulted initially or have been replaced.) A careful diagnosis of the reasons for key account unhappiness must be made, and a decision to stop or continue the action program, in its original or modified form, made after discussion with appropriate key account personnel.

Key Account: Unsuccessful/Supplier Firm: Unsuccessful (Cell D): Neither side is happy with progress of the action program. A decision to continue the program in the present form would be wasteful. However, before the program is totally abandoned, both key account and supplier firm personnel should revisit the original action program objectives and action steps to test their validity, and see whether appropriate modifications can be made.

Desired objectives may not be realized because of the failure of planned action steps. In addition, changes in objectives and strategy, at both key account and supplier firm, occur over time as a reflection of environmental imperatives and internal organizational changes. The key account strategy and action programs and, relatedly, the supplier-firm/key-account relationship may need to be adapted. The key account plan thus becomes a living document, rather than the output of a sterile exercise simply to satisfy senior management.

Planning Process Control

In addition to focusing on the current key account plan, the key account manager must control the planning process *per se*. She must ask, "Did the key account planning process produce the best possible strategy and action programs?"

An answer to this question requires an audit function separate and apart from controlling specific strategy and action programs. Conducted by the key account manager in consultation with the key account director, the audit's purpose is to assess the quality of planning process for the key account. Among the sorts of questions to be asked are:

- How thorough was the situation analysis? Did we secure satisfactory data from the key account regarding its external and internal realities, objectives, and strategies? If not, why not? What might we do to improve matters for the next planning cycle?
- How good a job did we do in developing planning assumptions? To what extent did the assumptions developed in previous years' plans hold up during the operating period?
- Did we do a good job isolating opportunities and threats?
- On our side, was the planning process a team effort? Did all personnel fulfill their assignments to the best of their abilities? Were there certain types of information that we were unable to secure? Which are these? Did we secure appropriate levels of cooperation from elsewhere in our organization in developing the plan? If not, why not? How might we improve things for the next planning cycle?
- Were the processes employed for strategy and action program development appropriate? Did they show a good mix of hardheaded realism and creativity?
- Do we have the systems in place to measure the value of our action programs? Are we able to distinguish between the sorts of action programs that deliver customer value and result in increased revenues and profits, and those that do not?
- Do we do a good job in implementing our action programs? Do these fail? If so, is it because planned resource commitments do not materialize, or for other reasons?

- Do we use the key account plan as a living document? Do we have in place a system of "steering control" for account review? Are course corrections made early when planning assumptions are found to be faulty?
- What elements of the planning process were particularly noteworthy? Which elements provided superior data, insight, creativity, and so forth?
- Did our planning process sufficiently engage personnel at the key account?

Audit results should identify those parts of the process that worked well and those that worked less well. The conclusion of the audit should be a set of action steps to improve the process for the next planning cycle.

Note that this audit function is driven by the key account manager and addresses his planning performance in the context of an overall supplier-firm system for key account planning. If shortcomings are identified, they should be addressed in the next planning cycle. The audit function should be clearly distinguished from the responsibility of the key account director continually to upgrade the entire planning system based on audits from the entire set of key account plans prepared by multiple key account managers.

SUMMARY

Key account management must put in place a set of managerial processes that ensure that key account plans are developed and implemented appropriately and that the supplier firm's relationships with its key accounts are enhanced and strengthened. Internally, several steps can be taken to ensure that key account teams are focused on achieving the supplier firm objectives at their key accounts. Externally, processes must be put in place to manage, carefully and deliberately, the interfaces between key accounts and the supplier firm. At present, significant innovation is occurring around the use of the Internet. Key account management must keep up to date with these developments and move toward adopting those processes that can improve the firm's relationships with its key accounts. Finally, the firm should implement the several different control mechanisms that are available for ensuring that key account management is on track at individual key accounts.

IV. CRITICAL ISSUES FOR KEY ACCOUNT MANAGEMENT

CHAPTER NINE

Partnering with Key Accounts

If the transition from the traditional sales force system to key account management represents a major shift in dealing with very important customers, then the transition from a competent key account management program to a partnership with key accounts is at least an equally major shift.[1]

A general definition of partnership is:

"a relationship . . . involving close cooperation between parties having specified and joint, rights and responsibilities."[2]

More specifically in the business domain, a partnership is:

"a tailored business relationship based on mutual trust, openness, shared risk, and shared rewards that yields a competitive advantage, resulting in business performance greater than would be achieved by the firms individually."[3]

For suppliers and key accounts, partnering involves working together to achieve specific long-run goals. These are secured via joint planning and coordination, information sharing, the absence of opportunistic behavior, and effective use of resources. Partnering is intermediate between arms-length relationships on the one hand, and joint ventures and vertical integration on the other.[4]

Partnering represents a level of intimacy beyond the traditionally successful key account relationship.[5] Indeed, partnerships involve a much deeper and broader mutually trusting commitment, involving transparency of otherwise confidential information, tailored to the parties' requirements that, if well conceived and executed, result in each party gaining significant benefits (and sharing risks).[6] In partnership relationships, problems experienced by one partner are also problems for the other partner.

Two important factors, based upon tough economic decision making, are responsible for supplier-firm/key-account partnerships becoming increasingly popular in recent years:

- Customer firms have realized that closer relationships with selected suppliers may enable them to be more competitive in their own markets.[7]
- Supplier firms have realized that partnerships, as a natural extension of successful key account management programs, may offer significant potential benefits for selected accounts.[8]

A particular feature of partnership relationships is that, whereas key account management programs were historically driven largely from the supplier side, partnership programs are just as likely to result from initiatives taken by the customer firm. Of course, partnership programs can only develop and succeed if both sides, buyer and seller, foresee and receive tangible economic benefits. And these benefits should exceed the incremental costs of developing and managing the partnership.[9]

EVOLUTION IN PARTNERSHIP DEVELOPMENT

Initiative from Customer Firms

Competitive pressures have led corporations to focus increasing attention on the procurement function as a means of improving their competitive positions. As a result, a variety of overlapping procurement strategies has evolved. These embrace supplier evaluation methodologies including preferred supplier programs,[10] supplier development activities such as advice regarding equipment, operating methods, and quality systems, and *strategic sourcing*.

EXAMPLE: Honda of America Manufacturing has fifty personnel devoted to supplier development. Small teams work on-site with key suppliers to identify goals of improving quality and reducing costs, and evaluating and modifying process to achieve those goals. With this training in process redesign, suppliers are expected to cascade the process to their own suppliers.[11]

Strategic sourcing seeks to determine the firm's most competent suppliers by gathering extensive data on their operations—for example, on work processes, cost build-up, and quality strategy. Frequently, multidisciplinary procurement teams conduct site visits to verify information, trouble-shoot quality problems, and seek ways to reduce costs. Performance improvement measures are selected, and targets negotiated to establish certification standards. Not only does achieving certification take considerable time and effort, ongoing reviews assess the supplier's performance and ability to retain customer certification.[12] Firms implementing strategic sourcing typically take control of the procurement schedule, issue greater numbers of RFPs and proposal revisions, and focus on life cycle costs, quality, and service, in addition to price.

Underlying this procurement behavior is the ageless tension between markets and hierarchies that leads to the following question:[13] Is the procuring firm better off working with a significant number of competitive suppliers? Should it vertically integrate backwards to bring the source of supply in-house? Or should it work with a reduced number of selected suppliers in partnership arrangements?

The advent of strategic sourcing suggests that many firms believe that, in some circumstances at least, the third option is most beneficial[14] and that adversarial relationships with large numbers of suppliers is counterproductive. In particular, they believe that significant benefits may derive from a reduction in the supplier base and the development of partnership relationships.[15] Of course, a supplier reduction does not *per se* lead to development of *partnership* relationships, and dealing with a smaller number of suppliers may be as adversarial as dealing with many.[16] Customers pursuing supplier partnerships believe that:

- Focused attention on developing a limited number of suppliers is more effective in spending multidisciplinary team resources to improve supplier operations, reduce costs and hence input prices.
- Internal operating costs may be reduced via faster running times, reduced working capital (including improved inventory management), scheduling flexibility, more efficient ordering procedures, faster delivery, reduced investment costs and improved quality.

- A smaller supplier base reduces the administrative costs of dealing with suppliers. These include, for example, reduced sales representative visits, fewer supplier assessments, fewer bids to manage and evaluate, simpler management of accounts payable and coordination costs.
- Closer relationships provide security of supply, priority in times of scarcity, improved problem solving, participation in value analysis programs, reduced time pressure, risk sharing via participation in product design, reduced development times, and better access to technology.

EXAMPLE: As the result of its partnership with Federal Express, Fujitsu moved its distribution center to Memphis (FedEx's hub). FedEx orchestrates the arrival of computer components from suppliers throughout Asia, oversees the assembly of personal computers, and ships them out. Fujitsu has reduced customer delivery time from ten days to four.

- The procuring firm may be able to offload (outsource) a set of noncore (yet often important) activities that are of little value in the firm's competitive battles.

EXAMPLE: Under severe offshore competitive pressure in the low-end copier business, Xerox formed a delivery-focused partnership with Ryder Truck. With Ryder's help, Xerox reduced its number of logistic centers from ten to two. It also outsourced to Ryder and others such functions as supplying warehouse equipment, performing preassembly tasks, product delivery and installation, customer training, and old equipment removal. Not only were overall costs reduced, sales force time was freed up for selling activities.[17]

Some of these customer benefits occur in the short run. Others such as securing preferred access to new and developing technology, are long run in nature.[18] Of course, not all benefits necessarily accrue to all customer firms in partnership relationships. Nonetheless, there is a rich set from which to evaluate partnership potential. In general, partnerships are only likely to be successful if each side receives roughly comparable benefits.

EXAMPLE: In its enhanced supplier program (ESR), Mobil Oil develops partnership-type relationships with such firms as Schlumberger, a supplier of oil field services. The results are dramatic. Mobil has reduced overall costs by 29% and computing costs by 36%. In addition, it has secured staff reductions of 25%, and been able to sell off 66% of oil fields accounting for 10% of production.[19] Schlumberger and other suppliers secure increased business with Mobil.

Several phased normative models have been developed to aid firms that believe partnership arrangements with suppliers may be beneficial. The six-stage process in Figure 9.1 combines the thinking behind several models:[20]

EXAMPLE: In 1995, MasterCard's (MC) new Global Purchasing organization used such a model to rationalize its purchases of printed material. MC spends tremendous sums on printing, production, and design for direct marketing, product/service brochures, policy binders, and corporate and brand advertising secured from a variety of vendors. MC selected a single partner to man-

---

- **Stage I: Preliminary**
  Establish the strategic need for partnership development, form a team to explore possibilities, confirm top management support.
- **Stage II: Identify Potential Partners**[21]
  Determine selection criteria, identify potential partners.
- **Stage III: Screen and Select**
  Contact potential partners, evaluate partners, decide on partner targets, and secure agreement to move ahead with a limited number of target accounts.
- **Stage IV: Establish the Relationship**
  Partners explore mutual philosophies, establish benefits, design linkages, appoint key people to critical roles, come to grips with critical issues (e.g., reduced cost for buyer but greater dependency; contract predictability but give up proprietary information).
- **Stage V: Build the Teams**
  Bonding based on personal relationships, multilevel linkages start to be developed, purchasing becomes one of several interface units rather than the only unit, institutional power-based system shifts to collaboration and consensus.
- **Stage VI: Alignment**[22]
  Bonding based on added value and problem solving, early integration of information systems, supplier's resources focused around buyer's needs, important dynamic changes within the organizations, sometimes problems of managing relationships.
- **Stage VII: Fused Organizations**
  Ideally single source agreement, build value through innovation, identify serious threats throughout the value chain, significant changes in operations and organization resulting from the partnership.

FIGURE 9.1: A Partnership Development Process

age all MC pre-press activities on-site, providing it with significantly greater control over printing quality and consistency.

Initiative from Supplier Firms

From the perspective of supplier firms, the increasing acceptance of key account management is fertile ground for the development of key account partnerships. Over a period of thirty to forty years, corporations have increasingly come to view their major accounts (current and potential) as significant assets. In a very real sense, partnership formation is a natural evolution of the trend to key account management.

In addition, the growth of strategic sourcing has led supplier firms to view partnership relationships as a means of avoiding the more harmful effects of aggressive procurement practices. As firms reduce their supplier bases, supplier firms are searching for ways of enhancing value for both organizations. Indeed, rather than viewing partnership formation as a defensive move, creative key account managers may be able to preempt customer adoption of the least favored elements of strategic sourcing.

Many benefits may accrue to supplier firms that form successful key account partnerships:

- Long-term customer commitment (possibly single source relationships)
- Reduced uncertainty through improved information flow, including advance notice of end-market changes and customer responses
- Faster response to customer needs, leading to extra current business and the ability to supply new products before competitors
- Cycle-time reductions and greater operating flexibility, leading to cost reductions and improved profit margins
- Differentiation from competition; possibly locking competitors out of important accounts
- More success in dealing with other customers via improved reputation and better technical capabilities. This leads to improved quality (both tangible and intangible benefits), technological developments and so forth.[23]

Cautions for Considering Partnerships

Despite the many potential benefits from closer buyer-seller relationships, partnership formation is no panacea for either buyer or seller. Potential concerns for customer firms include:

- *Too much emphasis on few suppliers.* This can affect security of supply when problems occur at the supplier, including manmade disasters such as strikes as well as natural disasters such as fires, floods, and earthquakes.

EXAMPLE: In 1999, many PC manufacturers faced significant disruption in their manufacturing operations as the result of the Taiwan earthquake which caused major interruptions in the delivery of computer chips.

- *Increased Organizational Stress.* For key accounts, partnering represents a different way of doing business that may lead to severe organizational difficulties. In addition, the firm may become embroiled in labor issues at its suppliers. Relatedly, some supplier firms may be forced to unionize to secure business from customers whose unions have made agreements regarding unionized suppliers.

EXAMPLE: In the late 1980s, British Rover was forced to intervene in a labor dispute at a supplier when management offered a lower-than-acceptable wage increase to its workers.

- *Negative Competitor Effects.* Since customer firms often have the same suppliers as their competitors, improved performance from a supplier firm/key account partnership may lead to benefit leakage to competitors. Relatedly, partnering with a restricted number of suppliers may cut the account off from technological advances made by other suppliers.[24]

Potential concerns for supplier firms include:

- *Too much emphasis on few customers.* The supplier firm risks the loss of significant business from revocation of partnership agreements into which considerable resources have been sunk. For example, customer expectations may be raised beyond the supplier's ability to deliver.

- *Foreclosed Options.* A partnership agreement with an attractive customer may foreclose the supplier from conducting business with the partner's competitors, in part because of the benefit leakage issue (see above).
- *Limited supplier firm ability to address new market opportunities.* In an era of significant technological change, partnership arrangements may lock suppliers into the "wrong" customers, those unable to keep up with the developing technology. Furthermore, buyers may use partnership agreements to place locked-in suppliers under undue price pressure.[25]

Notwithstanding these issues, in many circumstances partnerships just do not make sense, such as when volumes are small and little potential for mutual advantage can be foreseen.[26] In other cases, the customer firm may prefer to keep a group of competing suppliers; it may neither trust nor want close involvement with suppliers, or may already have a sufficient number of partnership relationships.[27]

From the perspective of the supplier firm, we can identify several characteristics of organizations that would make poor partners. The less favorable ones are those that:

- only negotiate on price
- don't keep promises
- have a deal mentality
- insist on detailed contracts
- don't like long-term commitments
- have adversarial relationships with suppliers and a reputation for frustrating them
- turn supplier problems into reasons for punishment rather than opportunities to find solutions
- have little interest in supplier benefits
- are closed-minded to supplier suggestions
- are reluctant to share information
- lack managerial processes for working other organizations
- lack active top-management support
- have weak cross-functional teamwork

Notwithstanding the potential value of partnership relationships, the supplier firm should be aware that circumstances may change and build contingent actions into its planning framework in the event that the early promise of a partnership relationship is no longer fulfilled.[28]

IDENTIFYING PARTNERSHIP OPPORTUNITIES[29]

We have identified various factors leading both key accounts and supplier firms to consider forming partnerships. Now we present a procurement framework that is useful in identifying both the potential for partnerships in general, and the type of partnership in particular.

The Procurement Portfolio Framework

Two dimensions can describe the type of product purchased by a key account—purchase importance and supply risk:

- *Purchase importance* focuses on the long-term potential impact of product purchase. Thus, if purchase volume were high relative to total purchases, the potential for financial savings and/or the impact on the key account's product quality would likely be significant.
- *Supply risk* focuses on both product availability and its importance for the company's future.

By identifying "high" and "low" levels of each dimension and combining the dimensions as shown in Figure 9.2, we develop a 2 × 2 *procurement portfolio* framework. As we shall see, this framework is useful for classifying purchased items into one of four matrix cells: noncritical, leverage, bottleneck, and strategic.

The characteristics of each cell provide insight into potential key account procurement strategies and the likelihood that partnering may be attractive. In general, situations with low supply risk lead customer firms to exploit their buying power. In situations with high supply risk, they attempt to use procurement strategies to create competitive advantage. These predispositions lead to different considerations for partnership opportunities, and suggest different strategies for supplier firms.

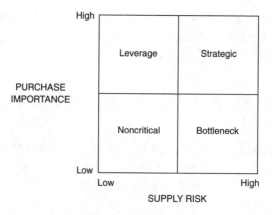

FIGURE 9.2: A Procurement Portfolio Framework

- *Noncritical products* have low supply risk and low profit impact. These commodity-type items are readily available from numerous suppliers. Since the customer buys in low volume, and supplier firm margins are typically thin, potential cost savings are generally low.

These *products* offer customers few partnership benefits. Because many suppliers can compete for this low profit impact business, implementing an efficient procurement system optimizes customer return. The potential for a supplier firm to interest a customer in a partnership is only likely as part of a multiple-product procurement agreement, or if it can offer extra benefits via important additional services.[30]

- *Leverage products* have low supply risk but potentially high profit impact. As with *noncritical* products, numerous suppliers compete for this business and substitutes are readily available. Although supplier margins are likely thin, and the potential for price reductions low in the current supplier environment, high purchase volume implies that potential cost savings may be significant.

These *products* offer customers the potential for significant cost savings and represent the most likely area for implementation of strategic sourcing. The dangers these strategies pose for the supplier firm include more adversarial account relationships, eroding margins, increased demands for services, and reduced flexibility. However, despite these potential problems, a creative supplier firm may identify opportunities to improve the value offered these customers.

As a result, it may be able to establish longer-term relationships, develop preferred customers, upgrade the customer portfolio, and secure higher profits.

Because of the high profit potential driven by large volume purchases, leverage products are far more susceptible to partnership opportunities than noncritical products. Since price is a major factor in the total cost of procuring leverage products, the supplier firm's strategic thrust should be to increase account market share. To the extent that significant cost experience curve effects and scale economies are available, lower prices for multiyear or guaranteed high-volume contracts via partnership relationships may benefit both customers and supplier firms.[31]

The supplier firm should consider pricing for long-run volume growth via life-cycle costing, for example, marginal cost pricing in the short run to secure volume to cover fixed costs in the long run. It should also contemplate acquisition of competitor suppliers to increase potential volume. In addition, it should improve the product line, use its geographic scope to offer attractive prices worldwide (if appropriate), and suggest more streamlined product offerings. Finally, it may persuade the account to relax noncritical specifications, design tighter to specifications, use lower cost components, and consider outsourcing to reduce costs.

Depending on circumstances, bundling several products together, or unbundling products, may improve value for customers. A particular concern should be to remove nonvalued services from a bundled offer.[32] In addition to a focus on price, suppliers should consider other cost-related elements offering supplier advantage. These may include guaranteed quality to eliminate incoming inspection, improved logistics (including cross-docking), just-in-time deliveries for low-to-zero inventories, automated invoicing, integration of product sale/use and production scheduling, and electronic-based ordering systems.[33]

In addition to focusing on the direct supplier/customer relationship, the supplier firm can enhance its position by creating demand further down the channel by engaging in brand-building activities such as advertising and customer loyalty programs. Through such programs, the supplier firm can develop a database on end-use customers that can be used for direct communication to pull its products/components through the system.[34]

- *Bottleneck products* are purchased in low volume. Hence, they have low profit impact in procurement but serious consequences for the account if supply problems occur. These products may have one or more of several characteristics—unique specifications, dependent on supplier's technology, few (if any) substitutes, inability to inventory because of storage risk, fluctuating and unpredictable usage, and production-based scarcity due to low demand and few supply sources.

Because their nonavailability may lead to a shutdown of the customer's production system, the major procurement challenge is to ensure availability, if necessary at extra cost. Because of their critical role, the lack of substitutes, and few suppliers, competent suppliers may find that partnership arrangements are beneficial to customer firms.

- *Strategic Products* have high supply risk. Since they are purchased in high volumes, they also have high profit impact. Continuous product delivery is critical for customer operations and purchase price is a significant component in the price of the customer's product. As with bottleneck items, these products may have unique specifications and supplier technology may be important. Because few technically competent suppliers are available, production-based scarcity makes changing suppliers difficult.

These products offer the greatest potential for partnership opportunities. Not only are they strategic for customers, they have high profit impact. The ability to secure products with the best available technology in the required volume is critical to the customer's success. As a result, a high level of cooperation with the supplier(s) is in the account's interest and the development of a partnership relationship may be highly beneficial. A partnership relationship locks in a valued supplier for products with today's technology. However, as cycle times reduce, bringing new ideas to commercial reality faster, it assures fast access to products from tomorrow's technology, assuming that the supplier remains at the technological cutting edge. From the supplier's perspective, its ability to deliver considerable value makes this sort of customer a prime target for a partnership relationship.

The foregoing analysis suggests that the four strategic procurement situations lead to essentially three approaches with regard to partnerships:

- For *noncritical products* there seems to be little value in partnerships for the customer firm. Pursuing such relationships is therefore likely to be wasted effort for supplier firms.

- For *leverage products,* the potential for partnerships is based on the customer's ability to secure lower costs. Hence, the supplier firm's challenge is to attempt to achieve efficiencies via a higher account share position in exchange for lower total cost to the account.
- For *strategic and bottleneck products,* the supplier firm should seek partnerships by focusing on developing and exploiting proprietary technology, reducing cycle times, developing tailored products, offering superior service and support, and improving the account's supply chain.[35]

Regardless of the particular actions the purchasing portfolio framework suggests, key account managers who have performed an effective situation analysis should be fully cognizant of key account needs and anticipate their customer's likely actions. In particular, they should be ready for introduction of supplier certification programs and other strategies, since effective response typically takes time. Relatedly, they need to be knowledgeable about quality practices in both their own organizations and the key account. If such programs have not been introduced, key account managers should consider proactive moves, using the portfolio framework as a guide, by developing creative ideas to add value and reduce costs in a partnership context that help to cement the key-account/supplier-firm relationship.

Partnership relationships are a means to an end, not an end in themselves. Since procurement portfolio analysis suggests that the potential for such relationships may be constrained, partnerships should not be force-fit in situations where they are inappropriate. Indeed, as with any interorganizational relationship, the potential for failure is always present (see below).[36] More broadly, the purchasing portfolio framework may provide supplier firms with a useful way of segmenting their key accounts into those seeking noncritical, leverage, and strategic and bottleneck product accounts.

New Business Opportunities

Although the four procurement categories embrace products and services currently being purchased by the account, they do not cover all potential partnership opportunities. Specifically, they do not include activities currently conducted in-house by the account that have the potential for being outsourced.

One feature of the business landscape is the waxing and waning of management fashion. In the late 1960s, the received wisdom of managing major corporations was to form conglomerates.[37] These organizations, highly diversified in many products and markets, operated on the rationale of spreading risk. More recently, conglomerates have largely gone out of fashion as increased competition and pressure from the financial community has led to a refocusing and narrowing of organizational missions. An outgrowth of mission focus has been a search for core competence as companies have sought to identify the factors that bring them success in their markets. By focusing on core competencies, the theory argues, the firm is better able to compete. Such a "back to basics" approach leads to consideration of outsourcing noncore activities that, though important, need not be conducted in-house.

This outsourcing potential has offered considerable opportunities for supplier firms to engage in partnership activities. Among the areas often outsourced by firms are payroll, computer systems management, copying activities, and security and legal services.

However, outsourcing is increasingly moving away from support activities to areas that are more central to the organization's operations. As global competition intensifies, and product development cycles shrink (concurrent with organizational downsizing), some firms find themselves with insufficient research, development, and operational resources to do what has to be done. Critical strategic questions focus on identifying the competencies that the firm *must have* to compete in the future, and those that do not fall into this category. Following this sort of analysis, companies are turning to outsource activities that were previously a mainstay of their operations. In the process, they are learning how to develop and manage relationships with suppliers in pursuit of competitive advantage.[38] Of course, customer firms must be concerned that in outsourcing production operations to "helpful" suppliers, they are not paving the way for later forward integration and tough competition.

From the perspective of the supplier firm, the better it understands its key account, the more likely it will be able to identify such customer opportunities, and so improve its long-run position.

A PARTNERSHIP DEVELOPMENT MODEL

Numerous partnership formulation models have been developed to aid organizations contemplating supplier-customer partnerships. Here we present a particularly useful model based on real-world experience that has been successfully field-tested.[39] The model is a systematic method for ensuring that both parties gain maximum advantage from the partnership. However, as with any model, the major benefit is not so much in the scoring and calculations, but rather in the full discussion of critical issues that the model structure enables. More importantly, great care should be taken in setting realistic expectations for the partnership. Before implementing the model, each firm should agree to follow through on all of the steps.[40]

The model comprises three major building blocks: drivers, facilitators, and components (Figure 9.3). Drivers set expectations for *outcomes* of the partnership, which in turn provide *feedback* to the components, drivers, and facilitators.

Drivers are compelling reasons to form a partnership; the stronger the drivers, the greater the partnership potential. In this model the drivers are:[42]

- *Asset/cost efficiencies* including the potential for cost reductions via integration of activities and/or development of specialized equipment and processes

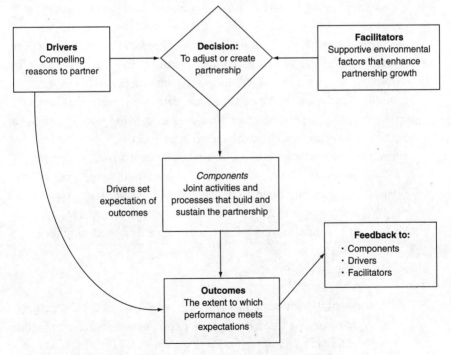

FIGURE 9.3: A Partnership Development Model[41]

- *Customer service improvements* such as reduced inventory, shorter cycle times, and more timely and accurate information
- *Marketing advantages* including improving marketing strategies, easing entry into new markets, providing better access to technology and innovations
- *Profit stability/growth* secured through long-term volume commitments, reduced sales variability, joint asset use, and so forth

Supplier firm and key account teams typically comprise eight to ten members per firm with various roles and organizational levels. Each team independently generates individual driver items, then rates their strengths using the guide in Appendix 9.1. All items are then exchanged prior to a joint discussion that strives for consensus. Items should be as specific as possible since objectives will be set and results measured against these objectives.[43]

Facilitators are universal and situation-specific supportive factors that enhance partnership growth. Universal facilitators should be present in any relationship. Situation-specific facilitators are likely to enhance the probability of success, but their absence does not imply failure. In this model, the universal facilitators are:[44]

- *Corporate compatibility*—the similarity of culture and business objectives
- *Managerial philosophy and techniques*—attitude toward employee empowerment, approach to quality, the relative importance of teams, etc.
- *Mutuality*—the ability of the management team to put itself in its partner's shoes—typically expressed as a willingness to develop joint goals, share sensitive information, and take a long-term perspective
- *Symmetry*—the importance of each firm to the other's success on such dimensions as relative size, market share, financial strength, productivity, brand image, company reputation, and level of technological sophistication. (A good example is the Coca-Cola/McDonalds partnership. McDonalds is Coke's largest customer, Coke is McDonalds largest supplier.)

Situation specific facilitators are:

- *Exclusivity*—implying that neither firm will work with direct competitors
- *Shared competitors*—a good example is PepsiCo as a shared competitor for both McDonald's and Coke—prior to the spin-off of its fast food operations (Burger King, Taco Bell, Kentucky Fried Chicken).

- *Physical proximity* of the two organizations
- *Prior history* of a successful relationship
- *Shared end users*—strengthens partnership opportunities because of a common target

Whereas drivers are generated and rated independently, facilitators are rated by supplier and customer together, using the guide in Appendix 9.2.

The combination of drivers and facilitators determines whether or not a partnership should be formed. It also suggests the partnership type, according to the framework in Figure 9.4.

- *Type I* is basically short-term in focus and involves single organizational units. Supplier and customer recognize each other as partners, and coordinate planning and other activities on a limited basis.
- *Type II* is long-term in orientation and involves multiple divisions and functions. The supplier and customer integrate activities.
- *Type III* embraces a significant level of operational integration. Each firm views itself as an extension of the other. No ending date is foreseen.

The drivers and facilitators jointly determine the potential for different types of partnership. Partnership components and their implementation determine the actual type of realized partnership—I, II or III.

FACILITATOR SCORE				
	Low	Arm's Length	Type I	Type II
	Medium	Type I	Type II	Type III
	High	Type II	Type III	Type III
		Low	Medium	High
			DRIVER SCORE	

FIGURE 9.4: The Propensity to Form a Partnership[45]

Components are the joint activities and processes that management establishes and controls throughout the life of the partnership. They make the relationship operational and help managers create the benefits of partnering. This model has several components: [46]

- *Joint planning* which may range from sharing existing plans to developing joint strategic plans together
- *Joint operating controls,* including the ability of either party to change operations for the good of the partnership
- *Communications* both on a day-by-day and nonroutine basis, via multiple modes, and a willingness to share both good and bad news
- *Risk and reward sharing* invoking the core concept of "shared destiny"
- *Trust and commitment* involving loyalty to each other and to the partnership, and long-term focus
- *Contract style,* wherein the strongest partnerships have the shortest and least specific agreements, and maybe no written agreement at all [47]
- *Scope,* concerning the number and complexity of value-added steps, and the amount of business involved
- *Investment,* such as shared assets, joint investment in technology, exchange of key personnel, joint R&D, placing the supplier's plant on the customer's site, reflecting high levels of financial interdependence [48]

Each component is evident in every partnership but may be implemented at either a low (Type I), medium (Type II) or high (Type III) level (Figure 9.5).

Because interorganizational commitment increases from Type I through Type III partnerships, in practice, Type I partnerships are the most numerous; Type IIIs the least.

After working through the partnership components it is quite likely that the parties will agree to a different level of partnership than was apparent from the drivers/facilitators analysis. Specifically, the components analysis clarifies the expectations for each partnership type. Neither firm may be ready for the intense relationships required of higher level partnerships.

Outcomes are specified based on a series of strategies and action programs. These are related to the drivers, and are developed regardless of the agreed partnership. Establishing success measures is essential—one set for the customer, and one for the supplier. Generic outcomes include:

FIGURE 9.5: Partnership Component Levels[49]

	Low	Medium	High
Planning			
Style	• On *ad hoc* basis	• Regularly scheduled	• Systematic: scheduled *and ad hoc*
Level	• Focus on projects/tasks	• Focus on process	• Focus on relationship
Content	• Share existing plans	• Performed jointly, eliminate conflicts in strategies	• Performed jointly, at multiple levels, including top management, objective to mesh strategies; each party participates in other's business planning
Joint Operating Controls			
Measurement	• Performance measures developed independently and results shared	• Measures jointly developed and shared; focus on individual firm's performance	• Measures jointly developed and shared; focus on relationship and joint performance
Ability to make changes	• Parties may suggest changes to other's system	• Parties may make changes to other's system after getting approval	• Parties may make changes to other's system without getting approval
Communications			
Nonroutine	• Very limited, usually just critical issues at task/project level	• Conducted more regularly, done at multiple levels; generally open and honest	• Planned as a part of the relationship; occurs at all levels; sharing both praise and criticism; parties speak the same language
Day-to-Day Organization	• Conducted on *ad hoc* basis, between individuals	• Limited number of scheduled communications, some routinization	• Systematized method of communication; manual or electronic; communication systems linked
Balance	•Primarily one-way	• Two-way but unbalanced	• Balanced two-way communications flow
Electronic	•Use of individual system	• Joint modification of individual systems	• Joint development of customized electronic communications
Risk and Reward Sharing			
Loss tolerance	• Vey low tolerance for loss	• Some tolerance for short-term loss	• High tolerance for short-term loss
Gain commitment	• Limited willingness to help the other gain	• Willingness to help the other gain	• Desire to help other party gain
Commitment to fairness	• Fairness evaluated by transaction	• Fairness is tracked year to year	• Fairness measured over life of relationship
Trust and Commitment			
Trust	• Trust limited to belief that each partner will perform honestly and ethically	Partner is given more trust than others, viewed as most-favored supplier	• Implicit, total trust; trust does not have to be earned
Commitment to each other's success	• Commitment of each party to specific transaction or project; trust re-earned	• Commitment to a longer-term relationship	• Commitment is to partner's long-term success; commitment prevails across functions and levels in both organizations

(continued on next page)

FIGURE 9.5: Partnership Component Levels[49] (*continued*)

	Low	Medium	High
Contract Style			
Time frame	• Covers a short time frame	• Covers a longer time frame	• Contracts very general in nature and evergreen; alternatively entire relationship on a hand-shake basis.
Coverage	• Contracts specific in nature	• Contracts more general in nature	• Contract does not specify duties or responsibilities; rather, it only outlines the basic philosophy guiding the relationship
Scope			
Share	• Partnership activity repre-sents a very small share of business for each partner	• Activity represents a modest share of business for at least one partner	• Activity covered by relationship represents significant business to both parties
Value-added	• Relationship covers only one or a few value-added steps (functions)	• Multiple functions/units involved in the relationship	• Multiple functions and units involved, partnership extends to all levels in both organizations
Critical activities	• Only activities relatively unimportant for partner's success	• Activities important for each partner's success included	• Activities critical for each partner's success included
Investment			
Financial	• Low or no investment between the two parties	• May jointly own low-value assets	• High-value assets may be jointly owned
Technology	• No joint development of products/technology	• Some joint design effort; may be some joint R&D planning	• Significant joint development; regular and significant joint R&D activity
People	• Limited personnel exchange	• Extensive exchange of personnel	• Participation on other party's board

- *Financial performance:* Increased revenues, profit increases, smoothing out profit flows
- *Process outcomes:* Improved service, reduced costs
- *Competitive advantage:* Better positioning, improved market share, knowledge

Once in place, the partnership should be developed and monitored on a continuous basis via frequent periodic reports and less frequent update meetings. Successful execution should pave the way for expanding the partnership's scope.

This model has been used successfully in several partnership situations:

- Establishing a new partnership: Allied-Signal and CSX
- Diagnosing an existing relationship: Goodyear and Yellow Freight
- Strengthening a key relationship: Texas Instruments and Photronics

In addition, the model is useful for implementing relationship management in the two organizations by institutionalizing the language of drivers, facilitators, and components.

REQUIREMENTS FOR SUCCESSFUL PARTNERSHIPS

By examining at the experiences of several successful and unsuccessful partnerships, we can identify a number of factors critical to developing successful partnerships.[50] These may be usefully grouped into those issues that are more strategic in nature, and those that are more operational. Strategic issues include a common philosophy and consensus on partnership development, top-level commitment, a deep concern for quality, formalism, and a mutual desire for success. Operational issues include a long-term focus, sensitive management of organizational linkages, and high levels of information flow. Partnership examples are summarized in Appendix 9.3.[51]

Strategic Issues

COMMON PHILOSOPHY AND CONSENSUS ON PARTNERSHIP DEVELOPMENT

Perhaps most necessary for successful supplier-firm/key-account partnerships is that both parties have clear and agreed-upon expectations regarding the purpose of the partnership and the manner in which it will develop. For example, in one partnership, the two parties agreed "to establish a trusting, long-term relationship that achieves enhanced profitability and advantages for both organizations." These goals were to be accomplished by:

- Creating and sustaining a team environment which fosters mutual respect, commitment, open communication, and pride
- Continuous improvement of product quality, service, and each organization's cost structure
- Improvement of communications and interface systems (e.g., order entry, billing)

- Obtaining an understanding of each other's manufacturing processes, capabilities, and limitations through free exchange of information
- Leveraging off each organization's experience to identify and take advantage of opportunities
- Committing to equal sharing of gains and savings
- Identifying and solving mutual problems with a sense of urgency and care

TOP-LEVEL COMMITMENT

Since partnership agreements are strategic for both supplier firm and key account, each organization should buy into the relationship at the highest level. Unless key personnel from each organization are committed to the partnership, display leadership, and understand clearly the roles and responsibilities that are necessary to make the partnership successful, significant disappointment may lie ahead for both partners.

This commitment is demonstrated most forcefully by appointment of a senior executive as "executive partner" for the key account (Chapter 4). This individual, by virtue of his position, is able to make commitments for the organization as a whole. Although day-to-day management of the account rests with the key account manager, the executive partner is available to deal with difficult issues, and leads the annual key-account/supplier-firm meeting. This role is even more powerful if imbued with a long-time horizon whereby the nominated executive remains as partner even though his formal organizational duties may change with promotions and lateral experience-gaining shifts in responsibility.

A DEEP CONCERN FOR QUALITY

Customers want high-quality products from their suppliers. Furthermore, quality standards have risen generally as such management practices as quality assurance audits and quality improvement activities have spread across many industries. In addition, significant employee empowerment has led to a focus on quality in other dimensions than product *per se*.

Many firms have turned to services to secure this advantage. Others have adopted a more holistic view of quality, focusing on the totality of the supplier-firm/key-account relationship.[52] Xerox, a leader in developing partnership relationships, likes to define a relationship defect as, "any output from either customer or supplier that does not meet the negotiated requirements of either party." Xerox applies total quality tools in attempting to drive the defect rate to zero.[53]

FORMALISM

For partnerships to function effectively, a well-crafted overall agreement should be defined and negotiated. A joint planning process, modeled after the key account plan, should identify critical customer needs, and opportunities to add value and cut costs. It should produce agreements on goals, mission, and operating principles, including quality improvement objectives. It should also specify what is acceptable and unacceptable behavior, for example, who gets to see what information, and how to handle costs and technology.

Other agreements should embrace measurement metrics and monitoring procedures, specification of multilevel organizational relationships, and other communication processes. In addition, the parties should agree on problem-solving processes, conflict resolution mechanisms, and provision of human and other resources. Confidentiality agreements, especially when advanced technology is shared, and ownership agreements on joint-technological development may also be necessary, especially when the fruits of development can be used in other businesses. Not only should the operations and performance of the partnership be monitored on a continuous basis, periodic high-level meetings should assess both partnership performance and the efficacy of the control mechanisms.

The desired impact of partnership formalism is to change the dynamic between supplier and customer in a significant manner. In the traditional relationship the core focus is the procurement act. In a partnership, the relationship *per se* is central, based on fairness, honesty, reciprocity, and openness, leading to the development and nurturing of mutual trust.[54] The critical factor driving procurement is the key account's success in its marketplace, and orders for the supplier firm occur almost as a by-product of the partnership.

MUTUAL DESIRE FOR SUCCESS

A critical factor in successful partnerships is a genuine desire for success on both sides. Inevitably, in relationships as complex as those we are describing, mistakes will happen, individuals will make errors, and "relationship defects" will occur. However, if each side displays a passion for success, these errors will lead to a positive spiral of improvement and success, rather than a downward spiral of mutual recrimination and failure.

Operational Issues

LONG-TERM FOCUS

Partnerships should not be thought of as short-term activities. Rather, both sides should enter them with a shared vision of joint long-run strategic advantage. Partnerships may involve the integration of systems, routines, and processes, and may require employees to develop new sets of skills. Thus they need to be managed for mutual long-run gain.

SENSITIVE MANAGEMENT OF ORGANIZATIONAL LINKAGES

Typically, the nature of partnership relationships is highly complex, involving a dense web of multiple actors from each partner. Sometimes personnel act as individuals, and sometimes as members of multifunctional, multiorganizational teams that bring stability to the developing relationship and coordinate diverse knowledge. Furthermore, the web of linkages may spread far beyond the supplier firm and key account to embrace the supplier firm's supplier(s) and other supplier firm customers. Critical relationships must be managed both among individuals within each organization, and among individuals across organizational boundaries.

Successful management of these various relationships requires a key account manager with enormous skill, who can rely on effective multilevel human resource strategies in both organizations. Many people are involved, each with their own individual need profiles, likes and dislikes, and personality traits. They work in different functions, with various roles and responsibilities, and have different levels of power and authority. Furthermore, they operate in different corporate cultures with different value systems.

> **EXAMPLE:** In 3M's corporate account organization, corporate key account teams are not only multifunctional in nature, they cross many different business units in attempts to identify opportunities for 3M's developing technologies.

A successful partnership must harness this heterogeneity in the service of attaining mutual goals. At the same time, it must avoid the potentially destructive conflict that is endemic in complex social systems. Thus, instead of viewing heterogeneity as a negative, it should be seen as a considerable strength. The partnership, as the mechanism for developing intra- and interorganizational trust, becomes a learning organism reaching for ever higher overall organizational performance.

HIGH LEVELS OF INFORMATION FLOW

Successful partnerships break down the barriers between functions and organizations. An important vehicle for developing seamless relationships is extensive information development and sharing throughout the partnership. Information flow occurs both in real time—for example, faxing materials rejection slips— and for forward planning, such as technology developments, design initiatives, project schedules, and marketing strategies.

Extensive information flow turns the partnership entity into a truly open system. The supplier firm needs to know early on the demands its customer's customers are placing on its customers. The customer needs early warning of emerging technological developments from the supplier, so it may build these into its future plans.

> **EXAMPLE:** Industrial gas manufacturer BOC has replaced its traditional fax/e-mail/telephone system with one based on the Internet to improve efficiency in the order/delivery cycle. Customer partners place orders via BOC's restricted access web site, screened for price and selection, based on their bulk-purchase agreements. They are able to check order status, shipping, and other continuously updated information. BOC allows these customers to access to its own inventory data. In return, customers give BOC access to their cost accounting systems to avoid reentering data.[55]

Finally, partnership members should continuously benchmark their relationship against other supplier-customer relationships and build these results into the process for upgrading their own relationship.[56]

A BLUEPRINT FOR
UNSUCCESSFUL PARTNERSHIPS

Earlier in the chapter we identified a series of reasons why either the supplier or customer firm might decide not to enter into a partnership. Regrettably, even if the conditions initially seem propitious for a partnership, many supplier/ customer partnerships fail. The reasons are numerous, and we highlight just a few.

Key reasons for failure are that the partners just do not clearly understand the time it takes to establish and maintain the partnership and the resources required. (Perhaps one or the other firm has too many partnership agreements.) As a result, even with a well-developed agreement, a partnership may fail because of poor implementation, including inadequate inter- and intra-organizational communication. Relatedly, the partners lack real understanding of the needs and competencies of the other party such that the business rationale for the partnership is not well-developed, the choice of partner and/or the partnership strategy may have been incorrect, and hoped-for results are not quantified. In addition, insufficient attention may be given to anticipating potential conflicts, such as joint product development leading to disputes over intellectual property rights.

Mobil has identified several stumbling blocks to successful supplier-customer partnerships.[57]

- Mistrust
- Nonaligned goals
- Personnel (personal) conflicts
- Ineffective communications
- Turf protection/job security
- Company policies/procedures
- Management apathy/commitment
- Nonaligned organizations

- Fear of losing control
- Fear of loss of competition
- Different business cultures
- Historic business cultures/ processes
- Noneffective resource use
- Exploitation of either party by the other

Over and above these problems, changed circumstancees may cause a rupture or at least a severe modification of the relationship. For example, procurement management may change, due to managerial succession or as the result of an acquisition; if the new procurement executives operate with a different purchasing model, a long-term partnership may dissolve overnight. If the market is rapidly changing, the key account may be unable to move sufficiently swiftly and the supplier firm may seek a more flexible partner. And if the key account suffers from profitability pressures, it may attempt to modify its supplier relationship and place renewed emphasis on price.

EXAMPLE: In late 2000, suppliers to DaimlerChrysler complained that the vaunted collaborative relationships forged between Chrysler and its suppliers in the 1990s were disintegrating. With Chrysler under severe profit pressure, the "give-and-take" in meetings was being replaced by one-sided demands from Chrysler executives. As Chrysler strove to reduce costs, suppliers said that the goodwill, developed slowly over several years, was being destroyed.[58]

Product failure may also lead to change:

EXAMPLE: In late 2000, Ford and Bridgestone/Firestone were engaged in increasingly public acrimony over the performance of Firestone tires on the Ford Explorer. Dating to the friendship between Henry Ford and Harvey Firestone, the Ford-Firestone partnership endured for most of the twentieth century. However, during the 1990s, failure of Firestone tires at high speeds in hot weather was alleged to have caused well over 100 deaths in rollover crashes, and in summer 2000 a massive recall was announced. While tire failure seemed little disputed, Firestone executives suggested that stability of the Ford Explorer might be a contributing factor, in particular Ford's recommendation of relatively low air pressure in the tires. The future of the partnership seemed in doubt.

See Appendix 9.4 for a partnering self-audit.

SUMMARY

In recent years, both supplier and customer firms have seen benefits in developing partnership agreements. Although they are no panacea, in part because many organizations are not ready for them, such agreements are increasingly widespread. Supplier firms contemplating partnership arrangements might employ the procurement portfolio framework as a conceptual device for suggesting the type of partnership it might conclude with a customer. Potential partners wishing to move ahead should do so only with a thorough understanding of what they are getting into; we suggested one partnership development model that can be very useful in surfacing the relevant issues. Partnerships succeed only if some basic requirements are followed; equally, several precursors of partnership failure can be identified.

CHAPTER TEN

Global Account Management[1]

It is an inescapable fact that, as we embrace the twenty-first century, the world appears to be getting smaller. Increasingly, corporations around the globe are re-defining the geographic scopes of their businesses.[2] No longer content with op-erating solely in their home countries, the search for business opportunities is leading them far from home to new countries, on new continents.[3]

From the perspective of the individual supplier firm, this advancing multina-tionalism inevitably means that its customers are increasingly operating in many areas of the globe. For domestically focused supplier firms, whether Brazilian, British, Swedish, Japanese, or U.S., the implication is that the traditional ways of interfacing with their major customers may no longer be adequate.

Regardless of where the multinational customer's headquarters operations are based, as it expands globally, it requires supplier firms in these new geo-graphic domains. The current domestic supplier is one of several potential choices. Others include local suppliers in the new geographies and other multi-national suppliers. If the present supplier is able to satisfy its customer's needs in a particular geography, it is a potential supplier there. If it can leverage its ca-pabilities from other geographies into the new geography, and satisfy meta-level customer needs related to managing its operations on a worldwide basis, it brings added value to the relationship, and enhances its potential for increased business. If it cannot satisfy these local and meta-level needs, it faces the possi-bility of losing even its historic domestic business.

Global account management can provide a major competitive advantage.

Customers of supplier firms with successful global account management programs know that around the world, their problems can be dealt with quickly. Furthermore, for companies wishing to expand globally, it is not just a question of having the right product delivered to the right location, it's getting it done fast.[4] Speed is an increasingly important competitive weapon; a well-designed global account management system can deliver speed to customers.

In recent years, many business organizations around the world have adopted some form of key account management, and national account programs have become widespread. In addition, as economic trading blocks such as the European Union, NAFTA, Mercosur, and ASEAN have matured, some companies have developed regional (multinational) account programs. These regional programs may represent an incremental step (training ground) *en route* to global programs or they may reflect marketplace realities. These realities include customers' regional organizations and/or the presence of regional trading blocks. However, regional programs may hinder the development of truly global account programs.

Notwithstanding the development of regional account programs, reacting to the pressures noted above, perhaps the fastest growth area in key account programs at the present time is *global account management*. Although many varieties of global account programs exist, they enjoy the common characteristic that, typically, each account is assigned a global account manager with responsibility for developing customer relationships, and pursuing revenue opportunities at the key account, around the world.[5]

In Chapter 1, we noted several influences leading to increased competition in general, and increased global competition in particular. Increased exposure to the global marketplace has led to many new experiences, changes, and challenges for all corporations. From the customer perspective, it has increased exposure to alternative suppliers, technologies, and services, and led to changes in how key suppliers and products are selected. As decision making shifts from multidomestic to global, these new decision-making processes often involve new decision makers, contacts, and networks.

In addition, implementation of supply chain initiatives and increased international movement of professional staff with different experiences from different national cultures, proficient in different management practices, has spread best practice and expertise around the organization. Indeed, whereas some customers are building strong relationships with preferred suppliers, increased competition has nonetheless raised their expectations and demands.

In the face of these changes, supplier firms must develop new systems and processes to address their customers' evolving requirements and to enhance their own positions at their key accounts. Thus, a narrow focus at, say, the national level is too restrictive and may lead to serious errors of judgment if the customer is developing strategy at a broader level. For example, a national account program focused on a Brazilian customer will likely be inadequate if that customer is implementing a "Latin American" strategy. Even more serious is a national account strategy for a customer that is truly global.

> **EXAMPLE:** Ivy Inc.*, a major European chemical supplier, negotiated a long-term global supply contract with a European customer. Despite the "global" nature of the agreement, Ivy based the contract on the assumption of production and delivery in Europe since that represented almost all of the customer's business. Shortly after the contract was signed, the customer significantly increased its operations in the United States. Although it had not been consulted in drawing up the contract, Ivy's U.S. subsidiary was forced to supply the customer at a loss.

In this example, had the supplier firm been thinking globally it might, at the very least, have involved its U.S. subsidiary in the negotiations, and taken into account the potential impact of its agreement on the subsidiary's operations.

Typically built on the foundation of in-place national account programs, global account management programs are in their infancy; however, the early reviews are positive.[6] Notwithstanding considerable difficulties in measuring hard business performance, anecdotal reports of successful results are widespread. These include improved revenue growth, increased account penetration, acceptance by customers of products based on new technologies, identification of specific pieces of business that would not otherwise have surfaced, improved customer satisfaction, increased competitive advantage, and enhanced ability to share best practice around the supplier's organization. In addition, suppliers secure enhanced knowledge of customers, and multiple individual firm/global account relationships are improved.

In this chapter, we focus on key factors leading to the initiation of global account management, and those elements critical to program success.[7] The chapter is not meant to be a thorough discussion of global account management. Rather, it should be seen as building on prior chapters. For this reason, we focus largely on those elements that differentiate global account management from key account management at a more restricted geographic level.

INITIATING A GLOBAL ACCOUNT MANAGEMENT PROGRAM[8]

In the face of new global experiences, multinational companies are increasingly turning to global account management. The specific triggers for program development are various but can be simply categorized as either externally or internally driven.

Externally Driven Global Account Programs

Major customers of the supplier firm typically drive the external impetus for global account management. As the global perspective of these customers increases, and they operate in more individual countries, they wish to be treated globally by key suppliers. In particular, they require consistently high service levels via a single interface. Frequently, they experience problems with the supplier in individual countries, and request an account relationship that ensures their concerns are considered at a high organizational level. Specific though related triggers may include the following.

Inadequate Global Support. The customer does not receive uniformly satisfactory supplier support in the various countries in which it operates. These shortfalls may include product availability and/or product, technical, or logistic support, unavailability of information in different languages, and unacceptable delivery dates for only "slightly modified" products. Shortfall locations may range from countries where the supplier puts in major effort but is performing poorly, to those with low organizational priority. Indeed, some countries may fall outside the responsibilities of a specific organizational unit in the supplier firm, yet be extremely important to the customer.

Global Price Discrepancies. As its global information systems develop, the customer discovers differences in prices for similar products, from the same supplier, delivered at different points around the globe. It realizes that these cannot be accounted for solely by variations in transportation costs, duties, VAT and other taxes, and exchange rates. Of course, in many cases, supplier firms deliberately set different prices for different locations by practicing geographic segmentation, so as to extract the optimum level of surplus from various geographic markets.[9] Perhaps, correctly, the customer believes overcharging is occurring in some countries and desires price rationalization. In addition to price comparability, customers also require consistency in such terms of trade as discounts, credit terms, and freight costs. Also, because of deficiencies in its own information systems, the customer may require the supplier to provide information on its global spending patterns.

EXAMPLE: In the office equipment business, Canon finds that because of fragmented procurement, current and potential multinational customers frequently require different products in each country (sometimes at each site). Furthermore, the value attached to individual products, and hence the prices, differs from location to location.[10]

Global Procurement Initiative. The customer believes that better value for purchased products can be attained by developing a global procurement process that eliminates incompatible systems and equipment. Thus, it can leverage its buying power, simplify contact with suppliers, standardize products, and ensure uniform product and service quality. In addition, it may be able to improve inventory management, simplify invoicing, shorten time to market, centrally source identical products for delivery in all locations around the world, and maintain supplier information such as price, delivery, and performance in one location. Indeed, by aggregating its global procurement information by product type, and making comparisons with benchmark data, the customer firm can objectively measure its procurement performance and develop appropriate strategies. The customer also believes that global procurement may minimize the impact of changing regulations and tax and currency fluctuations.

For customers moving in the direction of global procurement, suppliers must globalize their logistics and other practices, coordinate resources globally, and offer global coverage with a single point of contact. They must introduce new products and processes simultaneously around the world rather than on a rollout basis, and provide data, including product/country sales data, globally on a comparable basis. Being able to provide this data may serve as a competitive advantage if the account's systems are not up to the task. Indeed, a shift to global procurement by a major customer may open up the possibility of sole vendor status for the supplier.

EXAMPLE: As multinational firms have adopted global branding strategies, there has been a shift to use single advertising agencies worldwide. For example, in 1994, IBM consolidated its entire global advertising ($400 to $500 million) from over forty agencies to Ogilvy and Mather Worldwide.[11] Other multinationals have similarly moved all of their telecommunications business to a single supplier such as AT&T.

Such global procurement decisions place enormous pressures on local (national or regional) suppliers and may lead to their losing long established business.[12] However, the location of some procurement decisions may be fluid for individual products. As an FMC country manager in Asia explained, "As global procurement management becomes more effective, price discrepancies at different national locations are identified and procurement decisions brought into corporate. However, for specific raw materials, global procurement managers may have less knowledge of supply issues than individual country managers. As a result, supply shortages may occur at individual local plants. These shortages lead to rejection of production budgets by local manufacturing organizations, and procurement decision making tends to shift back locally."[13]

Internally Driven Global Account Programs

The internal impetus for global account management is typically some notion of corporate direction that, the supplier firm believes, will be enhanced by treating major customers in a global manner, and hence lead to increased sales and profits. The firm may act for one of the following reasons:

Respond to Global Opportunity. The firm may observe that multiple country markets are growing rapidly for some of its customers. As these customers become more global, it sees substantial opportunities for sales of its products and services.

Rationalize Customer Relationships. Relatedly, although a capital-goods firm's major relationship with an international customer is in the customer's home country, over time the customer's purchases may be installed at its foreign subsidiaries. Because the firm's own foreign subsidiaries were little involved in the original sales activities, its account maintenance investment may be less than optimal. As a result, the firm finds it has little centralized information on the location, use, and/or performance of its products, leaving it vulnerable to competition.[14]

Seek Competitive Advantage. A global account management system may allow the supplier firm to gain competitive advantage by helping its customers globalize their activities. It may demonstrate the value of acting more globally by encouraging cross-border technology transfer, global rationalization of raw material input procurement, leveraging scarce resources more effectively, and improving scale economies. It may also collaborate in market research studies to define the most appropriate country opportunities, and assist with country-specific issues such as introductions to government officials and noncompetitive suppliers, site location, capital equipment procurement, labor issues, and introductions to potential customers.

In the context of offering such benefits, the supplier firm gains deeper understanding of its accounts, broadens its set of relationships, and increases both company and individuals' capabilities. As a result, global account management *per se* may offer significant competitive advantage.

EXAMPLE: Howard Katzen, former vice president of national and global accounts marketing for Xerox, asserts that former competitor Kodak exited the copier industry in part because of its unwillingness to make a global account management commitment similar to Xerox's.[15]

EXAMPLE: In 1993, Asea Brown Boveri, comprising several hundred quasi-independent companies, introduced a pilot project in global account management program with seven globally active customers. A deliberate decision was made to minimize external information flow about the program. "The main reason for this restraint was to keep the strategic advantage of this innovative concept."[16]

Leverage Global Resources. In order to conduct its business operations, the supplier firm may put in place a state-of-the-art global infrastructure—for example, telecommunications and/or logistics—to secure major competitive advantage and preferred supplier status. Such a system may allow customers to receive fast answers to inquiries and/or to implement procurement decisions anywhere in the world expeditiously. As noted earlier, speed is an increasingly important competitive weapon, and a global account management system can deliver speed to customers. When speed is critical, more traditional elements of the marketing offer such as price and terms become much less relevant.

Leverage Customer Relationships. Sometimes, a diversified supplier firm comprises several business units, each with its own set of customers, competitors, and underlying technology. If top management sees opportunities to provide major customers of individual business units with products based on the technology of sister units, a global account program, located at corporate, may be designed to identify and exploit these opportunities.

Avoid Problems in Organizational Relationships. A global account management system may be necessary to avoid potential organizational disasters.

> **EXAMPLE:** In March 1999, the entire Canadian affiliate of KPMG, the major accounting firm, defected to competitor Arthur Andersen because, as CEO J. Spencer Lanthier put it, KPMG is "structured as a federation of firms rather than a global business." The following week, KPMG announced a major restructuring "to remove national barriers to serving global clients."

GLOBAL ACCOUNT STRATEGY

In Chapter 2, we identified several types of relationship a firm might have with its key accounts, and presented alternative portfolio approaches for developing key account strategy. Many of the issues discussed there were general in nature, applicable at a national, regional (multicountry), or global level. Here we focus largely on global account selection. However, we first consider introduction of a global account strategy.

Introducing a Global Account Strategy

As we have reinforced throughout this book, because the resource commitment required to conduct key account management properly is substantial, it should not be entered into lightly. This is especially true for global account management, where the resources required to manage accounts on a global basis are significantly greater than for purely domestic key accounts.

World-class key account management programs operate within a structure provided by broad-based marketing strategies. However, many corporations develop their marketing strategies only to find that the implementation focus is on just a limited number of key accounts. When the firm operates at the global level, not only does the overall global account management thrust follow from a global marketing strategy, but strategy for the global accounts serves as a major foundation for the broader-based strategic thrust.

Regardless of the supplier firm's long-term objective for its global account program, a phased introduction is preferable. Like key account management in general, introduction of global account management is a complex activity and, typically, a high-visibility organizational event. Regardless of the thoroughness of the firm's plans and its attempts to capture best practice, problems will doubtless occur and programs will have to be modified.

Furthermore, because of the potential large-scale impact on the organization, internal political issues must be addressed. Resistance to introduction of global account management is frequently observed on the part of geographic regional directors and country managers who anticipate a reduction in their own power and autonomy.[17] In addition, buy-in must be secured from critical senior executives and a common set of expectations and measures developed to ease the change process.

EXAMPLE: When Hewlett-Packard's global account management program was first introduced, many managers saw it as a fad. However, within two years, 85% of those who did not believe in the program were no longer in their positions at HP. Those in key country management positions were given two or three opportunities to buy in to the program. Those seen as obstacles were encouraged to pursue other opportunities.[18]

Far better to make these changes with a limited number of global accounts, and then grow the program, than to rush headlong into a major effort that later requires substantial reengineering with the associated organizational and human costs. Consider, for example the experience of European Chemical*.

EXAMPLE: For many years, European Chemical (EC) conducted a form of key account management at a national level. In the mid-1990s, a goal of closer focus on customer needs led EC to develop a new organization based on seven industry sectors for which it would develop global marketing strategies. Implementation of the new organization led directly to identification of twenty-one global accounts distributed across the seven sectors. EC management developed an account-planning template and held a series of two-day workshops to develop key account plans.

Several months into the process, EC management became concerned about two major issues—key account selection and global account manager appointment. Selection of key accounts was not rigorously performed; rather, key managers made "top-of-the-head" choices. Furthermore, some of the "global" accounts were not truly global, but were dominant regional accounts having little activity outside their regions. In addition, the role of global account manager was not defined clearly, leading to haphazard selection of managers. The organizational level ranged widely from senior to quite junior executives; these latter were quite unable to engineer and organize meetings between high-level key account and EC executives.

By contrast, Dun & Bradstreet started small, yet grew its global account program significantly as it gained experience. Initiated in 1995 with ten global accounts, in early 1997 there were twenty-seven, with one hundred by 1999.[19]

Selecting Global Accounts

A thorough, rigorous selection procedure for key accounts in general is essential. Because of the scope of operation and the resources involved, selection of global accounts is even more important.[20] Over and above the basic criteria discussed in Chapter 2, global accounts should most likely operate in at least two or three continents, with a significant (and growing) percent of the account's business conducted outside its home market. Potential accounts should be receptive and ready for a global relationship, in particular, the account should not view global account designation simply as a means to extract price concessions. In addition to considering these criteria, supplier firms should develop individualized criteria related to their own specific goals for global account management.

EXAMPLE: 3M, seeking to identify opportunities for its numerous technologies, commenced its search for global key accounts with the global *Fortune*

500. In addition to the key account criteria noted earlier, 3M looked for a bias for innovation and creativity measured by R&D spending as a percent of sales. The current relationship was irrelevant to selection; indeed, for some global key accounts, there was no prior relationship whatsoever!

Key account management should only be introduced if it adds value to the supplier-firm/key-account relationship; a similar caution is relevant for global account management. First, global account management makes little sense unless the customer's operations are located in several different countries. For this reason, we distinguish between customers that are *strategic* for the firm and the subset of those accounts that is *global* in nature. For example, the U.S. Postal Service and U.S. Steel may both be strategically important customers for a supplier firm, yet since their operations are essentially U.S.-based, it is probably inappropriate to treat them as global accounts. Such firms should be managed at the national level, but distinguished from regular national accounts and treated specially because of their strategic importance to the corporation as a whole.

Second, important customers may operate in many different countries, yet if their business is inherently local in operation, global account management may add little or no value.

EXAMPLE: Shell operates numerous drilling sites in various countries around the world. Schlumberger provides oil field services to Shell on short-term contracts at many of these sites. However, all of Shell's drilling-related decisions are made locally by oil field personnel. In the late 1990s, neither firm saw any value in a significant global account relationship.

Third, even though the nature of a customer's business may be congenial to a global management approach, its internal systems and decision-making processes may make such an approach infeasible or at least without value at the present time.[21] Indeed, the supplier firm may anticipate considerable heterogeneity across its account base even for those accounts that appear on the surface to be equally multinational in scope.

Furthermore, no matter how thorough the global account selection process, errors may occur or the supplier firm may find that, over time, individual global accounts no longer meet the selection criteria. In such cases, appropriate steps should be taken to deselect the account from its global management program. Finally, the entire set of criteria employed for global account selection may be expected to evolve over time.

ROLES AND RESPONSIBILITIES IN GLOBAL ACCOUNT MANAGEMENT

Top Management Commitment

In Chapter 3, we noted the importance of top management support for key account management in general; this support is even more important for the much more broadly scoped global account management. Top management sponsorship and support are necessary conditions for diffusing potential organizational conflict (see below). However, this support must be consistent, continuous, and demonstrated in various different ways, preferably by the CEO.[22] It may be exhibited through frequent internal company communications on the value of global account management—for example, through management meetings, speeches to company groups, and articles and interviews in the internal company periodical; it may also take the form of performance-based awards related to success with global accounts.

> **EXAMPLE:** Betz and Dearborne's success depended on reducing costs for customers. Each year, the CEO presented awards to those global account managers, and their managers, who were able to demonstrate the highest levels of savings (documented by customers). The meetings at which the awards were presented had high visibility within the firm and were attended by the entire top management cadre. In addition to receiving their awards, winners enjoyed immense status in the organization.

An executive partnership program is a particularly valuable device for both demonstrating top-level commitment to global account management in general and providing significant value-added to global customer relationships in particular. The basis of executive partner programs in this context is the "adoption" of a global account by a member of the firm's top management cadre. Linkages between this senior manager and the global account may be driven by a global account director acting as a broker and/or by a strong suggestion from the CEO that each member of the managerial elite should participate in at least one or two of these relationships.

A high-level reporting relationship for the global account director, for example, equivalent to the geographic region directors can send a particularly powerful message. The global account director may act as the "champion" of global account management or the "champion" and director may be different people, with the "champion" being a member of the executive committee.

The global account director attempts to ensure that global account management budgets are protected from short-term cost cutting. He also plays a critical role in ensuring that top management support is unflagging by continually feeding it such information as regular (monthly/quarterly) reports and *ad hoc* data on global account successes. In addition, selected positive information, via memoranda, Web site, newsletter, CDs and the like, is communicated throughout the organization to help build a global account culture. Finally, the global account director develops global account initiatives to be agreed on, and possibly executed, by the CEO.

A particularly valuable device for cementing top management support is the global account steering committee. Executive partners, the global account director, selected global account managers, and key geographic region executives (see below) meet periodically (at least annually) to discuss global account management issues and resolve disputes. This committee is especially powerful if the CEO is an active member. Global regional directors would not wish to be seen as having pursued their own parochial interests in the face of a CEO-supported global account management program!

Just as with national-based key account management programs, introduction of global account management provides significant opportunities for intraorganizational conflict. Global account management is frequently involved in conflict between domestic divisions and international, and among various geographic-area divisions, in addition to traditional inter-functional and inter-business conflicts. Methods for dealing with each type of conflict include setting and communicating expectations, and communicating results on a continuous basis.

EXAMPLE: In the mid-1990s, Marriott Hotels introduced a global account management program. In the first six months of the program, fifty customer presentations were made. In the same time period, 250 internal presentations were made as a means of preempting internal conflict![23]

Notwithstanding the importance of top management commitment for successful global account management, global account personnel must be able to demonstrate to senior executives that the program is not just another layer of overhead, but rather delivers value-added to the corporation in terms of documented results.

Global Account Managers and Global Account Teams

As noted earlier, the global account manager (GAM) is responsible for developing relationships, and identifying and exploiting opportunities for the supplier firm at the global account around the world. GAMs spend a significant amount of time with their global accounts, and in addition, most find it necessary also to spend large amounts of time within their own organizations, securing required resources and coordinating internal firm activities. Typically, individual GAMs are located in the head office (or most significant) country of their global accounts; indeed, they may even secure office space at the global account.[24]

In Chapter 3, we discussed the roles and responsibilities of key account managers. The roles and responsibilities of the global account manager are little different in type, but the planning and strategy task is more complex. Furthermore, the stakes are higher in terms of opportunities and threats, the sets of global account relationships are broader in scope and more senior in level, and the information network is global rather than local.

Just as key account managers at the national level typically represent their own firms in dealing with various key account business units, so global account managers should have the authority to speak for the entire company around the world, including geographically autonomous profit centers. However, operating globally may not be as simple as operating nationally. For one thing, the supplier firm's international presence may comprise a variety of different organizational forms including not only independent entities but also joint ventures, partnerships, or equity participations with various levels of ownership. A similar pattern may hold for the global account, making it difficult to identify the purchase decision process(es). Because the number of potential contacts at both the key account and the supplier firm is so large, it is imperative that the global account manager maintain up-to-date directories of them all.

Because of the broader geographic scope and heightened complexity of supplier-firm/global-account relationships, a global account team that may be cross-functional, cross-divisional, and cross-level must support the GAM. Team members may include not only functional experts—for example, in R&D, logistics and marketing—but also key executives responsible for account business in various countries, frequently national account managers (NAMs) for the key account. Ideally, team members should have had prior team membership experience (or at least undergo teamwork training) and, since they are based in multiple countries with varying cultures, be well-schooled in cultural diversity issues.[25]

EXAMPLE: IBM's global account managers are supported by International Sales Centers (ISCs), established in all geographies. The ISCs both resolve international marketing issues and provide worldwide support for GAMs pursuing international sales opportunities. International sales specialists who are thoroughly familiar with both the roles and capabilities of IBM's international support groups and the issues and complexities of international business support GAMs by identifying and coordinating appropriate IBM resources.

EXAMPLE: Siemens's top management believes that understanding individual national cultures is so important for successful global account management that it has developed a forum in which local contact managers from eighty countries meet with global account managers and make presentations on culture, market strategies, and the appeal of Siemens's products.[26]

Global account team members may be the GAM's direct reports, or they may report through other organizational units and have only dotted line responsibility to the GAM. Regardless, the GAM must get things done by demonstrating his value, by persuasion, and by exercising a high degree of team leadership. In some companies, including IBM, global account managers have the right of veto over personnel responsible for the global account locally.

SMOOTHLY FUNCTIONING GLOBAL ACCOUNT TEAMS

Since global account managers typically function through cross-functional, cross-divisional, cross-level global account teams, it is important that team members are appropriately selected and trained.[27] If the thrust of the global account program is developing new business, previously disinterested executives may join a global account team.

Global account team members play several major roles:

- Support the GAM in developing an information base about the account, identifying opportunities and threats, and generally assisting in planning, strategy making, and action program development
- Execute action programs developed in the global account strategy
- Continually collect and disseminate information about the global account
- Develop relationships with relevant personnel at the global account
- Interact as necessary with supplier firm personnel to form a cohesive global account team

When the GAM secures business from global account headquarters, locally based team members, experienced in dealing with their national cultures, manage the transition from global procurement to implementation in the national setting. If this "receiver" or "inbound" role is not well staffed, many issues may fall through the cracks in the transition. It is also important for the GAM to convince the global account that team members will be sensitive to its issues in the implementation process.

EXAMPLE: British liquefied gases multinational, BOC, seeks business from Japanese companies opening up operations in its Britain. BOC employs Japanese nationals locally so as to assure its Japanese customers of its sensitivity to their needs.

A simple yet effective way method of tracking the sets of responsibilities for managing global accounts is to develop a customer-country matrix in which the GAMs, locally based NAMs and other team members for each global account are clearly identified.

GLOBAL ACCOUNT MANAGEMENT AND THE CORPORATE ORGANIZATION

Corporations conducting business in many countries around the world typically manage their geographically diverse operations via either an international division or a geographic-area structure.[28] In general, the greater international operations as a proportion of corporate revenues, the more likely that firms implement a geographic-area structure. A typical structure might comprise four divisions—for example, North America, Europe (including the Middle East and Africa), Asia/Pacific, and Latin America. In such organizations, geographic region directors and their country-manager direct reports have at least top-line, and frequently also bottom-line responsibility. Regardless of the particular organizational form, introduction of global account management must occur in the face of some preexisting organization.

A variety of different organizational forms is available for global account management. We identify three alternative approaches—matrix, market-integrated, and the new region.

The Matrix Organization

When corporations seriously embark on global account management, the matrix organization is frequently the chosen organizational form. In this section we focus on reporting relationships, measurement of results, and pros and cons of the matrix structure

REPORTING RELATIONSHIPS

In the matrix organization, global account management is matrixed with the preexisting geographic area structure.[29] The GAM is responsible for planning, strategy making, action program development, implementation, and high-level relationship building. However, much day-to-day supplier firm/global account interaction at dispersed account locations around the world is conducted by personnel in local sales and support structures (for example, R&D, technical service, and logistics). These employees report (solid line) through their own geographic and/or functional organizations. Typically, the more senior of these personnel, such as national account managers for the key account, have dotted line reporting relationships to the global account manager.[30]

The GAM, operating "horizontally in a vertical world," typically reports to a local geographic-based manager at either a country or geographic region level, but also to a senior manager with customer responsibilities.[31] This second manager may be a global account director to whom all GAMs report or, perhaps, an industry (market sector) director who has planning and strategy responsibility for one or more market arenas on a global basis.

> **EXAMPLE:** At Milliken, the major textile organization, global account management operates within some form of high-level market segmentation, for example, by industry. Individual key accounts are selected within each industry targeted by the corporation, for example, distribution, health care, and education.

In practice, across corporations, a variety of reporting relationships can be identified; typically, the GAM reports on both a geographic and customer-focused basis. Each relationship may range from a strong solid line to a weak dotted line.

If the preexisting geographic area structure comprised strong regional managers, the initial relationship of GAM to geographic manager is likely to be a strong solid line. Conversely, the relationship to a customer-focused manager is likely to be a dotted line. However, over time, as the global account management program earns credibility, it is likely that the relationship of the GAM to customer-focused manager becomes stronger as the geographic relationship weakens. Within the geographic-area structure, some organizations transition to a situation where that relationship becomes solid line, and the relationship between GAM and geographic-based manager is described as little more than "care and feeding."

SUPPORTING STRUCTURES

In order to do their jobs effectively, global account managers may require a variety of support structures.

Headquarters account managers (HAMs). In its original matrix organization for global account management, Hewlett-Packard (HP) also identified a role for headquarters account managers (HAMs). Whereas GAMs typically resided in the headquarters cities of their global accounts, HAMs were their representatives at corporate headquarters. The HAMs' mission was to "champion the critical needs and significant opportunities of the global account within HP headquarters, and to establish HP as a strategic vendor through long-term sales growth and customer satisfaction."[32]

HAMs worked with GAMs on developing new business opportunities, and on technical, pricing, and strategy issues to support the global customer relationship. Other benefits of the HAM program were as a focused channel for product divisions into global account management, developing a network of resources across customer industries, and the sharing of best practices in global account management among the various HAMs and hence to the GAMs.[33]

Regional Account Managers. Because of a concern for excessively large span-of-control, multi-country regional account managers are often a critical element in a fully functioning global program.[34]

EXAMPLE: In Unilever's structure, key account managers in a country report to a national account manager for that country. However, the key account manager for a specific account, for example, Wal-Mart in Argentina, also reports (dotted line) to a regional account manager (RAM) for Latin America. The RAM, in turn, reports to Unilever's global account manager for Wal-Mart.[35]

MEASUREMENT

In the geographic-area/global-account-manager matrix structure, regardless of the specific nature of reporting responsibilities, sales to individual global accounts are typically accrued in the various local geographies where sales are made and/or product is delivered.[36] In particular, revenues (profits) secured in the global account's head-office country/region accrue to the GAM's geographic (local/regional) manager.

In addition to securing revenue (and profit) for their geographically organized managers, GAMs have global revenue responsibility that cuts across the geographic organization. In those cases where GAMs were formerly national account managers (NAMs) in the global account's home (or most important) country, a measurement system that weights international revenue growth more heavily than domestic growth may be necessary to attain the appropriate level of GAM effort internationally. Ideally, GAMs should also have some form of profit contribution or P&L responsibility. However, not only are leading companies hampered by the inability of their systems to produce this data, even developing global revenue data by account is often a significant challenge.

MANAGING IN THE MATRIX STRUCTURE

The major argument for the matrix organization is that attention is given to both the geographic and customer dimensions. Furthermore, since the preexisting organization was likely based on geographic areas, the matrix structure represents an organizational evolution, less disruptive than a full-scale organizational change with all its associated political ramifications.

The major problem with the matrix system is the potential conflict it engenders. The GAM must deal with two different pressures:

- First, her geographic superior is concerned to optimize performance in the specific geographic area of responsibility
- Second, in optimizing account performance globally, the GAM's responsibilities cut across geography

The conflict arises because decisions leading to global performance optimization may cause suboptimal performance in a particular geographic area (and vice versa), at least in the short run. Several types of conflict arise:

- To fulfill his global responsibilities, the GAM must travel to a different region or country. Such trips are wasteful from a narrowly construed geographic perspective. The GAM's geographic superior not only suffers the opportunity loss of GAM time, he must also finance the direct out-of-pocket trip cost.

- To secure a particular global contract (perhaps previously awarded regionally or nationally), the GAM has to agree to lower than normal prices. Although the supplier firm gains from the global contract, revenues and profits accruing to some geographically based managers are negatively affected. In addition, these managers face potential pricing problems with other customers.[37]

- Potential future global business requires spending in a specific geographic region. However, the likely major beneficiary of future sales revenue is not the region of a GAM's superior, but a sister region.

Ideally, potential conflict should be dealt with preemptively by developing a customer-focused global account management culture, driven from the top of the organization, that leads the entire firm to do what is best for the customer. The goal should be to bring geographic area executives "on board" in accepting global account management as a positive organizational innovation. Of course, it is likely that, in the preglobal era, regional executives experienced customer-related problems associated with the geographic structure. The supplier firm must develop systems and processes to address these and other potential problems. Possible actions include:

- International travel and other expenses additional to GAMs' local and regional responsibilities are funded outside the regional structure as a corporate budget item
- Shadow earnings systems developed such that:
  - geographic local and regional managers secure credit for global revenues earned outside their areas of geographic responsibility by GAMs located in their geographies
  - revenues earned from global accounts headquartered outside their home geographies are counted fractionally greater (for example, 1.5 times) than revenues secured from locally based customers.

Clearly, in each of these cases, appropriate changes must be made in revenue and profit objectives and/or quotas. Alternatively, global P&Ls are developed for global accounts and these accounts are removed from local P&L statements. Local management is measured on customer service levels.[38] Relatedly, global account directors may play a significant role in the evaluation process for both global account managers and executives responsible for dealing with global accounts locally.

Other supportive processes are:

- Regular biannual meetings are held to discuss global account issues (as noted above). Attendees include senior geographic managers, GAMs, executive partners, and/or other high-level managers (preferably including the CEO) who are committed to global account management.
- Because of their organizational positions, executives senior to the GAM are able to negotiate global/geographic conflicts. Two important roles are the global account director and the global account's executive partner. The biannual meeting mechanism (noted above) should reduce the number of conflicts raised to these organizational levels.
- Senior executives have both geographic and global account responsibilities. As a result, they understand geographic/global account tradeoffs firsthand, and are less likely to act parochially.

EXAMPLE: In one iteration of its global account program, in addition to the conventional geographic area structure comprising several regional directors, Citibank developed ten global planning units based on industry. Each GAM reported (solid line) into one of these planning units. In addition to their geographic responsibilities, each regional director had global responsibility for two or three of the ten industries.

The Market-Integrated Global Account Organization

In the previous section, we indicated that matrix organizations combining geographic area and global account management dimensions tend to evolve over time; the geographic reporting relationship becomes weaker and the global reporting relationship stronger. Some corporations have taken this progression to its logical conclusion by essentially eliminating their geographic area organizations.

EXAMPLE: In 1995, IBM scrapped its geographic organization and introduced a global sales force so it could serve customers across the globe and avoid turf battles between regional sales managers.[39] Initially GAMs reported into eleven industrial sectors, later reduced to six.

EXAMPLE: Asea Brown Boveri (ABB) was traditionally organized as a matrix of global product segments/business areas and countries/regions. Initiated in 1993, by 1999, about twenty customers in such industries as fine chemicals, pharmaceuticals, automobiles, and utilities were managed in its global key account management (GKAM) system. In its latest reorganization, ABB departed from the geographic organization by eliminating budgets by country. Henceforth, budgets were to be set only by product segments/business areas.[40]

In these firms, the critical organizational dimension is no longer geography but is based on market, typically industry. What may have been planning organizations in a geographic-area structure become line organizations as the geographic dimension essentially disappears. Locally based personnel responsible for the local operations of global accounts have strong relationships with the GAMs who, in turn, now report directly into their respective industry groups.

EXAMPLE: In one of Chase Bank's global business units, each key account manager has two roles. First, each is the GAM for one or more accounts based in her country of domicile, for example, Sony if based in Japan. Second, she is the local account manager for the Japanese subsidiary operations of U.S.- or European-based key accounts.

Revenue and profit responsibilities are exclusively the responsibility of market (industry) executives. As a result, global account management is budgeted by industry. Of course, these organizations must maintain a geographic structure for such functions as corporate image making, governmental relations, and "care and feeding" of locally based personnel. However, no longer do revenue, cost, and profit responsibility reside in the geographies. Indeed, expense budgets by geography no longer exist. Expenses in a particular geography are essentially the summed expenses of individual industry activities in that geography.

The major advantage of this organizational form is a complete alignment of the firm to its major customers. Externally, by focusing the organization on customer industry, GAMs secure superior information on industry trends and can add significant value in conversations with key account personnel. Internally, clarity is brought to lines of authority and responsibility. No longer is there discussion of solid and dotted line reporting relationships, nor any need for shadow revenue and expense systems to mitigate the global/geographic conflict.[41]

The New Region

In the "new region" approach, global customers are pulled out of the regular geographic area structure and managed in a new "region." This approach is less traumatic than development of the market-integrated global account organization just discussed, inasmuch as the geographic area structure remains intact, albeit with less power and responsibility than previously. The new region concept may be implemented in two ways.

FULL SEPARATION

The global accounts are completely separated from the existing geographic regions and placed in a new "global accounts" region. New region management has complete authority and responsibility for the development and management of these accounts. Global account managers no longer have to work through local personnel reporting through the geographic structure. Rather, totally new structures are developed for local sales, servicing, technical support, and so forth that report into the "global accounts" region. These local structures operate side by side with the residual geographic structures that retain those customers not selected as global accounts. Many individuals who previously operated within the geographic regions transfer to the new "global account" region.

Global account managers no longer have to use persuasion with the geographic regions to obtain resources to serve their global accounts. Instead, the key resource allocation issues are decided at a higher level, between the global account region head and the geographic heads. Resources required to serve global accounts now rest exclusively within the global accounts region, not in the geographic regions.[42]

PARTIAL SEPARATION

In this approach, the geographic region structure remains intact but a new "global accounts" region is added. The selected global accounts and the global account management organization are placed in the new region. However, local implementation still occurs through the geographic regions. Thus, compared to full separation, the geographic region head retains responsibility for global accounts, but with a difference.

For nonglobal accounts, the geographic head has full authority and responsibility, as previously, and is measured and rewarded based on his performance in the geographic region. For global accounts, the geographic region head is directly responsible for revenues secured within the region, but is only measured and rewarded based on the *global performance* of those accounts. Hence, the geographic head is highly motivated to work with global account mangers to help them meet their objectives of increased performance from global accounts.

EXAMPLE: Van Leer Packaging supplies steel drums to the oil and chemical industry. In October 1995, Van Leer lost a major contract, in France, with the French oil company, Total. This loss occurred largely because Van Leer's British subsidiary, which had a close relationship with Total (UK), refused to offer price concessions for a Europe-wide agreement. After a management shake-up, Van Leer introduced the partial separation system as a way of securing less provincial thinking by its country heads.[43]

* * *

Regardless of which organization form is chosen, implementation of global account management has an important impact on the various national account management systems and individual national account managers. First, those in-place national account managers responsible for the local activities of a new global account now have new responsibilities and an additional reporting relationship, to the GAM. The implications of this change must be clearly spelled out for the local organization so that these NAMs become functioning members of the GAM's team. Second, introduction of a global account management program, and the newly elevated status of global accounts, may spur introduction of national account programs in those areas of the organization without them. Such an organizational change should aid in fulfilling their enhanced responsibilities for the local activities of several global accounts.[44]

GLOBAL ACCOUNT PLANNING

In Chapters 5 through 7, we discussed at length a variety of systems and processes to improve key account planning. In many cases, systems that operate at the national level are equally useful at the global level. However, because of time and distance issues, they may take on added importance in a global context.

The Nature of the Global Account Plan

Although the global account plan is no different from the key account plan in concept, its requirements can range widely. For example, if the firm already has in place a well-run system for developing national (or multicountry regional) account plans, developing a global plan largely involves providing value-added over these national account plans. The GAM considers the global procurement focus of the key account, and makes global decisions on customer-focused investments.[45] However, if a planning system is not in place at the local level, global account plan development is a much larger enterprise. The global account manager may have to train local personnel to develop local situation analyses as part of the foundation on which the global account strategy should be developed.

Just as with national account plans, the GAM should ensure that customer executives are involved in the global account planning process, and that they agree with the objectives, strategies, and action programs that are developed. The GAM should schedule a formal annual global account review and also involve key account personnel in the two- to three-day annual planning meeting.

In general, the same philosophy and structure underlying the key account planning process are appropriate for global account planning. However, because of the physical distances and time zones involved, the global account plan may be more important than national account plans as a road map to guide day-to-day actions at the account. It is even more important to develop templates for the global account plan, and to set delivery dates for individual elements to be completed. A well-developed global account plan should comprise several action programs, each containing a series of action steps to be undertaken by combinations of global account and supplier firm personnel around the world.

Information for Global Account Planning and Implementation

Substantial quantities of information are required to develop and appropriately implement the global account plan. Although the global account manager is responsible for developing the situation analysis and driving strategy development, she needs several forms of assistance to complete this task. Certainly, members of the global account team are an important resource, but the GAM also needs broad-scale data including account industry trends and global economic forecasts. This sort of information could be provided by a marketing staff group reporting to a global account director, or by an industry-focused organization.

The global account plan, developed to a standard format, provides the foundation for day-to-day account management. As such, it should be updated periodically by designated personnel (typically the GAM) as new information becomes available and action steps are completed. These tasks are facilitated by an electronic information infrastructure that maintains the customer's global account plan and provides differential access to members of the account team and customer. Plan sections may be kept confidential at the GAM's discretion. The plan should include an executive summary that functions as a briefing document for senior executives meeting with global accounts. The planning system should also provide for success reporting, and a "chat room" for conversations about global account issues.

The importance of a well-developed information infrastructure cannot be overstated, for global account management must deal with the tyranny of distance and time zones.[46] It is especially critical when global accounts require some form of standardized prices and/or service around the world. For a GAM based in Paris, it is simply far more difficult to communicate with company and customer personnel in Beijing than in London, not least because work days do not overlap. In order to reduce the barriers of time and geography, the supplier firm should invest in some form of *Lotus Notes,* e-mail, or a proprietary electronic system that is available to both company and global account personnel.[47] Regardless, the GAM should schedule global account team conference calls at least quarterly.[48]

A well-designed information system offers numerous benefits. The most obvious is increased speed of communications, response, and decision making, and reduction in costs (e.g., decreased travel). In addition, conversations have an audit trail, and the system has a group memory that team members can access and which allows information dumping by individuals around the world. The memory function, which reduces communication redundancy, is the means by which the global account manager can manage implementation and updating of the global account plan.

> **EXAMPLE:** Hewlett Packard's (HP) *AccountNet* has a simple web-based format comprising both private (customer confidential) and public documents. For a global account, private documents are posted instantly and viewable only by account team members. Public documents are viewable by any HP Intranet user, but posting is delayed for formatting and review. Each global account team sets up its own file structure, and agrees on key information needs for managing the account. Typical categories of information include account overview and organization charts, account team organization charts, account news, big deal list (sales opportunities), account plans, sales plans, account proposals, and forecasts.[49]

Financial Systems to Monitor Global Account Plan Implementation

Although a variety of action planning objectives may be set for global accounts, fundamental business objectives for any account management system concern revenues and profits.[50] In order to assess appropriately the effectiveness of global account management, the firm needs a system that integrates local information into global performance. The global account manager should have at his fingertips data on the various revenue streams that together comprise the "top line." In addition, he should be provided with account share in different geographic areas, and volumes and prices by product with the appropriate comparisons to history and plan.[51] Not only does the GAM require this information to develop the global plan and make appropriate resource allocation decisions, global customers will want to know this information if only to check their own data.

Unfortunately, few companies today are able to identify global revenues "at the touch of a button," and measurement of global account profitability or profit contribution seems far in the future for many multinational firms. Of course, the development of such systems is not a simple task. Indeed, for many firms, local revenue and cost information around the world may be located in different formats on different computer systems in what is often a managerial morass.[52] In addition, the supplier firm has to deal with multiple currencies and floating exchange rates. Notwithstanding these problems, there is an old saying in management that "if you can't measure it, you can't manage it." Since global accounts are such an important element of the firm's future, tackling the measurement problem should become a major corporate priority.

Managing Contracts

Contract management for global accounts requires a complex information system embracing both global arrangements and unique local terms and conditions, with information available to interested supplier executives on a need-to-know basis. Initial system development may be difficult, involving the integration of various national legacy systems into a global pricing and service framework.

EXAMPLE: At IBM, a central support organization of International Order Management Specialists (IOMS) provides global account managers with a package of internationally acceptable contracts complete with technical details and local list prices. Global account managers have access to a range of "prefabricated" offers including prices, delivery terms, and product performance. In addition, they have the ability to offer aggregate volume discounts, or they may ask a central organization to make a globally binding pricing decision.

IOMSs prepare agreements for customer signature, receive and validate the agreements, communicate them within IBM, and load them onto appropriate local fulfillment systems. The IOMSs, in turn, are supported by a central organization with global access both to IBM's product portfolio and the customer stock of installed IBM products.

Once an IBM International Customer Agreement (IICA) agreement is signed at the global level, it is passed to local customer entities and IBM companies. Local customers and corresponding IBM companies agree to conduct business under IICA negotiated terms, thus eliminating inconsistent country-by-country agreements.

THE GLOBAL ACCOUNT MANAGER

In this section, we focus on those individuals who occupy global account manager positions. In most cases, our discussion is supplementary to the material in Chapter 4. Our discussion embraces skill sets; recruiting and selecting, training and retaining global account managers; and performance measurement and compensation.

Skill Sets

Key account managers require business management, boundary spanning, relationship-building, leadership, and team-building skills to operate effectively. These skills are no less important for global account managers. Indeed, GAMs face the added difficulty of employing these skills in a global context, in multiple cultures, in multiple languages, across immense geographic distances (both physical and time zones), often within a geographically based organizational context that is inhospitable to global initiatives.

As a result, in addition to the extensive set of skills required for successful key account management, the global account manager requires a degree of sensitivity, perspective, and experience that a national account manager may not need to develop. Specifically, the GAM must be an internationalist, possessing a global outlook, an international perspective, and an awareness of, and tolerance for, cultural diversity.[53]

Recruiting, Selecting, Training, and Retaining Global Account Managers

RECRUITING AND SELECTING

Finding candidates with the appropriate set of skills for such high-profile, high-visibility positions may not be an easy matter. Each firm must develop its own specific requirements, but typical candidate criteria include international outlook, multilingual ability, and significant experience working in foreign countries. Furthermore, appointment of people with high levels of credibility within the organization not only eases the job of the GAM, it sends a powerful message about the importance of the global account program. For example, several of 3M's corporate account managers were previously general managers in various countries (Ireland, Portugal, Ecuador). If these criteria can be met in a candidate with significant and successful key account management experience, the supplier firm secures the added benefit of ensuring that the basic business skills are already in place.

As a result, for companies with functioning national account programs that decide to embark on global account management, the current set of national account managers is an obvious source of potential global account managers. Indeed, a process for recruiting GAMs, used by more than one major corporation, is simply to elevate a set of NAMs to global account status—in effect, to expand their territory. The major benefit of this approach is that the NAM already has significant knowledge of the global account, typically based on experience in the account's most important market. The major negatives are that individual NAMs may not be currently functioning at a high level, even in the national context. Even if they are, they may not possess the elevated set of skills, contacts, perspective, and experience necessary to be successful at the global level. In sum, the wholesale promotion of NAMs to GAMs, without the appropriate training, development, and weeding-out mechanisms, is ill conceived. Not only may individual account management fail, significant human resource costs may ensue.

EXAMPLE: A major U.S. industrial company with a successful national account program introduced global account management. One key account manager, born and raised in Dayton, Ohio had been very successful with his Cincinnati-based key account. However, this individual had rarely traveled outside Ohio and, when appointed, did not have a passport. Six months into his tenure as global account manager he had to be removed from his position. Shortly thereafter he left the company.

Because of the extensive responsibility and requirement to operate at a high level in the customer organization, key account managers must report at a senior level in the supplier firm. The message that the GAM position is an important job has a major impact on recruitment. For example, personnel with international experience, even up to the level of country manager (as noted earlier for 3M), may both have the desired international credentials and be attracted to, and retained in, such senior level positions.

Several firms have put considerable investment in identifying criteria for the "ideal" global account manager.

EXAMPLE: Based on research with global account managers, senior management, and customers, software company Oracle developed criteria for global account manager selection and performance evaluation. Oracle uses an ideal GAM profile to create personal development programs for each global account manager.[54]

As global account programs expand in importance and scope, the requirement for global account managers will expand concurrently. Firms embracing global account management should consider developing systems that produce a talent pool of GAMs in waiting. Such systems would identify potential GAMs, and ensure they are provided with the opportunities to gain the appropriate skills and experience both through training programs and appropriate job assignments, for example, international and general management.

The foregoing discussion focused on internal candidates. Although powerful arguments can be made for internal appointments, the GAM position is so important that, in the absence of top quality internal candidates, the firm should enter the external labor market rather than appointing unqualified internally sourced personnel.

As with key account managers in general, the selection process should be rigorous, involving a panel of, or multiple interviews with, senior executives. The process should be to some degree standardized and the interviewers themselves should be experienced in global account management.

EXAMPLE: When the Marriott Corporation introduced its global account program, it selected eleven GAMs to serve its thirty Alliance Accounts. Each candidate completed a battery of psychological tests and was interviewed sequentially by two vice presidents to a standard format. The selection was conducted by a committee comprising the five vice presidents who conducted the interviews, and the executive vice president. Final recommendations for each position were approved by J.W. Marriott Jr., chairman and CEO.[55]

TRAINING

Regardless of how well the candidates qualify for GAM positions, some level of training is probably valuable, if only to establish commonality in systems, processes, and language. Furthermore, even a high-functioning national account manager may need assistance in broadening the scope of his planning expertise from national to global. Learning how to manage a far-flung network of team members, operating a global intranet system, selling to international customers, managing international projects, and multicultural and foreign language training may also be appropriate.[56] A particularly valuable type of training is in global account planning. Properly designed, a several-day training program can have as an output an embryonic global account plan. In addition, a variety of technical matters may be introduced such as international contracting and legal issues surrounding imports and exports.

The appropriate training system should be based on a formal skills assessment and closely related to the recruitment and selection processes. For example, a recruitment process that simply promotes NAMs to GAMs would probably benefit from a fairly standardized training approach inasmuch as significant common requirements are likely across many candidates. By contrast, in situations where GAMs are recruited from many different backgrounds and experience, a custom-tailored approach addressing specific needs may be more effective. Potential areas for training may include high-level selling, negotiations, relationship development, and cultural sensitivity.

Regardless of the initial training, a program of ongoing skill and knowledge development will ensure that the global account management force is the most effective it can be. For example, within the past couple of years, many GAMs would have benefited from education on such global trends as the Asian crisis and recovery, worldwide use of the Internet, and introduction of the "euro." Such education may be delivered in a variety of forms ranging from classroom seminars to web-based educational forums using either inside or independent training organizations.

Of course, the pressures of managing global accounts typically make it difficult for GAMs to find time for training. Dun & Bradstreet's certification process puts pressure on GAMs to find the time.[57] IBM has long had a credentialing program in which its GAMs complete assignments and take an examination. Described by some as a mini-MBA in international marketing, the program demands that IBM GAMs attend three weeks of classes spread over eighteen months. Although the GAM is the focal point of the global account management system, many support team members may also benefit from similar training.

RETAINING

The ability to retain high-performing global account managers is directly related to the level of corporate support for global account management, and the rewards associated with the position. Since these managers are probably highly sought after by competitors, the supplier firm should continually monitor job satisfaction levels and make appropriate responses.

> **EXAMPLE:** International package delivery firm DHL has a well-developed global account management program focused on twenty-eight accounts. Relatively few of its managers have left DHL, but those who do leave frequently wish to return. They find that their new companies fail to provide support levels for global account management equivalent to those they were used to at DHL.[58]

The GAM position is extremely important to the supplier-firm/global-account relationship, and those who fill it need significant time to comprehend fully the nature of their challenges, and to develop a basic set of functioning relationships. As a result, the position should not turn over every couple of years. Rather, a minimum time on the job is probably three to five years with many global account managers retiring from their positions.

Regardless of cause, when the time comes for a new global account manager to be appointed, a substantial hand-over period should be budgeted in which the outgoing GAM plays a significant role in the transition.

Performance Measurement and Compensation

PERFORMANCE MEASUREMENT

Measuring performance at the GAM level is significantly more complex than for key account managers operating at the national level. Desired performance measures may differ little from those discussed previously—for example, level and growth of sales revenue, share of business, profit contribution, and product mix. However, the supplier firm must also be concerned with such issues as multiple currencies, currency hedging, and the like in developing *hard* performance measures. Less than optimal data systems may make use of standard performance measures extremely difficult, if not impossible.[59]

The problem occurs when individual firm operations around the world use different data management systems. Indeed, it may be impossible to secure data for a valuable performance measure such as sales growth simply by pulling together global account revenue data electronically, although this may be obtained by paper and pencil methods. However, gathering global profit and profit contribution data may be well nigh impossible until global data systems are put in place.

Because such system difficulties may make it difficult to secure *hard* measures, relatively more attention should be paid to *softer* measures, collected in various ways, via a balanced scorecard approach. If balanced scorecard measures are well-chosen, good performance on the scorecard should lead to long-run *hard* measure success.[60] Candidate *soft* measures include customer satisfaction measures, in part account specific, and related diagnostics such as communications and responsiveness. These data may be collected in a structured manner, possibly by third party organizations.[61] For a large global account, several tens of respondents may be appropriate. Benchmarks should be developed for the various measures so that progress may be measured over time.

In addition, unstructured interviewing of global account executives by geographic region, executive partner, and/or industry sector personnel may provide valuable information on GAM performance. Other particularly valuable performance measures are identification of opportunities, and execution against the global account plan. Examination of the degree of implementation provides information on the GAM's planning, relationship building, and global team leadership performance.

Regardless of the specific performance measures employed, they should be focused on global performance and be related to the objectives, strategy, and action programs set forth in the global account plan. To the extent possible, the proposed actions and anticipated results should be shared with, and agreed to, by individual global accounts.

COMPENSATION

Regardless of the form of global account management organization, and the particular metrics used as the basis for GAM compensation, the compensation process should be global in scope and driven by corporate. The funding should fall outside any geographic area organization.

The GAM has high levels of responsibility and should be compensated accordingly. Compensation levels send powerful messages regarding the importance of the organization position, and appropriate levels are crucial in securing and retaining top level personnel. Current practice seems to remunerate GAMs equivalently to second-level sales managers managing perhaps a fifty-to-seventy-person organization, often in schemes comprising both salary (predominantly) and bonus, with specific criteria for both.

> **EXAMPLE:** Huckberry Inc.*, a major industrial company, compensates global account managers with both salary and bonus. Salary adjustments are based on such factors as customer satisfaction, revenue growth, and quality of account planning and execution. Bonus is based on specific targeted revenue opportunities, teamwork, product line balance, and a measure of personal growth.

In especially well-developed global compensation systems, the GAM sets targets for global sales team members whose pay is based in part on the extent to which these are achieved. In any event, recognition of global team effort via some form of team awards may also be appropriate.

> **EXAMPLE:** IBM global account managers set objectives for team members working at least 50% of their time for the global account, in various organization units, in various countries around the world. Performance evaluations are passed onto local managers. In addition, IBM operates a system of personal contribution bonuses for employees worldwide who work with global accounts. These payments are made at the discretion of global account managers, and are designed to encourage support of global account initiatives.[62]

SUMMARY

In this final chapter, we moved beyond key account management in general to address perhaps its most complex form, global account management. The introduction of global account management, still in its infancy, represents a major investment for those organizations that embrace this new approach. In these firms, the customer dimension plays a major line organizational role at the global level, either matrixed with a geographic organization, as a dominant component in an industry-focused organization, or as a stand-alone division.

Such a major change can only succeed with full and public support from the top of the organization. Not only must the CEO and the top management cadre be fully behind the program in spirit, resources must be spent to develop new management paradigms, to install new information systems, and to secure and train high-quality personnel for global account manager positions. Organizational devices must be instituted to support this effort by dealing with the high level of complexity, by managing new internal corporate alignments, and by mitigating potential organizational conflict. Global account management is expensive but, if well managed, may be a significant source of competitive advantage.

Whatever global account program the firm decides to implement, it should be designed with flexibility in mind, not least because localized business practices, in local cultures, differ around the world. For example, even though the firm may have several global accounts, these probably differ in the degree to which they are pursuing global procurement initiatives. Indeed, firms with strong histories of decentralized management may be extremely cautious about such centralization. They may, for example, require localized product offerings despite the promise of savings from global standards.

Nonetheless, the future for key account management in general, and global account management in particular, is an exciting one. As a major organizational innovation, global account management promises competitive advantage, increased customer satisfaction, and superior performance for those companies that make the necessary investment. Adopting a global perspective is clearly becoming an important element in key account management; and global account management is here to stay.[63]

EXERCISES: ANALYTIC MATERIALS FOR KEY ACCOUNT STRATEGY DEVELOPMENT

The seven major exercises presented here, including several subexercises, can enhance your skill at developing key account strategy and action programs:

1. Analysis of the Key Account
2. Analysis of Competition
3. Analysis of the Supplier Firm
4. Planning Assumptions
5. Opportunities and Threats
6. Developing Key Account Strategy
7. Information Requirements for Improved Key Account Plans

Exercise 1: Analysis of the Key Account

The purpose of this analysis is to gain a sufficiently detailed comprehension of the key account so that the supplier firm is able to clarify the key account's objectives, strategies, and action programs. As a result, the supplier can anticipate the key account's needs and identify its personnel and processes such that it is well placed to set and achieve its own objectives at the account. These exercises are fully comprehensive. The key account manager should make careful judgments between her scarce time resources and the appropriate depth of analysis.

KEY ACCOUNT FUNDAMENTALS

This exercise provides background to the key account analysis. The questions are not the only ones that might be asked, but they provide a good sampling of possible questions. Information is required in eight separate areas. This information is used to develop implications for the supplier firm.

Background Questions
1. *Ownership:* How does the overall organization fit together in terms of parent companies, subsidiaries, ownership interests, and so forth? Who are the directors, principal owners? What role do they play in the corporation? Do they rubber stamp the CEO's decisions or are they more independent? Where are corporate offices located? Is the key account a public company; if so, where are its shares listed?
2. *Organization:* Is the organization centralized with significant power at corporate headquarters or do individual subsidiaries operate more or less autonomously? If the key account is a global organization, does it operate with a domestic U.S. division and a separate international division, with geographic area divisions, with global product divisions, or some other kind of structure? How are developments in telecommunications, computer technology, and the Internet affecting the key account's organizational structures and processes?
3. *Top management cadre:* Who are the CEO and other members of the top management group? Are they being successful? Do they have the confidence of the board of directors or is there a difficult relationship? What is known about their business and management philosophies? What type of

corporate culture are they trying to instill? In particular, have they articulated a vision and/or values for the corporation? If yes, what are the vision and values?

4. *Locations:* Where are the accounts fixed assets located? Where are its plant locations? What are its capacities? How many employees does the account have? How are they distributed across locations?

5. *Corporate Actions:* What important actions has the key account taken recently as regards major resource shifts, significant capital spending, mergers, acquisitions, divestitures, joint ventures, R&D initiatives, new product introductions, increased internationalization, new market entry, use of the Internet, participation in B2B exchanges, and the like? How successful have these been?

6. *Financial Performance:* What has been the key account's revenue and profit history both overall and for relevant business units? What is the trend in return on assets? What is the trend in its stock price? What is the trend in earnings per share? What is the debt/equity ratio? How is its debt rated? What ratios are important to the account? How does it compare to major competitors in performance?

7. *Future Prospects:* What is the long-run outlook for the key account? Does it face any significant legal or regulatory problems? How is it perceived by the financial community? Do the majority of financial analysts recommend sell, hold, or buy? Why?

8. *Timing:* What are the time cycles for the key account, for example, the budgeting cycle? What are important dates, e.g., the fiscal year and annual meetings? Is there a periodicity to important announcements, e.g., CEO meetings with financial analysts?

What are the implications of this analysis for the key account?
What are the implications of this analysis for the supplier firm?

STRATEGIC KEY ACCOUNT ANALYSIS

Mission
The basic purpose of this exercise is scope out both the key account in general and the individual business units with which the supplier firm currently is, or might contemplate, conducting business.

1. Identify the mission (market/product scope) of the key account. The statement of mission typically comprises two elements: a statement of market

scope (including types of customers) and a statement of core products, services, or technologies. (Be sure to identify where in a vertical system of value-adding functions the key account is operating.) If the account does not have a clear statement of mission, do your best to infer the mission. If the key account is a multibusiness enterprise, a statement of mission is required both for the key account as a whole and for the particular individual business units that the supplier firm is currently targeting, or may in the future target, for effort.

Corporate Mission Statement

Business Unit(s) Mission Statement(s)

What are the implications of these missions for the key account?
What are the implications of these mission statements for the supplier firm?

External Analysis

The purpose of this exercise is to identify and analyze the various markets addressed by the key account that have relevance for the supplier firm's products and services. As a result, the supplier should identify the various environmental forces impinging on these markets, identify trends in needs of the key account's customers, identify trends in its competitive threats, and identify specific individual competitor threats. The overall purpose of this analysis is for the firm to develop a clear understanding of the key account's challenges and opportunities as the basis for developing its own key account strategy.

Market Analysis. Complete the following steps:

1. How large are the markets the key account could address, given its mission?
2. Describe the product(s) and/or service(s) currently offered by the key account.
3. Identify the types of customer that currently purchase the key account's products and services, specifying the value(s) each is securing from these products (services), and how these required values might be changing over time.
4. If there are well-defined market segments in the markets addressed by the key account, identify these segments, their sizes, and growth rates, and in-

dicate how they differ from each other in customer values sought. Which segments has the key account targeted, what are its market shares, and what are the critical success factors?

5. How secure are the key account's market shares? Is the key account likely to improve (suffer a decline in) its market shares? If so, why? If not, why not?

6. Identify the types of customer that could potentially purchase the key account's products and services, specifying the value(s) each might secure from them and how these required values might be changing over time. What would have to happen for these customers to be addressed? What are the critical success factors for serving these customers?

7. What other customers might the key account serve, given its mission, but for which the technology is currently not available?

What are the implications of this analysis for the supplier firm?

What are the implications of this analysis for the key account?

Environmental Analysis. Identify critical environmental trends affecting, or likely to affect, the key account's product/market as a whole in the short, medium, and long term. Indicate how any specific trend might be important to the key account. Among the environmental trends that should be considered are economic, technological, demographic, legal, regulatory, political, and socio-cultural. Complete the Environmental Analysis Worksheet (Figure E1.1).

Competitive Structure Analysis. Identify the various types of competitor faced by the key account; specify key competitors by name, and identify the particular threats each poses to the key account: If appropriate, identify these threats by market segment:

- Current direct competitors
- Potential new direct competitors
- Current indirect competitors
- Potential indirect competitors
- Supply chain competition: suppliers integrating forward, buyers integrating backwards

What are the implications of this analysis for the key account?

What are the implications of this analysis for the supplier firm?

Competitor Analysis. Focus on the key account's major competitors:

1. Summarize market and market segment sizes, growth rates and market shares of the key account and its major competitors.

Economic
Trends:
Implications for key account:
Implications for supplier firm:

Technological
Trends:
Implications for key account:
Implications for supplier firm:

Demographic
Trends:
Implications for key account:
Implications for supplier firm:

Legal
Trends:
Implications for key account:
Implications for supplier firm:

Regulatory
Trends:
Implications for key account:
Implications for supplier firm:

Political
Trends:
Implications for key account:
Implications for supplier firm:

Socio-cultural
Trends:
Implications for key account
Implications for supplier firm:

FIGURE E1.1 Environmental Analysis Worksheet

2. Identify the key account's position in the various markets where it competes. Complete the Competitive Position Matrix for the key account (Figure E1.2).

What are the implications of this analysis for the key account?

What are the implications of this analysis for the supplier firm?

Customer Analysis. In addition to questions asked in the market analysis:

1. Who are the key account's major customers? Is the customer base changing?

2. Is there a significant change in industry concentration for the account's customers?

3. Are the account's customers' needs changing? In what ways?

	Market Segment Characteristics				
Key Account Status	New Market Segment	Rapid Growth	Growth Rate Slowing	Mature	Decline
Dominant					
Strong number 2 or 3					
Tenable position					
Laggard					
Niche player					

FIGURE E1.2: Competitive Position Matrix

This chart should be completed for each business unit or division of the key account at which the supplier firm is attempting to secure business.

4. Are changes occurring in their buying practices?
5. What are the critical demand-sensitive elements?

What are the implications of this analysis for the key account?

What are the implications of this analysis for the supplier firm?

Summary of External Analysis. The foregoing analyses are summarized.

1. Identify the ways, if any, in which the foregoing analyses would differ from similar analyses conducted by the key account's own executives. If serious disagreements with these analyses are evident within the key account, highlight these key differences by those individuals that hold opposing positions.

What are the implications of this analysis for the key account?

What are the implications of this analysis for the supplier firm?

Internal Analysis

The purpose of this exercise is to assess the key account's ability to address its external environment. In particular, this section assesses the key account's strategic thrust and its competence, leading to an analysis of strategic coherence.

Strategic Thrust Analysis. The purpose of this analysis is to identify the long- and short-run objectives, strategies, and action programs set by the key account that have relevance for the supplier firm.

1. What are the key account's corporate and relevant business unit objectives? Identify the types of objective (i.e., profit, profitability, growth, market share, cash flow) and the specific short-run and long-run performance targets (i.e., how much, by when).

2. What specific opportunities and threats has the key account identified in its target markets and which does it intend to address?

3. In each market segment the key account is addressing, how is it positioned? In particular, what are its major customer targets, major competitor targets and core strategy?

4. How would you characterize other elements of the key account's business strategy, for example, finance, operations, human resources, and R&D?

5. Has the key account taken (or is it likely to take) any specific actions to modify its business such as acquisitions, divestitures, or strategic alliances? How do you assess the implications of these actions for its ability to achieve its objectives?

6. What specific action programs has the key account put in place either to increase customer value or to reduce costs?

Key Account Competence. The purpose of this analysis is to assess the resources available to the key account to implement its strategic thrust.

1. What do you consider the key account's relevant strengths and weaknesses?

2. In those business units relevant for the supplier firm's current and potential business, what has been the key account's performance? In particular, what are the trends in sales volumes, shares in targeted market segments, and profitability?

Analysis of Strategic Coherence. The purpose of this analysis is to assess whether or not the key account's strategic thrust is reasonable in light of its assessed competence.

1. In light of your external and internal analysis of the key account, what is your assessment of the account's objectives, strategy, and action programs? In particular:
   a. Do you think the objectives are feasible?
   b. Do you think the key account can achieve its objectives with the strategy you outlined?
   c. Do you think the key account's action programs can be successfully implemented to achieve its objectives?

What are the implications of the analysis for the key account?

What are the implications of this analysis for the supplier firm?

KEY ACCOUNT NEEDS ANALYSIS

The purpose of this analysis is to clarify the needs the key account will satisfy by purchase of the supplier firm's, or a competitor's, products/services.

1. Describe the specific needs, such as problems requiring resolution and/or opportunities being made available, that the key account is attempting to satisfy in future purchases. Consider functional, economic, and psychological needs

2. Regarding products or services currently being purchased by the key account, how well are the several competitive suppliers satisfying the key account's various needs?

3. For this question, be creative! What ways might be available for the supplier firm to help the key account:
   a. Increase its unit sales
   b. Increase its prices
   c. Reduce its costs
   d. Reduce its investment
   e. Reduce its risk

4. What organizational characteristics is the key account seeking in a supplier? In particular, how do the supplier firm and its competitors rate in terms of:
   a. Accessibility?
   b. Responsiveness?
   c. Preparing customized offers
   d. Keeping promises?
   e. Understanding critical customer issues?
   f. Communications?
   g. Being easy to do business with?
   h. Competence?

5. Use the answers from questions 1 through 4 to write, in order (from most important to least important), the criteria that the key account overall is expected to use in making future purchase decisions.

6. Complete the Key Account Needs Satisfaction Worksheet (Figure E1.3) for each major competitor in each application domain.

   What are the implications of this analysis for the key account?

   What are the implications of this analysis for the supplier firm?

Critical Key Account Needs (in order of importance)	Importance Weights (a) (sum to 100)	Supplier Firm Rating (b) (1 to 10 scale)	Supplier Firm Weighted Rating a × b
1.			
2.			
3.			
4.			
5.			
6.			
7.			
8.			
	100		Total _____

Critical Key Account Needs (in order of importance)	Importance Weights (a) (sum to 100)	Competitor A Rating (b) (1 to 10 scale)	Competitor A Weighted Rating a × b
1.			
2.			
3.			
4.			
5.			
6.			
7.			
8.			
	100		Total _____
etc.			

FIGURE E1.3: Key Account Needs Satisfaction Worksheet

BUYING ANALYSIS

The buying analysis comprises several individual analyses designed to provide insight into the manner and process by which the key account makes its procurement decisions.

The Procurement Process

The purpose of this analysis is to identify the key account's procurement process. For many purchases, a time-bound sequence of steps can be identified. These steps typically involve such activities as information gathering, information transmission, and decision making; they occur in a predictable sequence, sometimes at predictable times; and involve individuals who can be identified playing various roles.

1. Develop a flow chart from the triggers that set the procurement sequence in motion until the final decision. Use a rectangle to indicate an activity that does not require a decision; use a diamond to indicate a decision fork; indicate the people involved in each activity noted in the various rectangles and diamonds. Be sure to consider fully both the roles of individuals within the key account and those of persons from other organizations, such as the key account's customer, distributors, and third party organizations that may impact the process (Figure E1.4).

2. For each step in the process, ask the following questions:
   a. Why is this step in the process?
   b. Where is it done?
   c. Why is it done there?
   d. When is it done?
   e. Why is it done then?
   f. Who does it?
   g. Why do they do it?
   h. How is it done?
   i. Why is it done this way?

3. Ask the following questions of the process?
   a. Is this process stable? What events could occur that would modify the process?
   b. Where are the places in the process that the firm could most meaningfully interface?

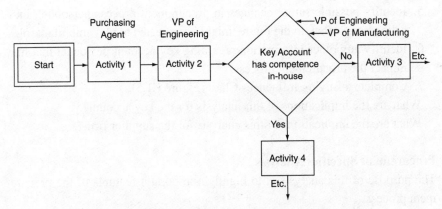

FIGURE E1.4: Example of Procurement Decision Flow Chart

    c. What sorts of actions could the firm take that would improve its probabilities of securing business?

What are the implications of this analysis for the key account?

What are the implications of this analysis for the supplier firm?

Decision-Making Participants Analysis

The purpose of this analysis is to characterize the important players in the key account's procurement process.

1. Make a list of all of the people involved in the procurement process that you identified in the buying analysis.
2. Identify their career history, former employers, organizational positions (on an organization chart), subordinate and superordinate reporting relationships, organizational future and potential career track, social style, informal and cross-functional relationships in the key account. In addition, identify the roles they play in the procurement process, e.g., decision maker, influencer, specifier, gatekeeper, spoiler, champion, and information provider. Be sure to indicate the degree of power and influence each person has in the procurement process.
3. Identify the key issues that each of these individuals is expected to consider in making a recommendation or decision in the procurement process. In answering this question refer to the results from question 2 and 3 in the Key Account Needs Analysis.
4. Make an assessment of the extent to which each of these players is favorably inclined towards the supplier firm's products and services versus those of competitors, and vice versa.
5. Identify possible future changes in procurement process personnel, indicating people that, in the future, might be expected to play important roles.
6. Identify any other information regarding key account personnel that may impact the procurement process.
7. Complete a Buying Influences Chart (Figure E1.5).

What are the implications of this analysis for the key account?

What are the implications of this analysis for the supplier firm?

Procurement Specifics Analysis

The purpose of this analysis is to highlight important features of the procurement process.

1. Does the key account have a formal supplier rating program? If so, what are the various procurement criteria, and how is each supplier and poten-

Influencers	Perceived Influence in Purchase Process (%)	Main Criteria for Deciding Among Potential Suppliers	Comments

FIGURE E1.5: Buying Influences Chart
(Note that the relevant players may change from decision to decision.)

tial supplier rated? Complete a chart with a structure similar to Figure E1.3.

2. Are purchase contracts drawn up centrally by head office personnel or by personnel in individual locations?

3. Describe the type of contractual agreements typically entered into by the key account (e.g., annual contracts versus spot purchases; contracts well specified with amounts and delivery dates versus "open-to-buy" contracts with specific quantities and delivery dates negotiated later with decentralized units). What types of contracts might the firm expect the key account to enter into?

4. Does the key account pursue a policy of actively seeking many potential bids? Or does it prefer to select a limited number of suppliers with which it can develop close relationships? What criteria does it use for sharing business?

5. Does the account have policies that prohibit sole suppliers? If the firm is currently sole supplier, what might cause the account to share its business with competitors?

6. Does the firm have policies regarding not dealing with supplier firms for which it would represent a large percent of production?

7. Does the key account follow a policy of working closely with one supplier to develop product specifications, then shop the specifications to seek the cheapest source of supply, regardless of the initial supplier's efforts? Or, does the key account provide some reward for specification development in the form of guaranteed purchase volume?

8. How dependent is the key account on the supplier firm? If supply were unexpectedly cut off, would this cause a significant problem for the account or could it easily secure its requirements from another supplier?

9. What is the key account's policy regarding internal sourcing? If the supplier firm puts in extensive development efforts, does it risk losing this business to an internal division?

10. What is the key account's budget cycle and how does it affect purchase decisions?

11. Is the key account moving any of its purchases into B2B auction markets via the Internet? If so, for what product categories?

12. Describe the type of decision process the key account must go through to make the impending purchase. The following categories may offer useful insight.

    a. Straight rebuy (i.e., product previously purchased, well-established purchase criteria, several well-known potential suppliers)

    b. Modified rebuy (i.e., potential replacement of traditional product choice, purchase criteria well developed)

    c. New buy (i.e., purchase criteria poorly developed, significant uncertainty in purchase, potential to change existing systems)

What are the implications of this analysis for the key account?

What are the implications of this analysis for the supplier firm?

Exercise 2: Analysis of Competition

The competitor analysis comprises several individual analyses designed to provide insight into the competitive threat(s) faced by the supplier firm at the key account.

COMPETITIVE STRUCTURE ANALYSIS

The purpose of this analysis is to develop the structure of competition.

1. Identify the firm's major competitors (current and potential) at the key account, those most likely to frustrate achievement of its objectives in the long run. Recall that competitors come in several forms:
   - current direct competitors
   - current indirect competitors
   - supply chain competition: suppliers integrating forward, buyers integrating backwards (i.e., self-production by the key account)
   - potential new direct competitors
   - potential indirect competitors

COMPETITIVE ANALYSIS

For each competitor that represents a significant threat, answer the following questions:

Capabilities and Weaknesses

1. What major strengths can the competitor bring to bear at the key account? What are its weaknesses or vulnerabilities?
2. What are its operating procedures? How good a job does the competitor do in product quality, service quality, new product development, delivery, payment terms, pricing, and so forth?
3. How does the competitor organize to address the key account? Who are the key players at the competitor? Who is the key account manager? What do we know about their decision-making styles and the personal relationships they have with key account personnel?

4. What is the competitor's overall relationship at the key account? What is this assessment based upon (e.g., long-term high-quality service; long-standing personal relationships; brand name; ability to react quickly to problem situations)?

5. Complete the Value Chain Analysis worksheet (Figure E2.1).

Summary: Where does this competitor have: (i) a cost advantage? (ii) a value advantage?

- technology
- product design
- raw materials
- manufacturing/operations
- marketing
- physical distribution
- customer service
- administration
- other area

What options does the competitor have to reduce costs and increase value to better position itself at the key account?

6. Complete the Competitor Analysis Matrix (Figure E2.2). Note that this analysis involves multiple competitors.

The purpose of completing the firm/competitor assessment matrix is to compare the firm and its major competitors' strength at the key account, from the key account's perspective.

Step 1: Factor Identification: Use the results from prior analyses to answer the following question: "What business strengths (skills, resources, and relationships) would any firm have to possess to become the favored supplier at the key account?" (You should have no more than ten items; six to eight is preferred. Combine similar items to arrive at a final list.)

Step 2: Factor Weighting. How do you weight these items in terms of importance? Allocate 100 points to the various items; the more important items receive higher numbers of points.

Step 3: Competitor Firm Ratings. How do the several competitors (supplier firm and major competitors) rate on possession of each business strength, where 1 = low possession and 10 = high possession.

Step 4: Develop Factor Scores: Multiply the importance weightings (in column 2) by the corresponding ratings in column 3 to produce the figures in column 4 for the supplier firm and each competitor.

	Supplier Firm Superior to Competitor	Supplier Firm Inferior to Competitor	Competitive Parity
Competitor A: Value Analysis			
Technology			
Product design			
Raw materials			
Manufacturing operations			
Marketing			
Physical distribution			
Customer service			
Administration			
Competitor A: Cost Analysis			
Technology			
Product design			
Raw materials			
Manufacturing operations			
Marketing			
Physical distribution			
Customer service			
Administration			

FIGURE E2.1: Value Chain Analysis Worksheet

Step 5: Develop the Business Strengths Scores. Sum the figures in each column 4 for the supplier firm and each competitor.

Step 6: Compare the total business strengths scores for the supplier firm and its various competitors; what do you learn from this comparison? Compare the individual weightings for the various competitors; what do you learn from this comparison?

Step 7: Using the results from prior analyses, identify those persons from the key account that would disagree with significant elements of this analysis. Which persons and which elements are important?

What are the implications of this analysis for the supplier firm?

Competitor Performance and Strategy

1. How much key account business does this competitor do? What is the competitor's share of business at the account? What are the trends? Is it profitable business for the competitor?

2. Does the competitor have any existing contracts with the key account? When are these up for rebid or renewal?

1) Business Strengths Criteria: What business strengths must any supplier possess to be successful at this key account?	2) Weights for Business Strengths Criteria	3) Supplier Firm	Supplier Firm Rating 4) Column 2 × Column 3
1.			
2.			
3.			
4.			
5.			
6.			
Total			_____

1) Business Strengths Criteria: What business strengths must any supplier possess to be successful at this key account?	2) Weights for Business Strengths Criteria	3) Competitor A	Competitor A Rating 4) Column 2 × Column 3
1.			
2.			
3.			
4.			
5.			
6.			
Total			_____

1) Business Strengths Criteria: What business strengths must any supplier possess to be successful at this key account?	2) Weights for Business Strengths Criteria	3) Competitor B	Competitor B Rating 4) Column 2 × Column 3
1.			
2.			
3.			
4.			
5.			
6.			
Total			_____

Figure E2.2: Competitor Analysis Matrix

3. What are the competitor's current objectives at the key account?
   - Increase/hold share of key account's business
   - Increase/hold profits from key account business
   - Increase/hold cash flow from key account business
4. What strategies:
   - Has the competitor employed in the past?
   - Is the competitor employing now?
   - Could the competitor employ in the future?
5. What action programs is the competitor currently conducting at the key account?
6. What is the true nature of the competitive challenge? What should the supplier firm be most concerned about?

What are the implications of this analysis for the supplier firm?

Projection of Competitor Actions

1. What will the competitor do to reduce costs to better position itself at the key account?
2. What will the competitor do to increase value that will better position it at the key account?
3. What objectives will the competitor set at the key account?
4. What strategies will the competitor employ?
5. What specific action programs will the competitor implement?
6. What other specific resource allocations will the competitor make at the key account?
7. How will the competitor view and respond to our proposed initiatives?

What are the implications of this analysis for the supplier firm?

Repeat the Competitive Analysis for each significant competitor.

Exercise 3: Analysis of the Supplier Firm

The purpose of this analysis is to assess the firm's position at the key account as a vehicle for making decisions regarding future actions.

HISTORICAL PERFORMANCE

1. What has been the supplier firm's historic sales, market share, and profit performance at the key account? What are the trends? The data to be analyzed should include sales revenues (and units), market share and profit (contribution) versus objectives. Where appropriate, these data should be broken out by such dimensions as product/product line, key account business unit, application, and geography of consuming unit.
2. What have been the key contributing factors to the firm's performance? For example: what major sales has the firm secured? Why was it successful? What major sales has the firm lost to competitors; why was it unsuccessful?
3. What is the status of current contracts? What is the status of current purchases in progress? How is the firm positioned versus competition in current selling activities?
4. To the extent that the supplier firm has any partnership, joint venture, or strategic alliance relationships with the key account: How have they performed? What is the status of these relationships?

What are the implications of this analysis for the supplier firm?

RELATIONSHIP ASSESSMENT

1. Referring to the Key Account Buying Analysis, how do important players at the key account feel about the various elements of the supplier firm's offer (e.g., products, services, delivery)? Why? Where are the potential trouble spots?
2. Has the firm been delivering on its promises to the key account? If not, why not?
3. In general, how well has the supplier firm been doing in:
   a. Meeting or exceeding key account expectations.
   b. Developing solutions to existing problems
   c. Solving new and/or unrecognized problems

4. What results is the firm securing from its customer satisfaction studies?
5. Is the business relatively secure or are competitors being seriously considered as replacements? Where has the supplier firm performed well? Badly?
6. How secure is the competitor's business? Is it likely the supplier can pry the account loose from the competitor? Where has the supplier firm performed well? Badly?
7. Who are the key players on the supplier firm's key account team?
   a. How do important players at the key account feel about them? Where are the potential trouble spots? Complete the Interpersonal Relationship Chart (Figure E3.1).
   b. How should their performance be rated? Are there any problems with expertise? Is there any confusion regarding roles and responsibilities?
   c. Are there any gaps that should be filled?
   d. How do they feel about the key account? Are any members taking the account for granted? If so, what actions should the supplier firm take to ensure continuous improvement and avoid complacency?
8. In general, how do you assess the quality of the supplier firm's business relationships versus competition? Identify how the firm stacks up against its competitors in the various areas in which the supplier firm and key account interface.

Key Account Personnel	Relevant Supplier Firm Personnel	
Name, Organizational Position	Name, Organizational Position	Nature of the Relationship

FIGURE E3.1: Illustration of an Interpersonal Relationship Chart

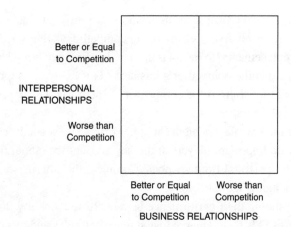

FIGURE E3.2: Business Relationship versus Interpersonal Relationships Matrix

9. In general, how do you assess the quality of the supplier firm's interpersonal relationships versus those of the competition?
10. Complete the business relationships versus interpersonal relationships quality matrix (Figure 3.2).
11. Should the supplier firm change the nature of the formal relationship with the key account?

What are the implications of this analysis for the supplier firm?

Assessing Firm Behavior: Corporate, Business-Unit and Related Functional Areas

1. To what extent have any changes in corporate and/or business unit strategies—e.g., major resource shifts, acquisitions, divestitures, joint ventures, or R&D initiatives—impacted the key account relationship since the previous planning cycle? If so how?
2. Have any changes in functional area strategies—e.g., marketing, operations, R&D, or human resources—since the previous planning cycle impacted the key account relationship? If so, how?
3. Have any changes in organization structure, climate, or processes since the previous planning cycle impacted the key account relationship? If so, how?
4. In looking forward, what planned (or contemplated) actions by corporate and/or the business units and related functional areas could impact the supplier-firm/key-account relationship? In what manner?

What are the implications of this analysis for the supplier firm?

RESOURCE AVAILABILITY

1. How do the supplier firm's capabilities and limitations relate to key account needs? What is the supplier firm's most critical weakness that could limit its ability to maintain or increase business with the key account?
2. Complete the Critical for Success/Supplier Firm Competence Matrix (Figure E3.3).
3. Is the allocation of required resources to the key account consistent with the supplier firm's overall marketing strategy?
4. What action programs has the supplier firm planned for this key account in the past? Were they fully implemented? What results were achieved?
5. Does the firm have adequate capacity to satisfy key account product/service requirements? Where are the bottlenecks?
6. What new supplier firm products can impact its business at the key account? Are any supplier firm system changes such as product delivery and customer service likely to impact the key account.

What are the implications of this analysis for the supplier firm?

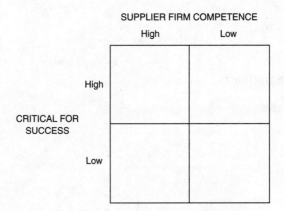

FIGURE E3.3: Critical for Success/Supplier Firm Competence Matrix

Exercise 4: Planning Assumptions

What are the principal planning assumptions upon which the key account plan should be based:

Assumptions about the key account:
1.
2.
3. (etc.)

Assumptions about competitors:
1.
2.
3. (etc.)

Assumptions about the supplier firm:
1.
2.
3. (etc.)

Any other assumptions:
1.
2.
3. (etc.)

Exercise 5: Opportunities and Threats

The purpose of this analysis is to identify opportunities for new business and threats to current business at the key account. This may be accomplished by use of the eight-cell matrix (Figure E5.1) and the related Figure E5.2.

PRODUCTS

ORGANIZATIONAL UNIT	Existing		New	
	Existing	New	Existing	New
APPLICATION Existing	1	2	3	4
New	5	6	7	8

FIGURE E5.1: Opportunity and Threat Identification Matrix

Each cell represents a distinct area of opportunity or threat for the firm. For each cell that is relevant for the firm at the key account, using the framework below:

a. Describe each current or potential piece of business in each cell.
b. Identify the key account's anticipated purchases in this and the upcoming planning period (e.g., calendar year).
c. Identify the probability that the firm will be successful in the upcoming period.
d. Calculate the firm's expected value of sales revenues (a × b).
e. Assign a priority to each piece of business: 10 = high priority, 1 = low priority.

1. Plot each piece of current business on a Business Trend/Competitive Strength (Figure E5.3).

Note that:
   • The horizontal axis represents the trend in demand for the products of the supplier firm and its competitors for a particular application in a particular key account organizational unit.

369

FIGURE E5.2: Opportunity and Threat Identification Matrix

Product/ Organization/ Application	Description of Business	Anticipated Purchases Current Year	Anticipated Purchases Next Year (a)	Success Probability Next Year (b)	Expected Value (a × b)	Firm Priority*
Cell 1						
Existing/ Existing/ Existing						
Cell 2						
Existing/ New/ Existing						
Cell 3						
New/ Existing/ Existing						
Cell 4						
New/ New/ Existing						
Cell 5						
Existing/ Existing/ New						
Cell 6						
Existing/ New/ New						
Cell 7						
New/ Existing/ New						
Cell 8						
New/ New/ New						

*1 = low priority, 10 = high priority

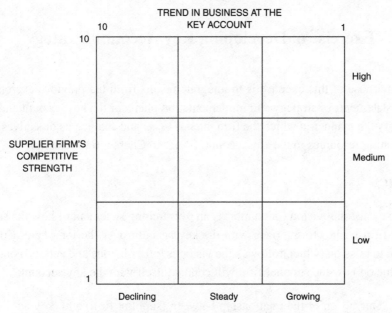

FIGURE E5.3: Current Business: Opportunities and Threats Matrix

- The vertical axis represents the key account manager's assessment of the supplier firm's competitive strength at the key account.
- Locate in the matrix the position of each of the supplier firm's products at a particular application/organizational unit.
- Draw a circle centered on this position that represents the volume of key accounts purchases from all competitors.
- Represent the supplier firm's fraction of the key account's business by shading in the appropriate part of this circle.

What are the implications of these analyses for the supplier firm?

Exercise 6: Developing Key Account Strategy

The purpose of this exercise is to integrate results from the previous exercises into statements of strategy and implementation plans for the key account and to specify the manner in which the firm intends to set and achieve its objectives by allocating resources to the key account. (Refer to Chapter 6 for examples.)

VISION

The key account vision (or charter) is an overarching statement of how the supplier firm wishes to interface with the key account over the long haul. Compared to mission (which follows), the vision is loftier in tone and acts as more of a guide on how the supplier firm will conduct itself with the key account:

> "Our vision of the relationship between (supplier firm) and (key account) is that . . ."

MISSION

State the firm's mission at the key account. The mission should encompass a statement of the types of customer in the key account that will be served, for example, business unit, functional area or geography, and the types of product or technology that will be offered for sale. This statement should be sufficiently broad to encompass future growth in the relationship but not so broad as to place no constraints on the firm's activities at the key account.

> "Our focus at the key account is to offer [products and technologies] to the key account's [business units, functions, geographies] . . ."

A COMPLETE KEY ACCOUNT STRATEGY

Objectives
State the objectives you want the strategy to achieve. Do this in steps as follows:
1. Identify the dimensions of objectives you want to achieve over the next three to five years. For example, do you seek to increase sales revenues, increase market share, improve profits, generate cash flow, or what?

2. Which of your objectives is the most important (primary), second most important (secondary)?
3. How will you measure your performance? In absolute numbers? As a growth rate? As a yield percent (e.g., ROI)?
4. What level of performance are you setting for primary and secondary objectives?
5. How do these performance objectives compare to the firm's historic performance?
6. State your objectives.

EXAMPLE: "During the next three years we shall increase profits at the key account from $15 million in 200X to $25 million in 200Y."

Strategic Focus

Describe briefly the broad focus of your efforts. How, in broad terms, you intend to achieve your objectives? Do this in the form of a statement similar to the example below. Note that the statement has two parts: a brief description of what, generally, you intend to do, followed by a clear description of how you intend to do it.

- Recall that strategic focus actions fall into two broad categories: those designed to maintain and increase sales volume and those designed to improve key account profitability.
- Subcategories to maintain and increase sales volume include: maintain current uses, expand current uses, displace competitor's products, and open up new applications.
- Subcategories to improve key account profitability include: raise prices, improve product mix, reduce operating costs, and reduce financing costs (e.g., reduce accounts receivable, inventory carrying costs)

EXAMPLE: "We shall reach our objectives by targeting those business units in the key account that, up to present, have had little experience with nucleobenzide. Specifically, we shall show them that nucleobenzide molding offers substantial opportunities for growth and profit."

Positioning

The purpose of positioning is to influence the key account's behavior. Once it has been decided what behavior should be influenced, positioning requires decisions on three key dimensions: target contacts, competitive targets, and core strategy.

1. Identify the firm's objectives in developing its positioning statement(s). Recall that the firm may wish to seek a favorable conclusion to the purchase process by influencing the key account's decision-making criteria or the key account's perception of its various options, or to modify the purchase decision *per se*—for example, influence the scope or timing of the decision or influence the set of personnel in the decision.

2. Develop the positioning statement:
   a. **Target contacts:** These are the individuals within the key account, e.g., influencers or decision makers, that it is important to convince regarding the positioning objectives.

EXAMPLE: "Our major efforts will be focused on convincing the key account's technical director and her direct reports of the value of our new technology."

   b. **Competitor targets:** These are the competitors that the firm views as most likely to frustrate the firm in achieving its objectives.

EXAMPLE: "Our central thrust will be directed against our primary domestic competitors of alternative forms of nucleobenzide, specifically Dow, Du Pont, and Union Carbide. Secondarily we shall build a defensive position against Hoescht and Bayer who, we anticipate, will enter the market with new technology within the next three years."

   c. **Key persuasive argument:** These are the key benefits that will cause the customer targets to behave in the way that you require, rather than be influenced by a competitor.

EXAMPLE: "Our key persuasive argument to the key account's technical director and her direct reports will be that using Tanide increases throughput. Specifically, we shall show that by using Tanide, rather than Corfide (major competition), molding time is reduced, cleaning time is reduced because of fewer deposits in the mold, and the need to clean flashing from the part is eliminated."

Strategic Action Programs

The action programs implement the strategy for the key account. Whereas the development of strategic focus and positioning statements is largely conceptual, action programs identify specific steps that the firm will undertake to implement the strategy. Implementation programs typically have a shorter time horizon than strategies; an individual positioning statement may be associated with several action programs.

In this section you identify action programs that are critical to strategy implementation. Each action program has two major elements: objectives and action steps. After you have developed each action program, you should identify the priority level of each action objective—high, medium, or low—and schedule the various tasks.

Examples

Objective: "The key account will conduct tests on our new device. On the basis of our superior performance characteristics, the chief engineer will recommend that our device, rather than Alpha Inc.'s, be used to power the key account's new product.

Action Steps:

Quarter 1: Secure agreement to test our product against Alpha's

Quarter 2: Formulate agreement on test criteria

Quarter 3: Run test

Quarter 4: Evaluate results, discuss with key account, secure initial order"

Objective: "The key account's marketing VP will agree that co-branding with our firm will significantly increase the key account's sales volume.

Action Steps:

Quarter 1: Design consumer survey to test brand name combinations

Quarter 2: Formulate agreement on test criteria

Quarter 3: Administer survey, analyze results

Quarter 4: Present results, secure commitment"

Force Field Analysis. For each strategic action program, the key account manager should complete a force field analysis. This analysis involves identifying the activating and resisting forces for the specific action program:

| Key Account Personnel | Relevant Supplier Firm Personnel | | | |
Name, Organizational Position	Name, Organizational Position	Nature of the Relationship	Action Objective	Action Steps

FIGURE E6.1: The Interpersonal Relationship-Building Action Plan

Activating Forces

How might these forces be enhanced?

Resisting Forces

How might these forces be converted into activating forces or at least diminished?

Interpersonal Relationship-Building Action Programs
The programs are based on the Interpersonal Relationship Chart (Figure E3.1). This chart is extended to include action objectives and action steps for each relationship in the chart (Figure E6.1).

Agreements on Resource Commitments
In this exercise we identify the specific resources required to implement the key account plan and manage the key account, specify when the resource is required, and identify the particular individual or group responsible for providing that resource. Complete the chart in Figure E6.2.

Budgets and Forecasts
Budgets and forecasts represent the detailed performance requirements set for the key account. These include absolute levels and trends in such measures as sales revenue, gross profit and/or profit contribution, expenses and sales to expense ratios, both in total and broken out by product/product line, organization unit, and application, where appropriate. Budgets and forecasts relate directly to performance objectives set in the key account strategy but are much more detailed. Indeed, they function as a managerial tool to track performance through the operating period. Typically, annual budget items are disaggregated and specified by quarter or by month. Complete the chart in Figure E6.3.

A similar format can be used for both aggregated and disaggregated data.

Resource Type	Specific Required Resource	When Required	Responsibility
Information Systems			
Administration			
Field and technical service			
Logistics			
Manufacturing/operations management			
Applications engineering			
Development, design, and product engineering			
Finance			
Legal			
Control			
Sales development			
Marketing research			
Senior management			
Director of key accounts			
Supplier Firm's Supplier			
(etc.)			

FIGURE E6.2: Required Resources for Implementing Action Programs

	Quarter 1	Quarter 2	Quarter 3	Quarter 4	Total
Sales Revenues:					
Plan					
Actual					
Variance					
Direct Expense:					
Plan					
Actual					
Variance					
Profit Contribution:					
Plan					
Actual					
Variance					

FIGURE E6.3: Budgets and Forecasts for the Key Account

Exercise 7: Information Requirements for Improved Key Account Plans

The purpose of this exercise is to identify information requirements for developing improved key account plans. Whether such a plan is the first written plan or builds off a base of plans developed in prior years, at the conclusion of the process it is likely that information gaps that could not be filled in the time frame of the planning process will have emerged.

In this exercise, these information gaps are identified, the person(s) (key account or supplier firm) or organizations (e.g., industry associations) that have the information are noted, and responsibility is assigned for collecting the information for the next planning period. The raw material for completing this exercise should be collected throughout the planning process as information requirements become evident.

Information Required	Individual Organization with Information	Supplier Firm Personnel Responsible for Collecting Information
1.		
2.		
3.		
etc.		

Appendix 1.1: Calculating the Cost of Serving Customers

	Top 20 %	20 to 40%	40 to 60%	60 to 80%	80 to 100%
Number of Accounts (a)					
Average Number of Calls per Account per Annum (b)					
Average Cost per Call (c)					
Total Calling Cost per Account ($d = b \times c$)					
Total Cost for All Accounts ($e = a \times d$)					
Average Revenue per Account (f)					
Average Percent Gross Margin per Account (g)					
Average Gross Margin per Account ($h = f \times g$)					
Total Gross Margin for All Accounts ($j = a \times h$)					
Total Profit/Loss for All Accounts ($k = j - e$)					

Appendix 2.1: Examples of Evolving Firm Commitment to Key Account Management

In this appendix, we profile the experience of several companies as they increased their over-time commitment to key account management. What is specially noteworthy is the evolution of these programs and the long time spans over which that evolution occurred.

Murata Erie North America

Murata Erie North America (MENA) is the domestic subsidiary of a global manufacturing company (sales over $2 billion, over 22,000 employees) headquartered in Kyoto, Japan. It has three U.S. production facilities, with over 1,200 employees, that historically interfaced with customers through manufacturers representatives and distributors.[1]

MENA started a national account program in April 1985; this was scrapped in September 1986. Several reasons were adduced for its failure:

- Critical company personnel did not understand the concept of a national account program.
- Role definition was vague.
- The program was not supported by top management.
- Persons with key account responsibility were not well trained and coached.
- Managerial egos were upset by the program.
- Customer selection criteria were ineffective.

In sum, involved company personnel said the firm moved too quickly.

In October 1986, soon after the initial national account program was scrapped, MENA recognized that significant business opportunities were available at Motorola; however, strategic coordination among different business units would be necessary to exploit these opportunities. Rather than develop a formal key account program, a single individual was assigned to be key account manager; the opportunity was sufficiently attractive that top management was committed. In July 1989, one more key account individual was added to the program and four additional customers were selected for key account focus. Throughout this phase, the key account role was reactive, improving internal communication by acting as an information clearing house via data accumulation and analysis.

In September 1989, a formal international key account program was developed by MENA's parent company; it included five North American customers. In September 1990, the North American customer list was expanded in consultation with MENA's European affiliates and approved by the parent. In August 1991, MENA underwent a reorganization; employees were added to the national account function and the program streamlined. A critical event was agreement on a new vision statement:

> The Multinational Account Management Group is chartered with insuring the collective focus and direction of global resources for managing sales growth and profitability on an international basis for designated North American–based multinational customers.

In March 1993, the customer list was refined; in August 1993 an account manager/support person was added and further adjustments made to the customer list.

Among the factors leading to changes in the program over time were development of a better understanding of customer needs, recognition of growth opportunities, and changing market dynamics. Internally, the key account focus led to increased sales/profit and market share, which in turn solidified top management support. Other positive factors were development of rigorous selection criteria for both key accounts and account managers, publication of a process and procedure document that clarified role definitions, improved company direction and strategy overall, and related changes in the MENA organization. With these changes came increased understanding of MENA's capabilities; additional resources were allocated to key accounts and to training and education, and international participation increased.

MENA executives identified many reasons why their successful key account program should be strengthened and revitalized. Externally, the business environment continues to evolve: in particular they see increased globalization, geopolitical changes such as developing market economies as former totalitarian states shift to privatization and deregulation; global economic growth and increasing numbers of joint ventures and alliances. Customer needs and behavior are also changing including an increased focus on quality (e.g., ISO 9000 certification) and greater concern with environmental issues such as ozone depleting substances (ODAs). Other changes include design, administrative and manufacturing cycle time reduction, shorter product life cycles, requirements for 100% on-time delivery and electronic data trasnsmission, introduction of specific performance measurement criteria for suppliers, and supplier reduction programs. MENA has also noticed customers' core competencies changing as they make technological advances, diversify product lines, and alter the way they go to market.

In addition, MENA has identified partnering opportunities that, with a focus on value-added, are viewed by customers as providing competitive advantage. MENA realizes that it must demonstrate flexibility and a willingness to change, make firm commitments to training/education and continuous improvement, share technology, and develop synergy across a broad product offering; the reward is preferred vendor status.

MENA has taken several steps to reinforce the value of its key account program with senior management. It has improved communications by institutionalizing account planning, developed performance criteria, conducted rigorous profitability analysis, and provided periodic reports and information on key events. It has enhanced the skill and experience level of key account personnel via rigorous personnel assessment, training and education programs, and networking with senior management.

MENA's plans include increasing empowerment of key account personnel, broadening key account management experience via international travel, better communications, and greater participation in industry associations, increasing training/education, and changing the compensation system. Increased resources will be placed in the key account program, top management involvement will increase and MENA employees will learn more about key accounts. Finally, customers will be chosen more selectively and MENA/key-account computer interfaces will become more sophisticated.

Appleton Papers Inc.[2]
In the early 1970s, Appleton Papers' (AP) major markets, served by direct sales representatives, were the business forms industry, converters, and commercial printing. With the forms industry growing, the customer base consolidating into larger accounts, and increased acceptance of its products, capacity-constrained AP developed its first key account program. Eight national account representatives, reporting through two national account sales managers to a director of national accounts (reporting to the director of sales), were set up as an independent organization. The program focused attention on key account headquarters and regional plant locations. Championed by the director of national

accounts, but with little top management involvement, the program focused on building relationships. It achieved modest success but, when its director was replaced by a person without national account experience, the sharp key account focus was diluted; product lines, customers, and people were added, and the organization became overloaded.

The early 1980s saw a transition phase. As AP continued to grow, the program was refocused on national accounts. The national account manager position was elevated as four NAMs now reported directly to the director of sales. Relationships, typified by handshake agreements, continued to develop with individual customers and top management involvement increased to a limited extent. However, the NAMs traveled extensively to all customer field and headquarters locations and, despite a closer relationship with the sales organization, territory infringement was a significant issue; ultimately this organization was deemed inefficient. Concurrently, customer consolidation continued, competition increased, and more sophisticated procurement practices led to the replacement of handshakes with formal agreements.

In the late 1980s, the NAMs once more reported to a director of national accounts (reporting to the vice president of sales) and concentrated their efforts on key decision makers at headquarters locations. Field sales assumed the relationship role at plant locations. Inside personnel supported the program to a greater extent and top management involvement increased. The requirement for improved communications has been aided by electronic methods. Because of further consolidation of Appleton's customer base, the NAMs currently report to two national sales managers each with responsibility for both national accounts and field sales for one half of the country.

The current structure is buttressed by greater attention to quality processes and increased partnering as the focus of key account relationships has shifted from AP's product and manufacturing concerns to customer requirements. Account plans are developed and distributed, and periodic reviews keep both AP and its accounts focused on important issues and the search for mutual opportunities. Individual NAMs have become more sophisticated (mirroring increased customer sophistication) and now undergo training for proposal and contract development, and negotiation skills. Top management involvement, evolving from occasional customer visits to participation in account strategy development and regular top level interaction, is believed critical to success.

In 1997, Appleton Papers was awarded the first National Account Management Innovation (NAMI) award for its Seal of Excellence Program. This program involves an independent research firm surveying Appleton's customer's customers with the aim of providing data to improve customers' service delivery processes and better meet their customers' needs. Appleton reports analysis results to customers and offers to assist with improvement steps. In addition, by conducting many such studies, Appleton secures detailed information on the factors driving satisfaction for its customers' customers.

AP believes it must continue to push the envelope of quality relationships. NAMs must continue to align key account plans with customer objectives, increase service levels, and become computer literate. Supplier and key account quality processes must be integrated, the level of computer tie-ins increased, progress reporting against specific customer requirements improved, and top management's commitment to be involved fully practiced.

Freddie Mac[3]

Freddie Mac (FM) is a publicly chartered stockholder-owned profit-making corporation committed to housing finance. It purchases mortgages from originators such as banks and mortgage bankers, packages these mortgages into pools, and sells and insures mortgage-backed securities collaterized by those pools to investors via security house distributors. It provides financing for over 10% of U.S. homes. It has roughly three thousand suppliers of which ten were identified as major national suppliers, market influencers with complex needs.[4]

FM first explored a national account system in 1987 by conducting a national account seminar and benchmarking in-place national account programs. In 1988, a recommendation to develop a national account system was rejected, but in 1989 a prototype key account system was developed. An initial departmental hire was made the following year and the first account (Citibank) was assigned. By the end of 1990, when a second account was added, the operational structure comprised a small core relationship management team and limited/cross-functional matrix support groups, including risk management, operations, legal, and mortgage finance. However, no formal controls/processes were in place.

The key account program grew rapidly in 1991. By year end, three more accounts had been added and the operational structure—including three relationship managers, a credit function, formalized cross-functional matrix teams, and prototyped functional matrix team integration—developed. Some control systems were in place, in particular formalized credit processes and controls, and departmental procedures. By the end of 1992, as the program matured, cross-functional matrix teams were integrated, and team charters and vision statements were developed to assist in generating performance criteria. Control systems had developed and included formal Resolution Trust Company

(RTC)/FDIC operating processes and controls, formal account plans, a customer credit file system, regular management reporting, sales compensation review and implementation, and formalization of a national account selection process.

FM executives believe the national account program has been successful. Critical elements included an initial focus on intercorporate organizational development, sustained top management support and decision making (versus "wait-and-see" attitudes), and a long-term view. Other important issues were integration with other organizational functions, effective resource management, and recognition that the program might conflict with existing selling structures. In particular, a flexible view of annual performance measurement and approaches to compensation that considered long-run measures (differing from short-run) for the regular sales force was critical.

Phonics Inc.[5]

In 1974, ELECOM, a French leader in electronics, purchased the local subsidiary of a Swedish telecommunications company, Swedecom, and became a significant force in French telecommunications. In the early 1970s, several customer-focused changes led to a heightened importance of managing these customers. Included were a growth in size and regional dispersion of customer organizations, centralization/coordination of purchasing, increased need for interoffice communications, requirements for more complex products, greater service requirements, and evolution of maintenance contracts. As a result, ELECOM set up an informal structure, a three-person Paris-based Contracts Operations Management (COM) unit, for dealing with important public-sector customers. COM's major role was coordinating calls for tender and transmitting these to branch offices for dealing with operational issues at customers' dispersed locations. In 1978, the then seven-person COM was renamed the Key Account Management (KAM) Unit to reflect a shift from managing contracts to managing relationships.

In 1985, ELECOM was merged into a major French telecom manufacturer, Phonics, which became the undisputed leader in the French market. The KAM group, located in the Phonics BD division, continued to expand and, by 1990, comprised fifteen persons managing forty key accounts. However, account selection was not formalized but based largely on historical patterns and current size. Within the KAM group, two separate manager-led teams were formed, one each for public and private key accounts.

By the early 1990s, several changes occurred in Phonics' product offerings.

Specifically, customers demanded "private networks" comprising voice, data, and image transmission; Phonics' strategy became one of offering global telecommunications solutions to customers. The KAM group was renamed the Private Network Division (PND) and key account managers coordinated the offerings of the several Phonics' divisions, based on their in-depth knowledge of customer requirements. Customer buying operations became more complex, sometimes with the emergence of multiple buying centers, as their requirements evolved, driven by the competitive environment faced by their own customers. Increasingly, in-depth knowledge of the customer's environment was necessary for supplying the appropriate telecommunications products.

By 1991, fifty key accounts (in the top two hundred French companies) represented 50% of Phonics BD revenues. The PND group was reorganized into seven industry sectors, each with a sector manager to whom reported several key account managers, each with responsibility for one or several accounts. Selection of key accounts was formalized; a two-person team monitored a backup list of two hundred potential key accounts, and elementary strategic plans were developed for each account.

Post 1993, a decision that industry sectors revenues should be in the FF200–300 million range led to a reduction in industry sectors to five (the public/private split was not maintained), and the name KAM was reinstituted. Two major accounts were removed and placed at corporate due to perceived political and strategic importance. Several regionally based customers were removed from KAM responsibility and placed with managers located adjacent to their head offices. A special key account correspondent position was developed to improve coordination between branch offices and the KAM unit, and a special "project" unit was set up within KAM to focus on project sales and management, regardless of customer sector. Finally, the entire KAM unit has become more professional: comprehensive strategic plans are developed for the unit as a whole, for the various sectors, and for each individual account.

Appendix 3.1: 3M's Corporate Accounts Program

In the early 1990s, 3M offered over 45,000 products. In its drive for innovation, it set strict goals on operating managers for new product introductions: in any year, 20% of revenues had to be derived from products based on technologies that were unavailable five years previously!

As one approach to help meet these goals, 3M introduced a corporate accounts program with the aim of leveraging its core competencies and technologies across customers in its fifty operating units (in over sixty countries) run by general managers with bottom-line responsibility. Initially piloted with two customers, by the late 1990s the program embraced over twenty customers, selected not on the basis of current volume, but on several parameters believed indicative of potential volume.

Corporate account managers, mostly each responsible for two corporate accounts, report to corporate marketing. They spend 20% of their time making connections with 3M personnel in its fifty different operating units and persuading them to take a 3M, as opposed to an operating unit, perspective. For another 20% of time, they make linkages between customer personnel and 3M personnel for specific identifiable application possibilities. The bulk of time (60%) is for developing the 3M-customer relationship and understanding where 3M technologies might be applied.

Corporate account managers are required to have multibusiness, multifunctional, and international experience. At each account, they are supported by a customer action team comprising cross-business-unit, cross-functional, cross-national members (e.g., manufacturing, logistics, information technology, R&D, sales management, marketing, division management) that assists in developing and implementing a corporate account plan. In its R&D laboratories, 3M has a well-known 15% rule allowing its scientists time to work on their own projects.[1] In a similar fashion, team members use their 15% of work time voluntarily to join the corporate account team.

Each account has an executive sponsor, reaching the level of vice chairman, who is responsible for global growth at that account (measured by a global sales reporting system), and who assists the corporate account manager in breaking down internal barriers. Corporate account managers also seek executive sponsors within their accounts to assist in identifying appropriate contacts. Corporate account managers see their role both as representing 3M to the customer

389

firm but also in representing the customer to 3M by assisting in identifying the appropriate organizational contacts.

Corporate account managers are measured by hard dollar revenues, with a goal of twice the average 3M growth rate. However, perhaps more important measures are the level of interaction between the two companies, and such pipeline measures as, for example, joint technology development and joint product development.

Appendix 3.2: Objectives for a Key Account Manager Position Developed by a Major U.S. Manufacturer

- Assure that the capabilities, plans, and programs of the supplier firm (SF) are synthesized and clearly in front of the customer at all times. Similarly, the strategic intent of the key account (KA) should be coordinated and made available to the respective SF business units.
- Take the lead in developing a national procurement plan for all KA's product needs:
  - Provide a multibusiness perspective to future volume and planning requirements
  - Coordinate potential joint-venture opportunities
  - Develop the necessary programs and alliances that make us indispensable
- Develop a supply chain management initiative with the KA. This will involve multibusiness and multichannel opportunities for mutual margin improvement by eliminating unnecessary cost from the supply chain.
- Provide the direction for product R&D, working closely with the KA's technology development department and providing a liaison role to the SF's product development center.
- Become the strategic issues coordinator. Tactical involvement includes forecasting and production issues. Strategic involvement includes response time, competitive assessments, marketplace trends, raw material and product cost trends.
- Provide guidance and interface with additional SF businesses that have the potential to be part of the corporate program with the KA, helping to clarify issues, responses, etc.
- Develop and track a set of key measures of customer satisfaction for the total business that will mirror for our respective organizations the KA's perception of our combined performance.
- Conduct and participate in formal and informal business reviews both internally and with the customer to ensure total commitment to customer satisfaction.

Appendix 5.1: Securing Data on Key Account Requirements

Data on the preferences for, and tradeoffs among, alternative product and service attributes of different individuals in the buying process must be obtained in order to fashion offers at key accounts. Essentially two sorts of methods are available for securing this data—direct and indirect.

Direct Methods: Essentially, direct methods involve asking respondents what attributes (and levels of attributes) they require. They can be asked their preferences for one attribute (level) versus another and preference tradeoffs between one attribute (level) and another. These questions can either be asked individually or in a group. This approach reveals respondents' views on individual attributes (levels).

However, individuals rarely make judgments and decisions about individual attributes *per se;* rather they make judgments and decisions about market offers that combine a whole set of product and service attributes. As a result, indirect measures have become increasingly popular.

Indirect Methods: These methods overcome the negative feature of direct methods. Individuals make judgments about market offers that reveal implicit preferences for attributes (levels); the related tradeoffs can then be calculated. The most popular method for developing this insight is *conjoint analysis.*[1]

In conjoint analysis, respondents are presented with different market offers. Each offer might comprise several product and service attributes. For example, suppose a computer company is seeking to make notebook computer sales to a key account. Important product attributes might be processing speed, hard drive memory, and working memory. Important service attributes might be delivery time and service contract. In addition, price and terms would probably be important. However, to keep the example simple, we focus just on product attributes and illustrate with an example.

Suppose notebooks come with two processing speeds (100mHz, 133mHz), two hard drives (2GB, 4GB), and two sizes of working memory (32MB, 64MB). Combining these three attributes produces eight different notebook design profiles. A typical respondent ranking is shown in Figure A5.1.

Not surprisingly, this customer has the highest preference for a notebook computer with a 133mHz processor, 64MB working memory, and a 4GB hard

| | Hard Drive | | | |
	2GB		4GB	
Working Memory	32MB	64MB	32MB	64MB
Processor speed:				
100mHz	8	7	6	5
133mHZ	4	2	3	1

FIGURE A5.1: Illustration of a Respondent's Preference Rankings for a Notebook Computer in a Conjoint Analysis Task

drive; also unsurprisingly, her least preferred option is for a 100mHz processor, 32MB working memory, and a 2GB hard drive. The ranking of the other combinations reveals the customer's preference for the various attributes. These can be calculated using conjoint analysis. In this example, on a relative scale, the value placed on processing speed is "2," the value for the hard drive is "4," and for working memory is "1," so that the relative importance of the processor is 29%, the hard drive 57%, and working memory 14%.

To conduct a conjoint analysis the following steps are recommended:

- Determine attributes and attribute levels: Secure information from key account personnel regarding the attributes and levels of attributes they would consider in making a choice.
- Select attribute profiles to be measured, using either all combinations (full factorial design) or a specially selected set (orthogonal design). For simple choices, a full factorial design can be used; this is typically not feasible for complex choices.
- Choose a method for stimulus representation, e.g., verbal description, pictures, prototypes.
- Select a response method and collect data, e.g., rankings or ratings of alternatives, selection and relative preference for profiles presented two at a time (i.e., pairwise comparisons).
- Choose a method of data analysis: a variety of software packages are available.
- Analyze the data: develop the attribute importances and utilities for each attribute level.
- Use the results: develop an offer or offers for the key account; decide how to present.

Appendix 6.1: Key Account Profitability Analysis

Typically, firms have ongoing systems that measure product profitability. However, systems for measuring customer or account profitability are more rare. In this illustration for a manufacturing company, we demonstrate the translation from product income statements to customer income statements.[1] Furthermore, we show two different methods for allocating customer-oriented overhead costs—simple allocation based on sales revenue, and allocation based on activities.

Step I. Suppose, for example, a particular firm sells three products—A, B, and C. The product income statements are shown in Figure A6.1:

FIGURE A6.1: Product Income Statements

	Product A	Product B	Product C	Total
Sales Revenues	$4,330,000	$6,400,000	$7,001,000	$17,731,000
Cost of Goods Sold	$3,175,000	$4,120,000	$5,213,000	$12,508,000
Gross Margin	$1,155,000	$2,280,000	$1,788,000	$5,223,000
Other Operating Costs				$4,023,000
Operating Income				$1,200,000

Cost of goods sold includes all product costs incurred in the manufacturing process; for simplicity, assume these comprise direct labor, raw materials, and factory overhead. In developing the product gross margins, total *cost of goods sold* ($12,508,000) must be correctly assigned to the various products. Although the direct labor and raw materials components can be easily assigned since, as variable costs, they change directly with unit sales, the overhead element is a more complex issue. Traditional methods involve assigning overhead on some rate base such as direct labor hours or machine hours. More recent approaches involve the use of activity-based costing (ABC) methods in which overhead elements such as machine set-up, receiving, engineering, and packing are isolated and assigned to the various products based on actual activity.[2] We assume that ABC methods have been used here to arrive at appropriate cost allocations in developing the various gross margins.

Other operating costs includes customer-specific costs such as sales force, field service, technical assistance, order processing, and delivery. In Figure A6.1, these have not been assigned to products, although companies frequently do allocate such costs on the basis of sales revenues or some other cost driver to arrive at product net incomes.

Step II. The revenue distribution for the three products to the three accounts is shown in Figure A6.2:

FIGURE A6.2: Product Revenue Distribution by Account

	Product A	Product B	Product C	Total
Account I	$1,030,000	$3,100,000	$5,250,000	$ 9,380,000
Account II	$ 550,000	$2,800,000	$1,001,000	$ 4,351,000
Account III	$2,750,000	$ 500,000	$ 750,000	$ 4,000,000
Total	$4,330,000	$6,400,000	$7,001,000	$17,731,000

Step III. From the product income statements, we can develop customer income statements simply by allocating the *cost of goods sold* for each product according to its proportion of sales revenues at each account. The result is three partial customer income statements providing gross margins per account (Figure A6.3). In this illustration, the wide gross margin distribution occurs because of the manner in which the various factory overhead expenses are absorbed, reflecting the particular needs placed on the factory by each of the three key accounts.[3]

Step IV. The challenge now is to calculate the net margins per account by allocating *other operating costs* ($4,023,000) among the three accounts. Basically, we can proceed in two different ways. One approach is to allocate these costs to accounts on the basis of sales revenues. Such an allocation leads to the income statements in Figure A6.4.

We note that the firm earns considerable profits at Account I but loses money at Accounts II and III.

FIGURE A6.3: Partial Customer Income Statements

	Account I	Account II	Account III	Total
Sales Revenues	$9,380,000	$4,351,000	$4,000,000	$17,731,000
Cost of Goods Sold	$4,452,000	$4,353,000	$3,703,000	$12,508,000
Gross Margin	$4,928,000	($ 2,000)	$ 297,000	$ 5,223,000
Other Operating Costs				$ 4,023,000
Operating Income				$ 1,200,000

FIGURE A6.4: Customer Income Statements
(Other Operating Costs by Simple Allocation)

	Account I	Account II	Account III	Total
Sales Revenues	$9,380,000	$4,351,000	$4,000,000	$17,731,000
Cost of Goods Sold	$4,452,000	$4,353,000	$3,703,000	$12,508,000
Gross Margin	$4,928,000	($ 2,000)	$ 297,000	$ 5,223,000
Other Operating Costs	$2,128,000	$ 986,000	$ 909,000	$ 4,023,000
Operating Income	$2,800,000	($ 988,000)	($ 612,000)	$ 1,200,000

Step V. The second approach is to allocate the various elements of *other operating costs* to accounts on the basis of actual activity. Suppose that these elements are sales force, field service, technical assistance, order processing, and delivery, and that the total cost of each activity is:

Sales force	$ 875,000
Field service	$ 773,000
Technical assistance	$ 950,000
Order processing	$ 550,000
Delivery	$ 875,000
Total	$4,023,000

These costs are allocated to accounts as follows:

Sales force: Based on actual costs for key account managers (e.g., compensation, travel and entertainment [T&E], assistants) and estimated time spent by the field sales force.

Field service: Based on estimated time spent with the three accounts: account I—29%; account II—42%; account III—29%.

Technical assistance: Based on estimated time spent with the three accounts: account I—30%; account II—30%; account III—40%.

Order processing and delivery: Based on ABC methods. The numbers of deliveries and orders processed for the three accounts are shown in Figure A6.5. This figure also shows the calculation of rate base (cost per unit) (cost divided by total number) for order processing and delivery. From this rate base, the order cost and delivery cost per account are simply calculated by multiplying the number of orders/deliveries by their respective rate bases.

FIGURE A6.5: Allocating Order Processing and Delivery Costs by ABC Methods

	Account I	Account II	Account III	Total	Cost	Rate base
Number of Orders	750	400	350	1,500	$875,000	$583
Number of Deliveries	110	65	45	220	$550,000	$2,500
Cost Allocations:						
Order Processing	$275,000	$162,500	$112,500	$550,000		
Delivery	$437,000	$233,000	$205,000	$875,000		

The final allocation of the elements of *other operating costs* among the three accounts is shown in Figure A6.6.

FIGURE A6.6: Other Operating Costs Allocated by Activity

	Account I	Account II	Account III	Total
Sales Force	$ 425,000	$ 225,000	$ 225,000	$ 875,000
Field Service	$ 224,000	$ 325,000	$ 224,000	$ 773,000
Technical Assistance	$ 285,000	$ 285,000	$ 380,000	$ 950,000
Order Processing	$ 275,000	$ 162,500	$ 112,500	$ 550,000
Delivery	$ 437,000	$ 233,000	$ 205,000	$ 875,000
Total	$1,646,000	$1,230,500	$1,146,500	$4,023,000

These figures lead to the customer income statements in Figure A6.7:

FIGURE A6.7: Customer Income Statements
(Other Operating Costs Allocated by Activity)

	Account I	Account II	Account III	Total
Sales Revenues	$9,380,000	$4,351,000	$4,000,000	$17,731,000
Cost of Goods Sold	$4,452,000	$4,353,000	$3,703,000	$12,508,000
Gross Margin	$4,928,000	($ 2,000)	$ 297,000	$ 5,223,000
Other Operating Costs	$1,646,000	$1,230,500	$1,146,500	$ 4,023,000
Operating Income	$3,282,000	($1,232,500)	($ 849,500)	$ 1,200,000

The net income by customer using a simple sales revenue basis for allocation of *other operating costs* (Figure A6.4) produced quite different account-level figures for operating income:

	Account I	Account II	Account III	Total
Operating Income	$2,800,000	($988,000)	($612,000)	$1,200,000

Appendix 7.1: Outline for the Key Account Plan

Executive Summary

Situation Analysis
    Analysis of the key account
        Key account fundamentals
        Strategic key account analysis
        Identifying and addressing key account needs, and delivering
            customer value
        Buying Analysis
    Analysis of competition
        Competitive structure analysis
        Analysis of specific competitors
    Analysis of the Supplier Firm
        Historical performance
        Relationship assessment
        Assessing firm behavior
        Resource availability
    Planning Assumptions
    Opportunities and Threats
        Protecting and expanding current business
        Securing new business
Key Account Strategy
    The key account vision
    The key account mission
    A complete key account strategy
        Performance objectives
        Strategic focus
        Positioning
        Action programs
        Agreements on resource requirements
        Budgets and forecasts

Appendix 8.1: Types of Data Collected from Customer Satisfaction Surveys[1]

Categories	Included in All Surveys
1 Overall	On an overall basis, how satisfied are you with our company?
2 Overall	How satisfied are you with the ease of doing business with our company?
3 Overall	Would you purchase products or services from our company again?
4 Overall	Would you recommend our company to an associate?
	Library of Categories: How satisfied are you with:
5 Billing	our billing and invoicing?
6 Business practices	the way we conduct business?
7 Communication	our company's overall communication efforts?
8 Communication	our telephone support systems (based on recent experience)?
9 Credits	our policies and procedures for issuing credits?
10 Customer impressions	our company as a business partner?
11 Customer service	the customer service we provide?
12 Customer support	the level of customer support we provide?
13 Delivery	the delivery of our products or services?
14 Design input	input relative to design or quality issues?
15 Documentation	the quality of printed support materials we provide?
16 Equipment service	the service we provide for your equipment?
17 Installation	our installation of equipment?
18 Literature	the literature we provide to describe our products and services?
19 Management	your interactions with our management?
20 Management	the commitment of our company's management to assist you?
21 Marketing	our marketing support programs?
22 New products	our effort to commmunicate the availability of new products?
23 Ordering	the effectiveness with which we process your orders?
24 Pricing	the procedures we use for providing quotes?
25 Product line	the diversity of our product line?
26 Product packaging	our product packaging?
27 Product quality	the quality of our products?
28 Relationship	your relationship with our company's personnel?

29	Sales	the personal commitment of our sales representatives?
30	Sales	our sales representatives' overall level of responsiveness?
31	Sales	the overall performance of our sales representatives
32	Sales	the accessibility of our sales representatives?
33	Service technicians	the performance of our service technicians?
34	Technical support	the level of technical support we provide?
35	Test standards	our procedures for maintaining and documenting test standards?
36	Warranties	the warranties we provide for our products?

Appendix 9.1: Assessing Drivers for the Partnership Development Model[1]

Drivers are strategic factors that result in a competitive advantage and help determine the appropriate level of a business relationship. For each driver, use the individual items to indicate the probability of your organization realistically achieving a benefit through forming a tighter relationship, by circling the appropriate number.

Asset/Cost Efficiency	No Chance				Certain
What is the probability that this relationship will substantially	0%	25%	50%	75%	100%
reduce channel costs or improve asset utilization?	1	2	3	4	5

- product costs savings
- distribution costs savings, handling costs savings
- packing costs savings, information handling costs savings
- managerial efficiencies
- assets to the relationship

1

If you rated efficiencies 3, 4, or 5 and if the advantage is either a sustainable competitive advantage or it allows your firm to match benchmark standards in your industry, circle the 1 above.

Customer Service	No Chance				Certain
What is the probability that this relationship will substantially	0%	25%	50%	75%	100%
improve the customer service level as measured by the customer?	1	2	3	4	5

- improved on-time delivery
- better tracking of movement
- paperless order deliveries
- improved cycle times
- improved preventive maintenance rates
- customer survey results
- process improvements

1

If you rated customer service 3, 4, or 5 and if the advantage is either a sustainable competitive advantage or if it allows your firm to match benchmark standards in your industry, circle the 1 above.

Marketing Advantage	No Chance				Certain
What is the probability that this relationship will lead to	0%	25%	50%	75%	100%
substantial marketing advantages?	1	2	3	4	5

- new market entry
- promotion (joint advertising, sales promotion)
- price (reduced price advantage)
- product (jointly developed product innovation, branding opportunities)
- place (expanded geographic coverage, market saturation)
- access to technology
- innovation potential

1

If you rated marketing advantage 3, 4, or 5 and if the advantage is either a sustainable competitive advantage or if it allows your firm to match benchmark standards in your industry, circle the 1 above.

Profit Stability/Growth	No Chance				Certain
What is the probability that this relationship will result in	0%	25%	50%	75%	100%
profit growth or reduced variability in profit?	1	2	3	4	5

- growth
- cyclical leveling
- seasonal leveling
- market share stability
- sales volume
- assurance of supply

1

If you rated profit stability/growth 3, 4, or 5 and if the advantage is either a sustainable competitive advantage or if it allows your firm to match benchmark standards in your industry, circle the 1 above.

Add all your circled numbers. This represents the strength of your motivation to partner.

Scoring
Low	8–11 points
Medium	12–15 points
High	16–24 points

Note: The bulleted items under each driver are only suggestive and should be used only as examples. In practice, each potential partner is provided with a blank sheet of paper for each driver. Individual items are generated, scored, then exchanged.

The individual items within each driver should be specified as clearly as possible. Thus, under Asset/Cost Efficiency, the amount of product/cost savings should be stated as, for example, 7% per annum; or under Customer Service, improved on-time delivery from 70% to 90% where on-time is specified as before noon or after noon.

Appendix 9.2: Assessing Facilitators for the Partnership Development Model[1]

Facilitators are factors which provide a supportive environment for the growth and maintenance of a partnership. For each facilitator, use the individual items to indicate the probability of each facilitator being a factor in this relationship, by circling the appropriate number.

Corporate Compatibility	No Chance				Certain
What is the probability that the two organizations will mesh smoothly in terms of:	0%	25%	50%	75%	100%
	1	2	3	4	5

Culture?
- Both firms place a value on keeping commitments
- Constancy of purpose
- Employees viewed as long-term assets
- External stakeholders considered important

Business?
- Strategic plans and objectives consistent
- Commitment to partnership ideas
- Willingness to change

Management Philosophy and Techniques	No Chance				Certain
What is the probability that the management philosophy and techniques of the two companies will match smoothly?	0%	25%	50%	75%	100%
	1	2	3	4	5

- Organizational structure
- Use of total quality management (TQM)
- Degree of top management support
- Types of motivation used
- Importance of teamwork
- Attitudes toward "personnel churning"
- Degree of employee empowerment

Mutuality	No Chance				Certain
What is the probability that both parties have the skills and predisposition needed for mutual relationship building?	0%	25%	50%	75%	100%
	1	2	3	4	5

Management skilled at:
- two-sided thinking and action
- taking the perspective of the other company
- expressing goals and sharing expectations
- taking a longer-term view
- mutual respect

Management willing to:
- share financial information
- integrate systems

Symmetry	No Chance				Certain
What is the probability that the parties are similar on the following important factors that will affect the success of the relationship?	0% 1	25% 2	50% 3	75% 4	100% 5

- Relative size in terms of sales
- Relative market share in their respective industries
- Financial strength
- Productivity
- Brand image/reputation
- Technological sophistication

Additional Factors (Bonus Points)	Yes	No
Do you have shared competitors which will tend to unite your efforts?	1	0
Are the key players in the two parties in close physical proximity to each other?	1	0
Is there a willingness to deal exclusively with your partner?	1	0
Do both parties have prior experience with successful partnerships?	1	0
Do both parties share a high-value end user?	1	0

Scoring
Low   8–11 points
Medium   12–15 points
High   16–25 points

Note: The individual items comprising the four universal facilitators and the five situation-specific facilitators are suggestive; they are not meant to be inclusive and should be used only as a starting point.

Appendix 9.3: Examples of Partnership Agreements

We present data on three different partnerships that were active in the 1990s. First, we illustrate the sorts of aspirations that firms have for partnerships, then provide information on one successful and one unsuccessful partnership.

Partnership Aspirations: Hoover/Dow Chemical
When Hoover and Dow Chemical developed a partnership they executed a formal agreement (charter statement) that contrasted partnering with other types of buyer/seller relationship. They noted that:

> *partnering* transcends the traditional short-term relationship between customer and supplier in which each company focused on its own goals with minimal concern for the other's business needs. . . . The new partnering relationship is based on the shared strategic objective of satisfying the ultimate customer—the consumer of Hoover's products. The partnering relationship includes visibility and support at senior management levels of Hoover and Dow Chemical. Successful partnering will lead to a sense of mutual interdependence. Dow Chemical will become a preferred supplier; Hoover will become a preferred customer.

The two companies recognized that:

> . . . our shared strategic journey requires continuous improvement in our total business relationship [and that] success on the journey of continuous improvement requires that we mutually:

> - Commit to innovative new growth ideas;
> - Work together at the earliest possible stage of new product development;
> - Communicate effectively regarding our mutual goals and needs;
> - Eliminate wasteful activity in our supply chain;
> - Recognize the highest mutual quality standards as a way of life;
> - Assure competitive costs of products to Hoover customers;
> - Act in environmentally responsible ways;

- Commit to provide Dow with appropriate insight into Hoover marketing and customers.

The document concluded by noting that several subjects would be acted on to move the firms to their shared strategic objective and that they "pledge[d] to work together to build trust and to establish a long-term relationship characterized by candor and openness." The document concluded: "We can always be better; we will never be as good as we can be."

Successful Partnership: Cutting Tools Supplier/Manufacturer of Wheels and Tires

Beech Inc.*, a wheel and tire manufacturer, and Mercury*, a supplier of cutting tools, developed a successful partnership arrangement.[1] Previously, Beech had three cutting tool suppliers. When chosen as a partner, Mercury studied Beech's processes and expenditures on various types of tooling during the previous two years. In addition, it assessed Beech's long-term needs and management philosophy, and compared these factors with its own business objectives.

Beech needed tooling cost reductions and the services of an on-site engineer to supervise the use of cutting tools in its machining operations. It was willing to give the engineer authority to order cutting tools through the information network between the two firms. Mercury agreed to this arrangement and promised cost savings of 15% of Beech's cutting tool expenditures during the first year of the partnership. In fact, cutting tool costs were cut by only 12% but Mercury was willing to share the 3% difference from the 15% target. At the end of the first year, both firms agreed to extend the initial twelve-month contract. Although the engineer worked full-time during the first year of the contract, after cutting tool procedures were established, his on-site work declined by about 50%.

Target prices are set at annual meetings between the two companies, and revised at quarterly review meetings. If the cost of the tools exceeds the target cost, Mercury bears the cost, but if fewer tools are used, Beech pays an agreed amount. In cases of uncertainty, such as new product development projects that incur budget overruns, costs are shared. Mercury spends 10% of revenues on R&D. For problem-solving or process-improvement purposes, Mercury interacts with suppliers in related businesses as well as Beech's customers. For example, it initiated meetings to facilitate improvements between its suppliers of cutting tools and Beech.

For Mercury, this partnership arrangement has not only brought increased sales and profits, but has provided an industrial laboratory for testing new products and gaining experience in heavy machining applications. Its R&D activities in Beech's plant have enabled it to improve some of its tools and earn higher margins. For Beech, Mercury's expertise has improved the cutting process and increased productivity via reduced machine downtime and set-up charges. Problems are identified on a daily basis and resolved proactively. Beech has also enjoyed significant cost savings on cutting tools, and has reduced on-site stocks of cutting tools by 80%. Finally, the cutting tool engineer assists Beech in buying new machine tools and in relationships with the cutting oil supplier.

Unsuccessful Partnership: Ford/Lear

Following Japanese automobile practice, Ford's manufacturing strategy for the new Taurus, launched in 1995, embraced long-term supplier partnerships.[2] In particular, it outsourced such critical automobile components as seats.

For the new Taurus (and the Sable), rather than assemble seats in-house from materials delivered by contract suppliers (e.g., frames, cushions, motors), Ford outsourced the entire seat manufacturing process (except power seat tracks) to a single supplier, Lear. Concurrently, Ford closed down its internal seat-making capacity.

The nightmare that followed seemed to follow from unrealistic expectations from both sides, and a lack of supplier understanding by Ford. In fact, Lear committed to several seat programs for different auto models without the depth of engineering talent necessary to conclude them satisfactorily. Ford should have been able to identify this failing, but seemingly had no understanding of this underlying problem. Perhaps, also, Lear should have realized that orders were outstripping its competence. Either it did not know, or chose to accept the orders and hope for the best.

A further problem was that the order for the power seat track went to Johnson Controls (JC), Lear's major competitor in automotive seating. The two companies' parts had to work together, but the fierce competition between them was not conducive to the give and take required in a complex development project. Problems in the development process included a host of defects in the prototype stage—the actual seats were different from the design, seat back panels fell off, major gaps occurred between exterior pieces, parts broke during assembly, and recliner mechanisms did not work properly.

Among the causes identified for these problems were Lear's use of inexperienced engineers, lack of a sense of urgency, and missed deadlines. In addition, a less than full commitment by JC, including poor continuity of personnel at meetings, and failure to visit the pilot plant to assist with the prototype, exacerbated the difficulties. Finally, cost increase requests by Lear were deemed unacceptable by Ford personnel.

Overall the partnership enjoyed little of the trust that is endemic in successful partnerships. Rather, Ford's perspective on all suppliers seems to have been: "You can't trust them. If we beat on them hard enough we'll get them to reduce their prices." Although the new Taurus model eventually came in on time, within the design cost parameters, the relationship between Ford and Lear seemed to have been poisoned by Lear's performance during the prototype stage.

Appendix 9.4: World Class Partnering Self-Audit

Here, items are reproduced by permission of SAMA. The order of presentation reflects levels of agreement in a membership survey. A useful approach is to rate individual partnerships on these items on an agreement scale—1 = strongly disagree, 7 = strongly agree.

- The supplier is driven by a mind-set to add value to the account and to help it achieve continual rapid improvement in all aspects of quality and operations.
- Supplier management routinely provides technical support on a proactive as well as a troubleshooting basis.
- Senior management leads, involves, and empowers everyone who can add value. The key account manager acts as a catalyst.
- The supplier has an effective process for thoroughly understanding the unit's needs, organization structure, and its vital success factors. The supplier applies this process aggressively with the account's help.
- Mutual trust and respect are felt by both partners toward each other's values and cultures.
- Everyone at the supplier takes ownership, has a well-practiced set of disciplines, and a mind-set for continuously adding value.
- The partners join forces to define measurements and monitor their performances.
- The supplier has an effective system for evaluating its core strengths, applying them in ways to add value to the account, and achieve buy-in.
- On the basis of reviews, direction, and people/structural changes within either or both organizations, the partners modify their processes.
- The partners have a system for evaluating their fit and agreeing on it so that both recognize the values of the relationship.
- Cross-functional teams are formed from the best and most relevant talent available and work well together.
- The partners jointly work together to develop new business opportunities, to design new products/services, and to conduct market research.
- Together the partners jointly develop a vision, define all aspects, link everyone and all actions together, and enforce implementation of the business or relationship plan.

- Communications and information flows are accurate, timely, and effectively analyzed and managed in both customer and supplier organizations.
- The partners have a proven process for methodically evaluating every aspect of costs within all operations in which they link, and applying it to cut costs in both organizations.

Appendix 10.1: Global Account Management at Xerox [1]

Notwithstanding its recent difficulties, when it comes to matters of customer satisfaction and dealing with customers generally, Xerox is one of the world's more farsighted corporations. Xerox recovered from a disastrous financial and market share situation in the early 1980s, brought on by an excessively inward orientation and the arrogance of monopoly. It succeeded by launching a successful recovery program based on quality and customer satisfaction.[2] In the late 1980s, Xerox launched a pilot global account program with five accounts that by 2000 had grown to include over 100 customers worldwide, roughly half headquartered out of the United States.

Xerox defines global account management as: "an account management strategy for customers doing business internationally that provides a consistent level of quality of support."

Xerox employs several criteria for selecting global accounts. These include a desire by the customer for an enterprise relationship plan, and a request that its business be handled on a global basis. In addition, the customer should be migrating to enterprise-wide centralized decision processes, be a global corporation, represent a defined major opportunity, and use, or have the potential to use, the full range of Xerox's products and services.

Xerox's global account management program is built on the basis of key account management programs in individual countries. For example, in large countries such as the United States and Japan, a particular customer might be served by a Xerox key account manager. In other geographic areas such as Eastern Europe, the Middle East, Africa, and the Near East, a Global Business manager would provide an in-country link for the GAMs.[3]

Xerox's shift to global account management involved two key appointments: global account manager and focus executive for each global account.

Global Account Manager. The global account manager is typically also a national account manager for the global account, physically located near the key account's headquarters in that particular country. In addition to his more local responsibilities, the global account manager manages the key account business relationship on a global basis. In this capacity, he is responsible for developing the global account plan, and making sure the appropriate implementation occurs by coordinating worldwide resources. To complete this task, the GAM works through individual national and regional account managers, who in turn work through their local organizations.

The critical global account manager responsibility is to coordinate and leverage worldwide corporate resources for the account's benefit. Xerox believes that the GAM's ability to identify resources within Xerox raises the account manager's status in the customer organization. It also allows him to operate at a higher organizational level, thus providing advantage over competitors that call at a lower level. The global account manager is empowered and funded by the local organization, but is evaluated globally for Xerox sales volume and customer satisfaction. In turn, the global account manager's own management is tied into his global targets.

Assignment of individuals to global account management depends on the size and importance of the account. Some managers have responsibility for single accounts; others may manage two or three. In managing any one account, a global account manager may be in contact with upwards of one hundred Xerox personnel (sales representatives and others) who interface with the global account around the world. Typically, the Xerox global account manager deals at a fairly high organizational level with the customer in its home country. As a result, when he visits global account operations around the world, he continues to operate at this level. He is able to raise the level of contact for local Xerox personnel by a significant amount.

Focus Executive.[4] The *focus executive* is a senior Xerox executive who, at least for Xerox's major global accounts, has the "ear of the CEO." The key mission of this role is "to facilitate value-added executive-to-executive relationships to optimize account satisfaction, and facilitate profitable revenue growth."

In particular, the focus executive, who should be familiar with the account's key business processes, increases the level and breadth of executive relationships, and enlists the involvement of other Xerox executives in the countries where their account has a presence, forming a network of focus executives to build worldwide relationships with the customer. She helps to ensure that Xerox becomes the vendor of choice at the account. In addition, she should capture and communicate into the Xerox organization "the words of the executive customer" and champion the resolution of executive customer issues.

The critical criterion for this appointment is that, as the result of experience and organizational position, this executive can make things happen within Xerox. The focus executive is available to the global account manager when difficult issues arise and attends six-month status meetings with the global account.

* * *

In addition to these individuals, Xerox appoints executives in its geographic operating divisions as global support managers. These individuals, typically members of the national/regional account staff, assist global account managers in getting things done. They help global account managers based in their geographic areas to do business globally but also assist other global account managers whose accounts do business in their specific regions. Another key role is that of the global service manager, parallel to the global account manager, whose role is to ensure that the global account receives appropriate service around the world.

Among the devices employed to ensure globalization of the Xerox/global account relationship is a Global Master Agreement (or contract) which acts as an umbrella for individual product, services, or solutions addenda. This document is used by customers "to educate" local domestic operations on the manner in which they have asked Xerox to serve the account on a global basis.

Specific-country pricing, and terms and conditions, would be attached to this document and determined during the initial contract negotiation. Xerox also provides a Global Account Management Information System to track a customer's expenditures across 60-plus countries.

Success of the global account management program is measured by such metrics as increasing profitable revenue growth, customer share growth, customer satisfaction, and designation as preferred (or even sole) vendor.

NOTES

CHAPTER ONE

1. Some people prefer the terms "Strategic" or "Major" Account Management.
2. *The New York Times,* August 24 and September 15, 1998 and *Business Week,* September 7, 1998. Long-Term Capital Management, the hedge fund that was ultimately bailed out by Wall Street bankers on September 29, 1999 under urging from the Federal Reserve System, lost $150 million on August 21. Roger Lowenstein, *When Genius Failed,* New York: Random House, 2000, p. 146. Ciena's share price actually regained the $57 level in December 1999 and has since risen significantly higher.
3. Later in 2000, Freemarkets share price reached a low of $15.
4. *The Wall Street Journal,* August 11, 2000.
5. I recently encountered a sales organization in the floor coverings industry that had removed an entire layer of zone managers and left the regional sales managers with a span of control of around 30:1. One is forced to wonder how much "management" salespersons receive in such circumstances.
6. Some sales forces, in life insurance and private banking, for example, often have no territory organization; salespeople are free to pursue sales opportunities wherever they may be.
7. Henceforth, we shall just use the term product; however, the meaning may be product, service, or product and service as appropriate.
8. Salesperson specialization may occur within a single sales force or through the creation of multiple sales forces.
9. For the advantages and disadvantages of these various forms of sales force organization, see Noel Capon and James M. Hulbert, *Marketing Management in the 21st Century,* Upper Saddle River, NJ: Prentice Hall, 2001, Chapter 15.
10. Depending upon circumstances, various combinations of these "pure form" organizations may offer effectiveness/efficiency advantages.

11. For very readable and insightful material on globalization, see Thomas L. Friedman, *The Lexus and the Olive Tree,* New York: Anchor Books, 2000.

12. Developed by *Sales and Marketing Management* magazine. Calculated by summing average compensation for an experienced representative, field expenses, and benefits, and dividing by average number of sales calls per year. These numbers are somewhat lower than an earlier series developed on a different basis.

13. In oligopolistic market structures, relatively few suppliers typically account for a large percent of industry output.

14. For example, the percentages of industry sales accounted for by the top four global producers in various industries are civil aviation (over 95%), automobile tires (over 70%), automotive (over 50%), and information processing (over 40%).

15. *The Economist,* October 31, 1998.

16. John Howard, IBM UK Ltd., "Changes in Global Purchasing Strategy," presentation to conference on Global Account Management: Best Practice, Cranfield School of Management, Great Britain, January 30, 1998. Published mid-1980s data from the U.S. Bureau of the Census suggests that upwards of 50% of total production costs of U.S. manufacturers are accounted for by purchased materials versus 15% for direct labor costs. Charles A. Watts, Kee Young Kim, and Chan K. Han, "Linking Purchasing to Corporate Competitive Strategy, *International Journal of Purchasing and Materials Management* 31 (Spring 1995), 3–8.

17. Remarks by Mark Letner, VP Corporate Strategic Sourcing, Johnson & Johnson, to a class in "Developing and Managing Strategic Customers," B8699–02 Graduate School of Business, Columbia University, March 9, 2000.

18. Remarks by Mark Letner, *op. cit.* An American Express study (1988) classifies corporate purchases into four categories: specialty (capital)—29% of dollar spend (0.7% of transactions); direct (cost of goods sold)—49% (11.3%); indirect/MRO (managed indirect)—18% (78%) and sundry (unmanaged indirect)—4% (10%).

19. One measure of the increased importance of procurement is the rise of procurement executives to senior managerial positions. For example, Thomas Stallkamp rose through purchasing to become Chrysler's CEO.

20. "Dell Online," *Harvard Business School,* 9-598-116, Boston, MA: Harvard Business School, 1999.

21. As a result, procurement overhead has increased in many companies.

22. The importance of reducing input costs can be seen in the allegation that when Jose Ignacio Lopez departed General Motors for Volkswagen he took with him a 3,350-page printout listing 60,000 parts and suppliers for GM Europe with exact prices and delivery schedules. *Fortune,* April 14, 1997.

23. Marriott Corporation has developed such sophisticated sourcing systems and high levels of procurement expertise that 60% of Marriott's purchasing and distribution activities are performed for non-Marriott clients. *NAMA Journal,* 32 (Fall 1996). Other companies using their procurement skills to generate revenues include BellSouth, IBM, and Siemens. *The New York Times,* April 8, 2000. See also Robert E. Speakman, John W. Kamauff, and Deborah J. Salmond, "At last Purchasing Is Becoming Strategic," *Long Range Planning,* 27 (1994), 76–84.

24. For an interesting perspective on the role of procurement in creating competitive advantage, see *Leveraging the Strategic Nature of Procurement,* Chicago: A.T. Kearney, 1998.

25. The *core series* comprises effective procurement techniques, buyer/seller negotiations, financial essentials and legal aspects of procurement, and strategies for supplier diversity. The *intermediate series* includes commercial team negotiations, software acquisition licensing agreements, intellectual property law concepts, software contracting, and multicultural awareness. The *advanced series* comprises strategic cost management, managing strategic supplier relations, international trade and risk analysis, managing the cost of the supply chain, procurement and sourcing strategy development, and multicultural team development, John Howard, *op. cit.*

26. In late 1997, across twenty-eight purchasing categories, IBM's input price changes were never inferior to benchmarks, and averaged 4% superior, John Howard, *op. cit.*

27. Interestingly, despite the apparent success of this partnership for both Wal-Mart and P&G, Wal-Mart continues to deal with Sara Lee Corporation *(Sara Lee* cakes), *(Coach* handbags), *(Champion* sweatshirts), *(Ball Park* frankfurters), *(Playtex* bras), *(L'Eggs* panty hose) and many others on an individual brand basis.

28. Electronic marketplaces are typically classified as *vertical*—organized around a commodity or industry (e.g., plastics—www.plasticsnet.com, steel—www.e-steel.com, steel and other metals—www.metalsite.com, paper—www.paperexchange.com, chemicals—www.chemdex.com) or *horizontal*—based on generally required items (e.g., logistics, inventory, media, and credit). Exchanges may be *independent*—open to many buyers and sellers (e.g., FreeMarkets.com), or *private*. Private exchanges may be set up by *individual companies* seeking to procure products and services (e.g., General Electric) or based on *buying groups* (e.g., Covisint—General Motors, Ford, DaimlerChrysler, Nissan, Renault; Exostar—Boeing, Lockheed Martin, Raytheon, BAE Systems; Chipcenter—Arrow Electronics, Avnet; Elemica—BASF, Bayer, BBP, Dow, Ciba Specialty Chemicals, Rohm & Haas). Of course, the author does not warrant that any of the sites noted here will be operational when this note is being read! For a good introduction to B2B exchanges, see Arthur B. Sculley and W. William A. Woods, *B2B Exchanges: The Killer Application in Business-to-Business Internet Revolution:* ISI Publications, 1999.

29. *Business Week,* April 10, 2000, p. 162.

30. *The New York Times,* April 8, 2000.

31. In Volkswagen's new plant in Brazil, component suppliers operate various areas of the plant.

32. See *Fortune,* February 20, 1995, "Purchasing's New Muscle," which documents examples of reductions in numbers of suppliers.

33. One spur to Xerox's action was a late-1970s trip to Japan by Xerox executives that revealed it had nine times as many suppliers as its Japanese rivals! In 1985, Xerox was awarded *Purchasing Magazine's* prestigious Medal of Professional Excellence.

34. *The Economist,* December 7, 1996. In this process, some suppliers were forced to accept price cuts of up to 30%.

35. Portions of these data from *The Wall Street Journal,* August 16, 1991.

36. *The New York Times,* March 21, 1997 and July 23, 1997.

37. In a contrawise move, in 1991, Coca Cola abandoned its single agency for thirty or more agencies around the world. See *The Economist,* June 22, 1996.

38. Source: Abberton Associates. Data presented by Professor Malcolm McDonald at the Global Best Practices Seminar, Cranfield School of Management, January 30, 1998.

39. This section benefited from Tom Slaight, Bruce Klassen, and Frank McGinnis, *Strategic Account Management,* Working Paper, New York: A.T. Kearny, 1998.

40. See Dan C. Weilbaker and William A. Weeks, "The Evolution of National Account Management: A Literature Perspective," *Journal of Personal Selling and Sales Management,* 17 (Fall) 1997, 49–59, for a review of much of the key account management literature.

41. Here, the term "large" customers is used loosely; as discussed in Chapter 2, size is only one of several criteria that can be used to select key accounts.

42. Recently, a senior executive with a major company saw the Columbia Executive Programs brochure for the Key Account Management Program that mentioned the 80/20 rule. In a conversation about sending executives to this program, he said: "Forget 80/20. In my business it's nearer 98/2!"

43. Except as "goodwill" when companies are acquired for a price in excess of book value.

44. In many companies, the focus on large accounts has led to the term, "national accounts"; indeed, for many years, the major industry association (founded in 1964) was the *National Account* Marketing Association (NAMA). In today's globalizing environment this term is too restrictive; we use the term "key account" throughout the book. In 1999, NAMA was renamed the *Strategic Account* Management Association (SAMA). For an historical development of key account management, see Derrick-Philippe Gosselin and Aimé Heene, "A Competence-Based Analysis of Key Account Management: Implications for a Customer-Focused Organization," Proceedings of the 5th International Conference on Competence-Based Management," Helsinki University of Technology, Espoo (Helsinki), Finland, June 10–14, 2000.

45. Thomas H. Stevenson, "Payoffs from National Account Management," *Industrial Marketing Management,* 10 (1981), 119–124. However, the 23 sample firms did not, in general, report improved new product acceptance, improved forecasting nor, somewhat surprisingly, improved internal coordination.

46. Data presented by Professor Malcolm McDonald, *op. cit.*

47. *Strategic Account Management Innovation Study,* S4 Consulting and SAMA, 1997.

48. In recent years, several European scholars have become interested in key account management. For a review of a program of research in France, see Catherine Pardo, "Key Account Management in the Business-to-Business Field: A French Overview," *Journal of Business and Industrial Marketing,* 14 (1999), 276–290.

49. Data collected in a survey of two hundred executives from *Fortune* 1000 firms, in Robert E. Wayland and Paul M. Cole, *Customer Connections,* Boston: Harvard Business School Press, 1997.

50. In a recent study by Sanjit Sengupta, Robert E. Krapfel, and Michael A. Pusateri, "Switching Costs in Key Account Relationships," *Journal of Personal Selling and Sales Management,* 17 (Fall 1997), 9–16, the authors found that high customer switching costs were related both to high "objective" supplier performance in terms of account market share, sales, and profits, and high "subjective" performance in terms of meeting the key account's objectives, relationship continuity, cooperation, and customer satisfaction.

51. Nicole Adams, Jonathan Gillibrand, Dan Treinish, Kathleen Woodberry and Briana Zaldivar, "British Aerospace Regional Aircraft: Addressing the Need for Key Account Management," Term paper for "Developing and Managing Strategic Customers," B8699-02 at the Graduate School of Business, Columbia University, Spring 2000.

52. Joseph Gelman, Bruno Messer, Jochen Heck, and Claudia Uribe, "A Financial Institution in Latin America: An Application of Key Account Management," Term Paper for "Developing and Managing Strategic Customers," B8699-02 at the Graduate School of Business, Columbia University, Spring 2000.

53. For an interesting study of networks involving a Swedish multinational firm and three of its key accounts, see Robert Spencer, "Key Accounts: Effectively Managing Strategic Complexity," *Journal of Business and Industrial Marketing,* 14 (1999), 291–309. H. Hakansson is perhaps the leading scholar in addressing supplier/customer relationships via a network approach. For a good summary of this work, see David Ford, Lars-Erik Gadde, Hakan Hakansson, Anders Lundgren, Ivan Snehota, Peter Turnbull, and David Wilson, *Managing Business Relationships,* New York: Wiley, 1998. See also Hakan Hakannson and Ivan Snehota (Eds.), *Developing Relationships in Business Networks,* London and New York: Routledge, 1995.

54. *The New York Times,* January 21, 2001. A further contributing factor to Lucent's problems was an overaggressive drive for revenue growth leading to excessive price discounting.

55. Considerable research has demonstrated that people's level of satisfaction tends to be determined by the gap between performance expectations and perceived performance, rather than by the absolute level of perceived performance *per se.*

56. See, for example, J. Ross, "Why Not a Customer Advisory Board," *Harvard Business Review,* 75 (January-February 1997), 12, and Tony Carter, "Cultivation Council," *Selling Power,* 19 (May 1999), 100–102.

57. Of course, in some industries there may only be a few customers. As a result, concentration on a limited number of customers is inevitable.

58. See "BT: Telephone Account Management," Martin Bless and Christopher H. Lovelock, in Christopher H. Lovelock and Charles B. Weinberg, *Marketing Challenges: Cases and Exercises,* New York: McGraw-Hill, 1993, pp. 328–339.

59. This reason was one of the driving factors leading to the breakup of the Cordiant advertising agency into separate individual agencies *(The Economist,* April 26, 1997). A similar issue featured heavily in AT&T's decision to separate the long-distance business from the hardware business (now Lucent Technologies including most of Bell Laboratories). Major telecommunications firms were nervous about securing their equipment from a competitor telecommunications firm, AT&T. Lucent spent in excess of $100 million on an advertising campaign designed to develop a new corporate identity.

60. *Fortune,* July 19, 1999.

61. In a recent European study, key account customers were classified into three groups based on their perceptions of key account management: *the disenchanted*—supplier seen as unwilling to tackle "real" problems, *the interested*—key account management viewed as positive but too limited an effort, *the enthusiasts*—key account management seen as the solution to several problems in the supplier-customer relationship. Factors believed leading to more positive customer opinions were: greater perceived importance of the supplier's product, key account understanding key account management, high perceived ranking in the supplier's portfolio, centralization of the buying process, lack of environmental challenges that divert attention from the supplier's key account management efforts, focus on strategic choices that key account management supports, and open-mindedness. Catherine Pardo, "Key Account Management in the Business-to-

Business Field: The Key Account's Point of View," *Journal of Personal Selling and Sales Management,* 17 (Fall 1997), 17–26. A related study found that preference for key account programs increased among customers whose purchase decision making was multilevel, multifunctional and took a long time; these tended to be large for-profit organizations, Arun Sharma, "Who Prefers Key Account Management Programs? An Investigation of Business Buying Behavior and Buying Firm Characteristics," *Journal of Personal Selling and Sales Management,* 17 (Fall 1997), 27–39.

62. Among the reasons cited by respondents for not adopting a key account management system in the Stevenson study, *op. cit.,* were lack of qualified people for national account management personnel, and a customer base with few repeat purchasers. Another reason was a policy to treat all customers alike regardless of volume purchases; of course, the wisdom of such a policy should be seriously debated.

63. Edmund Bradford, "Using Total Customer Management (TCM) to Develop Profitable Key Account Relationships," *The Journal of Selling and Major Account Management,* 1 (February 1999), 29–48.

64. In recent years, several books on key account management have appeared, mainly by European authors. These include Ken Langdon, *Key Accounts Are Different: Solution Selling for Key Account Managers,* London: Pitman, 1995; John Rock, *Key Account Management: Maximising Profitability from Major Customers,* Warriewood, NSW, Australia: Business & Professional Publishing, 1998; Malcolm McDonald and Beth Rogers, *Key Account Management,* Oxford: Butterworth/Heinemann, 1998; and Peter Cheverton, *Key Account Management: The Route to Profitable Supplier Status,* London: Kogan Page, 1999.

65. The key account congruence model is developed from a more general congruence model originated by David Nadler and Mike Tushman in their *Strategic Organizational Design,* New York: Oxford University Press, 1997. In spirit, at least, the key account congruence model is also related to the McKinsey, 7-S Framework comprising strategy, organization structure, systems, values, skills, staff, and style. Thomas J. Peters and Robert H. Waterman, *In Search of Excellence: Lessons from America's Best Run Companies,* New York: Warner Books, 1988.

CHAPTER TWO

1. Some firms move in an opposite direction. For example, Delphi Automotive Systems, newly spun-off from General Motors, is seeking to expand its customer base and reduce its dependence on General Motors business. *The New York Times,* May 25, 1999.

2. *Strategic Account Management Innovation Study, 1997–1999,* S4 Consulting and SAMA, 1999.

3. Starting small and later expanding is consistent with Everett Rogers's "divisibility" factor for successful adoption of innovations. E. M. Rogers, *Diffusion of Innovations,* 3rd Edition, New York: The Free Press, 1983.

4. David Fritz, "Internal Selling throughout the National Account Life Cycle," *NAMA Journal,* 33 (Spring 1997), 1, 3.

5. For an interesting exposition of the value of vision statements, see J. C. Collins and J. I. Porras, "Building Your Company's Vision," *Harvard Business Review,* 74 (September–October 1996), 65–77.

6. We should note that, for multinational firms, some domestic customers, because of their size and scope, may be more important to the firm than other global customers

7. See "Citibank: Global Trade Systems," in Noel Capon, *The Marketing of Financial Services,* Englewood Cliffs, NJ: Prentice Hall, 1992. Originally, WCG had its own infrastructure and staff; financial results were calculated locally and consolidated globally. However, in the early 1980s, this group was eliminated and its activities merged back into local operations under pressure from local management concerned about the loss of significant business with its traditional clients. In the mid-1980s, WCG was reformed but with a "coordinating" role; local relationship staff were part of local operations but reported to both local and WCG management. Thomas W. Malnight and Michael Y. Yoshino, *Citibank: Global Customer Management,* Harvard Business School/The Wharton School case study, 1995. In recent years, Citibank's system has continued to evolve.

8. For a firm selling polyester fiber for use in tarpaulins, key accounts might be found among various different entities, for example, spinners, weavers, proofers, makers-up, distributors and truckers. See Noel Capon, *ICI Fibres Ltd.,* New York: Graduate School of Business, Columbia University, 2001.

9. *The New York Times,* October 20, 1998.

10. For example, because of the critical importance that Citibank places on human resources, it selects major U.S. schools of business as key accounts and assigns top managers to individual schools to build relationships.

11. Tai Dai, Mouna Khabbaz, Kathleen L'Esperance, Swati Rao, and Jessica Dee Rohm, "E-Tech: Chase Internal Technology Global Account Management Program," term paper for "Developing and Managing Strategic Customers," B8699-02, Graduate School of Business, Columbia University, Spring 2000.

12. Xerox employs a fivefold scheme, termed the customer relationship triangle, embracing, in order: supplier, authorized supplier, preferred supplier, sole supplier, and quality partner. Some authors complete a continuum of relationship integration by adding joint ventures and vertical integration. See Martha C. Cooper and John T. Gardner, "Building Good Business Relationships—More Than Just Partnering or Strategic Alliances," *International Journal of Physical Distribution and Logistics Management,* 23 (1993), 14–26, for characteristics of the different forms of relationship.

13. Although single source agreements offer numerous benefits, customers may be subject to supply shortages, especially if demand exceeds expectations. For example, in September 1999, Apple Computer announced that in part because of strong demand for its new line of Power Mac G4 desktop computers, it was receiving only 40%–45% of the microprocessors it expected from sole supplier, Motorola. *The New York Times,* September 21, 1999. Relatedly, in early January 2000, PC manufacturer Gateway announced that chip shortages from sole supplier Intel had caused a loss in fourth quarter 1999 revenues of $200 to $250 million! *The New York Times,* January 6, 2000.

14. See J. D. Burdett, "A Model for Customer-Supplier Alliances," *Logistics Information Management,* 5 (1992), 25–31, for discussion on contrasting approaches to buyer/seller relationships. See C. Jay Lambe and Robert E. Spekman, "National Account Management: Large Account Selling or Buyer-Seller Alliance," *Journal of Personal Selling and Sales Management,* 17 (Fall 1997), 61–74, for a comparison of buyer-seller partnerships (alliances) and other forms of alliance.

15. To qualify for this program the account has to place a specified proportion of its business with Armstrong.

16. For a recent empirical study on selection of key accounts, see James Boles, Wesley Johnson, and Alston Gardner, "The Selection and Organization of National Accounts: A North American Perspective," *Journal of Business and Industrial Marketing,* 14 (1999), 264–275. For an extensive survey on a British sample, see John Hurcomb, *Developing Strategic Customers & Key Accounts,* Bedford, Great Britain: Policy Publications, 1998.

17. In addition to the criteria considered in these categories, supplier firms might develop such criteria as share of the key account's relevant procurement budget, long-run market growth rates for key account markets, technological sophistication, management longevity, and centralized decision making.

18. *The New York Times,* November 4, 2000.

19. Reportedly many suppliers to General Motors focused their major efforts on other customers in the early 1990s when Jose Ignacio Lopez was aggressively cutting GM's procurement costs.

20. In Roger Lowenstein, *When Genius Failed,* (New York: Random House, 2000), the author notes that although Long-Term Capital Management (LTCM), the ultimately failed hedge fund, was a strategic partner of Merrill Lynch (ML), ML made relatively little profit from the relationship. Indeed, on one occasion, LTCM made $7 million at ML's expense because of a technical loophole in a loan document.

21. See, for example, the situation in the European plastic stabilizer market in the early 1980s. *Alto Chemicals Europe (A,B,C),* Lausanne, Switzerland: IMEDE 1986.

22. See Gordon Canning Jr., "Do a Value Analysis of Your Customer Base," *Industrial Marketing Management,* 11 (1982), 89–93, for an early example of customer-based profitability analysis.

23. Presentation by Tom VanHootegem, Director National Accounts, Boise Cascade Office Products, SAMA Annual Conference, Orlando, FL May 3–5, 1999.

24. *Strategic Account Management Innovation Study,* S4 Consulting and SAMA, 1998.

25. For its corporate accounts program, 3M deliberately does not use current sales volume as a criterion but employs several different parameters aimed at identifying potential business.

26. Some companies use, as a related criterion, the customer's potential to use a broad spectrum of the firm's products.

27. In a study of key accounts identified by their energy or telecommunications suppliers, Pardo identified three general perceptions of the key account program—disenchantment, interest, and enthusiasm. Several factors led to the disenchantment end of the continuum: the supplier's product was relatively unimportant to the key account; little was known about the key account program; the key account believed it was not viewed importantly enough by the supplier; the key account program was disconnected from the key account's major strategic choices; the key account faced major environmental challenges that the supplier's key account program could not address, and the key account did not place a high value on managerial innovation. Catherine Pardo, "Key Account Management in the Business-to-Business Field: The Key Account's Point of View," *Journal of Personal Selling and Sales Management* (Fall 1997), 17–26.

28. One variant of the compensatory approach is setting minimum cut-off scores for responses in step 3. In another variant, all potential key accounts must satisfy certain crite-

ria—for example, financial security; then the compensatory approach is used for a second group of criteria.

29. One firm developed a four-factor key account attractiveness index (KAAI) based on current and predicted two-year future sales revenue and contribution:

KAAI = (Sales revenue 200X) × (Contribution margin 200X) × (Anticipated percent increase or decrease in sales revenue 200X+2) × (Anticipated percent increase/decrease contribution margin 200X+2)

The KAAI index was transposed into a 1 (low attractiveness) to 10 (high attractiveness) scale, so that each key account received an attractiveness number between 1 and 10.

30. See "The Travelers," Noel Capon, *The Marketing of Financial Services,* Englewood Cliffs, NJ: Prentice Hall, 1992, pp. 395–412.

31. *Strategic Account Management Innovation Study,* S4 Consulting and SAMA, 1998.

32. Another approach arrays *account attractiveness* (high, low) against *relationship needs* (high, low). Attractive candidates for key account management are those with high *account attractiveness* and high *relationship needs*. Developed from Edmund Bradford, "Using Total Customer Management (TCM) to Develop Profitable Key Account Relationships," *The Journal of Selling and Major Account Management,* 1 (February 1999), 29–48.

33. This matrix is related conceptually to the GE/McKinsey market attractiveness/business strengths "Stoplight Matrix" developed for strategic planning purposes. See, Renato Fiocca, "Account Portfolio Analysis," *Industrial Marketing Management,* 11 (1982), 53–62.

34. "Expected value" is a valuable metric inasmuch as it combines both the potential available business *and* the subjective probability of success.

CHAPTER THREE

1. See Kevin Wilson, "Whatever Happened to Global?" *Velocity,* 1 (Spring 1999), 18–20, for a case study illustrating this and other problems.

2. For a recent empirical study of account management structure based on seven international firms with locations in The Netherlands, see Marion A. Kempeners and Hein W. van der Hart, "Designing Account Management Organizations," *Journal of Business and Industrial Marketing,* 14 (1999), 310–327.

3. Since, in some industries, these customers essentially operate in single locations, neither travel costs to multiple locations nor multilocational coordination are relevant issues.

4. For more detail on these options, see Benson P. Shapiro and Rowland T. Moriarty, *Organizing the National Account Force,* Cambridge, MA: Marketing Science Institute, April 1984.

5. Shapiro and Moriarty *op. cit.* indicate that sometimes manufacturing operations are specific to national accounts in these systems.

6. This system was traditionally used by IBM's National Accounts Division and by major apparel manufacturers selling private label clothing to large retail chains such as Sears Roebuck, J.C. Penney, and Kmart. Such accounts are sometimes termed "house accounts."

7. Other factors that may increase key account complexity are procurement processes that comprise many steps, for example, data gathering, specification development, prelimi-

nary proposals, and product testing, in part because of long lead times between process initiation and ultimate purchase.

8. Joint supplier-firm/key-account complexity is even greater when the key account's requirements for quality and service, for essentially the same product, differ among its geographically dispersed plants and/or the supplier firm's geographically dispersed production facilities operate at varying levels of technological sophistication.

9. If suitable high-caliber sales representatives are available for assuming this high degree of responsibility, these relationships may be managed through the regular sales force system.

10. For an early study addressing organization structure for key accounts, see Jerome A. Colletti and Gary S. Tubridy, "Effective Major Account Sales Management," *Journal of Personal Selling and Sales Management,* 7 (August 1987), 1–10.

11. As Mike Newman, a senior executive in 3M's corporate accounts group puts it: "the fact that we are a multidivisional, multifunctional, multiregional, multiplant, multiproduct company is not the customer's problem." Presentation to Global and National Account Management Seminar organized by the NAMA, May 1996, Scottsdale, AZ.

12. For the development of Nalco Chemical's corporate account's program, see "Case Study: Nalco Chemical," Chicago: NAMA, 1998.

13. Of course, significant key account manager training and product support, and new compensation plans, were required to implement this organizational change. In addition, the dismantling of previously existing product-division/customer relationships had to be sensitively addressed.

14. *The New York Times,* December 18, 1998.

15. Tony Millman and Kevin Wilson, "Processual Issues in Key Account Management: Underpinning the Customer-Facing Organization," *Journal of Business and Industrial Marketing,* 14 (1999), 328–337, agree on the critical nature of top management support. They also argue that cultural barriers to customer management must be removed, customer management must focus on the "total" supply chain, and "real" involvement with the customer must be facilitated.

16. José Luz, Cristina Ribeiro, Marilia Rocca, and Maurita Sutedja, "Key Account Mangement at ABN AMRO Equity Division," term paper for "Developing and Managing Strategic Customers," B8699-02, New York: Graduate School of Business, Columbia University, Spring 2000.

17. Personal communication, Bob Shullman, The Willard & Shullman Group, Greenwich, CT, October 2000.

18. John Chambers, CEO of Cisco Systems, reportedly spends 35 hours per week with customers!

19. The term "key account director" is used generically. Depending on the firm's size and organizational approach, the specific roles detailed in this section may be the responsibility of a single individual or several managers to whom key account managers or their managers report. Furthermore, a frequently used design is to appoint both a director of key accounts and a multifunctional policy group to provide guidance and counsel. In the remainder of this chapter, we use the term key account director for simplicity.

20. Anton Fritschi, "Global Key Account Management at ABB: Success Knows No (Country) Limits," *Fachzeitschrift für Marketing THEXIS,* 16 (Fall 1999), 26–29, original in German.

21. Functional and business silos are often reinforced by the compensation system. This problem was ameliorated at Boise Cascade Office Products when introduction of an Economic Value Added (EVA) system, including bonus payments based on company results, led to a sharp reduction in across-barrier problems when the issue involved servicing key accounts. Tom VanHootegem, Director of National Accounts, Boise Cascade Office Products, at SAMA Annual Conference, Orlando, FL, May 2–5, 1999.

22. Patti Boese, National Account Manager, Abbott Laboratories, Diagnostics, at Strategic Account Management Annual Conference, Orlando, FL, May 2–5, 1999.

23. VanHootegem, *op. cit.*

24. Both of these examples are taken from Doug Bosse and Joe Sperry, "The Impact of Organizational Alignment on Trust," in Roger Dow, Lisa Napolitano and Mike Pusateri (eds.), *The Trust Imperative,* Chicago: SAMA, 1998, pp. 161–167. Doug Bosse and Joe Sperry of S4 Consulting report that such intraorganizational "silo" behavior appears widespread in manufacturing firms. Personal communication, October 2000.

25. Benson Shapiro and Rowland T. Moriarty, "Support Systems for National Account Management Programs: Promises Made, Promises Kept," Working Paper, *Marketing Science Institute,* 1984, p. 35. For example, customers highly value knowing the status of an order in the supplier firm's manufacturing system. When working with a client in the apparel industry several years ago, we discovered it took several days to secure this information. Needless to say, customers were not happy at this level of service. In Michael Hammer and James Champy, *Reengineering the Corporation: A Manifesto for Business Revolution,* New York: Harper Business, 1994, the authors relate a similar situation at IBM Leasing. A customer who placed an order for a computer had to wait between five and seven days before it received a firm quote, even though the lapsed time to process the request averaged about 45 minutes. The reengineered process reduced the period to just a few hours. More recently, use of Internet technology has reduced the time even more dramatically.

26. These programs have various names: for example, focus executive (Xerox), partnership executive (IBM), assigned executive (Hewlett Packard), executive sponsor (Compaq) and customer alliance (Lucent). I am grateful to Howard Katzen for sharing his insight into these programs.

27. Tammy Madsen and George Yip, "Hewlett-Packard: Global Account Management A and B," Los Angeles: Graduate School of Management, UCLA, 1994. HP identified three types of assigned executive: *deal executive*—associated with an account for the life of a big sales opportunity; *technology executive*—associated with an account that required a strong understanding of HP's strategy, products, or technology, and *functional executive*—associated with an account that required a strong functional understanding of how HP did business in finance, manufacturing, human resources or communications.

28. In mid-1999, Xerox had 100 focus executives assigned to key accounts.

29. The author is currently leading the Columbia Initiative on Global Account Management. Senior executives with global account management responsibility from 3M, Citibank, Deloitte and Touche, Hewlett-Packard, Lucent Technologies, Milliken and Co., Saatchi and Saatchi, and Square D-Schneider meet every sixty days to benchmark and seek best practice in global account management. In addition, business school executive education programs focused on key account management may partly fulfill a similar function.

30. A particularly successful internal benchmarking program focused on the sales force was introduced in Rank Xerox. Covering operations in Europe, the Middle East, and Africa, the benchmarking team gathered many types of sales data, making country-by-country comparisons. They found eight cases, including sales by telephone and sales of high-end copiers, in which one country dramatically outperformed the others. Individual country managers were given aggressive goals and told to select three or four cases and to implement the successful practices *as is;* they were not permitted to modify the practice in year 1 for fear their modification might change a critical ingredient of the successful practice. By the end of year 2, the incremental sales revenue was $200 million, 3.64% of Rank Xerox 1995 revenues, *Fortune,* October 26, 1996.

31. In any event, the supplier firm should take a structured approach to the staffing problem by assessing the number of relationships by account and estimating the time required to effectively manage each relationship. This estimate can be compared with the time available—total time less time for other activities (e.g., planning, travel, administrative tasks, attending internal meetings) to identify the number of key accounts per key account manager. This problem is conceptually similar to sizing the sales force. See Noel Capon and James M. Hulbert, *Marketing Management in the 21st Century,* Upper Saddle River, NJ: Prentice Hall, 2001, Chapter 15.

32. A classic study of boundary role positions concerned the foreman, spanning the boundary between management and the work force; the subtitle is instructive. Tom Lupton, *The Foreman: Master and Victim of Double Talk,* Manchester, U.K.: Manchester Business School, 1968.

33. John H. Nordloh, "Put Your Key Accounts on a Pedestal and Keep Them There," mimeo, prepared for National Account Marketing (NAMA) Annual Meeting, May 1987.

34. *Strategic Account Management Time Allocation Study,* The Alexander Group and SAMA, 2000.

35. An early 1990s study identified common tasks performed by national account managers. These included developing long-term customer relations, engaging in direct contact with key customers, maintaining national account records and background information, identifying selling opportunities and sales potential of existing national accounts, monitoring competitive developments at national accounts, reporting results to upper management, monitoring and/or controlling national account contracts, making high-level presentations to national accounts, coordinating and expediting service to national accounts, and coordinating communications among company units serving national accounts, Thomas R. Wotruba and Stephen B. Castleberry, "Job Analysis and Hiring Practices for National Account Marketing Positions," *Journal of Personal Selling and Sales Management,* 13 (Summer 1993), 49–65. Other key account manager roles included introducing new products, responding to RFPs, negotiating supply contracts, addressing specific problems and introducing local sales representatives.

36. See "Wachovia Bank and Trust Company" in Noel Capon, *The Marketing of Financial Services,* Englewood Cliffs, NJ: Prentice Hall, 1992, pp. 450–471, p. 452.

37. Jan Carlzon is CEO of SAS, the major European airline; see Jan Carlzon, *Moments of Truth,* New York: Harper & Row, 1989.

38. Jon R. Katzenback and Douglas K. Smith, *The Wisdom of Teams,* Boston: Harvard Business School Press, 1993.

39. For key account teams, IBM uses the operating-room metaphor. Many specialists come together to work as a team to accomplish a well-defined goal.

40. In a global context, teams typically include various national account managers; in these cases conflict often arises because of individual geographic priorities (see Chapter 10).

41. A few years ago, Columbia Business School Executive Programs almost lost a major piece of key account business as the result of faculty-to-faculty conversation in a conference call with key account personnel. Two key account personnel inferred, incorrectly, that conflicts existed among the faculty regarding the precise definition of the educational program.

42. I am grateful to my colleagues Eric Abrahamson and Mel Ingold for insights on successful team performance.

43. Presentation by John Shaw, Honeywell, Inc., at SAMA Annual Conference, Orlando, FL, May 2–5, 1999.

44. As the winner of the Malcolm Baldrige and European Quality awards, Milliken is often benchmarked by companies seeking to improve their own quality processes.

CHAPTER FOUR

1. A related key account competency model identifies five basic arenas—abilities, personality, skills, knowledge, and critical behaviors. Mohr Development Inc., Ridgefield, CT, 2000.

2. See Catherine Pardo, "Key Account Management: Between Internal and External Networks (The Symbolic Aspects of a New Mission)," paper presented at the Euroconference TMR Programme of the European Union, Porto, Portugal, September 1996, for an empirical study of key account managers' network relationships.

3. Jon R. Katzenback and Douglas K. Smith, *The Wisdom of Teams,* Boston: Harvard Business School Press, 1993, p. 133.

4. A useful leadership framework identifies a variety of complex and often contradictory roles (and their associated competencies): *innovator* (living with and creating change, thinking creatively), *broker* (developing a power base, negotiating agreements, presenting ideas), *producer* (working productively, fostering a productive work environment, managing time and stress), *director* (visioning, planning, goal setting; designing and organizing, delegating), *coordinator* (managing projects, designing work, managing across the organization), *monitor* (monitoring and managing personal, collective and organizational performance), *facilitator* (building teams, managing conflict, using participative decision making), *mentor* (understanding self and others, communicating effectively, developing subordinates). Adapted by Professor Schon Beechler, Graduate School of Business, Columbia University, from work by Robert Quinn, University of Michigan, 2000. For an interesting perspective on key account leadership, see Beth Rogers, "The Key Account Manager as Leader," *Journal of Personal Selling and Major Account Management,* 1 (February 1999), 60–66.

5. Katzenback and Smith, *op. cit.* The well-known framework, GRIP, identifies four fundamentals of effective teamwork: **G**—goal clarity and commitment, **R**—Role clarity and accountability, **I**—interpersonal relations, and **P**—procedures for working effectively.

6. Over the past seventy years, findings from leadership research in organizational behavior and social psychology have been inconsistent. For a good overview, see J. P. Kotter, "What Leaders Really Do," *Harvard Business Review,* 68 (May–June 1990), 103–111.

7. TRACOM, *Social Styles,* Highlands Ranch, CO: TRACOM, 1993.

8. Developed from a behavioral perspective, Merrill and Reid conducted the original research to discover patterns of observable behavior that others use regularly to describe how people act. See David Merrill and Roger Reid, *Personal Styles and Effective Performance,* Radnor, PA: Chilton Book Company, 1981.

9. For example, Columbia Business School offers a skill-building executive education program, "Managing Interpersonal and Group Dynamics," that focuses on developing these behaviors.

10. See also James M. Kouzes, Barry Z. Posner, and Tom Peters, *The Leadership Challenge: How To Get Extraordinary Things Done in Organizations,* San Francisco: Jossey-Bass, 2nd Edition, 1995.

11. For example, Abraham Maslow, "A Theory of Human Motivation," *Psychological Review,* 50 (1943), 370–396 and Frederick Herzberg, "One More Time: How Do You Motivate Employees?" *Harvard Business Review* (January–February 1968), 53–62.

12. Based on Allan R. Cohen and David L. Bradford, *Influence Without Authority,* New York: Wiley, 1989, p. 79.

13. Garry Hannah, "From Transactions to Relationships: Study Reveals the NAMs Fundamental Challenges," *NAMA Journal,* 33 (Spring 1997), 4–6.

14. Thomas R. Wotruba and Stephen B. Castleberry, "Job Analysis and Hiring Practices for National Account Marketing Positions," *Journal of Personal Selling and Sales Management,* 13 (Summer 1993), 49–65.

15. Mohr Development Inc., Ridgefield, CT, 2000.

16. Relatedly, the British "Sales Qualification Board" has made significant efforts to develop occupational standards for key account managers. However, these have been severely criticized; see Tony Millman and Kevin Wilson, "Developing Key Account Management Competences," *Journal of Marketing Practice,* 2 (1996), 7–22.

17. The supplier firm should also consider its requirements for such personnel as bidding specialists, contract preparers, installers, and service providers whose skills may be required in key account management. To ensure that the appropriate skills are available when needed, a database of human resource skills, including language fluency for global account management programs, should be developed. In addition, the supplier firm should consider implementing a planning process that identifies skills required at particular key accounts, estimates the time required, assigns skilled human resources as and when needed, and tracks their availability for future assignments.

18. *Strategic Account Management Innovation Study,* S4 Consulting and SAMA, 1997.

19. Tom VanHootegem, Director National Accounts, Boise Cascade Office Products at SAMA Annual Conference, Orlando, FL, May 2–5, 1999.

20. Patti Boese, National Account Manager, Abbott Laboratories, Diagnostics, at SAMA Annual Conference, Orlando, FL, May 2–5, 1999.

21. *Strategic Account Management Innovation Study,* S4 Consulting and SAMA, 1999.

22. In action learning environments, educational objectives meld with producing tangible output directly related to organizational functioning.

23. R. S. Kaplan and D. P. Norton, "Putting the Balanced Scorecard to Work," *Harvard Business Review,* 71 (September–October 1993), 134–147. See also "Using the Balanced Scorecard as a Strategic Management System," *Harvard Business Review,* 74 (January–February 1996), 75–85, by the same authors.

24. Presentation by Dennis Lebsack, V.P. of Major Accounts, at Key Account Management Program, Columbia Business School, October 20, 1997.

25. *Strategic Account Management Innovation Study,* S4 Consulting and SAMA, 1998.

26. Data taken from the 1998 account manager compensation survey conducted for the National Account Management Association (NAMA). The response rate was approximately 25%.

27. Some of the ideas in this section are drawn from a presentation by Dr. Thomas E. Tice to Global and National Account Management Seminar (1996), organized by NAMA. Another important source is The Alexander Group, Scottsdale, AZ; see, for example, Steve Mermey, "Using Compensation to Improve Strategic Account Performance," *Velocity,* 1 (1999), 38–40.

28. Management might also consider the provision of stock options for high-performing key account managers.

29. Cash compensation is base salary plus variable compensation, typically commissions and bonuses. Cash compensation specifically excludes one-time sales contests, long-term cash incentive plans, deferred compensation, benefits such as paid leaves, and expense reimbursements.

30. Data taken from annual account manager compensation surveys currently conducted for SAMA by The Alexander Group, Scottsdale, AZ. The samples for these surveys were individual members of SAMA; the response rates approximated 25%.

31. Financial compensation for managers of key account managers from data collected in the same studies was: salary range (median), 1995—$42,000 to $163,000 ($87,500), 1997—$47,500 to $215,000 ($98,000), 2000—$44,000 to $220,000 ($106,000); total cash compensation range (median), 1995—$53,000 to $600,000 ($115,000), 1997—$58,000 to $300,000 ($128,000), 2000—$44,000 to $307,000 ($142,000).

32. Data taken from the 1997 account manager compensation survey conducted for NAMA, *op cit.*

33. In some cases it may be appropriate to set goals on a multiyear basis.

34. For methods of reducing the impact of compensation caps, see Thomas E. Tice, "Managing Compensation Caps in Key Accounts," *Journal of Personal Selling and Sales Management,* 17 (Fall 1997), 41–47.

35. Problems with this system include the cost of double compensation, administrative complexity, and potentially compensating local salespeople who play little role in securing sales. Other, less generous, systems are based on splitting the incentive compensation (e.g., 50:50).

36. Mermey, *op. cit.*

SECTION III

1. An oft-faced problem is the requirement to integrate a host of legacy systems and processes into a fully functioning system that deals with current requirements and can be modified to address future issues.

2. For a related approach to developing key account strategy, see, Edmund Bradford, "Using Total Customer Management (TCM) to Develop Profitable Key Account Relationships," *Journal of Personal Selling and Major Account Management,* 1 (February 1999), 29–48. See also John Hurcomb, "Developing Strategic Customers and Key Accounts: The Critical Success Factors," *Journal of Personal Selling and Major Account Manage-*

ment, 1 (February 1999), 49–59, and Ken Langdon, *Key Accounts Are Different: Solution Selling for Key Account Managers,* London: Pitman, 1995.

3. The children's story of the three little pigs who, respectively, built their houses of straw, sticks, and bricks is an appropriate metaphor for the importance of a thorough situation analysis. So, also, is the biblical parable of building a house on sand versus building a house on rocks.

CHAPTER FIVE

1. As, for example, in the Japanese *keiretsu* and major companies in the Chinese diaspora.
2. To secure data discussed in this section, see the section on information sources, later in the chapter.
3. This process may be aided by a knowledge-sharing specialist.
4. The following section is written from the perspective of a key account with a single mission. Of course, if the key account has multiple businesses, each with its own mission, these analyses must be conducted for each business that offers potential for the supplier firm.
5. Technologically available means within the firm's current technological competence.
6. For a thorough discussion of environmental factors, see Noel Capon and James M. Hulbert, *Marketing Management in the 21st Century,* Upper Saddle River, NJ: Prentice Hall, 2001, Chapter 2.1.
7. In Chapter 6, when we consider the supplier firm analysis, we discuss competitive structure and competitor analysis in more detail.
8. *Business Week,* May 1, 1995.
9. A useful technique for identifying key account needs is *prospective hindsight.* The end state desired by the customer is assumed to have been reached; the key set of questions focuses on what must have happened for this end state to have occurred. By this method, deeper customer understanding may be secured.
10. Another useful framework for key account customers embraces three types of need: *product need* related to the specific set of benefits embodied in the product; *process need* embracing compatibility issues regarding the customer's use of the product, such as logistics (delivery, palletization, packaging), technical service, and so forth; and *facilitation need* embracing responsiveness, speed of action—the approach to doing business. Tony Millman and Kevin Wilson, "From Key Account Selling to Key Account Management," *Journal of Marketing Practice: Applied Marketing Science,* 1 (1995), 9–21.
11. R. Stanat, quoted in *Australian Financial Review,* March 27, 1998.
12. Lewis Pinault, *Consulting Demons,* New York: HarperBusiness, 2000, p. 56.
13. Bhote has noted that value engineering is a useful approach the key account manager might use to help identify cost reduction potential for a key account. He suggests several possible solutions that might be offered regarding any item—eliminate, simplify, alter to accommodate high-speed method, use standard part, use lower-cost materials and/or processes, or use higher-cost material to simplify design/production. Other approaches include different fabrication methods, increased quality reliability, increased differentiation to secure a higher price, more customer-important features, better service, increased dependability, greater flexibility, and just-in-time delivery. Keki R. Bhote, *Supply Management,* New York: AMACOM, 1989.

14. For key accounts that are customers of its own direct customers, suppliers may be able to reduce input costs by forward integrating and cutting a direct consumer out of the value chain. This strategy may lead to significant conflict with direct customers but may be forced upon the supplier by the key account seeking to cut its costs.

15. *Strategic Account Management Innovation Study,* S4 Consulting and SAMA, 1998.

16. See Chapter 6.

17. *Strategic Account Management Innovation Study,* S4 Consulting and SAMA, 1997.

18. Tim Minahan, "Chrysler Elects Procurement Team Leader as its New President," *NAMA Journal,* 14 (Spring 1998), 8–9.

19. Significant opportunities may be available in this area, especially if the supplier has a lower cost of capital than the customer. Of course, the key account's cost of capital may not be readily accessible; for public companies it is often buried in the footnotes to financial statements.

20. Developed in part from a study conducted by IBM, and in part from Benson Shapiro and Rowland Moriarty, "Support Systems for National Account Management Programs: Promises Made, Promises Kept," Cambridge, MA: Marketing Science Institute, April 1984. In an interesting case study of a pharmaceutical company and its suppliers, Sean deBurca identifies three core dimensions of business relationships—*active involvement* comprising understanding, cooperation, commitment, and trust; *intimacy* comprising personal contacts, and *interdependency* including information flows, perceptions of importance, difficulty in finding a replacement and level of adaptation, Sean deBurca, "Perceptions of the Underlying Dynamics in Important Business Relationships," *Journal of Selling and Major Account Management,* 1 (Autumn 1999), 31–63.

21. Time is an increasingly important strategic variable. For example, a McKinsey study on high-tech products showed that new market offerings that, compared to projects that were on time and within budget, were on budget but six months late earned 33% less profit over five years. By contrast, projects that were on time but 50% over budget earned 4% less profit! Reported by Bernard Gracia, European Institute of Purchasing Management, at a conference on Global Account Management: Best Practice, Cranfield School of Management, Great Britain, January 30, 1998.

22. "Electronic Commerce at Air Products," 9-399-035, Boston, MA: Harvard Business School, 1998.

23. As many executives are aware, the airline industry in general has not yet learned this simple lesson!

24. CIF: *c*arriage, *i*nsurance, and *f*reight.

25. Example provided by Howard Stevens; presentation to Global and National Account Management Seminar (1996) organized by NAMA.

26. Note that at similar interest rates, inventory financed by suppliers is less expensive than inventory financed by customers because of the different cost bases employed.

27. In the bidding process, some companies require that suppliers be able to scale up deliveries by certain amounts in specific time periods (e.g., 20% in one month, 50% in three months).

28. Linda Cardillo Platzer, "Managing National Accounts," Report 850, *The Conference Board,* 1984.

29. A particularly telling metaphor for satisfying key account needs concerns Gulliver's ex-

perience on his arrival in Lilliput. Although he could easily have broken anyone of the threads that held him to the ground, the combination of all of the threads was sufficient to hold him fast!

30. This framework resembles one developed by Wilson and Jantrania—meet customer requirements, exceed customer expectations, anticipate and meet customer needs. David T. Wilson and Swati Jantrania, "Understanding the Value of a Relationship," *Asia-Australia Marketing Journal,* 2 (1994), 55–66.

31. *Strategic Account Management Innovation Study,* S4 Consulting and SAMA, 1999.

32. Personal communication, Joe Sperry, S4 Consulting, October 2000.

33. Personal risk was successfully employed in the computer industry in the 1970s and early 1980s: "You'll never get fired for buying IBM!"

34. See, for example, "Cumberland Metals Industry, A, B," 9-578-170/171, Boston, MA: Harvard Business School, 1994.

35. See Michael Hammer and James Champy, *Reengineering the Corporation: A Manifesto for Business Revolution,* New York: Harper Business, 1994.

36. Procurement processes in many companies are quite tortuous, consume large quantities of resources, and may be the targets of reengineering efforts.

37. See James C. Anderson and James A. Narus, "Business Marketing: Understand What Customers Value," *Harvard Business Review,* 76 (November–December 1996), 5–15, for a formal approach to measuring customer value.

38. Starting points are the account's organization chart and its internal telephone directory.

39. I am grateful to LaVon Koener for his insight regarding this matrix.

40. See, for example, Thomas V. Bonoma, "Major Sales: Who *Really* Does the Buying," *Harvard Business Review,* 60 (May–June 1982), 111–119.

41. A useful categorization of four phases of buyer intelligence embraces: Type 1, *commodity intelligence,* focuses on raw material costs and economics of the commodity. Type 2, *process intelligence,* focuses on process economics, suppliers' manufacturing facilities and processes (e.g., Polaroid's "Zero Base Purchasing" [ZBP]) and process capabilities, extending to use of suppliers' technology and design staff. Type 3, *technology intelligence,* focuses on developing technology worldwide. Type 4, *business intelligence,* focuses on environmental factors and looks at long-term supplier issues.

42. A well-documented example of an individual in a purchasing organization using a major purchase to advance his own individual goals is provided by Andrew Pettigrew in *Politics of Organizational Decision Making,* London: Tavistock, 1973, p. 266.

43. Recounted by a participant at Columbia Business School's Executive Program in *Key Account Management* who wishes to remain anonymous.

44. A variety of methods have been discussed by Lisa M. Ellram, "A Managerial Guideline for the Development and Implementation of Purchasing Partnerships," *International Journal of Purchasing and Materials Management,* 27 (Summer 1991), 2–8. More detailed descriptions of models in use can be found in Robert E. Gregory, "Source Selection: A Matrix Approach," *Journal of Purchasing and Materials Management,* 22 (Summer 1986), 24–29; and Paul S. Bender, Richard W. Brown, Michael H. Isaac, and Jeremy F. Shapiro, "Improving Purchasing Productivity at IBM with a Normative Decision Support System," *Interfaces,* 15 (May–June 1985), 106–115. Details of proposed models are in Ed Timmerman, "An Approach to Vendor Performance Evaluation," *Journal of Purchasing and Materials Management,* 22 (Winter 1986), 2–8; William R.

Soukup, "Supplier Selection Strategies," *Journal of Purchasing and Materials Management,* 23 (Summer 1987), 7–12; and Kenneth N. Thompson, "Vendor Profile Analysis," *Journal of Purchasing and Materials Management,* 26 (Winter 1990), 11–18.

45. Value engineering is the modification of designs and systems following a systematic and critical assessment of design and costs in relation to a realized value (value analysis).

46. Keki R. Bhote, *Supply Management,* New York: AMACOM, 1987, 1989.

47. An important issue for firms operating globally is the potential impact of currency fluctuations on procurement costs.

48. Reportedly General Motors' practice when Jose Ignacio Lopez was in charge of procurement.

CHAPTER SIX

1. For a more detailed treatment of competition in general, see Noel Capon and James M. Hulbert, *Marketing Management in the Twenty First Century,* Upper Saddle River, NJ: Prentice Hall, 2001, Chapter 5.

2. In some cases, direct competitors adhere to informal agreements regarding "ownership" of individual major customers.

3. This was reportedly Jose Ignacio Lopez' practice when at General Motors. Of course, the reverse situation occurs when the key account contemplates outsourcing some activity previously conducted in-house, representing potential business for the supplier firm.

4. The questions in this and the following analysis require data on both the competitor(s) and the supplier firm. Although the supplier firm analysis is presented after competitor analysis, the analytic system is best viewed as an iterative process. For more details on value chain analysis, see Capon and Hulbert, *op. cit.,* Chapter 6, pp. 166–172.

5. This analysis is conceptually similar to the Weighted Supplier Selection Model (Chapter 5, pp. 182–184).

6. *Fortune,* May 26, 1997.

7. *Strategic Account Management Innovation Study,* S4 Consulting and SAMA, 1997.

8. *Strategic Account Management Innovation Study,* S4 Consulting and SAMA, 1998.

9. *Strategic Account Management Innovation Study,* S4 Consulting and SAMA, 1999 and personal communication from Joe Sperry, S4 Consulting, January 31, 2001.

10. Number of complaints is another useful measure.

11. See, J. L. Heskett, T. O. Jones, G. W. Loveman, W. E. Sasser Jr. and L. Schlesinger, "Putting the Service–Profit Chain to Work," *Harvard Business Review,* 72 (March–April 1994), 164–174, and T. O. Jones and W. E. Sasser, "Why Satisfied Customers Defect," *Harvard Business Review,* 73 (November–December 1995) 88–99.

12. In David Ford, "The Development of Buyer-Seller Relationships in Industrial Markets," *European Journal of Marketing,* 14 (1980), 339–353, the author develops a relationship framework involving five variables—experience, uncertainty, distance, commitment, and formal and informal adaptations. Particularly interesting is the distance variable, where reduced distance implies closer relationships:

   • *Social distance,* the extent to which individuals and organizations in a relationship are unfamiliar with each other's ways of working
   • *Cultural distance,* the degree to which the norms, values, and/or work methods of the two companies differ

- *Technological distance,* differences in the companies' product and process technologies
- *Time distance,* the time that elapses between establishing a contact, placing an order, and transferring the product/service
- *Geographic distance,* the physical distance between the two firms' locations

13. Joseph P. Cannon and William D. Perreault Jr., "Buyer-Seller Relationships in Business Markets," *Journal of Marketing Research,* 36 (November 1999), 439–460, test a model of buyer-seller relationships in which four market and situational determinants—availability of alternatives, supply market dynamism, importance of supply, and complexity of supply—are related to six key relationship connectors—information exchange, operational linkages, legal bonds, cooperative norms, adaptations by sellers, and adaptations by buyers. David Wilson, "An Integrated Model of Buyer-Seller Relationships," *Journal of the Academy of Marketing Science,* 23 (1995), 335–345, identifies a variety of buyer-seller relationship variables—commitment, trust, cooperation, mutual goals, interdependence/power imbalance, performance satisfaction, comparison level of the alternative, adaptation, nonretrievable investments, shared technology, structural bonds, and social bonds.

14. For discussion of this and other key account issues, see John Barrett, "Why Major Account Selling Works," *Industrial Marketing Management,* 15 (1986), 63–73.

15. *Business Week,* October 5, 1998.

16. A version of this approach is used by Xerox Corporation.

17. For example, U.S. multinational (chemicals and machinery) FMC develops global account strategy in the context of both industry (market) and country strategies.

18. For example, business, division, or geographic location.

19. Figure 6.11 is presented as qualitative categories on each of the two dimensions. However, each dimension could be scaled to provide quantitative measures of position of individual entries in the matrix.

20. Creative new product development may also lead to improved profit margins.

21. These new business opportunities could also be arrayed in a similar manner to current business threats and opportunities (Figure 6.11).

CHAPTER SEVEN

1. Of course, the greater the degree of key account and supplier firm complexity, the more likely that multiple strategic elements will be required.

2. In summary, operational objectives should be SMART—*s*pecific, *m*easurable, *a*ttainable, *r*ealistic and *t*imely.

3. Of course, if profitability pressures are severe, the supplier firm may have to reduce service levels and hence fixed costs in attempts to achieve its performance objectives.

4. Although conflicts are present in the different elements of strategic focus, creative managers may find ways to pursue multiple elements simultaneously. For example, through R&D efforts, the supplier firm may develop new products with significant customer value enabling it to expand current uses and displace competitors' products. At the same time it may improve the product mix, increase prices, and decrease operating costs.

5. *Creeping commitment* describes the phenomenon of increasing customer commitment to a supplier that works with the customer from the earliest stages of the purchase process. Such suppliers are often able to influence purchase specifications in a favorable manner.

6. See also Anthony Parinello, *Selling to VITO (The Very Important Top Officer)*, Holbrook, MA: Adams Media, 1994.
7. For ease of exposition, in this example, we do not focus on individual decision makers.
8. Since a widely cited model defines customer satisfaction as a function of actual performance less expected performance, the key account manager should give significant thought to setting expectations of executives at the key account for the specific results of action programs.
9. Personal communication from Tom VanHootegem, Director of National Accounts, Boise Cascade Office Products, July 2000.
10. This section draws heavily on Benson P. Shapiro and Rowland T. Moriarty, "Support Systems for National Account Management Programs: Promises Made, Promises Kept," *Marketing Science Institute*, April 1984.
11. *The New York Times*, March 23, 1997 and March 25, 1997.
12. Because increased revenue from price enhancements drops straight to the bottom line, a small price increase may lead to a large increase in profit contribution.
13. See "Wachovia Bank and Trust Company," in Noel Capon, *The Marketing of Financial Services*, Englewood Cliffs, NJ: Prentice Hall, 1992, pp. 450–471, p. 453.
14. This is a particular problem for those service organizations where the strength of relationship to a supplier firm representative may be greater than to the supplier firm *per se*.

CHAPTER EIGHT

1. The supplier firm may be able to secure economies of scale for certain types of disseminating information, as well as presenting a unified presence to its entire set of key accounts. Thus, a computer-based library of presentation overheads that can be used and reused indefinitely significantly reduces the key account manager's efforts when addressing a group of key account executives. Similarly, a library of "boilerplate" enables the key account manager to respond to proposals more efficiently.
2. John Sylvia, FMC Corporate Marketing; presentation to northeast NAMA Chapter, Boston, September 29, 1995.
3. *Fortune*, September 7, 1998. See also Richard Allan Scientific example, Chapter 6, p. 204.
4. In some situations, because of the value added, the on-site person is financed by the key account.
5. "Shanghai Chlor-Alkali Chemical Company Ltd.: PVC" in Noel Capon and Wilfried Van Honacker, *The Asian Marketing Case Book*, Singapore: Prentice-Hall, 1999, pp. 544–560.
6. I am grateful to Bill Zimmerman, regional sales manager at Milliken Corporation and faculty member in the Columbia Business School's Key Account Management Program for his insights into this process.
7. *Business Week*, May 1, 1995, p. 53.
8. Such a "leverage list" is invaluable for reminding key account executives what the supplier firm has "done for them lately."
9. Robert B. Miller and Stephen E. Heiman, *Successful Large Account Management*, New York: Henry Holt, 1991, p. 17.
10. My thanks to Peter Palij for his insight into the potential role of the Internet.
11. Based on work by S4 Consulting.

12. S4 Consulting identifies three main reasons why people engage in collaborative information sharing: *reciprocity*—an expectation that they also will receive valuable information, *reputation*—recognition as an expert in a particular area, and *altruism*—just to help others.

13. Personal communication from James Guilkey, S4 Consulting, November 2000. See also *Business Week E. BIZ,* October 23, 2000, pp. EB 52–56.

14. Based, in part, on a presentation by SouthCo Inc. to SAMA Annual Conference, San Antonio, TX, May 21–24, 2000.

15. "Dell Online," 9-598-116, Boston: Harvard Business School, 1999, p. 15. The numbers are disguised but are broadly representative.

16. "Dell Online," *op. cit.,* p. 17. As the technology developed, Dell account representatives were able to create dynamic *Premier Pages* tailored to individual account needs.

17. Of course, the supplier firm must be careful to safeguard access to private internal information; most customers would be very interested in knowing the supplier firm's private thoughts about the customer or, indeed, other customers! It is important that internal and account-accessible information *not* reside on databases that are easily cross-searched.

18. SouthCo also has a function, operated in conjunction with distributors, that allows local salespeople to identify inventory situations around the world, easing stockout problems by finding products for customers.

19. The measure–inspect–problem-solve system is a fundamental principle of total quality management (TQM).

20. For a broader discussion of trust, see Chapter 9.

21. Conceptual process employed by Willard & Shullman, Greenwich, CT.

22. Of course, 3.9 is not a particularly good satisfaction score. Personal communication from Joe Sperry, S4 Consulting, November 2000.

23. In general, senior management in key accounts should be addressed via personal interview, but other data collection systems may be cost effective with less senior key account personnel. For example, satisfaction measurement for a global account may be most effectively conducted by telephone using multilingual interviewers.

24. Personal communication from Joe Sperry, S4 Consulting, November 2000.

25. The following examples provided by Bob Shullman, Willard & Shullman.

26. In recent years, the notion of "control" has come under some attack in the wake of the employee "empowerment" movement. However, recent well-publicized events should alert all managers to the necessity of installing appropriate control systems in their organizations. These include investment banker Nick Leeson's excessive trading in Nikkei futures in late 1994 and early 1995 that led to bankruptcy for the blue-chip British bank Baring Brothers. A second example is the illegal behavior (fraud and forgery) by a Sumitomo copper trader in a $2.6 billion trading scandal. On a personal note, the author's classmate, a rising executive in Citibank stationed in London, resigned following actions by a rogue trader in his organization that cost the bank millions of dollars in losses.

CHAPTER NINE

1. For an excellent treatise on supplier firm partnerships, see Jordan D. Lewis, *The Connected Corporation,* New York: The Free Press, 1995; see, also, Lisa Napolitano, "Customer-Supplier Partnering: A Strategy Whose Time Has Come," *Journal of Personal Selling and Major Account Management,* 1 (February 1999), 20–27. For a more popular

account of the rise in partnerships, see, "Partnerships," *Business Week,* October 25, 1999, 114–130.

2. Webster's Dictionary, New York: Macmillan, 1994.

3. Douglas M. Lambert, Margaret A. Emmelhainz, and John T. Gardner, "Developing and Implementing Supply Chain Partnerships," *The International Journal of Logistics Management,* 7 (1996), 1–17, p. 2.

4. In some cases, supplier-customer partnerships may be viewed as nonlegally binding joint ventures.

5. An interesting model of key account management (KAM) development identifies six supplier-customer relationship stages—pre-KAM, early KAM, mid-KAM, partnership-KAM, synergistic-KAM and uncoupling-KAM. Kevin Wilson, "Developing Key Account Relationships: The Integration of the Millman-Wilson Relational Development Model with the Problem Centred (PPF) Model of Buyer-Seller Interaction in Business-to-Business Markets," *The Journal of Selling and Major Account Management,* 1 (Summer 1999), 11–32.

6. In a working paper, Henderson (noted in Thomas Haller, "Partnering . . . Marketing Myth or Preemptive Business Strategy," *NAMA Journal,* 32 [Winter 1996], 1, 12–15) identifies two dimensions of partnerships. *Partnership in context* encompasses mutual benefits, commitment (e.g., shared goals, incentive systems, contracts), and predisposition. *Partnership in Action* includes shared knowledge, mutual dependency on distinctive competencies and resources (sharing knowledge, management skills, experience and product attributes), and organizational linkage (exchanging information, building personal relationships).

7. A significant amount of writing targeted at procurement and operations personnel has advocated supplier-customer partnerships. See, for example, Michael R. Leenders and David L. Blenkhorn, *Reverse Marketing,* The Free Press: New York, 1988; Keki R. Bhote, *Supply Management,* New York: AMACOM, 1987, 1989; P. Cousins, "Choosing the Right Partner," *Purchasing and Supply Management* (March 1992), 21–23.

8. From the supplier firm's perspective, the partnership model is consistent with Reicheld's work on customer retention and the increased value of customers over time, F. F. Reicheld, *The Loyalty Effect,* Boston: Harvard Business School Press, 1996.

9. A special form of partnership, *keiretsu,* has existed in Japan for many years, historically involving interlocking ownerships. More recently, such firms as Matsushita have eschewed ownership stakes but, nonetheless, retain close relationships with their major suppliers. For example, Matsushita's 260 *kyoei gaisha* (co-prosperity companies), accounting for around 20% of parts purchases, have their own club. Matsushita works closely with the club in training and quality control, sharing key technologies, and providing insurance and pension plans for employees. In addition, Matsushita works individually with *kyoei gaishi* firms, sharing key technologies and involving them early in the design stage of production. *The Economist,* April 15, 2000.

10. For example, General Motors (GM) uses a Source Performance Evaluation and Reporting (SPEAR) system that rates suppliers on a variety of dimensions. Suppliers serious about improving their rating submit an action plan to GM. If approved, GM employees act as consultants to improve performance on an individual basis. Leenders and Blenkhorn, *op. cit.*

11. *Strategic Account Management Innovation Study,* S4 Consulting and SAMA, 1999.

12. In a study on British organizations, third-party certification (e.g., ISO 9000) was believed to be inferior to customer-specific procedures, J. D. A. Galt and B. G. Dale, "Supplier Development: A British Case Study," *International Journal of Purchasing and Materials Management* 27 (Winter 1991), 16–22.

13. See Oliver E. Williamson, *Markets and Hierarchies: Analysis and Antitrust Implications,* New York: The Free Press, 1975.

14. Of course, a similar set of choices may be available for a supplier firm: sell to many customers, integrate forward, or sell to a limited number of major accounts with which it develops very close relationships.

15. See Peter Kraljic, "Purchasing Must Become Supply Management," *Harvard Business Review,* 61 (September–October 1983), 109–117, for an early paper on the strategic importance of the purchasing function.

16. Several writers have suggested that this is the reality for much of the automobile industry outside of Japan (for example, R. Imrie and J. Morris, "A Review of Recent Changes in Buyer-Seller Relations," *OMEGA,* 20 [September–October 1992], 641–652.

17. C. John Langley, Jr. and Mary C. Holcomb, "Creating Logistics Customer Value," *Journal of Business Logistics,* 13 (1992), 1–27.

18. As an example, one study showed that supplier-customer partnerships led to improved supplier quality, decreased numbers of suppliers, increased contract length, and increased supplier involvement in quality certification programs. These benefits were more likely with longer-established partnerships, T. Scott Graham, Patricia J. Daugherty, and William N. Dudley, "The Long-Term Strategic Impact of Purchasing Partnerships," *International Journal of Purchasing and Materials Management,* 30 (Fall 1994), 13–18.

19. Elwyn Watkins, *Enhanced Supplier Relationships,* MBA thesis, Bradford, Great Britain: University of Bradford Management Center, 1997.

20. In particular, Lisa M. Ellram, "A Managerial Guideline for the Development and Implementation of Purchasing Partnerships," *International Journal of Purchasing and Materials Management* 27 (Summer 1991), 2–8 and J. D. Burdett, "A Model for Customer-Supplier Alliances," *Logistics Information Management,* 5 (1992), 25–31. See also Chan K. Hahn, Charles A. Watts, and Kee Young Kim, "The Supplier Development Program: A Conceptual Model," *Journal of Purchasing and Materials Management,* 26 (Spring 1990), 2–7, which focuses more on process and includes such devices as development of cross-functional teams.

21. Rather than focus on classic supplier firm criteria discussed in Chapter 6, procuring firms are advised to continue to employ supplier evaluation programs but with more strategically based selection criteria. These include compatibility of firms' organization, culture, and top management, long-term supplier plans (e.g., expand, contract, change focus), and financial performance and stability. Other dimensions include technological innovation/design capability (willingness to share or partner), suitability, flexibility and location of production facilities (willingness to relocate or expand), communication ease, and local content laws, tariffs, and other trade issues (with foreign suppliers).

Bhote has developed a series of ten evaluation categories and weights (sum to 100) for customer firms evaluating suppliers that have a *strong* desire to enter into a partnership. These include financial strength, strategy, and experience (5), management commitment to excellence (10), design/technology strength (10), quality capability (15), cost competitiveness (10), service flexibility (5), manufacturing skills (10), cycle time concentration

(15), partnership extension to subsuppliers (10), and employee participative climate (10). In his system, potential supplier partners are rated on a 1 to 10 scale for their perceived performance on these criteria. The products of the weights multiplied by the ratings are summed to develop a total score, Bhote, *op. cit.*

22. See Richard G. Newman, "Single Source Qualification," *Journal of Purchasing and Materials Management,* 24 (Summer 1988), 10–17, for recommendations to customers on how to evaluate potential single sources.

23. Note that the Baldrige Award places great importance on managing and developing customer relationships. See Robert Landeros and Robert M. Monczka, "Cooperative Buyer/Seller Relationships and a Firm's Competitive Posture," *Journal of Purchasing and Materials Management,* 25 (Fall 1989), 9–18 for an insightful early paper on cooperative buyer-seller relationships.

From unprompted recall in a benchmarking study whose respondents were two hundred suppliers, manufacturers, and retailers that had entered into advanced supplier-customer relationships, A.T. Kearny identified eight major benefits of these relationships: increased sales and share (48%), lower costs (42%), reduced inventory (24%), special treatment/loyalty (20%), higher in-stock positions (18%), learning/testing new approaches (17%), smoothed demand, better planning/scheduling (17%), and closer relationships, better communications (14%).

24. In some cases, for example, Nissan, the company's desire to control its supplier base leads to purchase of equity stakes in suppliers.

25. There may also be potential legal issues in partnership relations. See Silverio Ostrowski and Tony Millman, "Are Buyer/Seller Partnerships Becoming Anti-Competitive," paper presented at the Seventh Annual International Purchasing and Supply Education and Research (IPSERA) Conference, London, April 1998.

26. See A. Akacum and B. G. Dale, "Supplier Partnering: Case Study Experiences," *International Journal of Purchasing and Materials Management* 31 (Winter 1995), 38–44.

27. For a series of viewpoints on trust in key account management, see Roger Dow, Lisa Napolitano, and Mike Pusateri, *The Trust Imperative: The Competitive Advantage of Trust-Based Business Relationships,* Chicago: NAMA, 1998. See, also, Robert M. Morgan and Shelby D. Hunt, "The Commitment-Trust Theory of Relationship Marketing, *Journal of Marketing,* 58 (July 1994), 20–38, and Jordan D. Lewis, *Trusted Partners: How Companies Build Mutual Trust and Win Together,* New York: The Free Press, 1999.

An interesting approach to trust from Trusted Advisor Associates, Morristown, NJ, holds that:

$$T = \frac{C + R + I}{S}$$

where, T = trust

    C = credibility (words)—"I can trust what he says about . . ."

    R = reliability (actions)—"I can trust him to . . ."

    I = intimacy (emotional security)—"I can trust him with . . ."

    S = self-orientation (motives, focus): low—"I can trust that he cares about (not self) . . ."

28. In a recent study, Desireé Blankenburg Holm, Kent Eriksson, and Jan Johanson, "Creating Value Through Mutual Commitment to Business Network Relationships," *Strategic*

Management Journal, 20 (1999), 467–486, the authors show that value creation in supplier/customer partnerships is strongly related to mutual dependence. Mutual dependence is driven by mutual commitment which, in turn, is based on the extent to which the business between supplier and customer is affected by other suppliers and customers of either party.

29. Material for this section is drawn, in part, from Robert M. Monczka and Jim Morgan, "Strategic Alliances Carry Supplier Relationships Beyond Good Partnerships," *Purchasing,* (August 18, 1994), 58–62, and a presentation delivered to a NAMA audience by Raymond C. Howick, Director Corporate Purchasing and Logistics, Sara Lee Corporation, May 15, 1991.

30. Companies are now using powerful software and the Internet to secure these sorts of products at much reduced prices. For example, at the Honeywell Mall web site, authorized users can find and order everything from office supplies to temporary personnel from on-line catalogs at prenegotiated prices, twenty-four, seven.

31. Writers in the quality literature generally believe that annual contracts lead to mutual suspicion and lack of cooperation. See, for example, J. M. Juran, *Quality Control Handbook,* New York: McGraw-Hill, 1988.

32. Frequently, supplier firms offer various types of service along with their products. Medium-sized customers often benefit from these services whereas large companies have this expertise in house. By offering a single bundled price, large customers pay more than they need; hence unbundling service is often a straightforward way to accede to large customers' price requests.

33. The ROI framework presented in Chapter 5 is a useful starting point for identifying potential value that may be delivered to customers.

34. Examples of this type of strategy are legion. Recent examples include the *"intel inside"* campaign by Intel, *NutraSweet*'s brand presence on diet soft drink packages, and the DuPont *Stainmaster* carpet.

35. Akacum and Dale, *op. cit.* identified several situations in which partnering arrangements were prevalent (parentheses added to show conformance to the portfolio framework). These included high-purchase-volume materials and components *(leverage),* products strategically important to the business *(strategic),* and materials for which no previous supplier had been able to meet the requirements *(strategic, bottleneck).* In addition, they identified specialized products requiring information and training for effective use and services requiring a better understanding of the process to facilitate cost reductions.

36. Research suggests that formal joint ventures have a considerable failure rate.

37. Of course, successful conglomerates still remain—notably General Electric, Tyco, and Virgin. See, also, "Premium Conglomerates," *The Boston Consulting Group,* 1997. In recent years, several previously successful conglomerates such as the Korean *chaebol* and the Japanese *keiretsu* have achieved less than stellar performance.

38. For some organizations, this approach means that the majority of operations are outsourced. For example, Benetton achieves high flexibility and low costs by outsourcing virtually all operations except purchasing, dyeing, and cutting. J. Carlos Jarillo and Howard H. Stevenson, "Cooperative Strategies: The Payoffs and Pitfalls, *Long Range Planning* (February 1991), 64–70.

39. This model was developed following detailed analysis of partnerships involving such or-

ganizations as 3M, AT&T, Allied Signal, CSX, Coca-Cola, Goodyear, McDonalds, Ryder Truck, Texas Instruments, Yellow Freight, UPS, Whirlpool, and Xerox.

For a more detailed description of the model, see Lambert, Emmelhainz, and Gardner, *op. cit.* For an excellent example of an application of the model, see, Paul T. Newbourne, "The Role of Partnerships in Strategic Account Management," *The International Journal of Logistics Management,* 8 (1997), 1–8.

40. Coopers and Lybrand Consulting operates a partnership development model based on eight items. We note the items and attributes of its high-performance partnerships:

1. How we treat clients	Long-term value of customers totally embedded in the organization
2. How we behave internally	Client needs paramount, organization irrelevant
3. How we sell/win	Are part of client's business planning process
4. Types of projects/services	The most strategic/impactful projects that the client does
5. How we have impact	Significant impact on client's EVA (economic value added)
6. How we achieve financial results	Long-term, high-profit based on value creation for the client
7. How we are organized	Cross-unit, global account team organization—compensation mostly for team performance
8. What is our image	Part of the client's performance model and best practices resource base

41. Lambert, Emmelhainz, and Gardner, *op. cit.,* p. 4.
42. Lambert, Emmelhainz, and Gardner, *op. cit.,* pp. 4–8.
43. Suppliers seeking partnerships with several different organizations of a single type, for example, distributors, might develop a standard set of drivers and weight the subcategories for importance.
44. Lambert, Emmelhainz, and Gardner, *op. cit.,* p. 7–9.
45. D. M. Lambert, M. A. Emmelhainz, and J. T. Gardner, "Building Successful Logistics Partnerships," *Journal of Business Logistics,* 20 (1999), 165–181, p. 170.
46. Lambert, Emmelhainz, and Gardner, *op. cit.* (see note 3), pp. 10–11.
47. Both supplier and customer should be careful regarding pure "handshake" agreements, as conditions may change. For example, in the late 1990s, Marvin Lumber and Cedar, the world's largest manufacturer of custom windows, was engaged in a bitter legal battle with its former partner, wood preservative manufacturer PPG Industries, over the performance of its PILT product. *The New York Times,* March 28, 1999.
48. For example, BOC places air separation plants on customer sites, and auto-assembly manufacturers are similarly sited within newer automobile plants.
49. Lambert, Emmelhainz, and Gardner, *op. cit.* (note 3), p. 12.
50. Rosabeth Moss Kanter, "Collaborative Advantage," *Harvard Business Review,* 62 (July–August 1994), 96–108, identifies "eight I's that create successful We's" for effective partnerships. These include: *importance* (to both parties), *interdependence* (each party needs the other), *investment* (each party demonstrates tangible signs of long-term commitment), *information* (extensive information sharing), *integration* (linkages developed so the partnership runs smoothly), *institutionalization* (relationship is formal and extends

beyond the people that created it), and *integrity* (the partners behave toward each other in honorable ways that enhance mutual trust).

Another approach considers seven Cs: *commitment* of the parties to succeed, *comfort* resulting from mutual confidence, *competence* in resources and solutions, *creation* of alignment and value for both parties, *capability* to deliver on agreements, *compliance* with regulatory issues and standards and *commerciality* from satisfying business goals—attributed to Jim Neffgen, Global Marine, Watkins *op cit.*

Several of these elements have been included in a three-phase model developed in the context of entrepreneurial organizations. Phase 1, *preconditions,* includes personal reputations, prior relations, and firm reputations leading to reduced uncertainty, expectations and obligations, and enhanced early cooperation. Phase 2, *conditions to build,* comprises a trial period where one firm is the initiator and mutual economic advantage is secured in which rules and procedures are put in place, clear expectations set, and reciprocity and trust developed. Phase 3, *integration and control,* comprises operational integration, strategic integration, and social control. Andrea Larson, "Network Dyads in Entrepreneurial Settings: A Study of the Governance of Exchange Relationships," *Administrative Science Quarterly,* 37 (1992), 76–104.

51. For an interesting empirical study on collaboration processes in buyer-seller relationships, see Sandy D. Jap, "Pie-Expansion Efforts: Collaboration Processes in Buyer-Supplier Relationships," *Journal of Marketing of Research,* 36 (November 1999), 461–475. Interestingly, goal congruence and interpersonal trust had nonsignificant effects on idiosyncratic investments in the buyer-seller relationship. Jap explains this finding in terms of a stage theory of interorganizational relationships such that these factors may be more important at early stages, but are less effective over time.

52. In essence, total quality management has migrated from manufacturing through product development and distribution to procurement, management practice, and marketing.

53. The Xerox Partnership Development Process has three generic goals: continuously remove defects from the relationship; reduce costs of nonconformance of both parties to the relationship; build a set of relationship management processes that meet the specified partnership goals—for example, account management, communications, problem solving. Xerox and other companies with quality strategies believe that business received is highly correlated with the "quality" of the account relationship.

54. For example, in trust-engendering action, Benetton has instituted a policy of purchasing specialized machinery needed by its suppliers to reduce their risk of fashion swings. Jarillo and Stevenson, *op. cit.*

55. A further benefit of the improved efficiency this system provides is a reduction in BOC's costs of inventory. *The New York Times,* April 19, 1999.

56. Some supplier-customer partnership arrangements involve training of partner personnel; others involve membership in supplier and customer advisory boards. For example, Boise Cascade Office Products has set up Customer Quality Councils that meet regularly to identify business improvement opportunities. See also J. Ross, "Why Not a Customer Advisory Board," *Harvard Business Review* 75 (January–February 1997), 12, for a good discussion of customer advisory boards.

57. Watkins, *op. cit.*

58. *Business Week,* October 9, 2000.

CHAPTER TEN

1. Some of the material in this chapter was developed from a best practice study funded by BOC, the British liquefied gases multinational firm.

2. A 1999 Lou Harris poll of CEOs identified *globalization* as the most important major trend followed by *improving knowledge management, cost and cycle time reduction, improving supply chains globally, multiple location manufacturing,* and *managing the use of more part-time, temporary, and contract workers.* Only 18% of respondents believed U.S. companies' competence in dealing with *globalization* was "excellent"; 70% rated it "fair." For an excellent work on globalization, see C. A. Bartlett and S. Ghoshal, *Managing Across Borders: The Transnational Solution,* London: Hutchinson, 1990. See, also, Thomas L. Friedman, *The Lexus and the Olive Tree,* New York: Anchor Books, 2000.

3. The Netherlands-based Nolan Norton Institute believes that many organizations are currently going through several, frequently sequential, developmental phases: downsizing, improving quality, becoming customer oriented, reducing cycle time and thinking global.

4. See George Stalk, Jr. and Thomas M. Hout, *Competing Against Time: How Time-Based Competition Is Reshaping Global Markets,* New York: The Free Press, 1990.

5. In a 1998 study, the authors found that customer demand for global account management had increased in the previous five years and was expected to increase further. U.S. suppliers were more aggressive than non-U.S. firms in implementing global account programs but, although suppliers in general were expecting to strengthen their programs, these tended to lag customer demands. David B. Montgomery, G.S. Yip, and B. Villalonga, "Demand for and Use of Global Account Management," Working Paper, Graduate School of Management, Stanford University, September 1998; see also David B. Montgomery and George S. Yip, "Statistical Evidence on Global Account Management Programs," *Fachzeitschrift für Marketing THEXIS,* 16 (Fall 1999), 10–13. See Kevin Wilson and Simon Croom, "Defining Global Account Attractiveness," *Velocity,* 1 (Spring 1999), 25 *et seq.* for results of a descriptive study on global account management, followed up in Simon Croom, Kevin Wilson, Tony Millman, Christoph Senn, and Dan Weilbaker, "How to Meet the Challenge of Managing Global Customers, *Velocity,* 1 (Fall 1999), 33–34, 44–46.

6. In David Arnold, Julian Birkinshaw, and Omar Toulan, "Implementing Global Account Management in Multinational Corporations," *Fachzeitschrift für Marketing THEXIS,* 16 (Fall 1999), 10–17, the authors point out that whereas, in general, multinational firms have responded to increased globalization by seeking scale economies in such functions as R&D, production, and financing, until recently, customer management has largely remained a local issue.

7. Of course, because global account management is in its infancy, over time we can expect a shift in the best practice envelope. Since 1998, the seven major firms of "The Global Forum"—ABB, Cable and Wireless, Dun and Bradstreet, IBM, Reuters, Xerox, and Young & Rubicam—have been meeting every sixty to ninety days to capture, share, and implement best practice in global account management. The Columbia Initiative in Global Account Management—3M, Citibank, Deloitte & Touche, Hewlett Packard, Lucent Technologies, Milliken and Company, Saatchi & Saatchi, and Square D/Schneider—has a similar agenda and meets with a similar frequency.

8. For an early paper on global account management, see George S. Yip and Tammy L. Madsen, "Global Account Management: The New Frontier in Relationship Marketing," *International Marketing Review,* 13 (1996), 24–42. For a series of strategic questions for firms with global account management programs, see Tony Millman, "From National Account Management to Global Account Management in Business-to-Business Markets," *Fachzeitschrift für Marketing THEXIS,* 16 (Fall 1999), 1–13. For a recent study of global account management practices, see Kevin Wilson, Simon Croom, Tony Millman, and Dan C. Weilbaker, "The SRT-SAMA Global Account Management Study," *The Journal of Selling and Major Account Management,* 2 (Spring 2000), 63–84. See also Kevin Wilson, Tony Millman, Dan Weilbacker, and Simon Croom, *Harnessing Global Potential,* Chicago, IL: SAMA, 2001.

9. Such variable pricing practices are the proximate cause of "gray markets." Interestingly, the ability of firms to price differently in separate European countries has been significantly reduced by the January 1999 introduction of the "euro," and the gradual phase-out of national currencies.

10. Sandy Flemming, "Global Procurement—A Universal Trend and How Canon Succeeds," *Fachzeitschrift für Marketing THEXIS,* 16 (Fall 1999), 42–43.

11. Such pressure from multinational consumer goods companies led advertising agencies to be early adopters of global account management programs. See, for example, Douglas M. Sanford Jr. and Lynda Maddox, "Advertising Agency Management of Domestic and International Accounts," *International Marketing Review,* 16 (1999), 504–517.

12. See "Basic/Black Zale Youngman Advertising Inc.," in Noel Capon and Wilfried Van Honacker, *The Asian Marketing Case Book,* Singapore: Prentice Hall, 1999, pp. 629–637, for an interesting example of these pressures in an advertising agency in the Philippines.

13. This situation is exemplified in the case of steel container manufacturer, Van Leer, in dealing with Total, the French oil and gas producer. The Total UK subsidiary was content with its local supplier and strongly resisted pressure from corporate procurement for Europe-wide purchasing. "Van Leer Packaging Worldwide: The Total Account, A, B, C, D, E," 598-(018-022)-1, Fontainebleau, France: *INSEAD,* 1996.

14. See the Manflex and Cadstar case studies in Tony Millman, "Global Key Account Management and Systems Selling," *International Business Review,* 5 (1996), 631–645.

15. Howard Katzen, presentation to NAMA's Global and National Account Management Seminar, Scottsdale, AZ, May 5–8, 1996.

16. Anton Fritschi, "Global Key Account Management at ABB: Success Knows No (Country) Limits," *Fachzeitschrift für Marketing THEXIS,* 16 (Fall 1999), 26–29, original in German.

17. This may be a particular issue in those older multinational organizations in which country managers have long enjoyed significant autonomy. See Bartlett and Ghosal, *op. cit.*

18. Tammy Masden and George Yip, "Hewlett Packard: Global Account Management, A, B," Los Angeles: Graduate School of Management, UCLA, 1994.

19. Dave Oulighan, Vice President, Dun & Bradstreet, presentation to SAMA Annual Conference, Orlando, FL: May 2–5, 1999.

20. For one high-technology firm that is a major proponent of global account management, the fully loaded cost of a global account manager exceeds $500,000 p.a.

21. Because of the United States' global political role, global key account management may mean something different for U.S. customers than for companies domiciled in other

countries. Thus, since the United States currently operates an embargo on Iraq, some European companies believe that similar restrictions might, in the future, be implemented in other countries. As a result, non-U.S. key accounts whose strategies involve sales to these countries may insist on strong non-U.S. suppliers to enable them to conduct commerce in these countries.

22. For the view of one CEO on the appropriate role to play in global account management, see Editorial Staff, "The Formula for Global Account Management Success: The CEO must champion strategic accounts to build a firm's global business," 1 (Summer 1999), *Velocity,* 14–17.

23. Croom, Wilson, Millman, Senn, and Weilbaker, *op. cit.*

24. For major global accounts, the GAM position is a full-time job; however, a GAM might handle two or three smaller and less complex global accounts.

25. In addition to cultural diversity issues *per se,* understanding differences in national governance systems (e.g., legal systems, tax codes) is very important. For papers that address cultural issues in key account management, see Tony Millman and Kevin Wilson, "Global Account Management: Reconciling Organizational Complexity and Cultural Diversity," paper presented at the 14th Annual Industrial Marketing and Purchasing (IMP) Conference, Turku School of Economics and Business Administration, Finland, September 1998, and Tony Millman, "How Well Does the Concept of Global Account Management Travel Across Cultures?" *The Journal of Selling and Major Account Management,* 2 (Winter 2000), 31–46.

26. "The Power of Intercultural Communication & Teamwork: How a $70 Billion Company Instituted Change to Become More Customer-centric," *Velocity,* 1 (Summer 1999), 19–21.

27. A Conference Board report (1996) identified several principal barriers to global teamwork (not specifically global account teamwork): geographic distances/time zones, differences in culture and language skills, organizational structure, appropriateness of team assignment, necessity of face-to-face meetings, oversight of team process, competing objectives or priorities.

28. The global firm may also operate global product divisions; frequently these are matrixed with a geographic structure. See Noel Capon, John U. Farley, and James Hulbert, *Corporate Strategic Planning,* New York: Columbia University Press, 1988. For simplicity, we base our discussion on the geographic organization.

29. In principle, the GAM's problem of cutting across the geographic organization is similar to the NAM dealing with a geographically organized sales force. However, it is significantly more complicated internationally in part because regional geographic heads frequently control other functions in addition to sales, and also have profit and loss responsibility.

30. Arnold, Birkinshaw, and Toulan propose an information processing approach to study the relationship between global account management and national sales organizations. David Arnold, Julian Birkinshaw, and Omar Toulan, "The Relationship Between Global Account Management and National Sales Organizations," proposal to the Marketing Science Institute, Cambridge, MA, July 1998.

31. Of course, if a major multinational firm is located in a small country, sales responsibility for the global account manager may be greater than for his/her country manager!

32. Masden and Yip, *op. cit.* (note 18). When first introduced, reaction to the HAM program

within HP was mixed. After a couple of years, 57% of GAMs funded half a HAM, 31% funded a full HAM.

33. Because of the humor associated with the term HAM, these positions were later renamed account program managers (APMs).

34. For more insight on this "intermediate" level of account management, see Christoph Senn, "Operating Globally: Not Without the Regional and Local Level," *Velocity*, 2 (1st Quarter 2000), 6–8, 43, and Tony Millman, "Regional Account Manager (Europe): Interesting Job Title, but What Does It Mean?," *Velocity*, 2 (1st Quarter 2000), 33–36.

35. The package delivery firm DHL operates a similar regional account manager structure. Edmund Bradford and Francis Rome, "Applying Total Customer Management at DHL: How One Leading Company Has Proved the Payoff," *The Journal of Selling and Major Account Management*, 2 (Autumn 1999), 117–123. At Cisco Systems, the role of regionally based Gateway Global Account Managers (GGAMs) is to ease the communications between individual global account managers and locally based national account managers responsible for their global accounts. Global account managers are also supported by global systems engineers (GSEs) and global service managers (GSMs), Jay Parr, *op. cit.*

36. Difficulties sometimes arise when sales occur in one geography, yet the product is delivered and used in another.

37. This is also an issue when matrixed product divisions are involved.

38. The Fritz Companies, San Francisco–based specialists in global transportation logistics, use this system.

39. *Business Week*, January 23, 1995.

40. Fritschi, *op. cit.*

41. Of course, such a market-based organization may still be matrixed with a product-division organization.

42. This type of organization is a global version of the self-contained key account unit discussed in Chapter 3.

43. "Packaging Worldwide," Van Leer, *op. cit.*

44. For one company's experience in merging different approaches to global account management resulting from a joint venture, specifically Concert, formed by British Telecom and AT&T, see Peter Naude and Donald McLean, "Watching the Concert: How Global Account Management Developed within the Concert Alliance," *The Journal of Selling and Major Account Management*, 2 (Autumn 1999), 13–30.

45. In a similar fashion, the function of corporate strategic planning is to provide value-added over a set of lower level (e.g., division or business unit) strategic plans, see Capon, Farley, and Hulbert, *op. cit.*

46. As one example of global information flow, in mid-1998, Hewlett-Packard's external web site comprised 90,000 pages, over 130 content areas, 25 country web sites, 3.5 million hits per day, growing at 20%–30% per month.

47. Video conferencing may also prove to be a useful communication device.

48. Hewlett-Packard's global teams schedule monthly conference calls with a five-topic agenda: business opportunities (state of the sales funnel, "must win" deal review, new deals), sales calls (new contacts, executive contacts), partner activities, account management (account reviews, relationship assessment, electronic solutions, solutions opportunities workshop, seminars and mailings), and teamwork (including other HP organizations).

49. Mike Cohn, Manager Global Sales Programs, Hewlett-Packard, presentation to SAMA Annual Conference, Orlando, FL, May 2–5, 1999.
50. Financial services firms also need a system to identify global risk.
51. A well-developed information system should be linked to the Internet so that global account managers have the ability to tap into various third-party databases that may provide valuable account information for planning and monitoring purposes. It should also be linked to customer information systems for disseminating, interacting, and workflow purposes.
52. Howard Katzen from Xerox opined: "It is the single most difficult thing I have done in my career . . . to break through the information management quagmire and establish a way in which we can count the business we're doing," *op. cit.*
53. For research on global account management competencies, see Tony Millman and Kevin Wilson, "Developing Global Account Management Competencies," paper presented at the 15th Annual Industrial Marketing and Purchasing (IMP) Conference, Graduate School of Business, University College Dublin, Republic of Ireland, September 1999. For global managerial competencies more generally see, for example, N. J. Adler and S. Bartholomew, "Managing Globally Competent People," *Academy of Management Executive,* 6 (1992), 52–65 and C. A. Bartlett and S. Ghoshal, "What Is a Global Manager," *Harvard Business Review,* 70 (September–October 1992), 124–132.
54. *Strategic Account Management Innovation Study,* S4 Consulting and SAMA, 1998.
55. David Townshend, VP Alliance Accounts, Marriott Lodging at Strategic Account Management Annual Conference, Orlando, FL, May 2–5, 1999.
56. Ensuring that GAMs understand cultural taboos is a particularly important matter. See, for example, Roger E. Axtell, *Do's and Taboos around the World,* 3rd edition, New York: Wiley, 1993.
57. Oulighan, *op. cit.*
58. Bradford and Rome, *op. cit.*
59. In a seven-supplier firm study, dominated by Swedish organizations, supplier firm performance was positively impacted by several variables. In this study, performance was a composite made up of variable sales growth, better coordination, greater responsiveness, and relationship development. The impacting variables were GAM tenure, high commitment to the global account management program throughout the firm and greater commitment to such internal support systems as global sales monitoring, global customer profitability systems, appointment of executive partners, and for GAMs—internal forums, specific evaluation and reward systems, and career development tracks. Julian Birkinshaw, Omar Toulan, and David Arnold, Working Paper, Stockholm School of Economics, 1999.
60. Dan C. Weilbaker, "Compensation Issues for Global Account Management," *The Journal of Selling and Major Account Management* 2 (Autumn 1999), 88–95.
61. In a study based on global account relationships between six European and U.S. firms and their accounts, Senn identified a variety of strategic (S), operational (O), and tactical (T) variables that were positively related to high levels of customer satisfaction. Variables related to *defining goals and objectives with global customers* were: systematic business partner analysis and selection (S), individual global customer strategy (S), systematic customer needs analysis (O), worldwide product and service consistency (O), and well-trained (T) and experienced global account mangers (T). Variables related to

aligning business processes with global customers were: good personal relationships with key decision makers (S), systematic contact management (S), partnership based on core competencies (O), clear hierarchical structure (O), cross-functional teamwork (T), and conditions for professional teamwork (T). Variables related to *safeguarding know-how and speeding the learning process* were: joint learning events (S), independent supervision and learning transfer (S), and quantitative (T) and qualitative customer performance measures (T). Christoph Senn, "Implementing Global Account Management: A Process Oriented Approach," *The Journal of Personnel Selling and Major Account Management,* 1 (February 1999), 10–19 and Christoph Senn and Martin P. Arnold, "Managing Global Customers—Benchmarks from an International Research Project," *Fachzeitschrift für Marketing THEXIS,* 16 (Fall 1999), 36–40.

62. Volker Kulessa, Christian Frank, and Rolf Stangl, "International Key Account Management in Investment Goods Industry—Example IBM," *Fachzeitschrift für Marketing THEXIS,* 16 (Fall 1999), 18–25, original in German.

63. The Global Forum (note 7) has identified several best practices in global account management—get an executive champion, measure customer satisfaction and act on the findings, GAM training, make account planning a priority, establish consistent, rational pricing and contracts all over the world, set up incentives that reward global selling, and consistent communication, internally and externally, *Velocity,* 1 (Fall 1999), 15–19.

APPENDIX 2.1

1. My thanks to Tony R. Coalson of Murata Erie North America for his kind cooperation in developing this profile.

2. Developed in part from a presentation at the 1993 NAMA Annual Marketing Conference and based in part on research by S4 Consulting.

3. Developed from "National Account Program," Freddie Mac, mimeo, undated.

4. Although, technically, mortgage originators "supply" mortgages to FM, they are treated as customers for FM's services.

5. Developed from C. Pardo, R. Salle, and R. Spencer, "The Process of Key Accountization of the Firm: A Case Study," *Industrial Marketing Management,* 22 (1995), 123–134.

APPENDIX 3.1

1. This system produced the ubiquitous "Post-it" notes product.

APPENDIX 5.1

1. This example and steps for conducting conjoint analysis is taken from Chapter 14 in Donald R. Lehmann, Sunil Gupta, and Joel H. Steckel, *Marketing Research,* New York: Addison Wesley, 1997, pp. 541–545, used with permission.

APPENDIX 6.1

1. For issues in key account profitability analysis, see Tony Millman and Mike Lewis, "Observations on the Marketing/Accounting Interface in Key Account Management," *Journal of Selling and Major Account Management,* 1 (October 1998), 10–21.

2. This illustration employs a simple version of ABC. For in depth discussion of ABC methods, see Charles T. Horngren, George Foster, and Srikant M. Datar, *Cost Accounting,* Upper Saddle River, NJ: Prentice Hall, 1997, Chapters 4 and 5.

3. For example, perhaps product batches are made more frequently for Accounts II and III; perhaps these accounts also order different versions of particular products that require greater processing.

APPENDIX 8.1

1. Prepared by Steven W. Lewis, Vice President, Development II, Inc., Woodbury, CT. These data are typically collected on 5-point or 7-point scales.

APPENDIX 9.1

1. Source: Douglas M. Lambert, Margaret A. Emmelhainz, and John T. Gardner, "Developing and Implementing Supply Chain Partnerships," *The International Journal of Logistics Management,* 7 (1996), 1–17.

APPENDIX 9.2

1. Source: Douglas M. Lambert, Margaret A. Emmelhainz, and John T. Gardner, "Developing and Implementing Supply Chain Partnerships." *The International Journal of Logistics Management,* 7 (1996), 9.

APPENDIX 9.3

1. A. Akacum and B. G. Dale, "Supply Partnering: Case Study Experiences," *International Journal of Purchasing and Materials Management,* 31 (Winter 1995), 38–44.
2. Excerpted from Mary Walton, *Drama of the American Workplace,* New York: Norton, 1997.

APPENDIX 10.1

1. For an example of the development of an individual supplier/customer global account management relationship, see Olivier Epinette, Gerard Petit and Pierre Vialle, "The Role of Interaction with Key Accounts in Organizational Learning: The Global One/Hewlett-Packard Case," *The Journal of Selling and Major Account Management,* 2 (Autumn 1999), 64–87.
2. *Xerox Corporation: The Customer Satisfaction Program,* 9-591-055, Boston, MA: Harvard Business School, 1991.
3. Managing a global account management system is a particularly difficult challenge for Xerox inasmuch as in many parts of the world Xerox operates, not as a wholly owned entity, but as joint ventures, for example, Fuji Xerox.
4. Xerox's term for executive partner.

INDEX

Abbott Laboratories Inc., 29, 88, 121
ABN AMRO, 84
Accessibility, 163
Account concentration, increasing, 9–10
Account profitability, 227–228
Account tiers, 58–59, 210
Achievement, annual review of, 262–264
Acquisition potential, 53
Action programs, 235–240
  analysis of, 152
  implementation of, 97–98
  interpersonal relationship-building,
    239–240
  modification of, 275–276
  strategic, 235–239
Action steps, 235–238
Activating forces, 239
Activity-based costing (ABC) systems, 52,
    394–395
Administration, 240
Air Products and Chemicals Inc., 163
Alexander Group, 131
Allied-Signal Inc., 300
Alpha Graphics Inc., 26

American Electric Power Company, 52
American Express Company, 159
American Honda Motor Company Inc., 283
Amiable social style, 111–113
Ammitari Puris Lintas, 29
Analytical social style, 111–113
Annual review of achievement, 262–264
Appleton Papers Inc., 384–386
Applications engineering, 242
Armstrong, C. Michael, 92
Armstrong World Industries, 49
Asea Brown Boveri Group, 87, 314, 329
Asset/cost efficiencies, 295
Association of South East Asian Nations
    (ASEAN), 7, 309
AT&T Company, 3
Authority, unclear, 31–32

Backward simulation, 127–128
Bain Consulting, 266
"Balanced scorecard" approach, 125
Behaviors that "bother" and "impress"
    buyers, 166–167
Benchmarking, 93

Best practices, 93–94, 254
Betz and Dearborne, 80, 133, 319
BOC, 156, 222, 305, 323
Boeing Company, 16, 243
Boise Cascade Office Products Corporation,
    52, 88, 121, 161, 236
Bonuses, 129
Boston Consulting Group, 158
Bottleneck products, 289–293
Boundary spanning skills, 108–109
Breadth of commitment, 39–41
Bridgestone/Firestone Inc., 307
British Aerospace Regional Aircraft
    (BARA), 24–25
British Rover, 287
Brown, Ron, 243
Buckman Laboratories International Inc.,
    266
Budgets, 245
Business management skills, 107–108
Business portfolio analysis, 151
Business relationships, 206–209
Business Week, 14–15
Buyer-driven (reverse) auctions, 14–15
Buying analysis, 171–187
    decision-making players, 176–181
    nature of the purchase, 185–187
    procurement process, 172–176
    purchase methods, 184
    sharing business, 184–185
    supplier rating programs, 182–184
Buying influences chart, 181, 182

Canon Inc., 312
Capabilities, competitor, 195
Capital, 247
Carlzon, Jan, 99
Caterpillar Inc., 173
Centralization in procurement, 12–13
Channel member-based organization, 6
Chase Manhattan Bank, 46–47, 329
Chat rooms, 268

Chrysler Corporation, 153, 161
Ciena Corporation, 3
Cisco Systems Inc., 43
Citibank, 44–45, 79, 99
Citigroup, 79
Clariant Corporation, 169
Clinton, Bill, 243
Closeness of relationship, degree of, 47–50,
    210
Coca-Cola Company, 31, 296
Coherence with firm strategy, 54
Collaborative networks, 266
Commissions, 129
Commitment to key accounts:
    analysis of, 39–43
    examples of evolution of, 382–388
    key account director and, 88–90
    organizational decisions based on,
        71–75
    by top management, 82, 319–320
Communications, 165
Compensation. *See* Financial compensation
Compensation caps, 130
Compensatory approach to key account
    selection, 56
Competence of supplier firm personnel,
    166
Competition, increased, 7–8
Competitive advantage, 300
Competitive structure analysis, 149,
    191–194
Competitive threat, 215
Competitor analysis, 149, 190–200
Competitor analysis matrix, 196–198
Competitor's products, displacement of,
    227–229
Competitor targets, 232–233
Complementary product suppliers, 45–46
Components, 295, 298–300
Conflict:
    global account management and, 320
    internal, resolution of, 253–254

key account director and, 94
top management and, 84
Conglomerates, 294
Congruence model, 33–35
Conjoint analysis, 169, 392–393
Contact density, 256–257
Content-driven web sites, 266–267
Contract management for global accounts, 335
Contract style, 298, 300
Control, 242
Core competencies, 294
Corporate account management, 77–79
Corporate actions, 143
Corporate compatibility, 296
Costco, 159
Cost reduction, 159–161
Costs of goods sold, 394–398
Credit for key account sales, 130–131
CSX Corporation, 300
Cultural fit, 54
Current business, maintaining and expanding, 215–217, 226–229
Current direct competitors, 191, 192
Current indirect competitors, 191, 193
Current profits, 51–52
Current sales revenue, 51
Current Technological Possibilities (CTP), 147, 148
Customer advisory board, 92–93
Customer analysis, 149–150
Customer complaints, 260
Customer feedback, 270–274
Customer indicators, 270
Customers:
  calculating the cost of serving, 381
  key accounts, See Key accounts
  large, 18–20
  pressures on traditional sales forces from, 9–18
  small, 20–22

Customer satisfaction, 270–274
  customer loyalty and, 204–205
  open-ended personal interviews, 273–274
  relationships to, 205
  surveys, 271–273, 400–401
Customer service improvements, 296
Customer value, delivering. See Key account needs
Customs Research Inc., 41

DaimlerChrysler, 51, 307
Dayton Hudson Corporation, 170
Debrief, 258–259
DEC (Digital Equipment Corporation), 16
Decision-making players, 176–181
Deere & Company, 79
Degree of closeness of relationship, 47–50
Delco, 11
Dell Computer Corporation, 13, 267
Denko company, 158
Depth of commitment, 40–41
Design, 242
Detractors, 178
Development, 242
Developmental key account analysis, 66–68
DHL International Ltd., 43, 58, 340
Direct customers, 45
"Double credit" system, 130–131
Dow Chemical Company, 163, 406–407
Drivers, 295–297, 402–403
Driving social style, 111–113
Dun & Bradstreet Inc., 317, 339

Eastman Kodak Company, 314
Ebbers, Bernard C., 207
Economic values, 156
80/20 rule, 18
Electronic commerce, 8
E-mail, 265
Emerson-Swan Inc., 162
Environmental analysis, 148–149
European Union (EU), 7, 309

Exclusivity, 296

Executive partner program, 90–92

Exercises, 345–379
Analysis of Competition, 359–363
Analysis of the Key Account, 346–358
Analysis of the Supplier Firm, 364–367
Developing Key Account Strategy,
372–378
Information Requirements for Improved
Key Account Plans, 379
Opportunities and Threats, 369–371
Planning Assumptions, 368

Expectations, meeting or exceeding, 168

Expressive social style, 111–113

External analysis, 146–150

External candidates, 118

Extranets, 266

Facilitators, 295–297, 404–405

Fallon McElligot Inc., 199

FedEx Corporation, 268, 284

Field and technical service, 240

Finance, 242

Financial compensation:
global account managers, 341–342
key account managers, 126–131

Financial performance, 300

Financial performance data, 143

Financial security, 53

Financing costs, 228

Firewall protections, 80

Firm behavior, assessment of, 210–211

FMC Corporation, 252

Force-field analysis, 239

Ford Motor Company, 11, 16, 46, 307,
408–409

Forecasts, 245

Forward simulation, 127, 128

Foundation knowledge, 265

Freddie Mac, 386–387

Fred Meyer Inc., 10

Fritz Companies, The, 93

Fujitsu Ltd., 284

Functional values, 156

Future prospects data, 143

Future sales volume and profit, 52–53

Future Technological Possibilities (FTP),
147, 148

Gatekeepers, 178

General Electric Company, 150

General Motors Corporation, 3, 11, 16, 46,
243

Geographic organization of sales force, 6

Global account management, 308–343
corporate organization and, 323–331
global account managers, 321–322,
336–342
initiating a program, 311–315
planning, 332–335
roles and responsibilities in, 319–323
strategy, 315–318
at Xerox Corporation, 412–414

Global account managers, 321–322,
336–342

Global account plan, 333

Global account steering committee, 320

Global account teams, 321–323

Global procurement, 13

Goodyear Tire and Rubber Company, 300

Gore, Albert, 243

Grace, Patrick, 15

Greenhill, Robert, 187

Grubman, Jack, 207

Headquarters account managers (HAMs),
325

Henkel Worldwide, 178

Hewlett-Packard Company, 59, 91, 92,
273–274, 316, 325, 334

High breadth/high depth commitment,
41–42, 74–75

High breadth/low depth commitment, 40,
72–73

High-priority objectives, 236
Historical performance, 201–204
Historic data, 165
Holland Hitch Company, 160–161
Honeywell Inc., 103
Hoover Company, 406–407
Human resources:
  benefits of key account programs, 26
  defined, 34
  key account director and, 86
  key account manager and, 95
  top management provision of, 83

IBM Corporation, 11, 12, 14–16, 59, 92, 93,
    99, 254–255, 260, 313, 322, 329, 339,
    342
ICICI, 55, 78
IKEA Systems, 172
Implementation control, 274–275
Incentive pay, 129–130
Indirect customers, 45
Information providers, 178
Information sources:
  for competitor analysis, 200
  for key account analysis, 187–188
Information systems, 240
  global account planning and, 333–334
  interorganizational relationship and,
    252–253
Infosys Technologies Ltd., 55
Inspiration-related currencies, 114, 115
Intangible personal rewards, 133
Interface simplification, 14
Interfacing with key account, 256–264
Intermediate objectives, 237
Internal analysis, 150–154
Internal candidates, 117–118
Internal divisions or business units, 46–47
Internal relationship phases, 42–43
Internet, 8, 20, 108, 265–269
Internet-enabled exchanges, 14–15
Interpersonal communication, 4

Interpersonal relationships, 206–209
Interrelationship-building action programs,
    239–241
Interviews, open-ended, 273–274
Intranets, 265, 266
Investment, reduction in, 161–162

Job assignments, extra, 132
Job modification, 132–133
John Bright company, 179
Johnson & Johnson, 12, 173
Joint operating controls, 298, 299
Joint planning, 298, 299

Katzen, Howard, 314
Kearney, A. T., 16
Kellog Company, 16
Key account analysis:
  buying analysis. See Buying analysis
  information sources, 187–188
  key account fundamentals, 142–143
  key account needs. See Key account
    needs
  purpose of, 141
  strategic. See Strategic key analysis
Key account attractiveness/account
    vulnerability portfolio, 64–67
Key account attractiveness/business
    strengths portfolio, 61–64
Key account competence analysis, 153–154
Key account complexity, 75, 76, 94–95
Key account culture:
  key account director and, 88–90
  top management and, 83–84
Key account director, 85–94, 242
Key account fundamentals, 142–143
Key account management:
  congruence model for, 33–35
  emerging system of, 18–22
  human resources. See Human resources;
    Key account managers
  organization, See Organization

Key account management (*cont.*)
　strategy. *See* Strategy
　systems and processes. *See* Systems and
　　processes
Key account management programs, 22–33
　benefits for key accounts, 27–29
　benefits for supplier firms, 23–26
　cautions, 29–32
　factors in securing commitment to, 33
Key account managers, 106–134
　complexity of job, 96
　localized, formalizing, 73
　matrixed, 74, 76
　objectives for, developed by major U.S.
　　manufacturer, 391
　recruitment and selection, 117–119
　retaining, 122–124
　reward system, 124–133
　role of, 94–104
　in self-contained key account unit, 74–76
　skill sets, 107–116
　training, 120–122
Key account needs, 155–171
　addressing, 168–171
　business relationship assessment and,
　　206, 207
　depth of value, 167–168
　meta-level relationship needs, 162–167
　return-on-investment (ROI) equation,
　　157–162
　securing data on, 392–393
　type of customer value, 156–157
Key account plan, 138–140
　aggregation issues across individual,
　　247–248
　communicating, 246
　control of. *See* Performance monitoring
　internal consistency in, 245–246
　key account strategy. *See* Key account
　　strategy
　ongoing internal commitment to, 252
　opportunities and threats, 214–218

　outline for, 399
　planning assumptions, 213–214
　situation analysis. *See* Situation analysis
Key account profitability analysis, 394–398
Key account relationship types, 45–47
Key account requirements trends, 215
Key accounts:
　benefits of key account programs for,
　　27–29
　commitment to, 39–43
　current vs. developmental, 66–68
　degree of closeness of supplier-firm
　　relationship, 47–50
　at different levels in the organization,
　　44–45
　as information source, 188
　interfacing with, 256–264
　partnering with. *See* Partnering with key
　　accounts
　relationships among, 79–80
　selecting. *See* Key account selection
Key account selection, 50–61
　criteria, 50–55
　general issues, 58–61
　using the criteria, 56–57
Key account strategy, 140, 221–245
　action programs, 235–240
　agreements on resource commitments,
　　240, 242–244
　budgets and forecasts, 245
　mission, 222–223
　performance objectives, 224–226,
　　228–229
　positioning, 229–235
　strategic focus, 226–229
　vision, 222
Key account team:
　building and management of, 100–102
　focus of, 251–256
　roles of, 101
Key account unit, self-contained, 74–76
Key buying incentive, 233

Key persuasive argument, 233
Key players, understanding, 179–181
Klepper, William, 110
Klepper leadership model, 110–113
Kroger Company, 10

Laidlaw Inc., 43
Large customers, 18–20
Leadership skills, 109–116
Lear Corporation, 408–409
Legal support system, 242
Leo Burnett Company, 199
Leverage products, 289–291, 293
Logistics, 240
Lopez, Jose Ignacio, 13, 15
Low breadth/high depth commitment, 41,
    74–75
Low breadth/low depth commitment,
    40–42, 72
Low-priority objectives, 237
Lucent Technologies Inc., 25, 41, 80

Magna International Inc., 153
Maintenance-new business sales
    organization, 6
Managerial philosophy and techniques, 296
Manufacturing/operations management,
    242
Manulife North America, 158
Market analysis, 147–148
Market and market segment objectives and
    strategies, 247
Marketing advantages, 296
Marketing research, 242
Market-integrated global account
    organization, 328–330
Market segment-based organization, 6
Marriott, J. W., Jr., 338
Marriott Corporation, 89, 320
MasterCard, 285–286
Matrixed key account managers, 74, 76
Matrix organizations, 324–328

McDonald's Corporation, 296
McKinsey and Company, 178
Medium-priority objectives, 237
Meetings, key account team, 254
Merck and Company, 93
Mercosur, 7, 309
Meta-level relationship needs, 162–167
Microsoft Corporation, 93
Milliken and Company, 16, 43, 79, 104,
    174, 175, 265, 324
Mission:
    key account, 144–146, 222–223
    organizational, 294
Mobil Oil Corporation, 125, 284–285, 306
Modified rebuy, 186
Moore Corporation, 58
Morgan Stanley, 187
Moriarty, Rowland, 163
Motorola Inc., 16, 22, 120
Murata Erie North America Inc., 382–384
Mutuality, 296

Nestlé, 16
New business opportunities, 217–219,
    293–294
New buy, 186–187
"New region" approach, 330–331
Noncritical products, 289, 290, 292
Non-key accounts, 59–60
Nonpersonal communication, 4
Nortel Networks Corporation, 242–243
North American Free Trade Area (NAFTA),
    7, 309
Norton Company, 165

Objectives:
    action program, 236–237
    analysis of, 151
    operational, 225–226
    organizational, 4–5
    performance, 224–226, 228–229
    positioning, 230–232

Objectives (*cont.*)
    pre-meeting plan and, 258
    supplier firm, 96–97
Ogilvy and Mather Worldwide, 313
Olin Corporation, 43
Open-ended personal interviews, 273–274
Operating costs, 227–228
Operational objectives, 225–226
Opinion leadership, 55
Opponents, 178
Opportunities, 214–218
    identification of, 214–215
    identifying and managing, 260–261
    partnerships and, 293–294
    protecting and expanding current
       business, 215–217
    securing new business, 217–219,
       293–294
Oracle Corporation, 338
Organization, 70–105
    commitment to key accounts and, 71–75
    defined, 34
    information on, 142–143
    key account director role, 85–94
    key account manager role, 94–104
    locating key account management, 77–80
    managing the transition, 81
    supplier firm and key account complexity
       and, 75–76
    top management role, 82–85
Organizational congruence, 86–87
Organizational currencies, 113–115
Organizational forms for global account
    management, 323–331
Organizational goal alignment, 87
Organizational interrelationships, 53–54
Organizational level, 80, 209–210
Organizational objectives, 4–5
Organizational stress, 287
Organizational unit, 77–80
Other operating costs, 395–398
Outcomes, 295, 298, 300

Outsourcing, 294
Owens Corning Composites, 121–122
Ownership information, 142

Partnering with key accounts, 48–49,
    281–307
    cautions for considering, 287–289
    defined, 281
    development model, 294–301
    development process, 285
    factors in popularity of, 282
    identifying opportunities, 289–294
    initiative from customer firms, 282–
       286
    initiative from supplier firms, 286
    partnership agreement examples,
       406–409
    reasons for failure, 305–307
    requirements for success, 301–305
    world class partnering self-audit,
       410–411
Past performance analysis, 154
PepsiCo, 296
Performance control, 269–274
Performance measurement:
    global account manager, 340–341
    key account manager, 124–126
Performance monitoring, 269–278
    implementation control, 274–275
    performance control, 269–274
    planning process control, 277–278
    strategy control, 275–276
Performance objectives, 224–226, 228–229
Personal interviews, open-ended, 273–274
Personal power, 176, 177
Personal-related currencies, 114, 115
Personnel changes, 257
Pharmacia & Upjohn Company, 125
Philips Electronics, 159, 172
Phonics Inc., 387–388
Photronics Inc., 300
Pipeline analysis, 255

Planning:
key account. *See* Key account plan
pre-meeting, 257–259
Planning process control, 277–278
Portfolio approaches, 61–68
Positional power, 176, 177
Positioning, 229–235
Position-related currencies, 114, 115
Potential direct competitors, 191–193
Potential indirect competitors, 191, 193
Pratt and Whitney, 150
Pre-meeting planning, 257–259
Premier Pages, 13, 267
Present data, 165
Price discrepancies, global, 311–312
Price increases, 159, 227
Price reductions, 159
Problem diagnosis, 93
Problem solving, 168, 259–260
Process outcomes, 300
Procter and Gamble, 14, 31
Procurement:
buying analysis. *See* Buying analysis
global, 312–313
process of, 12–15, 172–176
rising importance of, 10–12
strategies, 282–283
Procurement portfolio framework, 289–294
Product, sales organization specialized by, 6
Product applications, new, 227–229
Product engineering, 242
Product mix, 227
Profit, 20–21
current, 51–52
future, 52–53
Profitability analysis, key account, 394–398
Profit stability/growth, 296
Promises, 163–164
Promon Ltd., 16–17
Promotions, 132

Prophet, 53
Psychological values, 156
Purchase, nature of, 185–187
Purchase decisions, influencing, 230–232
Purchase importance, 289–292
Purchase methods, 184

Quality supplier relationship, 48

Reckit and Coleman, 16
Recognition, 132, 133
Recruitment process:
global account manager, 336–338
key account manager, 117–119
Redeployment, 123
Regional account managers, 325–326
Regional account programs, 309
Relationship assessment, 204–210
Relationship building skills, 108–109
Relationship-driven web sites, 268–269
Relationship-related currencies, 114, 115
Research and development, 247
Resisting forces, 239
Resource allocation. *See* Key account strategy
Resource availability, 211–213
Resource commitments, agreements on, 240, 242–244
Responsibility, unclear, 31–32
Responsiveness, 163
Retaining:
global account managers, 339–340
key account managers, 122–124
Return-on-investment (ROI) equation, 157–162
Review processes, 262–264
Reward system, 124–133
Richard Allan Scientific Inc., 204
Risk and reward sharing, 298, 299
Role relationships, 176–179
Routine information, 165
Ryder Truck, 284

Salary, 129
Sales and Marketing Management, 8
Sales development, 242
Sales force, 4–22
   changing nature of, 18–22
   key account manager and, 102–104
   negative effects of key account
     management systems on, 31–32
   organization of, 5–7
   pressures on, 7–18
Sales force support organizational approach,
   73
Sales revenue:
   current, 51
   future, 52–53
Sales volume, 226–227, 247
Salomon Smith Barney, 79
Schlumberger Ltd., 284–285, 318
Sears Roebuck and Company, 163
Selection process:
   global account manager, 336–338
   key account manager, 117–119
Self-contained key account unit, 74–76
Selling costs, increases in, 8–10
Senior executive responsibility, 73
Senior management, 242
Served Available Market (SAM), 147, 148
Shangai Chlor-Alkali Chemical Company,
   259
Shapiro, Benson, 163
Shared competitors, 296
Shared end users, 297
Shareholder value, 4, 5, 8
Sharing business, 184–185
Shell Chemicals Ltd., 161
Shell Oil Company, 78, 318
Siemens AG, 171, 262, 322
Situation analysis, 139–220
   competitor analysis, 190–200
   identifying information gaps in, 246
   key account analysis. *See* Key account
     analysis

supplier firm analysis. *See* Supplier firm
   analysis
Skill sets:
   global account manager, 336
   key account manager, 107–116
Small customers, 20–22
Snelshire, Richard, 244
Social Styles archetypes, 111–113
SouthCo, 268
Spar company, 54
Specialization, 66
Specifiers, 178
Spoilers, 178
Stallcamp, Thomas, 153
Status analyses, 254–255
Stevenson, Thomas H., 20
Straight rebuy, 186
Strategic action programs, 235–239
Strategic coherence analysis, 154–155
Strategic focus, 226–229
Strategic key account analysis, 144–155
   external analysis, 146–150
   internal analysis, 150–154
   mission, 144–146
   strategic coherence analysis, 154–155
Strategic objectives, 225, 226
Strategic products, 289, 290, 292, 293
Strategic sourcing, 13–14, 283
Strategic thrust analysis, 150–152
Strategic vs. global customers, 318
Strategy, 39–69
   commitment to key accounts, 39–43
   defined, 34
   degree of closeness of key
     account/supplier-firm relationship,
     47–50
   key account. *See* Key account strategy
   key account director role in, 86
   key account manager role in, 97–98
   key account relationship types, 45–47
   key accounts at different levels in the
     organization, 44–45

portfolio approaches, 61–68
pre-meeting plan and, 258
selecting key accounts. *See* Key account
  selection
types of key account relationships,
  45–47
Strategy control, 275–276
Sun Microsystems Inc., 92
Supplier firm analysis, 201–218
  assessment of firm behavior, 210–211
  historical performance, 201–204
  relationship assessment, 204–210
  resource availability, 211–213
Supplier firm competence/critical-for-
  success matrix, 212–213
Supplier firms:
  affirmative reductions in numbers of,
    15–17
  analysis of. *See* Supplier firm analysis
  benefits of key account programs for,
    23–26
  complexity of, 75–76, 94–95
  degree of closeness of key account
    relationship, 47–50
  global account management and. *See*
    Global account management
  as information source, 187–188
  objectives of, 96–97
  partnering with key accounts. *See*
    Partnering with key accounts
Supplier rating programs, 182–184
Supply-chain competition, 193–194
Supply risk, 289–292
Support systems, 240, 242–244
Surveys, 271–273, 400–401
Switching costs, 170
Symmetry, 296
Systems and processes:
  defined, 34
  interfacing with key account,
    256–264
  key account director and, 87

key account team focus, 251–256
performance monitoring. *See*
  Performance monitoring
planning. *See* Key account plan
role of technology, 264–269
top management provision of, 83

Tampa Electric Company, 55
Target contacts, 232
Task-related currencies, 114, 115
Team-building skills, 110
Team leadership behavior, 112–113
Technical assistance, 247
Technically Available Market (TAM), 147,
  148
Technology, role of, 264–269
Telefonica España, 17
Telesp Celular, 17
Tellabs Inc., 3
Texas Instruments Inc., 16, 300
Threats, 214–218
3M Worldwide, 22, 42, 44, 78, 80, 92, 99,
  117, 304, 317–318, 389–390
Timing cycles, 143
Top management support:
  for global account management,
    319–320
  for key account management in general,
    82–85
Total target compensation, 128
TRACOM Corporation, 111
Training:
  global account manager, 338–339
  key account manager, 120–122
Transaction-driven web sites, 267
Transactions data, 253
Travelers Insurance Company, 58
Trust indicators, 270
20/80 rule, 20–21

Unicharm Corporation, 158
Unilever, 325–326

Unit sales, increasing, 157–159
Urgent information, 165

Value chain analysis, 153, 195–196
Value proposition, 233
Values, 143
Van Leer Packaging, 331
Varityper, 123
Vendor relationship, 47–48
Vision:
  key account, 222
  organizational, 143
Vision statements, 43
Visteon Corporation, 11
Volkswagen of America Inc., 15

Wachovia Bank, 98
Wall Street Journal, The, 3
Wal-Mart Stores Inc., 14, 326
Weaknesses, competitor, 195
Weighted Supplier Selection Model,
  182–184
Win/loss analysis, 254–255
World Trade Organization (WTO), 7

Xerox Corporation, 15, 26, 42, 92, 284,
  302–303, 412–414

Yellow Freight System Inc., 300

ABOUT THE AUTHOR

Noel Capon is Professor of Business and Chair of the Marketing Division at the Graduate School of Business, Columbia University, New York. He was previously a faculty member at the Graduate School of Management, UCLA and Harvard Business School; he has also taught at INSEAD (Fontainebleau, France), University of Hawaii, Monash University (Melbourne, Australia), The Hong Kong University of Science and Technology, and the China European International Business School (CEIBS) in Shanghai and Beijing. In addition, he is director for Columbia's executive training programs in key account management, sales management, and competitive marketing strategy and is a frequent participant in other programs offered at Columbia's executive training center at Arden House. He also teaches and consults for major corporations throughout the world.

Professor Capon is widely published. His articles have appeared in: *Annals of Operations Research; Columbia Journal of World Business; Communication Research; Developmental Psychology; Harvard Business Review; Industrial Marketing Management; Journal of Advertising Research; Journal of Applied Developmental Psychology; Journal of Applied Psychology; Journal of Business Administration; Journal of Consumer Research; Journal of Financial Services Research; Journal of International Business Studies; Journal of International Forecasting; Journal of Management Studies; Journal of Marketing; Journal of Marketing Research; Lending for the Commercial Banker; Management Decision; Management Science; Public Opinion Quarterly* and *Strategic Management Journal.* In addition, he has contributed to numerous edited books and is editor for sections on *Marketing,* and *Sales Management and Distribution,* in the *AMA Management Handbook* (1994).

He commenced writing this book when he was Visiting Professor of Business, School of Business and Management, The Hong Kong University of Science and Technology.